Global Gothic

Gothic Church Building in the 20th and 21st Centuries

In memory of Walter Zanini, one of the first global art historians to appreciate and master both Brazilian modernism and European tradition. A quarter of a century ago, in São Paulo, he planted the seed from which this book grew.

GOTHIC CHURCH BUILDING
IN THE 20TH AND 21ST CENTURIES

GLOBAL GOTHIC

Barbara Borngässer & Bruno Klein, eds
with the collaboration of Bettina Marten

KADOC Artes 20

LEUVEN UNIVERSITY PRESS

This book appears in the peer-reviewed series KADOC Artes.

Funded by
DFG Deutsche Forschungsgemeinschaft
German Research Foundation

Cover: São Paulo, Brazil, Metropolitan Cathedral (Sé).
[Wikimedia Commons; photo Webysther Nunes, 2019]

ISBN 978 94 6270 304 9
D/2022/1869/17
NUR: 648

GPRC
Guaranteed Peer Reviewed Content
www.gprc.be

San Francisco, Grace Cathedral under construction (1928-1964), mural 1963. Scene from a sequence of paintings by Jan Henryk De Rosen on the right side aisle wall of the cathedral.
[© Michael Lampen]

Contents

1 Gothic Going Global

About This Book

Barbara Borngässer and Bruno Klein

Whether neo-Gothic architecture has ever come to an end is a matter of perspective. From an art historical point of view with a Continental academic tradition, it came to an end around the First World War, when modern architecture began to prevail. For the countries of the British Commonwealth deeply rooted in the Gothic Revival, it may look a little different, but that does not change the overall picture. Almost everything built in Gothic style since the 1920s was either shifted to expressionism or modernism, if seemed to have any similarities with modern architecture—if not, it was considered kitsch.

We ourselves believed that for a long time. It was only during a months-long teaching and research stay in Latin America in the 1990s that we began to suspect that such an assumption could be a construction. Our colleagues there, especially in Brazil, Argentina, and Mexico, were talking about and researching very seriously contemporary local neo-Gothic art. Since then, we have increasingly learned about the continuity in the construction of neo-Gothic buildings, especially churches; we knew that neo-Gothic architecture in the twentieth and twenty-first century is a reality that cannot be ignored and should be explored from an art historical point of view. Little by little, we realized how much of our specific interest was part of the developing postcolonial and global art history.

We conceived the book in this sense. It is, above all, not a summary, but only a first attempt to describe and explain global Gothic, intended to spur both further systematic considerations and more detailed research. The book will perhaps also help to broaden views and methods in the future.

The entire project benefits from the global spread of the "new" media in a digitized world; it often thrives on image-hungry and image-producing international tourism, which makes previously unimaginable quantities of objects visually accessible. Only by means of internet research could a large number of the churches presented in this book be identified as relevant at all. But it was a constant problem that the information obtained in this way usually did not meet scientific standards, for being too subjective, emphatic, or uncritical. Typically, the design of many of the buildings presented here are described in those sources as based on prominent examples such as the Notre-Dame in Paris, or the cathedrals of Chartres, Canterbury, or Lincoln. None of these stand up to scrutiny in detail. Such assertions rather indicate the melting of global ideas and local realizations. Perhaps the global Gothic style of the last hundred years owes more than ever to an idealized, not very realistic, image of Gothic architecture as it does to existing buildings.

The project was hit hard by another phenomenon of globalization—namely, the worldwide spread of SARS-CoV-2. Many of the authors of the project fortunately knew the objects they were dealing with from personal experience. Martín Checa-Artasu was able to complete his major South American research expeditions just before the outbreak of the pandemic and before being quarantined in Mexico. But many other planned on-site researches were no longer possible, especially in North America, Africa, and Asia.

1.01 Maboma, Democratic Republic of the Congo, formerly Belgian Congo. St. John the Baptist Church, with elementary school, boarding school, and teachers' seminary, probably 1930s. Maboma may illustrate many topics of this book, e.g. colonialism and postcolonial art history, Gothic as a continuing ideal Christian style, unknowingness of this widespread global phenomenon. [© LuAnn Cadd]

1.02 St. John's Cathedral, Brisbane, Australia. View to the west facade completed in 2009. John Loughborough Pearson and Frank Loughborough Pearson,1901–2009. [Wikimedia Commons; photo Kgbo, 2020]

1.03 Paulinum – Aula and University Church St. Paul, Leipzig, Germany. Erick van Egeraat, 2007-2017. [Wikimedia Commons; photo Stb-le, 2017]

1.04 Phủ Cam Cathedral, Huế, Vietnam, Ngô Viết Thụ, 1963-2000. [Wikimedia Commons; photo Lưu Ly, 2011]

1.05 Grace Cathedral, San Francisco, USA. Lewis P. Hobart, 1928–1964. [© Bruno Klein]

Nevertheless, we decided to publish the book even under these conditions, because there are never ideal conditions for such a project. And we remembered that many of the European missionaries who traveled to Central Africa in the late nineteenth century had nice plans for Gothic-style churches in their luggage. But before they could realize them, they were struck down by the deadly yellow fever.

The Deutsche Forschungsgemeinschaft (German Research Foundation) has generously funded the entire project over a period of three years. The Technische Universität Dresden (Dresden University of Technology) and the Sächsische Landesbibliothek – Staats- und Universitätsbibliothek (Saxon State and University Library) enabled the realization in many ways. We are pleased that the book, as one of the results of this research, can be published in the KADOC Artes series, because it is positioned in a good scientific framework and will get the desired international distribution. We would like to thank the numerous colleagues and friends and also the anonymous reviewers who repeatedly accompanied the project in various phases with critical, but always valuable advice. We are deeply indebted to the staff of KADOC, specially Luc Vints, Lieve Claes and Alexis Vermeylen and Leuven University Press with particular mention of Veerle De Laet and Mirjam Truwant for their support in the realization of this book, which we hereby present to the public.

Dresden, fall 2021

2
A New Old Architecture
Global Gothic in the Twentieth and Twenty-First Centuries

Bruno Klein

Continuities, Interruptions, Voids

Pope John Paul II consecrated the Almudena Cathedral in Madrid 1993 [Figs. 3.25, 3.26 and 3.27], and Pope Benedict XVI the Sagrada Familía in Barcelona in 2010 [Figs. 3.28 and 3.29] as well as the Templo Expiatorio in León, Mexico [Fig. 9.01], in 2012—all three are huge churches in Gothic or Gothic-derived forms.

But as important as these buildings are for their countries and cities, and as prominent as the consecrators were—none of these churches plays any role in the history of contemporary architecture. Yet, the monuments mentioned are only the tip of the iceberg of worldwide building activity in a Gothic idiom, which has been going on for over a hundred years. Ignorance of this architectural reality has much to do with the presumption that the "authentic," art historically recognized neo-Gothic and Gothic Revival[1] movements came to an end with the onset of modernism in the early twentieth century. Thus, almost everything built in a Gothic idiom since the First World War is mainly regarded to be nothing but kitsch.

Therefore, an intensive preoccupation with this modern or contemporary "Gothic" architecture may be regarded as an amount to a defense of kitsch. But the intention of this book is far from that! Its aims are scientific exploration and critical discussion of an often ignored, but widespread phenomenon. The authors analyze modern and contemporary architecture in a Gothic idiom in its cultural complexity, to shift the hitherto mainly art critical view to art historical and even cultural-historical studies. Both examination of the individual buildings and a broader systematic analysis of this contemporary Gothic style are only in formative stages. It is therefore even still difficult to define, describe, and explain the phenomenon in concrete terms. At the moment, only a first approximation on different methodological levels is possible.

Scientific investigation of this architecture has progressed in an unequal way in different countries, cultures, and continents. Mainly in Europe, this is most likely to happen in the field of monument conservation, as a matter of restoring, repairing, or reconstructing historic Gothic or neo-Gothic buildings. This has recently been shown by the short-term discussion on the forms in which the reconstruction of Notre-Dame in Paris should take after the fire of 2019. The general discourse about conservation will therefore be revisited at various points in this book.

The academic literature on our topic begins, of course, with publications on neo-Gothic or Gothic Revival, of which only the fundamental studies by Georg Germann and Michel J. Lewis[2] may be mentioned here. These works concentrate mainly on the eighteenth and nineteenth centuries and Europe.

Literature on the architecture of the twentieth century and on architecture globally is usually best when the research ties in with the works on historical neo-Gothic and the Gothic Revival. This is especially true for the English-speaking cultural sphere for mainly two reasons: on the one hand, the Gothic Revival never really came to an end, especially in Great Britain itself, and on the other hand, this style was carried from there to the whole world in order to contribute to

2.01 Dresden, Germany, Castle Chapel, 2013, reconstruction of the late Gothic vaults, destroyed 1737.
[© María José Ventas Sierra]

1 On the critical use of the terms neo-Gothic and Gothic Revival, see below.
2 Germann, *Gothic Revival*; Germann, *Neugotik*; Lewis, *The Gothic Revival*.

identity formation within the British Empire. Against this background, several important books emerged almost simultaneously in the mid-2010s. Among these are Alex Bremner's studies of "Imperial Gothic," which focus on the political reasons for and effects of the choice of style within the Empire's colonies.[3] These are complemented by the research on the Pugin reception and the "Gothic Revival Worldwide" by the group led by Timothy Brittain-Catlin, Jan De Maeyer, and Martin Bressani.[4] Both aspects, the colonial as well as the stylistic, have been reflected before in Brian Andrews's book on "Australian Gothic,"[5] which presents the persistence of the Gothic Revival on one continent.[6] More recent individual studies follow.[7]

Although no longer colonies, there are many publications on Gothic Revival in the United States and Canada.[8] Similar to England itself, and especially thanks to the work of Ralph Adams Cram (1863–1942), continuity is seen in the Gothic, which extends far into the twentieth century. Even Mies van der Rohe's Lake Shore apartment buildings in Chicago fit into this tradition.[9]

For the former colony of British India and its successor states, the study of twentieth-century Gothic architecture is still in its infancy. It does not seem to have progressed beyond basic work by Christopher London on the "Bombay Gothic" of the nineteenth century.[10]

The survival of the Gothic in Africa has only been explored in rudimentary form, and only in the former British colonies.[11] More far-reaching approaches emanate from the cultural-historical, critical colonialism research as presented by Fassil Demissie in his anthology, in which the entire phenomenon of colonial architecture in Africa is taken into consideration.[12] Nevertheless, large parts of the continent remain terra incognita with regard to the survival of Gothic architecture.

A remarkable upswing has recently taken place in research on colonial Gothic architecture in China up to its current reception. Here, above all, the numerous works of Thomas Coomans and his Chinese colleague Luo Wei 罗薇 must be mentioned.[13] In the meantime, their work has also been expanded by other researchers.[14] For neighboring Japan, only initial studies are available, especially on older, sacred Christian architecture since the late nineteenth century.[15]

For Latin America, knowledge of architecture in Gothic forms has improved significantly in recent years, thanks mainly to Martín Checa-Artasu. Together with Olimpia Niglio, he has presented numerous overarching systematic as well as individual studies.[16] The editors of this book have also published research on the transatlantic Iberian cultural area.[17]

In principle, most of these researches approach the subject of architecture in Gothic idiom in the twentieth and twenty-first centuries from the margins. This research subject has not yet arrived in the broader research. Instead, even today, the interest in architecture in the Gothic idiom is mainly bound to the initiative of individual scholars. This is evident, among other things, from the fact that several of the authors mentioned have published together in specific anthologies. Some of these scientists could be won as authors for this book, to obtain an overlapping image of the previously separated cultural spaces and regions.

The authors in this book attempt to be systematic in their approach, but cannot ignore the varying depth of research with respect to the topic. The primary concern was to cover the phenomenon of continuing building activity in Gothic forms as globally as possible, so that similarities and differences became recognizable and comparisons were possible. This was the reason for the division of the topic by continents and major regions; at the same time, however, taking into account the fact that there is hardly anyone to survey several of these areas.

A certain exception in this respect is the "world" of Gothic Revival, originating in England and spreading in the British Empire, which is still largely connected in the Commonwealth today. Comparable studies con-

3 Bremner, *Imperial Gothic*; Bremner, *Architecture and Urbanism in the British Empire.*
4 Brittain-Catlin, De Maeyer and Bressani, *A.W.N. Pugin's Global Influence. Gothic Revival Worldwide.*
5 Andrews, *Australian Gothic.*
6 Also: Andrews, "Pugin in Australia"; Wrainwright, *Pugin. A Gothic Passion.*
7 Randles, *Medievalism and the Gothic in Australian Culture;* King and Willis, "The Australian Colonies."
8 Andrews, *American Gothic;* Macdonell, *The American Pugins.*
9 Andrews, *American Gothic*, 142.
10 London, *Bombay Gothic.*
11 Bremner, *Imperial Gothic;* Bremner, *Architecture and Urbanism.*
12 Demissie, *Colonial Architecture and Urbanism in Africa.*
13 A small selection: Coomans and Luo Wei 罗薇, "Exporting Flemish Gothic Architecture to China"; Coomans, "Architecture to China"; Id., "Die Kunstlandschaft der Gotik in China"; Id., "East Meets West"; Id., "Gothique ou chinoise, missionnaire ou inculturée"; Id., "Pugin Worldwide".
14 Wolfendale, *Imperial to International*; Sweeten, *China's Old Churches.*
15 Löffler, *Fremd und Eigen;* Niglio, "La fortuna critica di John Ruskin in Giappone nella prima metà del Novecento."
16 A small selection: Checa-Artasu and Niglio, *El Neogótico en la arquitectura americana*; Checa-Artasu, "Religious orders and the expansion of Neo-Gothic architecture in Latin America."
17 Borngässer and Klein, *Neugotik global – kolonial – postkolonial;* Klein, "El estilo gótico global."

cerning the spread and reception of French Gothic Revival, on the other hand, do not exist.

To make syntheses at all possible, it was first necessary to make an inventory:[18] because there is no catalog of the relevant buildings, the authors first had to undertake this inventory themselves. A major concern of the individual essays is therefore to present material, compiled here for the first time, to an academic audience. So, the scales have tipped sometimes more toward presentation and sometimes more toward synthesis.

Differences between the individual chapters were determined both by the material and by the formation and interests of the authors. For **Europe**, for example, it was relatively easy to obtain information on such buildings in a Gothic idiom that, because of their modernity, have been integrated into the canon of architectural history, such as the Sagrada Família in Barcelona [Figs. 3.28 and 3.29] or the Grundtvig's Church in Copenhagen [Figs. 3.30 and 3.31]. But the literature on the Cathedral of Vitoria-Gasteiz [Figs. 3.14 and 3.15], also located in Spain, as well as on numerous other recent churches in Gothic forms, may be described as almost nonexistent. And because of the heterogeneity of a stock originating from different historical and cultural backgrounds, correspondingly different interpretive approaches were required.

For the **United States and Canada,** the situation is completely different. In these countries is a large, relatively homogeneous stock of churches in the Gothic idiom, especially from the first half of the twentieth century. However, apart from a few prominent buildings and their architects, this has not been systematically explored. So, it was necessary to work exemplarily, to recognize some common principles and to position contemporary Gothic in relation to older, well-known phenomena.

In a similar way, this also applies to **Australia and New Zealand**, although the inventory of buildings in the Gothic idiom is distributed there rather selectively.

Because research on this architecture in the subcontinent of **India** has hardly begun, it was necessary to develop a few initial guiding ideas that can be used to explore the stock in more depth in the future.

The three chapters just mentioned deal with strongly English-influenced regions of the world. The more or less proper research of these regions has already been pointed out. Because this does not apply to the areas of the former Spanish and Portuguese in **Latin America**, a different, two-pronged approach was chosen. This approach involved a broad inventory, as expressed especially in the chapter on the Spanish-speaking countries. Because there was no broad background on the continent for the continuing Gothic reception such as the Gothic Revival, it was necessary to focus on the different motives for building in these forms. In particular, the great importance of the Catholic orders emerged. Additionally, a depth sounding was made especially for **Mexico**. This chapter stands out among all the others because its author, Martín Checa-Artasu, is a sociologist and cultural geographer, and he could broaden the perspective on the continuing Gothic through a special professional methodology.

The fact that **Brazil** was formerly part of another empire—namely, the Portuguese Empire—is not the only reason for its separate treatment. In Brazil, much more than in the other South American countries, strong competition between historicist and modern architecture emerged throughout the twentieth century up to the present day; these traditions, however, are related to each other. The fact that more churches have been built in a Gothic style idiom than in a modern style idiom in the country in the last hundred years is a surprising finding of the research presented here.

In all the continents and major regions discussed so far, there is always a relatively uniform cultural or architectural historical background for the continuing reception of Gothic architecture in the twentieth and twenty-first centuries. For **Africa, China,**

18 A freely accessible database was created in parallel with this book: <http://www.deutschefotothek.de, and then search "glogo">.

and Japan, however, this looks completely different. For these areas, the European countries competed fiercely with each other during the period of colonialism, sometimes aggressively trying to compete through their ideas of architecture. And so the already stated heterogeneity of European architecture is reflected once again.

But it did not seem appropriate for the editors to divide these areas into art historical colonies and to view the architecture merely from the perspective of the colonizing countries. Rather, the attraction lay precisely in analyzing the competitive situations and viewing them in the context of the different confrontations with indigenous building cultures. In this context, the decades that have passed since the colonial era are of particular importance for Africa and China.

But such a theoretical claim is easier postulated than realized: there was only partial preparatory work for the chapters on **Africa and Japan**, so that scans rather than in-depth analyses could take place. For **China**, however, it is true that the research on the colonial Gothic there and the postcolonial treatment of it can be described as increasingly excellent, both in terms of content and method. The corresponding contribution by Thomas Coomans shows the conceivable dimensions of future research on the global Gothic.

Finally, the last chapter on the **wedding chapels** hints at where an architectural Gothic reception in the twenty-first century, largely stripped of its original contexts, may lead. This is neither to be evaluated positively nor negatively, but serves solely to establish that both imitative and creative Gothic adaptations continue.

The wedding chapels are especially widespread in the East Asian and Pacific regions. Surprisingly, this is exactly the area for which the fewest studies on the persistence of the Gothic in the twentieth and twenty-first centuries are available so far. It was not possible to fill this gap in this book. Therefore, instead of a separate chapter, at least some particularly characteristic buildings should be presented here, whose further systematic research is still pending.

In Indochina, especially in Vietnam, numerous neo-Gothic churches were built in the late nineteenth century during the period of French colonialism. However, even in the middle of the twentieth century, there were still corresponding new buildings or renovations; for example, the Basilica of the Virgin Mary (Phú Nhai, Fig. 2.02). In South Korea, not only churches such as the Choon Hyun

2.02 Xuan Phuong, Vietnam, Basilica of the Virgin Mary (Phú Nhai), 1916–1922, restored after partial cyclone-related destruction until 1933. [Wikimedia Commons; photo Hoangvantoanajc, 2011]

2.03 Seoul, South Korea, Choong Hyun Presbyterian Church, 1953. [mapio.net]

2.04 Seoul, South Korea, Kyung Hee University Seoul Campus, 1979–1999. [Wikimedia Commons; photo Vantharith]

2.05 Singapore, Saint Alphonsus, Novena Church, 2014–2017. [Wikimedia Commons; photo Exec8, 2018]

Presbyterian Church were built from 1953 [Fig. 2.03] but also the "Peace Hall" of Kyung Hee University (1979–1999): an auditorium with a façade that is a copy of the Brussels Cathedral [Fig. 2.04]. Most recent is the extension of Novena Church in Singapore (2014 to 2017)—a construction that features unusually exact imitations of nineteenth-century Gothic Revival Churches and at the same time, motifs that are only possible thanks to contemporary construction methods, such as the pillars hanging from the ceiling [Fig. 2.05].[19] These examples have not yet found their place in art history.[20]

The obviously asymmetrical research situation leads to various methodological problems. For example, with regard to the sources: as a rule, these are often not documents as known in classical architectural history, such as building dossiers and newspaper articles with concrete information, for example. More often, highly subjective printed or digitally published material was necessary for this research. Scientific or critical self-reflection hardly plays a role in this often merely hectographed literature, or in the countless in number, but scare in information and often identical internet entries. In those contributions, buildings and their protagonists are, however, usually emphatically celebrated. By contrast, cultural-historical and critical links are rarely found. Nonetheless, despite all its inadequacies, this material is often indispensable in a positivist sense as a source of construction data and actors, for example. And sometimes reading between the lines offers enlightening insights into mental backgrounds. The line toed when scientifically evaluating these sources is narrow.

On the other hand, however, it is precisely the generally accessible information from the internet that provides a hitherto untapped potential. In fact, it would hardly have been possible to compile such a quantity of examples if there were not so many photos, blogs, Wikipedia entries, which were created, because they obviously ignore any traditional art historical canon. Therefore, this book owes much to the new media and their corresponding research possibilities. The book's underlying assumption that there

19 This motif can be found almost simultaneously in the so-called Paulinum in Leipzig [Fig. 1.03].

20 Sacred architecture in the Philippines should also not go unmentioned: the Baclaran Church (officially, the National Shrine of Our Mother of Perpetual Help, 1953–1958), an important pilgrimage site south of the capital Manila, shows neo-Romanesque motifs inside and out. At first glance, this seems particularly evident in the façade, which, like the west façade of the Church of the Annunciation in Nazareth (1960–1969), especially borrows from the prominent twelfth-century Lombard building of San Michele in Pavia. Nevertheless, the façade of the Baclaran church also shows particularly strong similarities to the expressive neo-Gothic Grundtvig's church in Copenhagen (Fig. 3.30).

is a persistent broad, mentally shaped affinity for architecture in Gothic forms, for which there are various reasons and which is fed by many sources, is supported by these heterogeneous, unacademic sources.

Questions of Style

Neo-Gothic, Neugotik, Néo-Gothique, or Gothic Revival have long been common terms in the history of architecture, denoting a phenomenon that was a defining feature of architecture from the eighteenth to the early twentieth century.[21] In addition, during the main period of historicism, there were also other "neo-styles," such as neo-Renaissance and neo-Baroque on the European continent, or the short-lived sequence of various alternating English neo-styles in the decades around 1900. Today, other historicizing architectural styles have been added, in which construction takes place parallel to the current Gothic idiom: in the booming Gulf States, for example, there is a broad current of neo-Arabic architecture; Baroque palaces are also being built all over the world. In the tourism and entertainment architecture sector in particular, the adaptation of historical architectural styles seems to be unlimited. In addition, there are the countless reconstructions of lost buildings or entire city quarters, which are spread all over the world,[22] as well as attempts to develop a contemporary architecture from local historical models. Historicism in architecture is thus not merely of undeniable reality, but more present than ever.

It is possible to integrate contemporary architecture—operating more or less freely with Gothic forms and types—into the abovementioned context? Various observations contradict each other: on the one hand, the constantly updated revival of Gothic building forms and types has continued steadily since the eighteenth century, asserting itself as a relatively old and consistent phenomenon in comparison to numerous other younger or short-lived neo-styles. Moreover, the corresponding religious architecture of the twentieth and twenty-first centuries, which is the focus of this book, has a quality of its own that distinguishes it from most of contemporary historicizing building activities. It is not an only "postmodern" or "neo-historical" phenomenon, such as the contemporary city or palace reconstructions, but has historical roots that extend beyond the merely formal. Only the purely fictious assumption that the current of construction in Gothic forms has generally come to an end through modernism and modern architecture obscures this continuity. It is more productive to look at some continuities.

And vice versa: why should neo-Gothicism *not* continue? The idea of a universally uniform stylistic development is, in the words of the architectural historian Werner Oechslin, "a modern longing, not an adequate reference to historical diversity and reality!"[23] Moreover, nothing is less probable than the assumption that something approved stylistically, mentally, historically, and socially, as well as by building practice, could suddenly disappear only because of a new paradigm—namely, that of a supposed rational modernity in everything.

At the same time, neo-Gothic architecture has often been highly modern and innovative even in the technical sense: the scaffolding on the 157-meter-high towers of Cologne Cathedral, which was completed in 1880, seems to have been exemplary for corresponding constructions of the early skyscrapers, which at that time, were far from reaching such heights.[24] Steel skeleton constructions were also commonplace in many of the neo-Gothic buildings of the time.[25] The differences between Gothic and modern architecture in the twentieth century thus relate exclusively to forms and their syntax, while they are not distinguishable in terms of the techniques.[26]

Nevertheless, it is undeniable that the increasing importance of modern architecture has often blocked the practice of building in Gothic forms and almost brought it to a standstill. In Europe, the continent of mod-

21 Germann, *Gothic Revival*; Germann, *Neugotik*; Brook, *Gothic Revival*; Brittain-Catlin, De Maeyer, and Bressani, eds., *A.W.N. Pugin's Global Influence*; Amic, Le Men, and Coudert, eds., *Cathédrales*.

22 See, for example, Sigel and Klein, eds., *Konstruktionen urbaner Identität*; Kappel, ed., *Geschichtsbilder und Erinnerungskultur in der Architektur des 20. und 21. Jahrhunderts*; Brandt and Meier, eds., *Stadtbild und Denkmalpflege*. There are several contributions on the subject in: *Architectura. Zeitschrift für Geschichte der Baukunst*, 46 (2016), 2.

23 Oechslin, "'Quae sub humanum intellectum cadunt'", 128.

24 Steuer, "Industrialisierung und Domvollendung"; Schumacher, *Großbaustelle Kölner Dom*; Borger, *Der Kölner Dom*. In 1890, the 161-meter-high west tower of Ulm Minster was also completed. The tower of the Philadelphia City Hall (1901) is about the same height. The Singer Building in New York, completed in 1908, is considered to be the first real skyscraper, at 187 meters tall, it surpassed any the tower erected until then.

25 This is why it is possible to trace its effects far into the twentieth century in Michael Lewis, *Neo-Gothic architecture*. Not only the cathedral of Liverpool or Grundtvig's Church in Copenhagen are listed but also German expressionist architects such as Dominikus Böhm "the last great architect of the Gothic Revival," Fritz Höger and Hans Poelzig.

26 Not to forget the exception of some architects who insisted on the connection between medieval forms and techniques; for example, Ralf Adams Cram in the United States. Further details in Bettina Marten's contribution in this book.

ernism, hardly any church has been built in the Gothic idiom since the 1920s—with some exceptions, as mentioned, especially in Great Britain.

Where the storm of the concept of modernity blew less violently—in other words, mostly outside of Europe—"Gothic" construction was carried out much longer. There is often no sign of a real break in places where the neo-Gothic or Gothic Revival building tradition has been common since the nineteenth century. This applies to Australia[27] and North America,[28] but especially to the South American subcontinent.

In a global context, this particular Gothicizing architecture has benefited from postmodernism since the 1970s and 1980s. The construction of numerous churches was reactivated; many of these buildings had been started in the late nineteenth and early twentieth centuries, but building activity had ceased in the 1920s or 1930s, and the churches were in danger of falling into neo-Gothic ruins. Numerous of these have since been completed or are close to completion, such as the Santuario Guadalupano in Zamora, Michoacán [Figs. 9.02 and 9.03], where construction started in 1898, was interrupted between 1914 and 1988, and was finished in 2015.[29] A quite unexpected parallel is in the People's Republic of China, where the neo-Gothic churches of the former European colonials were demolished during the Cultural Revolution in the late 1960s and early 1970s, only to be restored shortly afterward.[30]

Such observations show that churches built in Gothic forms during the last decades may appear stylistically similar without belonging to the same cultural contexts: there are both buildings in the unbroken neo-Gothic/Gothic Revival tradition and others that are independent of it and stand for the Gothic variant of the increasingly widespread international historicizing stylistic pluralism that can take up any older form, even without any continuities or traditions in building practice. Therefore, it remains to be examined in each individual case which corresponding position the buildings occupy. Overlaps are possible. One should be careful not to ascribe a higher moral value to one direction or the other, because the discussion about truthfulness and seriousness in the reception of historical building forms, or the insinuation of arbitrariness in their use, is as old as historicism itself!

A New Style or Not? Difficulties in Terminology

One thing is certain: the end of Gothicizing architecture, which was supposedly heralded by the onset of modernism in the period around the First World War, did not take place. Rather, there were further, multilayered developments, as well as geographical asymmetries. Building in Gothic forms came under pressure almost only in Europe, but not at all on other continents. Thus, building in a Gothic idiom, which continues to this day, is primarily a non-European phenomenon. This means, however, that the terms "neo-Gothic" and "Gothic Revival," which originated in European building culture, cannot be easily applied to this global architecture.

But even further, "neo-Gothic" and "Gothic Revival" stem from historically defined cultural areas. To continue to use them without reflection would be to perpetuate the colonial division of the world for architectural history. Furthermore, it must be taken into account that there are different, not always consistent linguistic practices in different countries. Buildings in the tradition of German or French neo-Gothic can be named in English-language literature as "Gothic Revival," but this cannot be applied generally.

If the terms are nevertheless used further, then this is always done with a certain mental distance, especially since there are no new, better terms. There are even good reasons for not developing new terminology. If one were to introduce completely different terms from "neo-Gothic" or "Gothic Revival" for architecture in the Gothic style

27 Andrews, *Australian Gothic*, XX, sees the period 1840 to 1950 as a neo-Gothic period for Australia.

28 A publication has been announced for 2022 in which the intertwining of modernism and historicism in neo-Gothic buildings of the early twentieth century in Great Britain and America will be examined: Ayla Lepine, *Medieval Metropolis: The Middle Ages and Modern Architecture*, Bloomsbury Academic.

29 For more details, see the contribution on Mexico of Martín Checa-Artasu in this book.

30 Coomans, "Gothique ou chinoise, missionnaire ou inculturée?"; Coomans, "Die Kunstlandschaft der Gotik in China."

idiom that has been built grosso modo since the First World War, this would imply recognizing the exclusive claim of modernism to define all architecture in the twentieth and twenty-first centuries. On the other hand, to hold on to the old terms used synonymously here in a heuristic sense makes persisting stylistic and often also intellectual continuities recognizable.

The situation is somewhat different in the case of architecture that is doubtlessly in the modern style, but picks up Gothic structures and motifs. Because, as already explained, modern architects did not have a fundamental aversion to medieval Gothic, but rather one to its historicist remake, there was nothing to prevent the integration of supposed authentic Gothic principles into modern style. It therefore seems reasonable to continue to classify stylistically modern buildings, in which such principles reappear, as modern. After all, architecture of ancient temples and baroque castles, for example, was also adopted in modernity, without immediately speaking of "neo-antiquity" or anything similar. The selective use of certain formal elements and structures does not make modern architecture at once an old one, even not in postmodernism, but merely shows how problematic the definitions of strict stylistic boundaries are.

Introducing new stylistic terms would not only be cumbersome, it would also mean continuing the traditional thinking in clearly separable categories of immanent stylistic terms. Perhaps it is most neutral to speak of architecture in the "Gothic" idiom, because this excludes further inconscient implications.

Different Narratives: Gothic Architecture of the Twentieth and Twenty-First Centuries as a Mental, Religious, and Social Phenomenon

The phenomenon of stylistic survival or the revival of Gothic/neo-Gothic in the twentieth and twenty-first centuries is linked to the question of whether certain mental expectations were associated with it. An older history of art would perhaps have answered this question by saying that the "Gothic" or the "spirit of the Gothic" were according to anthropological constants, so that corresponding formal emanations would have to occur almost inevitably and repeatedly. Under less ideologically shaped conceptions, it is more obvious today to analyze precisely and in a case-oriented manner what the specific occasions and backgrounds to build in a Gothic idiom could have been—and still are.

From the eighteenth to the early twentieth century, "Gothic architecture"—and the neo-Gothic style derived from it—was often regarded as particularly sublime. This idea about the Gothic idiom has not yet been overcome. Because of this, Gothic was and is often considered to be particularly suitable for religious buildings, intended to elevate the soul. However, in the twentieth century this idea—and this is a central result of the research presented here—became independent of the discourse on current aesthetic and stylistic mainstreams. And so modern forms and structures could be integrated into contemporary "Gothic" and vice versa. The cathedral of the Brazilian capital Brasília, designed by the atheist Oscar Niemeyer,[31] for example, features a buttress and window architecture in which numerous Gothic formal and structural elements are transcended in an extreme way to give an adequate cathedral to the ideal modern capital [Fig. 10.15].[32] On the other hand, there are churches recently built, also in Brazil, of the "Heralds of the Gospel," an extremely conservative Catholic congregation [Figs. 10.18 and 10.19]. They

31 Fils, *Brasilia*; Underwood, *Oscar Niemeyer.*

32 Illustrations of most of the buildings mentioned in this introduction can be found in the corresponding geographical chapters.

were constructed in forms that strive to imitate medieval Gothic architecture as closely as possible. The Sainte-Chapelle in Paris, especially in its colorful nineteenth-century manner, seems to be the most important model. The freelance, modernist Gothic adaptation à la Brasília forms one pole of the current architectural Gothic reception, the Gothic imitation à la Heralds the other. In between lie numerous and above all, varied solutions. Liberal and, increasingly, conservative authoritarian movements stand side by side and both make use of Gothic architecture.

There is no longer a privileged religious access to art and architecture in specific stylistic forms. At best, there are claims to provide such access.[33] These are not to be neglected and in some specific cases, have certainly led to the building or ongoing construction of neo-Gothic churches in the twentieth century. However, neo-Gothic church architecture has become much too widespread worldwide in the last hundred years to be generally attributable to specific religious motives.[34] The construction of such churches has also been shown not to be typical for certain Christian confessions, because whether Catholics or Protestants, Lutherans or Anglicans—they can all build in a Gothic idiom. Particularly in North America or Australia, where the different confessions had to fear for their temporary dominance in the course of various waves of immigration, their "Gothic" churches often stand directly next to each other—formerly in competition, today in friendly neighborhoods and together shaping the cityscape. And finally, Gothic forms can be applied to buildings that only pretend to be religious ones, but, in reality, are not and only imitate them.[35]

A number of widespread similarities are emerging despite all the differences in the details. For example, over the past hundred years, the actors involved in the construction of Gothic churches have become increasingly aware that they were not building according to architectural mainstreams. This does not necessarily mean, however, that they are conservative in the political or religious sense—although this is often the case. But this phenomenon, too, must be considered in a more differentiated way. Thomas Coomans, for example, observed that Chinese Catholics, who today are once again building simple Gothic churches, were unable to notice the reforms of the Second Vatican Council, because of the decades of repression of the Christianity in China; these Chinese Catholics therefore held many opinions that were otherwise outdated in Catholicism.[36] In that case, building Gothic has to do with asynchronous information. While this may be a special case, it can generally be observed that in the course of its long history, the neo-Gothic style has been considered and used as something that deviated from, or even resisted, common norms:[37] as an anchor thrown into history during transitional times of accelerated change, in phases of mental disorientation, especially against a background of fear of marginalization and loss.[38] The historical assumption that the Gothic is always the opposite is still true today. Of course, similar things happen again and again in many fields and in many media. But it remains to be clarified how especially architecture in Gothic forms, although of European origin, was able to grow worldwide into such a role during in the twentieth century.

Yet this role is ambivalent: in Chile, several neo-Gothic churches were recently (autumn 2020) set on fire, because they were considered exponents of political and social reaction. The same happened to such buildings in China as early as 1970. Between extreme appropriation and extreme rejection, however, there is also a middle position for churches in Gothic forms.

Especially since the early twentieth century, the construction of churches in Gothic form is interpreted as an expression of public spirit and is also staged accordingly. Here, too, the roots lie in the nineteenth century, when cathedral building societies were founded.[39] These were essentially middle-class institutions that took on the task of completing medieval churches, while re-

33 Individual Catholic movements are relatively well studied in this respect, e.g., in: Pirotte, "Néo-gothique et fantasmes de chrétienté"; De Maeyer, "Pro Arte Christiana."

34 Quoting Gothic architecture in other contexts, such as in films or advertisements, can have different reasons that go far beyond the religious. In "Goth Culture," religion hardly plays a role.

35 See the contribution in this book by Barbara Borngässer about wedding chapels.

36 See the contribution of Thomas Coomans in this book.

37 Klein, "Warum Gotik."

38 Interesting reflections on the function of Gothic today can be found in Woodword, "The After-Lives of English Gothic," esp. 12–16, chapter: "Postmodern 'Gothic' and the commercial world."

39 See, for example, on the "Kölner Dombauverein": Pilger, *Der Kölner Zentral-Dombauverein im 19. Jahrhundert*; Pilger, "Die Entwicklung des Zentral-Dombau-Vereins bis zur Vollendung des Kölner Domes."

2.06 Lille, France, Cathedral, Poster, 1964.
[© Episcopal Archives Lille; photo Pascal Lemaître]

maining socially open at the top and bottom [Fig. 2.06].[40]

This is a quality lacking in many other modern large-scale building projects, which are erected for purely functional reasons, whereby their owners—and above all, their construction financing—are almost always anonymous. In such cases, no "capital of transcendence" can be gained from the preparation and actual construction process. But this is conversely possible in the construction of the new "Gothic" churches, which are built thanks to small, individual donations. In the era of turbocapitalism, this applies all the more. The slow, often difficult, but mostly continuous building processes are a real advantage here, because they document a sustained and widespread, above all, public interest in a building project that does not promise an immediate pecuniary gain. And they can refer to proven medieval building processes, imitating them without being antimodern. Because the idea of community-integrating, collaborative creation stood also at the cradle of movements from Arts and Crafts to Bauhaus, incunables of contemporary architecture.

In this sense, the numerous inscriptions in the Washington National Cathedral in Washington, D.C. (1907–1990) speak for themselves [Fig. 2.07]. And when money ran out during the construction of the Guildford Cathedral in England after World War II, finances were restored thanks to a buy-a-brick campaign: from the Queen to the common citizen, many people bought stones bearing their name. Sagrada Família in Barcelona—which, according to its statutes, may only be built through private donations—has virtually become a self-financing church in the course of the increased veneration of its architect Antoni Gaudí, in combination with international city tourism.

There is no question that such funding and participation always emanates from the center of the "good" society, which thus sets its standards and asserts its claim for its overarching community spirit. This is especially true in traditionally relatively homogeneous societies. But where European and indigenous cultures clash in the former colonies, this also expresses the claim to cultural-social superiority of the first group, serving, at the same time, its inner self-assurance.

Contemporary Gothic and Monument Preservation

In the case of the restoration of Gothic or neo-Gothic buildings, parallel tendencies to the phenomena described above can be observed in the twentieth and twenty-first centuries. During this time, restoration was not always only about scientifically based preservation and reconstruction but often also about participation. Examples are numerous around the world: when, for example, the neo-Gothic cathedral in Christchurch, New Zealand, built in the late nineteenth century according to plans by George Gilbert Scott,[41] was severely damaged in 2011 by earthquakes, its reconstruction seemed impossible and the diocese planned to demolish the ruins. Immediately, a massive public resistance arose.[42] As a result, the reconstruction of the church was decided in 2017. The case of Notre-Dame in Paris shows a development that at first glance appears different, but on closer inspection is similar: immediately after the fire in the spring of 2019, ideas of a repair in contemporary forms flickered for a short time, but these ideas soon evaporated in favor of a reconstruction of the state into which Eugène Viollet-le-Duc had brought the building in the nineteenth century. Above all, however, the well-intentioned but nevertheless authoritarian steering of the cathedral's rebuilding by the French president was quickly considered negative by public. Simultaneously, the extensive grants from large companies and financially powerful families to support reconstruction were criticized for marginalizing any possible commitment in favor of the Notre-Dame by small-scale, individual engagement. Consequently, the process of the reconstruction of Notre-Dame and the discourse about it seem to shift—slowly but continuously—to a more broadly socially accepted one.

Over the course of the twentieth century, heritage preservation neglected only for a brief period the principle to reconstruct as authentically as possible. Numerous buildings, especially the larger churches destroyed in Europe during the First World War in France and Belgium, were restored almost to their original state. This is true of cathedrals as badly damaged as those of Soissons or Reims,[43] as well as of a church completely razed to the ground such as Saint-Martin in Ypres [Figs. 3.18a-b & 3.19].[44]

This principle did not apply in such a strict way after the destructions of the Second World War. As a result, churches were often not rebuilt true to the original, but traces of their damage remained visible and contemporary elements were integrated. This was the case for Gothic churches from the Middle Ages as well as for the neo-Gothic ones from the nineteenth century, which were treated with far less respect.[45] The most famous example of this is probably Coventry Cathedral in England, which was not reconstructed after its destruction by German bombing in November 1940, but preserved as a ruinous memorial next to a completely modern church [Fig. 2.08].[46] On the other hand, St. Mary's in Lübeck [Figs. 2.09 & 2.10], or other churches in Germany, such as the Frauenkirche in Munich, were completely restored, albeit with extensive loss or failure to reconstruct the former interior. In the case of the Cologne Cathedral, which dates from both the Middle Ages and the nineteenth century, securing and repairing began in 1945, so that the cathedral could

2.07 Washington, D.C., United States, National Cathedral, supporter's inscription.
[© Bruno Klein]

40 From the beginning, such associations developed from educational to financial institutions, which were followed by the corresponding associations of the twentieth century concerned with the construction of new churches in historic forms.

41 Bremner, *Imperial Gothic*, 100–110 and 364.

42 Lochhead and Stocke, "Christchurch Cathedral."

43 Numerous older religious, art historical, and nationalist discourses culminated and forced themselves in an extreme way after the destruction of the cathedral of Reims in 1914 in World War I and its subsequent reconstruction. Gaehtgens, *Die brennende Kathedrale*. See also the review by Herklotz.

44 On Ypres, see below in the chapter about Europe.

45 Kappel, *Memento 1945?*

46 Campbell, *Coventry Cathedral*; the remarkable contrast between the ruin and the new building is further enhanced by the fact that immediately adjacent to this ensemble rises the Gothic Holy Trinity Church with its high crossing tower, which survived the bombing.

2.08 Coventry, England, Cathedral of Saint Michael. Ruins of the Gothic church, new cathedral and Holy Trinity Church.
[Wikimedia Commons; photo De-Facto, 2018]

be reopened in 1956 after the reconstruction of the neo-Gothic vaults in the main nave and transept. The cathedral of Reims, which was severely damaged in World War I, was not repaired until 1938, in other words, only shortly before the work had to be started in Cologne. Similar to Cologne is the case of Nantes Cathedral in Brittany, which was begun in 1434; neither cathedral was completed in the Middle Ages. Construction of the Nantes Cathedral, especially of the choir, was resumed from 1840–1891; the church was damaged by bombs in 1944 and was not yet fully restored in 1972, when during conservation works, a fire destroyed the entire roof. Only after that catastrophe was repair forced, so that the damages from different periods were finally eliminated in 1985.[47] Thus, even during the heyday of modernity, there were always large Gothic/neo-Gothic construction sites for conservation reasons, flanked by a myriad of others, smaller and less prominent.

However, especially in the field of heritage conservation and repair, there were and still are unmistakable tendencies to bring existing Gothic and neo-Gothic churches stylistically and typologically "up to date": in Britain, for example, Stephen Dykes Bower not only built churches in the twentieth century in the style of the Gothic Revival, but also restored numerous renowned buildings of the Middle Ages in this spirit, such as Westminster Abbey in London or the colleges in Oxford and Cambridge.[48] More significant perhaps is the case of the parish church of St. Mary Magdalene's in Goch on the Lower Rhine, Germany, where after the collapse of the Gothic tower in 1993, a new tower in updated form was built by 2003 [Figs. 2.11 & 2.12].[49]

Finally, since the 1990s, there has been a noticeable tendency for numerous damaged or destroyed Gothic churches in the former Eastern Bloc countries to be repaired, supplemented, or completely restored. These included buildings such as the St. George's

47 James, ed., *Nantes*. The church burned again on June 19, 2020, destroying the main organ in the west, but leaving the architecture essentially intact.
48 Symondson, *Stephen Dykes Bower*.
49 Horst, "Ein neuer Kirchenturm für die katholische Pfarrkirche St. Maria Magdalena in Goch."

2.09 Lübeck, Germany, St. Mary's, interior, 19th century.
[Archive Bruno Klein]

2.10 Lübeck, Germany, St. Mary's, reconstruction of the interior after the destruction of the church in the Second World War.
[Wikimedia Commons; photo De-Facto, 2018]

2.11 Goch, Germany, St. Mary Magdalen's, façade with tower before 1993 collapse.
[© Manfred Geurts]

2.12 Goch, Germany, St. Mary Magdalen's, Goch, Façade with tower after reconstruction.
[Wikimedia Commons; photo Steffen Schmitz, 2012]

50 Zimmerling, ed., *Universitätskirche St. Pauli.* For more details, see the contribution on Europe in this book.
51 Sächsisches Staatsministerium der Finanzen, ed., *Das Schlingrippengewölbe der Schlosskapelle Dresden.*
52 One of the very rare and truly marginal exceptions is the Catholic Cathedral of Our Lady of Moscow: built in 1911, profaned and partially destroyed during the Soviet era, it was restored to its original state and reconsecrated in 1996–2001.
53 Cheng, Davis, and Wilson, *Race and Modern Architecture.* See also the contribution of Thomas Coomans in this book.

in Wismar, which was severely damaged in World War II and then not rebuilt during the German Democratic Republic era, but has been consistently restored since 1990. In 1968, the Leipzig University Church, a Gothic and neo-Gothic building that shaped the cityscape and created the city's identity, was blown up for ideological reasons. After reunification, the so-called "Paulinum" was erected in its place, taking up the forms and structures of the lost original, both inside and out [Figs. 1.03 & 3.35].[50] In Dresden, on the site of the Gothic St. Sophie's church with neo-Gothic façade, which was demolished in 1962–1963, the Busmann Memorial Chapel was recently constructed. It contains parts of the original furnishings, but also a concrete choir polygon with reused tracery and a reference to a vault, which is indicated by steel ribs. If such attempts at reconstruction can be explained by the grief of contemporaries over the loss of the original churches, the reconstruction of the complicated curvilinear rib vault in the former Castle Chapel Dresden can no longer be answered by this argument [Fig. 2.01]. The chapel was demolished as early as in 1737, and its reconstruction was based rather on practical considerations as to how the palace, which had been badly ruined in World War II, should be converted into a museum. However, a realization was only possible after the technical and manual skills needed to fulfill this difficult task had been relearned.[51] Long before, when the old wooden ceiling in Eton College Chapel in England became infested with deathwatch beetles in the 1950s, a new fan vault was installed there—made of concrete, but covered with stone [Fig. 2.13]. Although such similarities between the churches in Dresden and Eton may seem coincidental, it is clear that the narrative of the special significance of Gothic architecture continues to lead to parallel phenomena in building conservation and restoration.

2.13 Eton, England, Eton College Chapel, new fan vault, 2nd half 20th century.
[Archive Bruno Klein]

Global Gothic as a Colonial and Transcultural Phenomenon

Any examination of the neo-Gothic global architecture of the twentieth and twenty-first centuries cannot be done without taking colonialism into account, because this architecture mainly exists in Western Europe or in European-influenced "mother countries" and their colonies.[52]

The Eurocentric colonial dominance is also indicated by the fact that there are no known direct connections between the various neo-Gothic building sites, building cultures, and practices around the world. It is always necessary to return to Europe to trace such connections. In the academic field, too, art history influenced by Europe is indispensable for identifying parallels and connections. This book itself is a good example of this. The Eurocentric perspective on the globally persistent architecture in Gothic idiom therefore cannot be ruled out for the moment, but should change once the discussion has started.

However, global neo-Gothic or Gothic Revival shouldn't be completely subsumed under the term colonialism or reduced to it. Although its spread, especially in Africa and Asia, is undoubtedly directly linked to historical colonialism and even racism,[53] the phenomenon as a whole is considerably more complex—even more so on other continents, especially considering the multilayered nature of colonialism itself. In addition to its different regional characteristics, it is important to note that this book focuses broadly on buildings from the era of decolonization, in other words, a classical period of transition that occurred differently from one colony to another. And even if former colonies, especially on the American continent, had long been independent during the period regarded here, it cannot be ignored that postcolonial battles for cultural sovereignty and independence continued to be fought there with the means of architecture. In North America, this was quite often a matter of surpassing European models, while in South America the focus was on the attempt to make a focused selection of specific models. What was considered culturally worthy—such as the Gothic architecture of France, England, and Germany—was adopted,[54] while the Gothic of the Iberian Peninsula was mainly excluded, because it was regarded as a rather undesirable model.

In addition, building churches in a Gothic idiom was often connected with a certain educational idea—either to set an example for the colonized people, or to set an example among the nationally and socially heterogeneous groups of colonizers. These are all phenomena of colonialism, postcolonialism, or second colonialism.

These "didactic" churches are particularly evident in the Christian mission in Africa, which emanated from both the Catholic Church and the various Protestant congregations. Especially in the central and southern parts of the continent, expansive colonization and missionary work went hand in hand. With the construction of the mostly Gothic churches, the entire population, both indigenous and immigrant, was to be Christianized, disciplined, and "cultivated." But the various nations also fought proxy wars by means of religious architecture. With decolonization, the construction of such churches with a mainly political background generally came to a standstill in the second half of the twentieth century, but not completely, because Christianization had outlasted the core phase of national colonialism.

In Latin America, the first, forced missionary work and colonialism were basically at an end when the churches under consideration were built in the twentieth and twenty-first centuries. Their construction must be seen mainly against two different backgrounds that overlap: on the one hand, a politically driven Christian sacralization of nations and, on the other hand, a widespread general interest in religion. Missionaries as well as builders were sent to or brought from Europe. Furthermore, Latin America and Africa seemed to be the ideal areas for a Catholic restoration. That may explain the strong rejection of the older colonial or newer neocolonial, in other words, baroque, ecclesiastical architecture in favor of new neo-Gothic churches during the first decades of the twentieth century. What was sought was a recourse to an idealized Christian architecture, which was not perceived as decadent or corrupted during the first phase of colonialism.[55]

At the same time, the interest in missionizing the indigenous population in general seems to have been relatively low in Australia and New Zealand. Accordingly, building churches there was not directed to this part of the population, but to the immigrant Europeans, for whom the architectonic culture of their countries of origin was exported, or who imported this culture themselves—always conscient of the contrast between the translocated European architecture and its now foreign surroundings.[56] In areas with ancient, but "advanced" civilizations that were considered to be almost on a par with European ones, such as India or Japan, building churches in Gothic style was more restrained. China is yet another case. There was no paternalistic colonization and missionary work of the entire country as in Africa, but churches in the Gothic style, especially after the suppression of the Boxer Rebellion, were built as monuments of victo-

54 In the "Manifesto Antropófago" published in 1928, the Brazilian intellectual Oswaldo de Andrade wrote: "we must treat European culture anthropophogagly, because we must eat it and digest all that is good in it; then we should bring out all this again in a more superior form, with a great deal of humour and critical spirit…" Andrade, *Manifesto Antropófago.*

55 In the United States, there was already a connection between abolitionism and neo-Gothic in the nineteenth century.

56 Andrews, *Australian Gothic*, 1.

ry. And once again the French colonies are to be evaluated differently: the closer they were to the mother country—especially the departments in North Africa at that time—the more they participated in the current modern architectural development of the mother country, because they were considered "truly French." In the more distant regions of Indochina, however, the "true" neo-Gothic style could still live on, even though its time was over on French soil itself.

A chapter in itself is formed by the United States and Canada, where the diffusion of Gothic architecture, especially in the twentieth century, was accompanied by a growing self-confidence of the countries, driven by the desire to catch up with Europe or even occasionally to outdo it. A strong indication of this is also "collegiate Gothic," the use of Gothic forms in university buildings; these institutions were intended to stabilize the present and guarantee the future.[57]

But even more strongly, churches, especially in Gothic forms, are continuously considered as mainly representative of the desired homogenous but differentiated society. It is not by chance that the most representative modern building type of the twentieth century in the United States, the skyscraper, was sacralized for a long time by resorting to Gothic forms.[58]

These observations suggest that there is an overarching motive for continuity in the building of "Gothic" churches in the twentieth and twenty-first centuries—namely, to construct, consolidate, strengthen, and dynamize identities. Those identities can be quite different, even ambivalent: identities should be newly imposed or restored if believed to be lost.[59] Of course, many different means could be activated for this purpose—whereby Gothic, which had advanced to a kind of canonical style for ecclesiastical architecture in Europe in the nineteenth century, was given the special role for providing the recognized symbolic form in the field of sacrality and religion.

A modernized Gothic, or rather Gothic adapted to modernity, can finally be understood as a hybrid form typical for the twentieth century. The use of mud bricks, especially in Africa, has led to independent building types for which there were no models in medieval European brick Gothic. Typical also was the integration of traditional regional ornamentation or of specific flora and fauna, the latter especially in gargoyles or the sculptural decoration of capitals.[60] In the Catholic mission territories under Popes Benedict XV (1914–1922) and Pius XI (1922–1939), a regionalization of the church was pursued, which included an increased adoption of local traditions and elements—a phenomenon which in current terminology could be called transculturation.[61]

The amalgamation of different models, which is rare in Europe and is more frequent in North and South America, should also be mentioned in this context. And the borderline to the transcultural is crossed, where the Gothic churches of the twentieth and twenty-first centuries did not encounter traditional European urban structures common from the Middle Ages to historicism. This is not only true for North American or Australian cities, where Gothic churches are often lined up along arterial roads, or where buildings built by different denominations are grouped together. Rather, in the new cities of the former African colonies, which were rapidly expanding in the twentieth century, churches in the Gothic idiom, for historical reasons, often serve as visual anchor points in an urban environment that appears unstructured. Some of these churches were built at geographically particularly prominent points; for example, in the capital of Uganda, Kampala, supposedly built like Rome on seven hills—which is a colonial projection—the dominant monuments of the Anglican Namirembe and the Catholic Rugaba Cathedral [Figs. 11.15 and 11.22] rise on the top of two of these hills. With their precious materiality and elaborate forms, all those churches serve today as antipoles to the often informal architecture of their surroundings.[62] However, they have this stabilizing function not only because of their form,

57 Köth, "Verortung in der Zeit."
58 Skyscraper churches represent a special form of combining sacral and profane architecture; Murphy, ed., *Skyscraper gothic;* Köth, *Wolkenkratzerkirchen.*
59 A significant example of the ambivalence of the use of Gothic architecture can be found in Vietnam: near a small French vacation village from the early twentieth century, which was abandoned after the independence of the country, a giant new resort was built in 2015 under the title "French Village" with a building in the center that is reminiscent of a French Gothic church. Considering that much of Vietnam's history in the second half of the twentieth century revolves around the political decolonization of the country, it is at least astonishing how easily the architectural paradigm of the colonization era could be adopted in the end. See fig. 14.07.
60 Australian examples in Andrews, *Australian Gothic*, 135, and the contributions on São Paulo (Brazil) and Quito (Ecuador) in this volume.
61 On the concrete and ambivalent impact of Holy See politics in China, see the contribution of Thomas Coomans in this book.
62 Introducing remarks especially for cities in Africa: Demissie, "Imperial legacies and postcolonial predicaments" and Id., "Colonial Architecture and Urbanism in Africa."

but above all as buildings of institutions for which it is important to gather the population and to penetrate and shape the environment in a religious way. The Gothic style, proven for ecclesiastical buildings, seems to be the most suitable means for this purpose, a style to be used again and again.

Gothic in the Twentieth and Twenty-First Centuries: An Architecture of Global Transfer

Below this general cultural level, how Gothic forms and building techniques were imitated, transferred, and adapted in concrete terms plays an important role. Corresponding scientific investigations are relatively numerous for the nineteenth century. Especially within the British Empire, there was an intensive exchange of people, ideas, plans, pattern books, etc.[63] During the twentieth century and outside of the Empire, the situation is more complicated for some reasons already mentioned: religious orders or societies have often taken on the role of transmitters.[64] But there were no longer globally uniform political or administrative structures that could have led to a uniform exchange of Gothic forms, nor did similar travel opportunities exist everywhere for persons and media. And another characteristic and important, but completely different phenomenon of twentieth-century architecture does not seem to have played any role in the continuation of architecture in Gothic forms: that of the exile of architects. On the other hand, there were and are, at first glance, surprising connections between the protagonists active on different continents.[65]

For this reason, too, the global Gothic of the last hundred years stands for the polycentric development of art and art historical discourse in the age of modernism and postmodernism. Its story can no longer be told in the traditional sense through dominant, familiar, and proven narratives. A multiperspectival view, as it is attempted here, can better do justice to these phenomena.

One benefit of this book is that it provides a—doubtless only sketchy, but at least global—overview of the differentiated building culture in Gothic forms in the twentieth and twenty-first centuries. Many, significant differences become apparent. But it is much more surprising to learn how many parallel and similar phenomena globally existed or still exist: To mention only the unrecognized survival of "classical" neo-Gothic or Gothic Revival worldwide, expressive adaptations of Gothic from Europe to Africa to China, postmodern reappearance of Gothic forms, Gothic as a style of forced Christian reactionism, and so on. However, not only are the forms often amazingly similar, but also the cultural and social constellations that led to the choice of those forms. All of this is only to learn in an overall view, which is not colonialist, but which focuses on the discourses that arise during and thanks to the increasing global networking and entanglement in respect to such a traditional, Eurocentric subject as Gothic architecture and its permanent, always new adaptations.

63 Bremner, *Imperial Gothic*; Andrews, *Australian Gothic*, 45–62.

64 See the contributions of Martín Checa-Artasu, Thomas Coomans, Bruno Klein, and Olimpia Niglio in this book.

65 On America and Australia, see Andrews, *Australian Gothic*, 42–43; on China, see the contribution of Thomas Coomans in his book.

3
Gothic in Europe after the "End" of Neo-Gothic

Bruno Klein

European architecture in Gothic forms presents itself during the twentieth and twenty-first centuries in different variations—they range from the detailed imitation of medieval models to extremely free appropriation. But they all have in common their location on a continent where medieval Gothic and historicist neo-Gothic had existed.[1] So the discussion of medieval or neo-Gothic models of the nineteenth century play an unparalleled role because of their sheer quantity, leading to adaptation or demarcation.

As large and varied as the number of such models was, so were the reasons for a stronger or weaker imitation of such churches in the last one hundred years: to mention unspecific religious feelings, to sentimentally reference an idealized Middle Ages, to attempt to revive the Gothic as a particularly uplifting and inspiring architectural style, and so on. And nationally oriented historical constructions, especially in the first half of the twentieth century, made also use of the Gothic style. But that, on the whole, should not be overestimated, because Gothic churches were often constructed entirely for local or regional reasons, without a view to the national.[2]

Despite the large inventory of Gothic buildings from the Middle Ages as well as neo-Gothic ones from historicism, Europe is not the focal point of neo-Gothic sacred architecture of the twentieth and twenty-first centuries. Rather, the development of Gothic architecture in Europe came to a virtual standstill in the period after the First World War. This was due to not only the new narrative of "modern" architecture, which was then developing into a leading discourse, but also an unspecific feeling was emerging, especially in the countries that had been the main places of the war, against prewar culture for being partly responsible for that disaster. A break with the immediate past was therefore obvious, also in the field of architecture. In addition, new tasks in residential and industrial construction were growing, while the construction of new churches was no longer perceived as a priority. What was nevertheless built in this respect was, in style and type, mostly new.

However, this was different in two major areas: first, where war damage made the restoration of the lost desirable. This was particularly the case in Belgium—Ypres will later be presented as an example of this—and in northern France. Buildings such as St. Vaast in Béthune [Figs. 3.02 & 3.03] were not really reconstructed, but rather rebuilt in the vague memory of what was lost.[3] Second, in the countries on the periphery of the great battlefields of the First World War a radical break with the past seemed less necessary. As a result, more than elsewhere, churches in the traditional, mainly neo-Gothic idiom continued to be built there. This was especially the case in Great Britain and the Nordic countries but also in Spain, which was not to experience its warlike crisis until 1936–1939 in the Civil War.

Continuity, repair, reconstruction, and modernity were entangled in the continuity of Gothicizing architecture and forms since the early twentieth century in Europe. It is hardly possible to find buildings that could stand for one single or even only a few of these themes. However, some individual or groups of churches may be identified that

3.01 Trondheim, Norway, Nidaros Cathedral, façade, mainly 20th century. [Wikimedia Commons; photo DXR, 2015]

1 For this reason, Eastern Europe doesn't play an important role in this context; however, the region is still far too little studied with regard to the neo-Gothic style of the twentieth and twenty-first centuries.

2 It seems that the "nationalization" of Gothic architecture was a mere phenomenon of art history. Famous and sometimes notorious for this are a number of publications from the time around the First and Second World War. For example, in 1918, Mâle, *L'art allemand et l'art français*, or, in 1950, Sedlmayr, *Entstehung der Kathedrale*. It should not be overlooked that there have also been repeated attempts to interpret Gothic architecture as an internationally unifying element.

3 Anonymous, "Cordonnier, Louis-Marie".

3.02 Bethune, France, Saint-Vaast, before destruction in World War I. [Postcard, archive Bruno Klein]

3.03 Bethune, France, Saint-Vaast, Reconstruction by Louis-Marie Cordonnier, 1924–1927. [Wikimedia Commons; photo Velvet, 2014]

3.04 Wellingborough, Northamptonshire, England, St. Mary's, Sir Ninian Comper, 1908–1931. [© Fioni Orsini]

3.05 Stratton-on-the-Fosse, Somerset, England, Downside Abbey, nave, Giles Gilbert Scott, 1925. [Wikimedia Commons; photo Hugh Llewelyn, 2017]

can be regarded as particularly characteristic of one or the other field. It is not paradoxical that the termination of such building projects belongs to the reality of twentieth- and twenty-first-century neo-Gothic in Europe.

Gothic Revival after World War I in Great Britain

England is certainly the country where the First World War caused the smallest break with neo-Gothic or Gothic Revival architecture in Europe. In addition, there were long-lasting and permanent processes such as industrialization and urbanization, not to mention the restoration of the Roman Catholic church hierarchy or the general Catholic Renaissance, which made it necessary to build new places of worship. The strong architectural tradition in this style continued, supported by people and institutions.[4] Perhaps most striking in this regard is the work of Sir Ninan Comper (1864–1960), who had studied architecture in the 1880s under George Frederick Bodley and spent his entire life building churches in the style of the Gothic Revival. His most famous work is St. Mary's in Wellingborough (1908–1931) [Fig. 3.04].[5]

Gothic Revival churches have been so common over the last hundred years that only a few of them can be mentioned here: very characteristic are a number of long-lasting building projects, some of which were planned or started as early as the nineteenth century and could only be completed in the twentieth or even twenty-first century.

An early example of this is the Catholic Church of Downside Abbey in Somerset.[6] Its construction was begun in 1873 with the transept according to the plans of Archibald Matthias Dunn and Charles Francis Hansom. Thus, it is an example of the "classic" Gothic Revival. In 1906 the chancel, due to plans by Thomas Garner, was consecrated. Giles Gilbert Scott completed the nave in 1925 [Fig. 3.05]; the crossing tower followed in 1938. While Scott kept back with his own stylistic inventions at the nave where he designed historical Gothic forms, the provisional façade shows quite new stylistic elements that are characteristic for his interwar style. Those forms appear clearly in his main work, the Liverpool Cathedral.

Its planning and construction extended from 1885 to 1978, so beyond the caesuras of the First and even the Second World War.[7] The industrial harbor city, which had grown rapidly since the late eighteenth century, had become the seat of an Anglican diocese in 1880.[8] Similar to Truro in Cornwall, which had become the center of a new diocese four years earlier followed by the construction of a new cathedral,[9] an equal monument was planned there. But while the neo-Gothic church of Truro was erected very quickly between 1880 and 1910, the process up to the consecration in Liverpool took much longer. A first draft from 1885 for a new cathedral by William Emerson was nothing more than a fantasy product, especially because not even the exact building site of the church was yet fixed.[10] Only in 1902 or 1903 was a competition held to finally select the winning design by the young, twenty-six-year-old Giles Gilbert Scott. [Fig. 3.06] The experienced neo-Gothicist George Frederick Bodley was then chosen as associate architect.[11] It is difficult to judge the results of this combination of an "old" and a "young" neo-Gothicist.[12] In any case, it was only after Bodley's death that Giles Gilbert Scott presented a stylistic turn. As a result, the former highly differentiated design of Liverpool Cathedral was drastically simplified. The central tower, whose dimensions were continually increased during the whole planning process, became at that moment finally the focus of the entire monument.[13] Details were to change several times during its construction from 1934 to 1942, but always with the aim of simplification and monumentalization.[14]

The permanent, processual transformation of the building project, which was originally deeply rooted in the English Gothic Revival of the nineteenth century, was not an obstacle, but the precondition for the completion of the

4 Bremer, *Imperial Gothic.*
5 Symondson, *Sir Ninian Comper.*
6 Bellenger, *Downside Abbey.*
7 A short characterization of the Liverpool Cathedral as the endpoint of the Gothic revival: Yorke, *Gothic Revival Architecture*, 58–59.
8 The new diocese had been separated from the old diocese of Chester.
9 Shearlock, *Truro Cathedral*; Brown, *The Story of Truro Cathedral.*
10 Kennerley, *The Building of Liverpool Cathedral*, 3.
11 Ibid., 17.
12 Ibid., 13–21. Bodley (1827–1907) had since long close professional and family ties with the Scott family. So, as a commissioner in the competition for Liverpool Cathedral, it could hardly have escaped to him that the grandson of his teacher George Gilbert Scott (1811–1878) and son of his late companion George Gilbert Scott Jr. (1839–1897) had submitted a design. However, after Giles Gilbert Scott was declared the winner and Bodley assigned to him as "senior partner," their relationship did not develop as expected. This was because Scott explicitly declared the Liverpool Cathedral design to be his own intellectual property. When Bodley died in 1907, Scott assumed sole responsibility for completing the project (Kennerley, *The Building of Liverpool Cathedral*, 31–36). About Bodley: Hall, *George Frederick Bodley and the Later Gothic Revival in Britain and America.*
13 Kennerley, *The Building of Liverpool Cathedral*, 53–54.
14 Lewis, *The Gothic Revival*, 180, sees the completed building of Liverpool as the synthesis of the two tendencies toward simplification on the one hand and pathetic architecture on the other.

3.06 Liverpool, England, Anglican Cathedral, modified draft by Giles Gilbert Scott 1909–1910.
[Kennerley, *The Building of Liverpool Cathedral*, 18]

3.07 Liverpool, England, Anglican Cathedral, execution, consecrated 1978.
[Wikimedia Commons; photo Rodhullandemu, 2021]

3.08 Guildford, England, Anglican Cathedral, Edward Maufe, interior, 1932–1961.
[Wikimedia Commons; photo Poliphilo, 2019]

building, finally consecrated in 1978 [Fig. 3.07]. Its closing design benefits from the architect's capability to modernize it in permanence. In fact, Scott was successful in building a series of other churches during his career,[15] including Ampleforth Abbey, North Yorkshire (1922–1924 and then 1958–1961)[16] and Oban Cathedral, Scotland (1935–1952), which can be considered examples for a further development of Gothic Revival architecture into the twentieth century. Stylistically, they are characterized by a simplification of forms, similar to the contemporaneous American skyscraper Gothic. Their move into the sublime is also characteristic of other, more monumental buildings by Scott, such as the Battersea Power Station and the Bankside Power Station, which is today's Tate Modern.

The affinities to modern architecture were even stronger in the work of the British architect Edward Maufe (1882–1974).[17] He also built numerous churches, which typologically and formally follow models from the Middle Ages or the nineteenth century. His main work is undoubtedly the Anglican Holy Spirit Cathedral in Guildford, Surrey. Designed around 1932/1933, its foundation stone was laid in 1936 and its consecration took place in 1961. Maufe intended to continue the tradition of medieval English cathedrals, but at the same time to create a contemporary church. The simplicity of the interior of Guildford Cathedral [Fig. 3.08] is similar to the somewhat older Grundtvig's Church in Copenhagen or the almost contemporary Hallgrim's Church in Reykjavík [Figs. 3.31 & 3.33].

St. Edmundsbury Cathedral in Bury St. Edmunds [Fig. 3.09 & 3.10] is a special example of stylistic continuity in church building from the Middle Ages through the nineteenth century to the present. Similar to Liverpool Cathedral, St. Edmundsbury Cathedral was the center of a newly established diocese in the wake of industrialization. However, it was not a completely new building, but an extension of the older St. James Parish Church from the early sixteenth century.[18] Fifteen years after the establishment of the diocese in 1944, in 1959, instead of a smaller Victorian chancel built by Gilbert

15 See Lewis, *Modernizing tradition*, esp. chapter 3: "The Church designs. Tradition in the Modern Age," 128–225, where those buildings are characterized stylistically as "sculptural."
16 For more information see:<https://historicengland.org.uk/listing/the-list/list-entry/1315767>.
17 Maufe, *Guildford*. Before publishing this chapter, it was unfortunately not possible to consult Dunmur, *Edward Maufe*.
18 Other older churches in England were also elevated to cathedrals of new dioceses during this period, e.g., in Leicester and Chelmsford. And there, too, extensions were made in Gothic forms, but these were not as large as in Bury St. Edmunds.

3.09 Bury St. Edmunds, England, St. Edmundsbury Cathedral, chancel (Stephen Dykes Bower) and "Millenium tower" (Hugh Mathew), 1959–2005.
[Wikimedia Commons; photo Martin Pettitt, 2015]

3.10 Bury St. Edmunds, England, St Edmundsbury Cathedral, interior looking east from the chancel toward the nave.
[Wikimedia Commons; photo David Diliff, 2014]

Scott, a new, elongated three-aisled choir was erected, according to plans by Stephen Dykes Bower.[19] It now towers above the older nave in height. A new transept arose at the intersection of the two parts of the building, and the crossing, generated in that process, was topped between 2000 and 2005 by a high tower, designed by Warwick Pethers, the last assistant of Dykes Bower. Small chapel extensions were added later.[20] Stylistically, the parts from the twentieth and twenty-first centuries are a modernized Perpendicular, much closer to any medieval model than Liverpool. If the free recourse to the Gothic served initially to invent a tradition with the first extension of the St. James Parish Church, such tradition was later reconstructed in Bury St. Edmunds by equal architectonic means, because it was the burial place of the national patron Saint Edmund. His relics were venerated in a huge abbey church, whose ruins lie behind the new cathedral. It picks up where the history of the monastery ended with the English Reformation in the sixteenth century.

Fragmentary Churches of the Neo-Gothic Style in the Twentieth Century: The New Cathedrals of Lille and Vitoria-Gasteiz

In other countries, historicist building projects also didn't come to a complete standstill. Historicisms occurred over the course of the twentieth century again and again in both the private and the public, profane building sector. Moreover, an abrupt change of style for pure artistic reasons would have been risky, even during construction of large sacred buildings, because it could endanger the financing: donors who wanted to support the previous ancient project had to be won back for the new one. It was therefore safer to continue largely unchanged. On the other hand, such a continuously pursued church construction could also gradually come into conflict with considerable social changes and finally become anachronistic—not for stylistic reasons, but as a project as a whole.

The situation in France was significant for this; in 1905 the separation of church and state had taken place. All existing cathedrals then belonged to the state, which, especially in the heated atmosphere following the pass-

19 Symondson, *Stephen Dykes Bower*, 61–79. Dyker Bower was not only responsible for restoration and maintenance of several of the most prominent historic buildings in England, but he was also the architect of new churches in different medieval styles; for example, the neo-Romanesque St. John the Evangelist Church, Newbury, or, the more late Gothic, All Saints' Church, Hockerill.

20 Pepin, *Cathedrals*, 194–196.

3.11 Lille, France, Cathedral Notre-Dame de la Treille, first model to the project by Charles Leroy from 1856. Frontispice.
[Hautcoeur. *Histoire de Notre-Dame de la Treille*]

ing of the relevant law, showed no interest in financing the construction of large new churches.

In this respect, the Gothic cathedral of Nantes was just lucky. Its construction, begun in the fifteenth century and for a long time interrupted, finally came to an end between 1840 and 1891, with the addition of a neo-Gothic transept and choir with ambulatory and chapels—only fourteen years before the separation of church and state.[21]

Less fortunate was the construction of the church—later cathedral—of Lille.[22] Started in 1856 according to a plan by Charles Leroy [Fig. 3.11], it was far from finished when it was elevated to cathedral in 1913, as was always intended. After a period of dormant construction work during World War I, its erection was resumed in 1919 and the transept was begun. In the 1920s, the building was technically and organizationally modernized, mainly to reduce costs but also to increase the speed of construction.[23] These measures were successful only in part. After all, working didn't stop during World War II and continued in accordance with the original plans of 1856. But a break came immediately after the ceremonial opening of the nave in 1947 and continued until 1954. At that time, just some lower parts had been built, and a radical change seemed inevitable: to complete the church as a whole, the construction of the clerestory was subsequently abandoned and a simple ogival barrel vault was added to the existing parts [Fig. 3.12]. Reduced in this way, the interior of the cathedral was then completed between 1955 and 1975. The façade remained an unfinished torso, which gave the building such a dilapidated aspect that even in the 1970s, one thought aloud about demolishing the entire cathedral.[24] Finally, a modern façade was finished in 1999 [Fig. 3.13].[25] Formally a cross-section of the nave behind it, the façade takes up Gothic elements and may be classified stylistically as an updated neo-Gothic from the end of the twentieth century.[26]

In contrast to Lille, where a neo-Gothic cathedral stuck in its initial stages could only be completed, with great effort, by abandoning the original design idea, the new cathedral in the Basque city of Vitoria-Gasteiz, entirely from the twentieth century, has remained stylistically uniform, but incomplete [Fig. 3.14].[27] The rapid industrial development of the late nineteenth century led to the layout of a new town, at Vitoria-Gasteiz, with the cathedral at its center. Doubtlessly, such a cathedral had to be Gothic in style.[28] Begun in 1907, and designed by Javier Luque

21 James, ed., *Nantes.*

22 Hautcoeur, *Histoire de Notre-Dame de la Treille dans l'ancienne collégiale de Saint-Pierre et dans la nouvelle basilique érigée en cathédrale par sa Sainteté Pie X le 25 octobre 1913;* Ulrich, ed., *Lille: la Treille, lumière du Nord.* See there, specifically for the continuing construction during the twentieth century: Vienne, "La Deuxième Phase du Chantier, 1919–1965," 114–137.

23 Wall and pillar cores were made of concrete and covered with stone. Pneumatic tools for stone cutting and modern cranes were introduced. Only stonemasonry, stonework, sculpture, and surface treatment remained to be carried out by the site's own workers. The rest—e.g., foundation work—was outsourced to independent companies. Vienne, "La Deuxième Phase du Chantier, 1919–1965," 116–119.

24 Vienne, "Admirateurs et détracteurs de la Treille."

25 Frémaux, "1999, La cathédrale enfin achevée."

26 In this context, the new construction of the façade and narthex of the monastery church of Sainte-Marie de la Pierre-qui-vire in Morvan, France, from 1991 to 1992 could also be considered: there, a neo-Gothic church was given a porch in an abstract, vaguely Gothic style. Apers, "L'abbaye 'Sainte-Marie de la Pierre-qui-Vire.'"

27 Marigorta, *Las dos catedrales de Vitoria*, especially 69–109. Numerous photographs of the project are published on the home page of the "Centro Vasco de Arquitectura - Euscal Herriko Arkitektura Ikerkundea": <http://intranet.pogmacva.com/en/obras/60046>.

28 Marigorta, *Las dos catedrales de Vitoria*, 71.

29 Marigorta, *Las dos catedrales de Vitoria*, 75. See also <https://es.wikipedia.org/wiki/Catedral_de_Mar%C3%ADa_Inmaculada_(Vitoria)> (23 February 2020).

and Julián de Apraiz, even the royal couple of Spain came to the laying of the foundation stone. But already in March 1914 the construction work stopped, because the budget was completely overdrawn. It was only resumed in 1946 after the dictator Franco promised to support the project.[29] In 1969, the church was vaulted and then consecrated. The concrete vaults made outer flying buttresses superfluous. Because of the expected costs, the crossing tower and the

3.12 Lille, France, Cathedral, interior. [Wikimedia Commons; photo Velvet, 2013]

3.14 Vitoria-Gasteiz, Spain, Model (inside the cathedral) of the original project for the new cathedral (Catedral Nueva) María Inmaculada by Javier Luque and Julián de Apraiz. [Wikimedia Commons; photo Zarateman, 2007]

3.13 Lille, France, Cathedral, façade, Pierre-Louis Carlier, Peter Rice, 1996–1999. [Wikimedia Commons; photo Velvet, 2015]

3.15 Vitoria-Gasteiz, Spain, Cathedral of Santa María Inmaculada today. [Wikimedia Commons; photo Tim Tregenza, 2013]

monumental double-towered façade were not executed; only a portico was erected in their place in 1973, when the construction came to an absolute end [Fig. 3.15]. The building is in some way a monument of the era of General Franco's dictatorship.

Like the Lille Cathedral, Vitoria-Gasteiz Cathedral is only theoretically complete, but in reality, it remains a torso in relation to the original project. In the end, there wasn't enough social approval to complete such ambitious projects.[30] So these churches remained unfinished for ideological or political, but not for stylistic, reasons. Under other conditions, neo-Gothic churches could be completed if they were not too much charged in an ideological sense and if the original plans were not followed too strictly or even orthodoxically.

Steady and Carefully Developed Neo-Gothic: Prague, Ypres, and Trondheim

St. Vitus Cathedral, Prague, begun in 1344, is one of those monumental buildings whose neo-Gothic construction process led to its completion beyond World War I [Figs. 3.16 & 3.17]. The choir and parts of the southern transept were erected, along with parts of the southern transept and the basements of the adjoining tower, when construction work was permanently suspended in 1419 as a result of the Hussite uprising and subsequent wars.[31] The work was resumed in the nineteenth century,[32] initially revolving around the architectural idea of completing the late Gothic south tower as the center of the cathedral. Finally, cathedral architect Josef Mocker designed the nave, which was built from 1873 onward and imitated the older parts of the fourteenth-century choir. He added a double-towered west façade, which was subordinate in height and mass to the torso of the south tower. According to these plans, the cathedral was largely completed when Mocker died in 1899. His successor, Kamil Hilbert, had to limit his own work mostly to structural details and the interior decoration. Therefore, the neo-Gothic completion of St. Vitus' Cathedral belongs to the nineteenth century in terms of both thought and architectural history, even though the building was not consecrated until 1929.

Nevertheless, the cathedral in Prague is an important example of the continuity and autonomy of large neo-Gothic construction sites that bridge historical ruptures: it was started when Prague still belonged to the Hapsburg monarchy and completed during the time of the Czech Republic.

The situation is completely different with the St. Martin's Church in Ypres [Figs. 3.18 & 3.19]. The Gothic building was begun in 1221 and finished with the erection of the tower between 1435 and 1475.[33] During the First World War, St. Martin's was completely destroyed, like the entire city, and it was reconstructed between 1922 and 1930.[34] The belfry of the city was rebuilt from 1931 to 1934, while the reconstruction of the market hall, which began in 1936, could only be completed in 1962.

The reconstruction of the Gothic church of Ypres could be interpreted as part of a more extensive rebuilding of the entire city, in which mainly lost objects with a high memorial and identification value were to be restored. Stylistic idioms such as Gothic weren't important in the context. In fact, the architect of the reconstruction, Jules Coomans, had been the master builder of Ypres since 1895, so he was ideally suited to the task.[35] But Coomans had also been one of the leading representatives of neo-Gothic in Belgium even before World War I. He advocated for the historical reconstruction of the city instead of a modern one: as a representative of the conservative and politically influential St. Thomas and St. Luke's Guild, founded in Belgium in 1863, he transferred its ideas of Gothic as the ideal church architecture in Ypres from the pre- to the postwar period.[36] So he didn't only help the tower of St. Martin's Church to its spire, which had been missing since the Middle Ages and

30 Other examples in Spain were the churches of Alba de Tormes, Castilla y León (Mesecke, "Repullés y Vargas, Enrique María"; <https://www.asturnatura.com/turismo/basilica-de-santateresa-de-alba-de-tormes/3382>), Son Severo, Mallorca (Liaño Gibert, "Rubió i Bellver"), and Arucas, Gran Canaria (Alemán Hernández; Martín Hernández. *Guía del patrimonio*, 116–118).
31 For the construction, restoration, and furnishing work between 1419 and the 19th century, see: Kuthan and Royt, *The Cathedral of St. Vitus at Prague Castle*, 355–423.
32 Ibid., 425–437.
33 Construction data from Masure and Houwen, *Ieper*, 6–8. Ypres was a diocese and St. Martin's a cathedral from 1559 to 1801. Since 1969, Ypres is a titular diocese. The designation "Cathedral" for St. Martin's has been retained for traditional reasons.
34 Rüter, "Coomans, Jules".
35 Masure and Houwen, *Ieper*, 8. De Maeyer, ed., *De St. Lucasscholen en de neogotiek 1862–1914*, 415.
36 De Maeyer, "Pro Arte Christiana," 166.
37 Masure and Houwen, *Ieper*, 8.
38 Nordhagen, *La cathédrale de Trondhjem*. Planning and implementation are described in more detail in: Meyer, "Cathédrale de Trondhjem. Aperçu abrégé de sa fondation, de sa decadence et de sa reconstruction actuelle," 1–30; Nordhagen, "Considérations sur la conception architectonique de la façade occidentale," 31–48; Kolsrud, "Le statuaire de la façade," 49–52; Albertsen, *Der Dom zu Drontheim;* Danbolt, *Nidarosdomen fra kristkirke til nasjonalmonument*; Fischer, *Domkirken i Trondheim. Kirkebygget i Middelalteren*, esp. vol. 2 with chapter XII "Restaureringen," 405–528, Summary "The Restoration," 584–585; Storemyr, *The Stones of Nidaros*.

3.16 Prague, Czech Republic, St. Vitus Cathedral, state 1887.
[Photo by Jindrich Eckert. Public domain]

3.17 Prague, Czech Republic, St. Vitus Cathedral, 2010.
[Wikimedia Commons; photo Jorge Làscar, 2010]

which he had planned as early as 1907, but he also designed numerous neo-Gothic furnishings inside the church, such as the choir screen and the organ loft.[37]

The restoration and reconstruction of Trondheim Cathedral, or Nidaros Cathedral, Norway, had a strong national connotation.[38] It was built successively from east to west from around 1183–1190 onward in place of a predecessor building. The west façade was erected from around 1300 onward, but it is unclear whether it was ever completed. The cathedral had already burned down in 1328 after a lightning strike, and further fires followed in 1432 and 1531. Severe storm damage in the following centuries was only repaired in a makeshift manner, so that the cathedral was a ruinous fragment in the early nineteenth century [Fig. 3.20].

After Norway achieved independence from Denmark in 1814 and became a new kingdom in personal union with Sweden (until 1905), the cathedral—burial place of Olav, the legendary first Christian king of Norway—was given the constitutional rank of a coronation church. After various, sometimes contradictory, renovation and restoration projects, the parliament passed a resolution in 1869 to reconstruct the cathedral. From 1841 the German-born architect Heinrich Ernst Schirmer was involved in the preservation of the cathedral, followed by Christian Christie, from 1872 until his death in 1906. While it was possible to restore, based on visible traces, the supposed medieval original of the eastern sections, it was more difficult to find a form for the upper parts of the nave and the west façade, because there was no longer any evidence to help reconstruction. This led to disputes about the design of these parts, so that the building process was abandoned between 1915 and 1923. It was not until 1930 that the nave vaults could be closed; the south tower was completed in 1964, and its northern counterpart in 1969.[39] Work on the sculptural program for the façade continued [Fig. 3.01].

While in the nineteenth century, reconstruction work was mainly based on traces, the result of twentieth-century building activity was a creative, in other words, pure neo-Gothic reinvention. If the dispute over the appropriate form of the missing sections led to an interruption, the idea to stop the entire completion of the cathedral as an outdated historicist project was never expressed.

The general movement for a full restoration of that Norwegian National Cathedral could not be broken by modernity, but there

39 Storemyr, *The Stones of Nidaros*, 82: "The west front is a major work in Norwegian art history, primarily because of the rich iconographic programme in which many eminent Norwegian sculptors participated. The niches of the three upper storeys are filled with life-size statues, but only five of them are actually copies of medieval ones. The last statue was put in place as recently as in 1984."

3.18 a-b Ypres, Belgium, St. Martin, before and after destruction in WW1. [Postcards, archive Bruno Klein]

3.19 Ypres, Belgium, St. Martin, after reconstruction. [Wikimedia Commons; photo Limo Wreck, 2007]

3.20 Trondheim, Norway, Nidaros Cathedral from north, 1762. [National Library of Norway]

3.21 Trondheim, Norway, Nidaros Cathedral, façade, Christie's project. [Trondheim Nidaros Domkirkes Restaureringsarbeider]

3.22 Trondheim, Norway, Nidaros Cathedral, façade, Nordhagen's first project. [Trondheim Nidaros Domkirkes Restaureringsarbeider]

3.23 Trondheim, Norway, Nidaros Cathedral, façade, Nordhagen's project 1921. [Trondheim Nidaros Domkirkes Restaureringsarbeider]

3.24 Trondheim, Norway, Nidaros Cathedral, façade, Thiis's project. [Trondheim Nidaros Domkirkes Restaureringsarbeider]

were delays caused by different modern considerations: the crisis regarding the continued construction of the façade was the result of a double, if not a triple, crisis. First, the old cathedral architect Christie had submitted a plan for the west façade, which he finally corrected in 1905 according to new archaeological evidence [Fig. 3.21]. After his death, a nationwide competition was held with five invitations, and the winner was immediately assured that he would take over the vacant position of the cathedral architect. The result, however, remained unsatisfactory. Only Olaf Nordhagen, who was invited with special permission, submitted a convincing design, which made him architect of the cathedral in 1909 [Fig. 3.22]. He subsequently revised his project to follow a plan that was approved by the Storting, the Norwegian parliament, in 1915. The first crisis about the design of the façade was thus just overcome, when Nordhagen himself initiated the second one: he withdrew his already approved design with the argument that it "did not give sufficient expression to our Nordic character. The towers were designed too 'English', while the cathedral should by no means look 'imported' but having a Norwegian appearance" [Fig. 3.23].[40]

40 Albertsen, *Der Dom zu Drontheim*, 94–95.

Trondhjems Domkirke

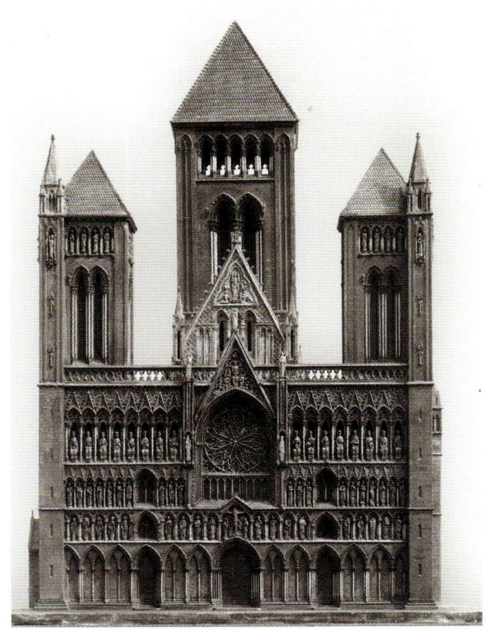

Behind this reflection about an appropriate national style was, however, something quite different: Nordhagen's new design represented, by no means, authentic historic Norwegian architecture, because there were no appropriate models for it. Rather, he simplified his plan in order to move it away from an architecture imitating historical models to a more sublime and expressive form. His turn corresponded to simultaneous artistic currents: Nordhagen's replanning of Trondheim Cathedral was paralleled by that of Giles Gilbert Scott in Liverpool.

But the construction of the Nidaros Cathedral was not only paralyzed by Nordhagen but also by the historian Julius Frederik Macody Lund. Macody Lund had been researching the reconstruction of Nidaros Cathedral for several years, when he claimed to have discovered that the medieval cathedral was built according to a system "ad quadratum." Accordingly, the nave vault had to be higher than planned, which in turn was important for the design of the adjacent west façade. Macody Lund was able to convince the Storting to stop further construction and to grant him funds to substantiate his theses. In the end, a commission of international leading conservationists and art historians[41] was set up to examine Macody Lund's theses. In 1922, the commission decided that Macody Lund's ideas were not sufficiently robust to be used as a basis for the further construction of Trondheim Cathedral and they should not delay its completion.

This seemingly curious story has a serious epistemological core : Reconstructions founded on subjective artistic invention came under increasing pressure, starting in the late nineteenth century, from supposedly scientifically based attempts. The assertion that, on the basis of art historical evidence, the design of neo-Gothic architecture in the twentieth and twenty-first centuries can be normatively determined was one of the guiding themes of this epoch and became relevant for numerous buildings.

In 1928, the architect Helge Thiis won another competition for the façade, and from 1930 he was in charge of the reconstruction work. He only slightly modified Nordhagen's final design, but he softened its severity with minor changes and additions, and he brought it closer to established art historical models, especially from England [Fig. 3.24]. Not that the design thus moved more in the direction of "modern" architecture—it was merely stripped of the pathos of the expressive architecture of the 1910s.

The Disappearance of Neo-Gothic: The Almudena Cathedral in Madrid and the Sagrada Família in Barcelona

With the Almudena Cathedral in Madrid and the Sagrada Família in Barcelona, the two biggest Spanish cities each have large, essentially neo-Gothic churches, both of which were begun in the late nineteenth century, but whose main structure was built in the twentieth and twenty-first centuries. Their ground plans are similar: they have polygonal choirs with an ambulatory and chapels; three-aisled transepts, three bays deep; and naves of six bays, in Barcelona five-aisled and in Madrid three-aisled but with bay-wide lateral chapels. Both churches are united by another strange phenomenon: Their original neo-Gothic structures and forms were more and more made to disappear during the building process!

Nevertheless, they could hardly be more different in terms of appearance and reputation. While in Barcelona, lines form in front of the building to visit it for an entrance fee, the magazine *El Confidencial* launched an online survey in 2016 to find out why Madrid's cathedral has so few visitors.[42]

In Madrid construction began with a neo-Romanesque crypt integrated into the otherwise luxurious neo-Gothic design of the cathedral, which was planned by Francisco de Cubas between 1883 and 1911. After the completion of that part, the building process was interrupted due to the high costs. Only after the end of the Spanish Civil War,

41 Paul Boeswillwald (President) (F), Camille Enlart (F), Gilbert Scott (GB), Frederick Moore Simpson (GB), Jules Brunfaut (B).
42 The following after Marten, "Die Almudena-Kathedrale zu Madrid," 141, with more detailed literature references.

when the Catholic Church became, under the dictatorship of General Franco, one of the most important pillars of the state, was the construction thought to be continued. Of course, the enthusiasm for the neo-Gothic style was over by this point, so it was decided to construct a building that stylistically better fit with the late baroque royal castle in front of it. The project of Fernando Chueca Goitia and Carlos Sidro emerged victorious from a competition held in 1944. Construction took place between 1950 and 1993, with a twenty-year break from 1965 to 1985. The interior, with a colorful wooden ceiling instead of the planned ribbed vaults, was completed in 2003 [Figs. 3.25, 3.26 & 3.27].

The Basílica i Temple Expiatori de la Sagrada Família (known as the Sagrada Família) in Barcelona was begun as a relatively conventional neo-Gothic building in

3.25 Madrid, Spain, Almudena Cathedral, model after the project by Francisco de Cubas.
[© Oronoz]

3.26 Madrid, Spain, Almudena Cathedral, choir.
[Wikimedia Commons; photo Luis Garcia, 2010]

3.27 Madrid, Spain, Almudena Cathedral, interior, completed 2003.
[Wikimedia Commons; photo Diego Delso, 2015]

3.28 Barcelona, Spain, Sagrada Família in 1908.
[*La Ilustració Catalana*, 3 January 1909]

3.29 Barcelona, Spain, Sagrada Família in 2017.
[Wikimedia Commons; photo C. Messier, 2017]

1882 on behalf of the conservative Associació Espiritual de Devots de Sant Josep.[43] The plans had been supplied by the diocesan architect Francisco de Paula del Villar y Lozano, who soon withdrew from the project, which was then entrusted to Antoni Gaudí. Born in 1852, Gaudí was deeply rooted in the architectural tradition of the nineteenth century. Gaudí first completed the already begun parts of the building, especially the crypt, but soon changed style and typology in line with the Catalan modernism, an artistic movement that took up regional building traditions and natural features to develop something new.

Nevertheless, in the early phase, in which the crypt was completed (1889) and the outer walls of the choir chapels were built (1893), he still leaned heavily on neo-Gothic forms [Fig. 3.28]. During this period, he also presented a new overall design, which still resembled a Gothic church in terms of its ground plan, although the forms of the upper parts became increasingly distant from it. In the designs produced after 1900, a completely new static system was then developed and original, expressive, organic decorative forms were created. In this phase, the building had almost completely distanced itself from Gothic or neo-Gothic formal ideals. Only a few basic elements still vaguely remind of medieval models, such as the choir with ambulatory, the multinave plan, the transept façades with portal gables and towers or the tracery. Above all, the Sagrada Família imitates and exaggerates the architectural pathos of the great Gothic cathedrals, and even their slow construction process, which in this church was deliberately staged in an anti-modern way.[44] It is unknown how the building would have been completed according to Gaudí's ideas, because the architect, who died in 1926 by an accident, permanently changed the architecture. Moreover, his office in the Sagrada Família was devastated during the Spanish Civil War and almost all documentation was lost. Thus, what was built at the Sagrada Família since then is at best an approximate reconstruction of a single, coincidental plan-

43 Bonet i Armengol, *La Sagrada Familia de Gaudí*.

44 It was forbidden to accept donations from ecclesiastical or state institutions.

ning moment [Fig. 3.29].[45] The fame of the church is based less on its sacred function, but rather profits from the increased veneration of its architect. It has mutated into a mystical building, where the extravagant formal inventions of a brilliant architect are adored.

While the neo-Gothic style of the cathedral in Madrid is hidden under its neo-Baroque exterior, the modern, expressive church in Barcelona grows out of a neo-Gothic core. The Almudena in Madrid is a state cathedral, formally a compromise to meet all the requirements of such building. In comparison, the Sagrada Família can be called a city cathedral. Its construction and form were founded on the individual spirituality of its clients and its main architect.

Both buildings—each consecrated by a pope—represent artistic counterparts of contemporary Spanish building culture.

National Gothic Revival: Copenhagen and Reykjavík

Since the completion of Cologne Cathedral in the nineteenth century, there has been a tendency to turn neo-Gothic buildings into national monuments.[46] However, any functionalization in a specific national sense was opposed at an early stage by the discovery that the Gothic style originally came from France and was therefore actually an original French style. Attempts to nationalize medieval Gothic, such as the definition of a "special German Gothic style," were limited to the study of historical architecture and played no significant role in neo-Gothic architecture in the twentieth century.[47]

On the other hand, Gothic architecture could also stand for a sublime style in an abstract sense, open to many different uses. This phenomenon had already been observed several times; for example, the "Catalanization" of the Sagrada Família by Gaudí, or in 1915 the cathedral of Trondheim was redesigned to make it less "English" and

45 For this reason, the Sagrada Família is not part of the UNESCO World Heritage of Gaudí Sites as a whole, but only the parts of it that were realized at the death of the architect.

46 Germann, "Der Kölner Dom als Nationaldenkmal"; Danboldt, *Nidarosdomen fra Kristkirke til nasjonalmonument*, esp. 290–304; Borger-Keweloh, "Mittelalterliche Dome als Nationaldenkmäler." Because this chapter is only concerned with buildings in Europe, the use of neo-Gothic architecture as a means of stabilizing dominant cultures on other continents will not be discussed here. On this phenomenon see the introduction of this book and specially: Bremner, *Imperial Gothic.*

47 Bushart, *Der Geist der Gotik und die expressionistische Kunst.*

3.30 Copenhagen, Denmark, Grundtvig's Memorial Church, façade, Peder Jensen-Klint and Kaare Jensen-Klint, 1921–1940.
[Wikimedia Commons; photo seier+seier, 2007]

3.31 Copenhagen, Denmark, Grundtvig's Memorial Church, interior, Peder Jensen-Klint and Kaare Jensen-Klint, 1921–1940.
[Wikimedia Commons; photo John Towner, 2016]

3.32 Reykjavík, Iceland, Hallgrím's Church, exterior, Guðjón Samúelsson, Hörður Bjarnason and Gaðar Halldórsson, 1935–1986.
[Wikimedia Commons; photo Cédric Liénart, 2018]

3.33 Reykjavík, Iceland, Hallgrím's Church, interior, Guðjón Samúelsson, Hörður Bjarnason and Gaðar Halldórsson, 1935–1986.
[Wikimedia Commons; photo Rob Young, 2012]

more "Norwegian."[48] Exactly at the same time, Peder Jensen-Klint, in Copenhagen, presented plans for a monument dedicated to Nikolai Frederik Severin Grundtvig, who had grown into the role of a Danish national theologian, poet, educator, and politician since his death in 1872.[49] The monument was combined with a church and was built between 1921 and 1940; after Peder Jensen-Klint's death in 1938, it was completed by his son Kaare. Meanwhile, the project had expanded into an housing estate with the church in the center [Figs. 3.30 & 3.31].[50] Seen from outside, Jensen-Klint's is a monumentalized Danish village church from the Middle Ages, which is more obvious in side views than from the often published expressive façade. Inside, the building presents itself as a radically unornamented, three-nave Gothic stepped hall with articulated pillars and ribbed vaulting, completely and strictly systematically built with bricks.[51] This interior in particular is impressive, with its unadorned, independent adaptation of forms of late Gothic brick architecture. The church belongs to the late work of the universal artist Jensen-Klint, who had previously built in both Baroque and Gothic styles, but who considered the Gothic to be the only "Nordic" architecture.[52] As in Trondheim, a Gothic style that was both ornamentally reduced and monumentalized was understood and staged in Copenhagen as an architectural expression of national Romanticism.[53]

This also happened a little later on Iceland, which had only been independent from Denmark since 1918 and where no Gothic and almost no neo-Gothic existed. However, the path to national neo-Gothic in Protestant Iceland was led via a Catholic detour: the state architect Guðjón Samúelsson had been commissioned by the head of the Catholic vicariate[54] in Reykjavík to build a church, for which he submitted a design in the spirit of Danish national Romanticism in 1921. This was rejected, however, because "the new church was to be combined with the Gothic style of the heyday of the Catholic Church."[55]

48 See note 40.
49 Faber, "1904–1929 A Time of Transition," esp. 173–175, "An unsurpassed monument"; Sestoft and Christiansen, *Guide to Danish Architecture. 1000–1960*, Vol. 1, 206–207; Jensen, *P. V. Jensen-Klint,* 288–391.
50 Jensen-Klint had only won second prize in a competition for a Grundtvig monument in 1913. This was to consist of only one tower. However, because he had planned to build a church along with the monument, he was commissioned to build it, especially because the model had been exhibited in Copenhagen City Hall and had received enthusiastic criticism. The overall project, which was finally realized, only developed during the construction period.
51 The church was built in yellow brick by seven specially selected craftsmen. Faber, "1904–1929 A Time of Transition," 173.
52 Repetzky, "Jensen-Klint, Peder Vilhelm".

The architect only reluctantly complied with this request, but eventually designed a neo-Gothic building, the Landakot Church in Reykjavík, built between 1925 and 1929.[56] Its walls are cast and not bricked, as was common for many buildings in Iceland at the time; the vaults are constructions of staff and wire mesh. The interior of the three-nave hall church with a circumambulatory choir, transept, and tower[57] is unadorned, similar to Grundtvig's church—here, too, the profiled pillars without capitals merge into arches and ribs. For the exterior buttresses, Guðjón Samúelsson was the first to apply the "columnar basalt style"[58] characteristic of his later work, which he saw as a means of giving Icelandic buildings a national look.[59]

The main work in this style is the Hallgrim's Church in Reykjavík, designed by the same architect and completed after his death by Hörður Bjarnason and Gaðar Halldórsson [Figs. 3.32 & 3.33].[60] It is a monumental three-nave, cross-ribbed vaulted building of the hall-type, behind a tower façade reminiscent of a rock motif. After long and complicated preliminary planning dating back to 1935, construction only began in 1945 and then progressed slowly, because forty percent of the financing for the church's construction was by donations. At Guðjón Samúelsson's death in 1950, the planning was not yet complete; the consecration did not take place until 1986.

In the course of its planning and construction, the church became a symbol of Icelandic independence. The whole process was accompanied by considerable Icelandic national propaganda, especially during World War II, when Denmark, which was then still connected to Iceland in royal personal union, was occupied by Germany from 1940 to 1945. Nevertheless, Guðjón Samúelsson cited the Grundtvig's Church in Copenhagen as a model, but described the style of the Hallgrim's Church as a synthesis of neo-Gothic and columnar basalt style, because "the Gothic style is considered the most beautiful style for church buildings. On the other hand, I wanted the sacred building to have the expression of the Icelandic landscape and surroundings."[61]

Meaning, Function, and Image of the Gothic

Hallgrim's Church is the last great building in Europe that was uniformly built according to the formal ideas about the "Gothic" period—it is also, however, an expression of a cultural construction, especially of the nineteenth century. The more attempts were made in the course of the twentieth century to realize new buildings and extensions as faithfully as possible in accordance with this historicist distillate, the greater was the danger of failure, as the cathedral of Lille in particular and some Spanish examples have shown. However, if the buildings and the designs for them were freed from the compulsion of an almost archaeologically exact repetition of medieval motifs and forms, they could succeed, as some northern European examples have shown.

However, it is hardly possible to define exact limits up to which a building can still be considered neo-Gothic or only Gothic-inspired. Characteristic of this is the Sagrada Família in Barcelona, which is almost only squeezed into the framework of a neo-Gothic building project from the nineteenth century at ground plan level, but which grows far beyond this in vertical direction. By contrast, numerous expressionist buildings that only used individual Gothic motifs, such as pointed arches or the tracery windows, were excluded from this chapter, as otherwise the number of objects would have become oversized and the focus on the survival of the neo-Gothic style defined in the nineteenth century would have become blurred.
There are some special buildings often overlooked because of their singularity, such as Paul Tournon's Sainte-Thérèse-de-l'Enfant-Jésus in the residential city of Élisabethville (municipality Aubergenville, Yvelines, France, 1927/1928), a modern adaptation of the thirteenth-century Gothic Sainte-

53 Because the location for the construction of the Grundtvig's Church was not fixed from the beginning, after the referendum of 1920, through which Northern Schleswig became Danish again, there were considerations to build the church in Dybbøl (German Düppel), which at that time had become Danish again, the place of the decisive Danish defeat in the Prussian-Danish War of 1864. The consecration of the church took place on September 8, 1940, a few months after the German occupation of Denmark in World War II.

54 Iceland only had religious freedom beginning in 1874. At that time, the first Catholic community was founded by French priests.

55 Hubertsson Seelow, *The modern architecture in Iceland in the first half of the 20th century*, 116.

56 Abrecht, *Architektúr á Islandi – leidarvísir*, 86/87.

57 A spire had been planned, but it was not built for reasons of cost. Abrecht, *Architektúr á Islandi – leidarvísir*, 86.

58 For more on this style, see Hubertsson Seelow, *The modern architecture in Iceland in the first half of the 20th century*, 123–126.

59 Hubertsson Seelow, *The modern architecture in Iceland in the first half of the 20th century*, 118, with a contemporary comment on the pillars: "It was there that the similarity to the rocks at Hofsós first appeared. This succeeded so well that the buttresses of the church in Landakot are much more beautiful than their models in old churches in southern countries."

60 Hubertsson Seelow, *The modern architecture in Iceland in the first half of the 20th century*, 144–152; Abrecht, *Architektúr á Islandi – leidarvísir*, 104–105.

61 Hubertsson Seelow, *The modern architecture in Iceland in the first half of the 20th century*, 147 and 149.

3.34 Élisabethville, France, Sainte-Thérèse-de-l'Enfant-Jésus, Paul Tournon, 1927–1928. [Postcard, archive Bruno Klein]

Chapelle in Paris [Fig. 3.34].[62] On the one hand, Sainte-Chapelle is imitated in Sainte-Thérèse-de-l'Enfant-Jésus much closer than was otherwise customary in the period, so that it is recognizable precisely and not just vaguely. On the other hand, however, a radical transformation took place through the use of modern techniques and materials.

For planning and construction of most of the churches with sporadic takeovers and free adaptations of Gothic forms, their sacred, religious function seemed to have been mainly in the foreground. They were built where they were needed as a result of industrialization and/or migration. This does not apply to other buildings to the same extent: Grundtvig's and Hallgrim's churches, for example, were planned before it was known where they were to be built. And when the reopening of the Sagrada Família construction site became apparent in the 1960s, protests arose, because the construction of a cathedral-like church in Barcelona was considered as a waste of money.[63] Thus, the construction of monumental neo-Gothic churches in Europe in the twentieth and twenty-first centuries was mostly successful if they could be connected with special ideas that lifted them above their purely ecclesiastical function. Such ideas were not uniform: romantic nationalism or the attempt to create – whatever – identity seemed to be most promising.

For example, the attempt to (re)construct identity after a devastating period as in Ypres. This resembles a recent example in Germany, where a free approach to Gothic building forms is combined with a reference to a historical model. According to the plans of the Dutch architect Erick van Egeraat, the so-called Paulinum, built between 2007 and 2017, of Leipzig University was officially the "Assembly Hall and University Church of St. Paul's" [Fig. 3.35].[64] Where it stands, once stood the Gothic/neo-Gothic Paulinerkirche, blown up for ideological reasons in 1968 during the German Democratic Republic. The dimensions, outline, and individual motifs of the new building's façade correspond with those of its lost predecessor, but its ma-

62 Mesecke, "Tournon, Paul". Further literature can also be found here. Tournon was, along with Auguste Perret, the most important French architect of the second quarter of the twentieth century in terms of the combination of tradition and innovation, particularly in the construction of churches. See also his Sacré Cœur Basilica in Casablanca (Fig. 11.27). Another contemporary interpretation of the Sainte-Chapelle is the Capilla de la Cruz de Cantera, in Mexico, León, Guanajuato (Fig. 9.09).

63 *La Vanguardia*, 9 January 1965, 24.

64 Zimmerling, ed., *Universitätskirche St. Pauli.*

3.35 Gerald Müller-Simon: Leipzig, Augustusplatz 2014. University buildings Augusteum on the left and Paulinum on the right (architect: Erick van Egeraat). The reflection of the modern church on the rain-soaked square shows the neo-Gothic façade of the former church blown up in 1968. [Universität Leipzig, Kunstsammlung Inv. Nr.: 4548/90]

terial and integration into a larger building complex make it modern. At first glance, the interior resembles a three-nave Gothic hall church, but with pillars hanging down from the vaults,[65] illuminated from inside, that do not reach to the ground [Fig. 1.03]. Parts of the ancient inventory rescued from the old church are presented in a museum-like manner.

The new building of the Paulinum in Leipzig was intended to build a bridge from the nineteenth and early twentieth centuries over the Nazi era and the German Democratic Republic period into the present.The fact that this was a building with a Gothic core unter a strong neo-Gothic shell did not play a major role in the vague reconstruction. This can also be seen from the fact that, together with the Paulinum, the classicist façade of the old university building has also been restored in a conjectural manner, even if that is nearly invisible: the Gothic church is a strongly anchored image in mentality for cultural, historical reasons, especially in Europe. Ecclesiastical Gothic architectures, or in its condensation in the metaphoric "Gothic Cathedral," are European memory spaces—what might be the main reason for their rather rare, but still continuous, construction during the twentieth and twenty-first centuries on this continent.

65 The motif of pillar heads hanging from the vault is also found in Novena church in Singapore at about the same time. Direct connections between the two buildings or their architects are not known. But obviously at the beginning of the twenty-first century it seemed to be interesting from an artistic point of view to problematize or ironize the traditional pillar-load system in buildings in Gothic forms.

4
Tradition in the Age of Progress
Notions on Gothic Church Architecture in the United States

Bettina Marten

Introduction

During the twentieth and twenty-first centuries, a complex richness of adaptations of Gothic architectural and decorative forms abound in the United States. In this multidenominational society characterized by heterogeneous waves of immigration, architecture in medieval, especially in Gothic, forms seems to be of particular importance: historically, it has apparently been able to form a supradenominational bracket, but it may now serve primarily to reassure a traditional majority society. Sacred buildings in Gothic idiom have an important, thoroughly social function, which is why their significance was never fundamentally questioned by other stylistic paradigms such as that of "modern architecture," although symbioses could also occur. More likely, the fronts of these buildings run within the historicizing architecture itself, between neo-Romanesque, neo-Gothic, neo-Renaissance, or neo-Baroque.

The decisive factor here is the transformation of Gothic forms into the local and confessional needs of a parish, depending on a building scheme developed by a ground floor pattern: from a cruciform ground plan rises a three-nave basilican church with a more or less pronounced transept. In their idiosyncratic heterogeneity, the complex large forms, which can be related to a variety of models in Europe, may be better summarized under the term "Gothic stylistic idiom" or "Gothic architectural vocabulary" than under the art historical style phases of the Gothic. Some churches are predominantly based on the models of French (cathedrals in Chartres, Paris, Laon, etc.) and English templates (here especially King's College Chapel). Other models are rarely copied literally, but are rather quoted. Pronounced copies are, for example, the Catholic Cathedral of St. Helena in Helena, Montana, which recalls the Votivkirche in Vienna; St. Martin's Episcopal Church in Houston (Texas) as a copy of the Elisabeth Church in Marburg (for both, see below); or the Roman Catholic St. Mary's Cathedral Basilica of the Assumption in Covington, Kentucky, built 1895–1915. While the interior design of the structure designed by Leon Coquard (1860–1923/1926) was modeled on the Cathedral of St. Denis, the architect of the main façade on Madison Avenue (1908–1910), David D. Davis (1865–1932), drew on the model of the Cathedral of Notre-Dame de Paris, although the planned towers, however, remained unfinished.

The Gothic stylistic idiom offered a high potential for acceptance that corresponded to a society that believed in progress, as did U.S. society since industrialization beginning around 1850. Cathedrals and churches in the Gothic style have belonged to the cityscape of *every* American city since the middle of the nineteenth century. In the search for an architectural language that would provide confessional identity not only for the various immigrant groups but also for the nation, the Gothic style became more significant as genuinely Christian architectural style than the classical architecture. This means a stylistic "framing" of cross-ethnic and cross-social needs concerning confessional and national identity in a modern world. In this way, the Gothic stylistic idiom is both a clear expression of a long tradition within a "short" U.S.

4.01 Washington, D.C., National Cathedral, plans by George Frederick Bodley and Henry Vaughan, 1907–1990.
[Washington, Library of Congress: LC-HS503-3784; photo Carol M. Highsmith]

history, without indigenous style, and its permanent transformation in a modern and forward-thinking society.

For this reason, cathedrals of different denominations in the same city appeared early on and competed with each other in their Gothic architecture, as the following examples demonstrate. Trinity Cathedral in Cleveland, Ohio (Charles Schweinfurth, 1901–1907) was originally planned as a neo-Romanesque building, but was executed as a neo-Gothic building by request of the bishop and the community. It is the antithesis of the Roman Catholic Cathedral of St. John the Evangelist (Patrick Keely, consecration 1852) in the same city. In Denver, Colorado, the episcopal Cathedral of St. John in the Wilderness (1909–1911, Tracy and Swartwout) is a reaction to the Roman Catholic Cathedral Basilica of the Immaculate Conception (1902–1912, Leon Coquard). In New York City, the Roman Catholic St. Patrick's Cathedral was followed by the Episcopal Cathedral Church of Saint John the Divine. In Chicago, the Roman Catholic Holy Name Cathedral (1872–1875, Patrick Keely et al.) was followed by the Episcopal St. James Cathedral (after 1871, Faulkner & Clarke architects). In San Francisco, the Episcopal Grace Cathedral (1928–1964, Lewis P. Hobart) with its French-style neo-Gothic construction corrected the neo-Romanesque, neo-Gothic architecture of the Catholic Cathedral of Saint Mary of the Assumption, built 1887–1891.

These examples illustrate that from the middle of the nineteenth century onward, the Roman Catholic denomination initially set Gothic stylistic idioms in the big cities with large cathedrals, which were followed shortly afterward and into the twentieth century by the Episcopal denomination with corresponding counterbuildings. Other Christian congregations (Anglican, Presbyterian, and free congregations) likewise opted for the Gothic architectural style for their places of worship. Thanks to this continuity, a complex infrastructure of protagonists also exists: there are proven practices of the conventions of donors, long-standing architects and architectural firms, and developed furnishing companies.

The intention of the following pages is decidedly not a listing of objects; in this context, that would hardly be manageable due to the sheer mass, especially because, so far, only outstanding buildings have been analyzed architecturally and historically in source-critical individual studies. The material base is gigantic, and scientifically reliable studies are rare, so that a great potential opens up for further research. Basic, reliable information about the properties is first provided by their listing on the National Register of Historical Places (U.S. National Park Service), if done. The selection of objects for the following case studies was guided both by their architectural significance and by the following aspects to initiate a wider discourse: to show the widest possible range of Christian denominational groups using the Gothic style; to demonstrate the broad geographical distribution within the country; to show that the Gothic style is not a matter for large cities but also for remote, rural areas; to address the importance of the urbanistic context, and the political and social relevance associated with these buildings; to address the network structures and backgrounds of the protagonists.

Actors and Aspects of Construction

Communities and Donors

Church construction in America is a common concern of the parish. But it is above all a task of the social elite, which not only consists of wealthy parishioners and philanthropists, but also includes the artistic elite.[1] The most urgent assignment is the fundraising as a social participation. Depending on the financial situation, the erection of a building could last for decades. In case of financial shortages, interruptions in construction were the logical consequence. Grants from major financiers such as the Heinz, Rockefeller, Duke, and Monaghan families acceler-

1 Williams, "The Iconography of the American City," 379–381.

ated the construction process considerably. Competing for the visibility of the individual parishes in the urban fabric, the church became an expression of confessional self-confidence. Site, size, furnishings, and materials are suitable to express the prosperity of the parish. The fame of the commissioned architect also contributed to the renown: wealthy communities could afford famous architects and artists.

Building Experts

Since the erection of cathedrals and churches, around 1900 and in later decades, became an important construction task, specialized architectural firms developed almost exclusively with this type of building. Among the most prominent of these firms were Cram, Goodhue, and Ferguson (Boston); Zantzinger, Borie, and Medary (Philadelphia); Pelton, Allen, and Collins (Boston); Frohman, Robb, and Little (Philadelphia); and Charles Z. Klauder. Their professional starting points were practical experience in the construction business or academia: James G. Rogers (1867–1947) studied at Yale University and at the École des Beaux-Arts in Paris, and George DeWitt Mason (1856–1948) received his training in an architectural office. Some architects worked exclusively for one denomination, such as John T. Comès (1873–1922) for the Catholic Church. Others were commissioned by different denominations; for example, Bertram G. Goodhue, designed for both the Catholic and Episcopal Churches. The Catholic Philipp H. Frohman received commissions mainly from the Episcopal Church. Ralph Adams Cram converted to Anglo-Catholicism in Rome, but received his most important commissions from the Episcopal Church. The church building was obviously also suitable for breaking racial laws in individual cases; the career of the Philadelphia-based architect Julian Francis Abele (1881–1950) cannot be explained differently. He was the first of African American origin to graduate from the School of Architecture at the University of Pennsylvania School of Design in 1902 and to receive an architecture diploma in 1903.[2] After the Second World War, the offices of Skidmore, Owings, and Merrill, and Hartmann-Cox Architects, among others, were active in this field. All these architects shared the search for the authenticity of the Gothic form, which was best learned during studies in Europe.

The church-building boom evident for the first half of the twentieth century led to the formation of an industry for church accessories, which produced, for example, pulpits, seating, and altars on a large scale and distributed them through sales catalogs. The Chicago-based Daprato Statuary Company Pontifical Institute of Christian Art was one such company that produced church accessories to sell in catalogs.[3] Glass windows were imported from Europe, mainly Germany[4] and France, or were produced by large specialized glass studios in the United States. Among the most famous glass artists was Charles Connick, who ran his studio near Boston. He worked together with Cram and Goodhue, among others.[5] Great studios for architectural sculpture were maintained, for example by Lee Lawrie, who was of German origin, by Corrado Parducci, who emigrated from Italy, and by John Angel from England.

Building Techniques and Materials

To Ralph Adams Cram, one of the most distinguished architects of the Gothic style, Gothic form was also linked to the choice of the right materials and techniques to achieve truthfulness. For him, an integral part of his backward-looking, romantic view was the ideal of the medieval Bauhütte, where all the trades came together.[6] This issue turned into a question of faith. As a result, Cram and his circle tried to work in traditional craftsmanship wherever possible, in order to achieve the most authentic Gothic result possible. However, he could not completely avoid iron reinforcements.

Colleagues such as Henry C. Pelton and Charles Collens or Lewis Hobart thought differently: they regarded the steel skeleton

2 His oeuvre contains more than 200 buildings. Webster, "Julian Francis Abele (1881–1950)," 2004; King, "Abele, Julian Francis (1881–1950)."

3 This large company had studios for Christian art not only in Chicago, but also in New York and Pietrasanta, Italy and also delivered to Canada. Sales catalogs offer a wide range of products. See Daprato Statuary Company in Chicago, *Creations in ecclesiastical art.*

4 The Bavarian Art Institute founded by Franz Xaver Zettler or the Mayer'sche Hofkunstanstalt founded by Joseph Gabriel Mayer, both situated in Munich, were popular German companies for glass windows.

5 Tannler, *Connick: his education and his glas work*; Connick, *Adventures in light and color.*

6 Macdonell, "The American Pugins," 95–105; Macdonell, *Ghost Storeys: Ralph Adams Cram, Modern Gothic Media, and Deconstructive Microhistory at a Canadian Church*; Shand-Tucci, *Ralph Adams Cram: An architect's four quests*; Cram, *Church Building.*

construction, which Cram rejected as a masquerade, as a great innovative element for transferring the Gothic skeleton construction method to the contemporary world. Modern architectural innovation was seen as the equivalent of the admired historical Gothic construction method, as long as the apparatus of forms remained in the same idiom. Hence, it was not only a matter of perfect adaptation to European Gothic, but also of recognizing contemporary time. The use of Guastavino tiles for vaulting offers an example in this respect.[7] In the second half of the twentieth century, these debates about the truthfulness of the material were no longer continued. On the contrary, innovative building materials were used without ideological discussions to create attractive buildings.

Notions on Gothic Stylistic Idiom: Selected Case Studies

Washington: The Question of Style for the National Cathedral

Architecture plays a central role as a mediating instance of historical constructions and national claims to validity, insofar as they attract attention through religious identity. This is particularly evident in Washington, D.C., the capital and place of national representation and identification,[8] where patriotism and religion are closely related [Fig. 4.01]. Consequently, the question arises as to the significance of denominations in linking and instrumentalizing religious community and national history. In this context, the architectural language is the visible expression of an action-guiding value system. Pierre L'Enfant's "Plan for a Federal City" from 1792 already provided the project of a large church for national purposes, which was renewed in 1891. Headed by the first bishop of the Diocese of Washington, Henry Yates Satterlee, the Episcopal Church endeavored "to fill the void of a national witness of basic religious sentiment in the USA with a cathedral building."[9] Because freedom of religion is guaranteed in the American Constitution (First Amendment of the Constitution), the chances of success of the project remained limited in this regard, even though the Episcopal Church received permission from the U.S. House of Representatives in 1893 to build a cathedral.

The new cathedral, designed by George Frederick Bodley (1827–1907) and Henry Vaughan (1846–1917), was not, as originally planned, built in the classicist style of state buildings, but rather in Gothic vocabulary, following the example of Westminster Abbey as an expression of the specifically Christian character: "we believe that if the Cathedral is Gothic the contrast between it and the magnificent classic buildings will be no loss but a positive gain in effect" (Satterlee). Gothic is the highest expression of Christian art. The close connection between the Anglican and Episcopal churches was clearly demonstrated by the attendance of the Bishop of London at the laying of the foundation stone on September 29, 1907. With the presence of President Theodore Roosevelt, the act took on the character of a national event. From 1907 on, the building was constructed using the traditional masonry technique. After Vaughan's death, Philip Hubert Frohman (1887–1972) and his partners Harry B. Little (1882–1944) and E. Donald Robb (1919–1942) took over the execution.[10] The last crop was added only in 1990 in the presence of President George H. W. Bush. Due to its elevated position on Mount Saint Alban, the National Cathedral occupies a prominent place in the city's silhouette, as a topographical response to the Capitol and the White House. At the same time, the construction of skyscrapers in the surrounding area was prohibited by law in order not to impair the prominent positions of these institutions in their symbolism. Thus, the cathedral was staged as the third national authority.[11] "While the site guarantees the presence of the church in the triumvirate of national powers, the church at the same time forms the counterpoint to state power."[12]

7 The so-called Guastavino tile, also known as Akoustolith, refers to a tile with excellent acoustic quality made by Rafael Guastavino with a special mix of materials, laid according to the medieval model. The Spanish-born Guastavino had the system patented after his immigration to the United States. Guastavino, *Escritos sobre la construcción*; Buchner, "R. Guastavino Co: five decades of construction," 255–265.

8 The following remarks are based on Minta, "A church for all purposes," 261–285, 262; Minta, *Staatsbauten und Sakralarchitektur in Washington D.C.*, 286–392.

9 Minta, "A church for all purposes," 266.

10 Ralph Adams Cram was brought in as a consultant, but his cooperation was quickly terminated at Frohman's request due to differences of opinion.

11 Minta, "A church for all purposes," 267.

12 Ibid., 268.

13 Tweed, "America's Church," 73. The cornerstone was laid in 1920; construction was interrupted in 1929 over the course of the Great Depression and during World War II. After 1953, after successful fundraising, the upper church was completed by 1960. The installation of the Trinity Mosaic of Venetian glass in the main apse completed the interior decoration in 2017.

In response to the Episcopal National Cathedral, the Roman Catholic Church prompted the construction of the Basilica of the National Shrine of the Immaculate Conception, which was built between 1920 and 2017. Situated in an elevated position near the Catholic University of America, it serves as national pilgrimage site [Fig. 4.02].[13] The architect Charles Donagh Maginnis (1867–1955) initially submitted a neo-Gothic design (1914–1915), but had to replace these plans with a neo-Romanesque, neo-Byzantine building after receiving objections from Bishop Thomas Joseph Shahan (1857–1932), who had taken the initiative, and the building committee. In the competition for the visibility of the various denominations in the capital, the Roman Catholics decided to establish an architectural antithesis to the National Cathedral in a firmly different architectural style.

New York and Surroundings

Newark Cathedral – "A fitting memorial to faith"[14]

The key concept for the Sacred Heart Cathedral in Newark, New Jersey originated from the cathedral as a monument to faith [Fig. 4.03]. First considerations concerning the idea of a new cathedral church appeared in 1859, six years after Pope Pius IX had established the Catholic diocese of Newark. With regard to the visibility of a monument, the choice of a location in a prominent position on Park Avenue with a view as far as New York is conclusive. In 1870 the Irish-born architect Jeremiah O'Rourke (1833–1915), entrusted with preliminary planning, set off on a journey through Europe to study Gothic cathedrals and met George Goldie in

4.02 Washington, D.C., Basilica of the National Shrine of the Immaculate Conception, Charles D. Maginnis, 1920–2017.
[Wikimedia Commons; photo Joseph Leonardo, 2012]

4.03 Newark, New Jersey, Cathedral Basilica of the Sacred Heart, Jeremiah O'Rourke, 1899–1954.
[Wikimedia Commons; photo Jim Henderson, 2010]

14 Quote from Bishop Bernard McQuaid at the laying of the corner stone on June 11, 1899. See Regan, *Gothic Pride*; McCarrick, et al. *The stained glass of the Cathedral Basilica of the Sacred Heart*; Flanagan, *Cathedral of the Sacred Heart*.

4.04 New York City, Cathedral of Saint John the Divine, plans by George L. Heins and Christopher G. LaFarge, begun 1892.
[© Nikreates / Alamy Stock Photo]

London, one of the leading representatives of neo-Gothic architecture in England. In 1897 O'Rourke's design in the style of Anglo-Irish Gothic was the winner of a limited competition. The cornerstone was laid on June 11, 1899. By April 1902, the walls of the nave had been completed as well as the galleries up to a height of about fifteen meters, the western façade, and the flanking towers up to the fourth floor.

At that time, however, differences started to emerge between O'Rourke and the Waldron company, which finally led to O'Rourke's dismissal in 1910. His successor, Isaac E. Ditmars (1850–1934), changed plans in 1913, initially to secure the statics of the building, but also to adapt the church to the models of French cathedrals, such as Chartres, Laon, and Reims. This meant, among other things, the insertion of wheel pattern rose windows in the west and transept façades. Ditmars reduced the height of the towers by a third and changed the shape of the tower domes. He also dispensed with external buttresses and battlements on the roof. By contrast, he favored more sculptures at the entrance. Innovative elements were the steel skeleton construction of the roof including the pointed tower, a heating tunnel in the basement and in the crypt, and the vaults made of Guastavino tiles. The interior decoration was completed by the consecration on October 19, 1954. In total, the construction costs, which initially were not to exceed $1 million, amounted to over $6 million, which was raised in various fundraising campaigns. The most conspicuous elements are the two towers turned at a forty-five-degree angle to the main façade, which seem to enclose the arriving visitor. As model for the cathedral, the St. Patrick Church in Elizabeth, New Jersey is mentioned, which was built between 1889 and 1901 according to drawings by William Schickel (1850–1907). Newark Cathedral offers an outstanding example of planning processes and plan changes that may proceed over the course of many years of construction, as does the following example of St. John the Divine in New York City.

New York City, St. John the Divine – The Unfinished

The Cathedral of St. John the Divine is the second largest episcopal church building on the East Coast following Washington's National Cathedral. With 11,200 square meters, the Cathedral of St. John the Divine is one of the largest sacred buildings in the United States [Fig. 4.04]. First ideas for the construction of the cathedral in New York City emerged as early as the late 1820s. But it was not until the economic boom of the 1880s, which anchored New York as the economic, cultural, and intellectual center of the North

American continent, that the project took concrete shape. The building was to become the symbol of the city's cosmopolitanism, an "American Westminster Abbey."[15] Sponsors featured the city's wealthiest families, including the Astors, Vanderbilts, Belmonts, Morgans, and Rockefellers. At the beginning of the planning in the 1890s, the Episcopal congregation of New York was the largest single congregation, with about forty thousand members. For this reason, the construction of a large church seemed justified as the seat of the diocese. Among the members were many of the richest and most influential families in New York, whose contributions and donations not only significantly financed the construction costs of the cathedral but also supported the inherent social institutions. The commitment to the disadvantaged remained the focus of the community work after World War II.[16]

The new building was intended as an antipole and in competition with the Catholic St. Patrick's Cathedral (1858–1879, James Renwick Jr.) at Fifth Avenue in Midtown East Manhattan. The prominently situated property at 112th Street in Morningside Heights (Upper West Side, Manhattan) purchased in 1887 supported this purpose. At the same time, it was to serve as the initial building for the development of a new urban center. Early debates on the architectural style led to a competition in 1888, which was won by the office of George Lewis Heins (1860–1907) and Christopher Grant LaFarge (1862–1938) with a Byzantine-Romanesque design influenced by the architecture of H. H. Richardson. Because the board of trustees preferred the neo-Gothic style, the design was modified. The most important change concerned the orientation: originally aligned to the north, the cathedral was now oriented at ninety degrees to the east, as is customary for churches. Although it lost its visibility from the south, it became a visual focal point at the end of West 112th Street. A further modification includes the seven choir chapels, which, as "Chapels of Tongues," were intended to symbolize New York's ethnic groups. Construction work began in 1892. Because of problems with the foundations, the work progressed slowly.

In 1911, when LaFarge was dismissed and Ralph Adams Cram was hired as chief architect, the choir, crossing, Chapel of the Redeemer, and St. Columba's Chapel were finished and ready for use thanks to provisionally moved-in walls. At that time, the Episcopal cathedrals in Denver, Boston, Washington, D.C., and the much-acclaimed Anglican Cathedral in Liverpool, in the United Kingdom, were under construction in Gothic style as well.[17] Because Cram was an avowed follower of the new Gothic style, he immediately began with conversion designs that incorporated the existing structural elements. Instead of low and broadly based English models, he oriented to French examples. His models included the cathedrals in Bourges, Paris, Amiens, and Reims as well as Wells in England. The installation of the triforium and the clerestory contributed to the verticality and openness of the space. Work was restarted in 1916 during World War I, but stagnated until 1925 due to financing difficulties. Subsequently, the nave, west façade (without towers), baptistery, and part of the north transept were built until their completion in 1933. In 1929, Cram presented a third modification plan, which provided for an approximately ninety-meter-high square tower instead of a pointed tower above the crossing. The number of entrances on the west side was to be increased from three to five. Over the course of the economic depression, work was interrupted again. In 1939 it was resumed, entailing changes in the vaulting of the choir to adapt it to the vaults of the nave.

The opening of the cathedral was celebrated on November 30, 1941. Already the next week, work had been interrupted again after the Japanese attack on Pearl Harbor. It was not until the 1970s that work resumed, including the establishment of a mason's guild where unemployed people were trained as stonemasons. They were supposed to create sculptures and continue the construction to make the cathedral a symbol of hope

15 Wickersham, *The Cathedral Church of Saint John the Divine*; Stern et al., *Metropolitan Architecture and Urbanism 1890–1915*, 396. During these boom years, the Metropolitan Opera House (1881–1884), Carnegie Hall (1889–1891), New York Botanical Garden (1891), Columbia University (1892), New York University (1892), Metropolitan Museum of Art (1894), City College (1897), and New York Public Library (1898), among others, emerged to compete with the urban development of the major European cities. Ramazzotti, "La cupola per St. John the Divine," 277–291. Landmarks Preservation Commission, June 17, 2003, Designation List 347, LP-2123 <http://nycnpc.org/db/bb_files/cathedral-church-st.johnthedivine-2003.pdf>.

16 Lemos McHale, *Cathedral Church of Saint John the Divine and the Cathedral Close*, 6.

17 See the contribution of Bruno Klein on Europa.

and rebirth of the city. During this time, the forty-five-meter-high south tower was built. The recession of the 1990s led to the bankruptcy of the mason's guild. Since then, the works have been suspended once again.

The portal figures, completed in 1997, designed by the English sculptor Simon Verity and executed by various employees of the mason's guild, illustrate representatives of the Old and New Testaments. Remarkable is the design of their consoles, which depict modern motifs such as New York skyscrapers, including the Twin Towers. At that time, the cathedral was two-thirds complete. The towers on the west façade, the transepts, the crossing, and the choir roof remained unfinished. In December 2001, a fire in the north transept caused great damage.

In addition to this large building, numerous Gothic-styled churches were built in the neighborhoods, such as St. Patrick's Cathedral in Midtown Manhattan; the Episcopal churches of St. Mary the Virgin and of St. Thomas (Fifth Avenue and 53th Street); the Church of the Heavenly Rest (Fifth Avenue and East 90th Street); the Church of the Intercession (Sugar Hill and Washington Heights); Holyrood Episcopal Church (715 West 179th Street and Fort Washington Avenue); or the Catholic Church of Vincent Ferrer (869 Lexington Avenue). They all made New York a center of Gothic-styled churches in the early twentieth century in the United States.

New York City, Riverside Church – Church as a multifunctional building

The interdenominational Riverside Church on the Hudson River, adjacent to the Morningside Heights and Harlem neighborhoods of the Upper West Side in Manhattan, provides the architectural home for a parish founded in 1922 by a group of progressive members of the American Baptist Church and the United Church of Christ [Fig. 4.05].[18] The main actors in this project were the modernist Baptist minister Harry Emerson Fosdick and philanthropist John D.

4.05 New York City, Riverside Church, choir, Henry C. Pelton and Charles Collens, 1926–1930. [Postcard, archive Bruno Klein]

Rockefeller, Jr. Their vision was to build a church open to all Christians on the edge of one of New York City's most prosperous neighborhoods.[19] John D. Rockefeller, Jr. appeared as main sponsor; he purchased the plot and financed the construction with further generous grants, which is why it bears the nickname "Rockefeller Church." As architect, Cram was the first to be thought of, because of his expertise in Gothic buildings. However, a collaboration failed due to Cram's conservative attitude. Rockefeller then invited a select circle of architects to realize Fosdick's social ideas in the new building: in addition to the church room, it should contain rooms for numerous other uses connected with the social and cultural engagements of the parish. It should be constructed with modern building materials and the necessary technical infrastructure such as heating and elevators. Architect Henry C. Pelton, who had previously distinguished himself with the Park Avenue Methodist Church, received the assignment. In search of the greatest possible authenticity, he and his partner Charles

18 See Pendo, *A Brief History of the Riverside Church*; Paul, "Chartres in Amerika," 287–300; Cook, "A Christian vision of unity," 137–178.
19 More than forty ethnic groups were counted among the parish.
20 Paul, "Chartres in America," 294. The cost of the construction is estimated at approximately $4 million. Between 1950 and 1959, in a second construction phase, the so-called South Wing, since 1985 the Martin Luther King Jr. Memorial Wing, was built by the office of Collens, Willis, and Beckonert in reduced Gothic style with underground parking. The extension was also financed by John D. Rockefeller, Jr.

Collens subsequently traveled throughout France and northern Spain for further study purposes. The Chartres, Laon, and Albi cathedrals ultimately influenced the final design. The building was executed as a steel skeleton construction between 1926 and 1930. The loads are carried by the steel skeleton construction; the buttressing is consequently purely decorative. Behind the façade, it conceals a multifunctional building with a church, sports hall, meeting room, kitchen, bowling alleys, and rehearsal rooms. The massive tower reaches the height of a twenty-two-story high-rise building at 120 meters. It contains further functional rooms accessible via elevators. The pictorial program of the sculptures, stained glass windows, reliefs, and capitals depict Christian motifs, biblical figures, outstanding personalities from philosophy, science, art, and history as well as historical events, resulting in an "all-encompassing syncretic world view, presented as a Christian apotheosis of the entire cultural history."[20] It is completed by the representation of a labyrinth in the floor of the church, modeled on the one at Chartres.

Riverside Church guarantees the outward transmission of traditional Christian values through its Gothic vocabulary of forms, while the building's construction and multifunctionality mark the latest technical achievements and space-optimizing concepts. The neo-Gothic style in its modern form seemed suitable to meet the changing spiritual and practical needs of modern urbanites.[21]

San Francisco, Grace Cathedral: Church Building in the Earthquake Zone

Grace Cathedral in San Francisco is one of the three major cathedral buildings of the Episcopal church in the United States, along with St. John the Divine in New York and the National Cathedral in Washington, D.C. [Fig. 4.06][22] Its predecessor, built in 1862, was destroyed by the great earthquake of 1906. With the donation of their demolished land on Nob Hill to the parish, the family of

4.06 San Francisco, Grace Cathedral, George F. Bodley and Lewis P. Hobart, 1928–1964. [Wikimedia Commons; photo Bobak Ha'Eri, 2009]

railroad magnate and banker William Henry Crocker made possible the construction of a larger cathedral at a prominent location in the urban fabric. As for Washington, D.C., G. F. Bodley (1827–1907) submitted a design shortly before his death. The cornerstone for this design was laid in 1910, but work stagnated thereafter; as a result, there were changes to the plan later on. In 1914 the foundations and the crypt, which was temporarily used as a church until 1931, were completed. With the advisory assistance of Cram architect Lewis P. Hobart (1873–1954) began the planning of the present cathedral in 1925, which was built in different periods between 1928 and 1964.

Following Hobart's death in 1954, the office of Weihe, Frick & Kruse was assigned to the site. Although they continued work according to Hobart's design, they significantly changed the east portal:[23] the planned open vestibule was replaced by a deeply cut step portal with wimpergs. The cathedrals of Amiens, Beauvais, and Paris, as well as churches in Catalonia, are cited as models for the construction. The attached Grace Chapel is modeled on the Sainte-Chapelle at Paris.[24] Photographs of the destroyed Grace Church

21 "In these seventy-plus years, the innovations in the twentieth-century neo-Gothic style of the Riverside Church have served the shifts in its ministry's leadership, mood, and emphasis in such a manner as to be a remarkably compatible and stabilizing entity in which beauty, symbol space and liturgy have consistently pointed to both the need to serve the human condition and the reality and presence of God." Cook, "A Christian vision of unity," 176. See also Gillwald, *Ein Primus der Sinnstiftung: Die Riverside Church.*

22 About the history of Grace Cathedral, see Lampen, *Grace Cathedral, San Francisco*. The journal *The Architect and Engineer*, Vol. 119, No. 3, December 1934 dedicated a thematic focus to the completion of the first construction phase with contributions from Lewis P. Hobart and the glass artist Charles Connick, among others.

23 Photographs by Hobart on the construction of the Grace Cathedral in the Weihe, Frick & Kruse Collection. <https://archives.ced.berkeley.edu/collections/hobart-lewis>.

24 Lampen, "Grace Cathedral," 4. The orientation toward French models is obvious, because Lewis P. Hobart completed his training at the Ecole des Beaux Arts in Paris and was able to study the buildings directly on site. Hobart himself drew size comparisons to Westminster Abbey and the cathedral in York. Hobart, "Cathedral," 12.

and the new Grace Cathedral illustrate that the new building was based on the design of the predecessor church, and obtained a visual continuity. Significant difference provides the rose window instead of a lancet window on the main façade.

The cathedral was originally planned as a stone building, but it turned out to be too expensive; for this reason, a steel skeleton construction with machined concrete material was executed.[25] This construction method reacted to the geological situation of the city at the San Andreas Fault with a constant danger of earthquakes. It compensates for seismic waves better than a massive stone structure.[26] The material properties of the concrete necessitate a simpler architecture without the decorative elements such as crops and pinnacles, for example, that are characteristic of French High Gothic buildings. The vaults were covered with Guastavino tiles and demonstrate contemporary modern construction methods as well. The earthquake catastrophe of 1906, the resulting destruction of the predecessor church, and the construction of the new cathedral are reflected in the murals [see fig. on p. 5]. Special pieces of decoration include a copy of the labyrinth from Chartres Cathedral[27] and, on the main portal, a cast copy of the Paradise Door of the Baptistery in Florence by Lorenzo Ghiberti, made by Bruno Bearzi after World War II and offered for sale on the open market.

In 1934, on the occasion of the completion of the first phase of construction (choir, Grace Chapel, transepts, and the adjacent three bays of the nave) by the provisional closure of the nave, Cram praised the building as "one of the most impressing, convincing and promising schemes for an American cathedral that has thus far been brought forward during the process of creating in America a logical and consistent architectural expression of Christian faith and the Christian polity."[28]

Grace Cathedral on Nob Hill was intended to be a prominent, widely visible point in the urban fabric, comparable to National Cathedral in Washington, D.C., but already in the 1950s this visibility was impaired by the immediate vicinity of various residential towers. Its orientation toward the west is due to urban planning and climatic aspects.

Detroit: Statements in Gothic Style

Every major city in the United States features a certain number of church buildings in the Gothic style: for example, Pittsburgh (Saint Paul Cathedral, 1906, Egan & Prindeville; First Presbyterian Church, 1905, Theophilus P. Chandler; Calvary Episcopal Church, 1905–1906, Ralph A. Cram; East Liberty Presbyterian Church, 1932–1935, Ralph A. Cram), Kansas City (St. Peter Catholic Cathedral, 1925–1927, Henry W. Brinkman), Atlanta (Cathedral of Christ the King, 1935–1937, Henry D. Dagit, Jr.), Indianapolis (Scottish Cathedral, 1927–1929, George F. Schreiber), Baltimore (Cathedral of the Incarnation, 1909–1955, H. Vaughn, B. Goodhue, and others), Boise (Idaho, St. John's Catholic Cathedral, 1906–1921, John E. Tourtellotte & Charles F. Hummel; Cathedral of the Rockies, 1958–1960, Harold E. Wagoner). The industrial city of Detroit provides numerous churches in a special urban context along Woodward Avenue, a broad main axis that runs from downtown Detroit to the outskirts of the city. The Catholic Cathedral of the Most Blessed Sacrament in Detroit (Michigan) is located on 9844 Woodward Avenue [Fig. 4.07]. Construction began in 1913 according to the designs of Henry A. Walsh (1867/1868–1940) from Cleveland, Ohio, but it was not until 1951 that George F. Diehl (1892–1976) completed the church with the west façade and the crossing tower, the latter modeled on the Notre-Dame in Paris. The façade towers, however, have remained fragmentary to the present day—the designated spires are missing. Work was nevertheless finished in time for the 250th anniversary of the community; the solemn consecration ceremony on November 17, 1951 was broadcasted live on local television. The massive stone building follows early Gothic models and is supplemented by

25 On this: Hobart, "Cathedral," 11–12; Smith, "Supplants Stone. Cathedral in Concrete," 27–28. Historic photographs by Ansel Adams document the construction process: <https://gracecathedral.org/architecture-2/>.

26 After the great earthquake of 1906, demands were made to construct new buildings taking into account the imminent danger. See Nishkian, "Earthquakes, hazards and protection," 23–25.

27 <https://gracecathedral.org/our-labyrinths/>.

28 *The Architect and Engineer*, 119 (December 1934), 3, 3: Notes and Comments.

4.07 Detroit, Cathedral of the Most Blessed Sacrament, Henry A. Walsh and George F. Diehl, 1913–1951. [Wikimedia Commons; photo Nheyob, 2015]

4.08 Detroit, Cathedral Church of St. Paul, Ralph Adams Cram, 1905–1907. [Wikimedia Commons; photo Andrew Jameson, 2008]

4.09 Detroit, Woodward Avenue Presbyterian Church, Sidney Badgley, 1911. [Wikimedia Commons; photo Andrew Jameson, 2008]

4.10 Detroit, Metropolitan United Methodist Church, William E. N. Hunter, 1916/1917–1922/1926. [Wikimedia Commons; photo Andrew Jameson, 2008]

4.11 Detroit, St. Joseph's Episcopal Church (today St. Matthew's-St. Joseph's Episcopal Church), James J. Nettleton, 1926. [Wikimedia Commons; photo Andrew Jameson, 2008]

4.12 Detroit, Central Woodward Christian Church (today Little Rock Missionary Baptist Church), George D. Mason, 1928. [Wikimedia Commons; photo Andrew Jameson, 2008]

High Gothic decorative elements including a statue gallery, rose windows, and tabernacle attachments with crops.

The Catholic church building may be viewed as reaction to the Cathedral Church of St. Paul, since 1912 the center of the Episcopal diocese of Michigan, which also resides on Woodward Avenue at the boundary of the Historical Center [Fig. 4.08].[29] The building, erected between 1905 and 1907 on plans by Cram, provides the architectural idiom on which the Cathedral of the Most Blessed Sacrament was based in variation a few years later. However, Cram's church building appears more compact. The main entrance is flanked by two massive buttresses, western towers are missing, and a square crossing tower remained unfinished. St. Paul's is situated next to Wayne State University. Education and religion, two central components of American society, are positioned here in programmatic proximity.

Along Woodward Avenue, a large number of churches in Gothic style are lined up like pearls on a chain.[30] Between the two poles of St. Paul's on the edge of the Old City district and the Cathedral of the Most Blessed Sacrament in the then suburb of Arden Park, sacred buildings of various denominations are lined up, which are to be interpreted as the neo-Gothic architecture statements of the respective parishes: Woodward Avenue Presbyterian Church (1911) [Fig. 4.09];[31] North Woodward Congregational Church 1911–1912;[32] Metropolitan United Methodist Church, designed 1916–1917, constructed 1922–1926 [Fig. 4.10];[33] First Baptist Church, 1909;[34] St. Joseph's Episcopal Church, 1926 [Fig. 4.11];[35] and beyond the Cathedral of the Most Blessed Sacrament are Central Woodward Christian Church, 1928 [Fig. 4.12];[36] First United Methodist Church, 1916;[37] and Grace Evangelical Lutheran Church, 1929–1930.[38] A similar row of church buildings can be observed on Peachtree Road in Atlanta, Georgia.

The Gothic-styled Hungarian Roman Catholic Church of Holy Cross at 8423 South Street in the Detroit suburb of Delray originated from a different social background. Built in 1924–1925 according to the plans of the Hungarian architect Henry Kohner (1884–1943), who came from Timisoara, this church is the spiritual center of Hungarian emigrants.[39] Kohner based his plans on representations of numerous churches in Hungary, Europe, and the United States.[40] In 1948 the Hungarian-born Andres Dauber was commissioned to execute the wall paintings. The stained glass windows of the Van Gerichten Company (Columbus, Ohio) in the transept were created by immigrant glass craftsmen.[41] The main altar, pulpit, and baptismal font, however, were supplied by the Daprato Statuary Company Pontifical Institute of Christian Art, Chicago. The church reflects the origins of the parishioners with its specific pictorial features reflecting a special iconographic program important for the Hungarian church.[42]

Beyond the Big Metropolises

Gothic-styled cathedrals and churches are not only present in the big cities. Prominent cathedral buildings have also been erected at smaller dioceses in remote areas, for example, the Catholic Cathedral of St. Helena in Helena, Montana [Fig. 4.13].[43] The architect of this church, built between 1909 and 1924, A.O. Von Herbulis (actually, Albert Olszewski, 1861–1928) from Washington, D.C., was charged with the design, because he was considered to have great expertise in Gothic architecture due to his education at the Polytechnic University in Vienna.[44] Of his two preliminary designs, the building committee decided on the variant that refers to an explicit model—the Votivkirche in Vienna, which Von Herbulis knew well. The towers in particular are copies. The reference to Europe is further strengthened by the stained glass windows, which were designed by the company F. X. Zettler from Munich.[45] In 1935 numerous earthquakes caused major damage; among others the south tower had

29 4800 Woodward Ave.

30 Tutag and Hamilton, *Discovering Stained Glass in Detroit*, 64–65; Collum, Krueger, and Kostuch, *Detroit's Historic Places of Worship*.

31 8501 Woodward Ave., by Sidney Badgley (1850–1917).

32 8715 Woodward Ave, by Hugh B. Clement (1862–1927), today St. John's Christian Methodist Episcopal Church.

33 8000 Woodward Ave., by William E. N. Hunter (1868–1947).

34 8601 Woodward Ave., by Guy J. Vinton (1859–1910), today Peoples Community Church.

35 8850 Woodward Ave., by James J. Nettleton (1862–1927), today St. Matthew's and St. Joseph's Episcopal Church.

36 9000 Woodward Ave., by George Mason (1856–1948), today Little Rock Missionary Baptist Church.

37 16300 Woodward Ave., by William E.N. Hunter.

38 12375 Woodward Ave., by J. Adam Fichter, today Prayer Temple of Love Cathedral.

39 The first Hungarian immigrants arrived at the end of the nineteenth century, followed by a second wave after World War I. A third, this time mainly political refugees, followed after World War II; the fourth wave followed in 1956 as a result of the Hungarian uprising against the communist regime. The members of the first two groups founded the parish. Tutag and Hamilton, *Discovering Stained Glass in Detroit*, 64–65, <http://detroitchurchblog.blogspot.com/2018/03/return-to-holy-cross-hungarian.html>.

40 Kohner was a construction manager and architect, trained in the United States. Tutag and Hamilton, *Discovering Stained Glass in Detroit*, 64–65; Collum, Krueger, and Kostuch, *Detroit's Historic Places of Worship*, 172–179, 239.

4.13 Helena, Montana, Catholic Cathedral of St. Helena, A.O. Von Herbulis (actually Albert Olszewski), 1909–1924.
[Wikimedia Commons; photo 2006]

4.14 Orlando, Florida, Cathedral Church of St. Luke, Frohman, Robb, and Little, 1922–1987.
[Wikimedia Commons; photo 2014]

to be rebuilt. Since the middle of the 1950s, the interior has been modified.

The Episcopal Cathedral Church of St. Luke in Orlando, Florida, was planned by the architectural firm of Frohman, Robb, and Little, who was also responsible for the National Cathedral in Washington, D.C., starting in 1922 [Fig. 4.14].[46] Construction of the cathedral in Orlando began in 1925, but was halted in 1926 due to financial problems caused by the economic depression in Florida. With the erection of a temporary wall at the end of the nave, the completed building could at least be used for church services after its consecration on Easter in 1926. It was not until 1986 or 1987 that the church, which is now brightly plastered, was completed according to the original plans: the choir area including the sacristy and the tower were added. The modern flying buttresses with attached pinnacles are the most obvious feature of the late addition. Only the patron saint is figuratively represented on the stepped portal in the main façade. Figure niches with pedestals and tracery canopies in the portal walls remain empty so far.

At the same time Philip H. Frohman received the order for the construction of the Episcopal St. Paul's Cathedral (since 1985)[47] in San Diego, California, in the Bankers Hill neighborhood. It was planned as a parish church with community center from 1920 onward. First, the community center was realized. The world economic crisis of 1929 and World War II impeded the construction of the church, which was completed only after 1950 in a reduced neo-Gothic style. Drafts from 1948 demonstrate a project in the English style with a dominant crossing tower. From the beginning, these plans proved to be too expensive for the congregation, which launched several fundraising campaigns for financing. Changes in the building regulations by the city administration, which, among other things, required the availability of parking areas, also re-

41 The stained-glass windows in the choir were created by Detroit Stained Glass Works. Tutag and Hamilton, *Discovering Stained Glass in Detroit,* 64–65.

42 Another example of the great importance of parishioners' origins in church design is St. Anthony of Padua (former St. Bernard's Church) locally known as the "Cathedral on/of the Prairie" in Hoven, South Dakota, former territory of the Sioux. Built in 1920/1921 to plans by architect Anton Lohman for a congregation of mostly German settlers, it refers on to Bavarian models. Carolyn Sands; Diane Filipowicz; Carolyn Torma (July 1979). "National Register of Historic Places Inventory/Nomination: St. Bernard's Catholic Church / St. Anthony's Church." <https://npgallery.nps.gov/NRHP/GetAsset/NRHP/80003731_text>

43 Regan, *Gothic Pride*, 176–177; Spencer, *Helena, Montana: The Queen City*.

44 His main client was the Catholic Church. Kervick, *Architects in America of Catholic Tradition.*

45 The windows in the clerestory were made by Charles J. Connick.

46 Cathedral Church of St. Luke (Orlando, Florida), *Centennial Book of the Cathedral Church of St. Luke*, <http://www.stlukes-cathedral.org/History.html/History.html/History_detailed.htm>. Cathedral Church of St. Luke (Orlando, Florida; Episcopal), *Church Records and History, 1900–1992.*

47 Koelsch, "A Gothic Architect in San Diego," 42–60.

4.15 Toledo, Ohio, Our Lady, Queen of the Most Holy Rosary Cathedral, John T. Comès, 1912–1925/1931. [Wikimedia Commons; photo Nheyob, 2013]

quired modification. The calculated costs increased with every delay. Instead of the original $600,000 planned in the 1920s, a sum of $1,250,000 would have to be raised according to the plans in 1947. With these conditions, it became increasingly difficult for the architect to produce a design that would meet all requirements.

Frohman initially insisted on a neo-Gothic building, originally intended to be a pure stone structure, but by the late 1940s the only concern was the rapid completion of the church. As a result, a concrete skeleton construction with artificial stone cladding was created. From the beginning, there was a dispute not only about money but also about the architectural style. The Southern California community envisioned a church in the neo-Renaissance or colonial style: "As originally presented to me St. Paul's was a problem in architectural design but not in architectural economics."[48] The designs that Frohman finally submitted were a mixture of Romanesque and early Gothic, dispensing with the tower.

Our Lady, Queen of the Most Holy Rosary Cathedral is the center of the Roman Catholic Diocese of Toledo, Ohio, established by Pope Pius X in 1910 [Fig. 4.15]. John T. Comès submitted the design for the new church in 1912; the beginning of construction was delayed until 1925, but already in 1931, during the Great Depression, the church was completed under the direction of William Perry. The work of the interior continued until 1940, the year of its consecration. The cost was $3.25 million. The cathedral building attracts attention mainly because of its finely crafted, openwork ornamental elements as well as stained glass and rose windows and pinnacles above the buttresses.[49] Especially the openwork ornamental elements refer to models of the Isabelline Gothic of Spain. Spanish motifs are also reflected in the interior, for example the barrel vaults, which are divided into star-shaped

48 Koelsch, "A Gothic Architect in San Diego," 49.

49 <https://toledodiocese.org/page/our-cathedral#_the_facade>.

compartments and reproduce Spanish artesonado ceilings. An authentic stone from the cathedral of Toledo in Spain, which was laid next to the cornerstone, creates a direct connection to the former capital of the Visigoths. The cathedral is the center of a multi-ethnic congregation, which consisted of the descendants of first Irish and German immigrants and was later strengthened by French, Hungarian, Italian, Mexican, Polish, Slovakian, and Afro-American immigrants. This plurality is also reflected in the artists who were commissioned to design the interior.

The Second Half of the Twentieth Century

Even after World War II, the Gothic style is still the focus of current semantic architectural considerations in America. The skeleton construction method is suitable as a metaphor for describing a design process: "Like Gothic building, planning is a skeleton whereon and wherein the works of art of many others will build up the beauty of the whole body."[50]

Beyond the big cities, churches in Gothic style, financed by wealthy residents, continue to be built, seamlessly continuing the prewar period.

For example, the Catholic Cathedral of the Holy Angel in Gary, Indiana (1947–1950), whose new construction required a community that grew rapidly after 1940 [Fig. 4.16]. Today's limestone building is modeled on the ecumenical Rockefeller Chapel of the University of Illinois, Chicago (1919–1928, Bertram G. Goodhue, Fig. 4.27). In 1956, the church gained a new dimension with the establishment of the Diocese of Gary by Pope Pius XII: cathedral status.

Another example demonstrates the continuity of Gothic style in that period, the Presbyterian Kirk in the Hills, Bloomfield Hills, Michigan [Fig. 4.17]. The parish was founded in 1947 in the Cedarholm area of Bloomfield Township.[51] Already in 1946, first drafts had been submitted by Wirt Rowland (1878–1946), but they were realized only after his death—from 1951 to 1958 by the firm of George D. Mason.[52] Self-made man Edwin S. George, who considered it necessary to establish a church community, provided the extensive, picturesque building site, and set up a foundation for the building starting in 1933.[53] The model for the building is the Cistercian Melrose Abbey in Scotland. The imposing Apostle's Tower, with its seventy-seven-part carillon dates back to the foundation of the Roy A. Fruehauf family, who made their fortune from the manufacture of semitrailer tractors.[54] Other artists of renown in church construction provided the architectural decoration, such as Lee

50 Allsopp, "Urban Planning for Delight," 55.

51 Meyer et al., *Detroit architecture: A.I.A. Guide*, 170. See also: <https://ilovedetroitmichigan.com/detroit-architecture/kirk-in-the-hills-presbyterian-church-bloomfield-hills-michigan/>. The name "Kirk" in the Hills is derived from the Old English word Kirk, meaning "church."

52 Smith, *Designing Detroit – Wirt Rowland and the Rise of Modern American Architecture*.

53 <https://detroithistorical.pastperfectonline.com/byperson?keyword=George%2C+Edwin+S.>.

54 About the philanthropy of the Fruehauf family see <https://www.singingwheels.com/kirk-in-the-hills-presbyterian-church.html>.

4.16 Gary, Indiana, Catholic Cathedral of the Holy Angel, 1947–1950. [Wikimedia Commons; photo Nyttend, 2012]

4.17 Bloomfield Hills, Michigan, Kirk in the Hills, Wirt Rowland, 1947–1958. [Postcard, archive Bruno Klein]

Lawrie, Corrado Parducci, and John Angel. In the area surrounding the Kirk in Hills, in the Cranbrook district, the Episcopal Christ Church in neo-Gothic style is located, built 1925–1928 according to plans by Oscar Murray from the office of Bertram Grosvenor Goodhue Associates.[55] It is significant that, on one hand, renowned models from the United States were used, as in the case of the cathedral in Gary, and on the other hand, renowned architectural firms with many years of experience and tradition were commissioned, as in the case of the Kirk in the Hills. The resumption of the Gothic style after World War II could support the assumption that there was a desire for the continuation of a prewar value system.

Modern tendencies of the Gothic style are evident in Harold E. Wagoner's National Presbyterian Church, Washington, D.C. (1966–1969) [Fig. 4.18], which is the third major denominational church building in the American capital apart from Episcopal National Cathedral and Catholic National Shrine. Already around 1930, after the founding of the Covenant-First Presbyterian Congregation as antecedent of the National Presbyterian Church, plans by Cram and Ferguson for the construction of the new church had been submitted, but they were not carried out.[56] Like the National Cathedral, the church built later was ennobled at the laying of the cornerstone on October 14, 1967 by the presence of a—in this case former—president, Dwight D. Eisenhower. The limestone-clad steel construction is given a reduced Gothic look with high, narrow lancet windows filled with glass windows from Willet Studios.[57] The design of the vault as plank framework of a ship's hull associates Noah's Ark as a safe haven. The simplicity of the rest of the furnishings is due to the concentration on the spoken word.

4.18 Washington D.C., National Presbyterian Church, Harold E. Wagoner, 1966–1969. [Wikimedia Commons; photo Farragutful, 2012]

Gothic Style in the Postmodern Era

With the emergence of postmodernism around 1980, the Gothic style in architecture became fashionable again. Buildings such as the Mildred B. Cooper Memorial Chapel in Bella Vista, Arkansas, by Euine Fay Jones and Maurice Jennings (1988), take over pointed arches (as steel constructions) and glass walls as striking motifs of Gothic architecture in the most abstract form [Fig. 4.19]. The recourse to Gothic is deliberately designed to evoke the spirituality of the "great age of faith":[58] "The Gothic was chosen for its enduring quality, a quality which is as awe inspiring today as it was in Fourteenth Century Europe."[59]

The innovation potential inherent in Gothic architecture was realized in an increasingly abstract form; for example, the Crystal Cathedral in Garden Grove, California, (now Christ Cathedral), made of steel and glass, was built between 1977 and 1980 according to a design by Philip Johnson. Its crystalline shape was the origin of its name [Fig. 4.20]. The imposing temples of the Mormons, for example in Washington, D.C.

55 <https://christchurchcranbrook.org/history-architecture/>. It originated from a foundation of the Booth family.

56 Apparently, the Cram and Ferguson office was commissioned immediately after the merger of The Church of the Covenant (Presbyterian) and First Presbyterian Church in 1923 with the planning of a new church building. About the merger, see McCartney, "The National Presbyterian Church and Its Heritage in Washington," in: Records of the Columbia Historical Society, 1960/1962, 206–223. For a depiction of their proposal, see Hayward, *Reproduced illustration of an architectural proposal for the National Presbyterian Church of Washington, D.C.*

57 About the iconographic program, see The National Presbyterian Church Communications Committee, ed., *Facets of Faith*. The windows by Tiffany and Booth from the predecessor building of the nineteenth century were also taken over.

58 Barry, *The Arkansas Designs of E. Fay Jones 1956–1997*, 63–66; Cordes, "Encore Delivered with Strength and Delicacy: Cooper Chapel," 52–57.

59 <http://www.cooperchapel.com/about.html>.

(1968–1974) and in San Diego (1984–1993), can also be affiliated with abstract forms of Gothic style.

Continuity in the Twenty-First Century

In the twenty-first century, the survival of the Gothic style idiom was initially ensured by restoration measures. Unfinished buildings have been completed, such as the Catholic Cathedral Shrine of the Virgin of Guadalupe in Dallas, Texas, a religious center for Mexican immigrants, which was built between 1898 and 1902 according to plans by Nicholas J. Clayton.[60] In 2005 the building was completed with the addition of the bell tower. Similarly, the Catholic Cathedral of St. John the Baptist in Charleston, South Carolina (1890–1907, Patrick C. Keely) received its bell tower only in 2010 according to designs by Ruben Solar [Fig. 4.21].[61] The two new towers reflect the design elements of the existing buildings, resulting in a harmonious appearance.

Gothic style was also taken up by the firm of Hartmann-Cox Architects, which in 2004, planned the Goodson Chapel on the campus of Duke University in Durham, North Carolina in the immediate vicinity of the neo-Gothic Duke Chapel (1930–1932) [Fig. 4.22]. The architects adopted characteristic design elements of it for their building, resulting in a subtle design continuity of the ensemble.

Between 2004 and 2006, the Central Lutheran Church of the Norwegian American congregation in Minneapolis, Minnesota was also expanded by the addition of the Northwest Tower [Fig. 4.23].[62] Building the west façade of the church 1926–1928 the flanking future towers, which remained unfinished then, were already prepared by the first two floors. A stylistic model for the Central Lutheran Church may have been St. Mark's Episcopal Cathedral in Minneapolis, built 1909–1910 according to plans by Edwin H. Hewitt, even though they differ fundamentally on the inside: while St. Mark's Cathedral demonstrates the classic two-story wall elevation, Central Lutheran Church has a bright church room with an open gallery zone.[63]

Completely new buildings in Gothic style are gaining popularity again, as St. Martin's Episcopal Church in Houston, Texas, testifies [Fig. 4.24]. Today's church of the parish, which was founded in 1952, was built between 2000 and 2004 according to plans by the Jackson & Ryan office in Houston,

4.19 Bella Vista, Arkansas, Mildred B. Cooper Memorial Chapel, Euine Fay Jones and Maurice Jennings, 1988. [Wikimedia Commons; photo LearningLark, 2012]

4.20 Garden Grove, California, Crystal Cathedral (today Christ Cathedral), Philip Johnson, 1977–1980. [Wikimedia Commons; photo Arnold C., 2007]

60 "History – The Cathedral at the Arts District," <https://web.archive.org/web/20120624064037/http://cathedralguadalupe.org/about/history.cfm>.

61 See Bergeron, "Centennial Completion," 15–16, <https://charleston.pastperfectonline.com/archive/7DC3E30A-221A-47EC-99F9-247687504562>.

62 Kristofer Coffman, "Central Lutheran. Minneapolis. Hennepin County. Minnesota.": <https://pages.stolaf.edu/locluth/project/central-lutheran/>.

63 About St. Mark's Episcopal Cathedral, see *St. Mark's: A Parish Church and a Cathedral, Minneapolis, Minnesota, The Cathedral Church of St. Mark;* Sicilia, *Building Honestly.*

4.21 Charleston, South Carolina, Cathedral of St. John the Baptist, Patrick C. Keely, 1890–1907, bell tower in 2010 by Ruben Solar. [Wikimedia Commons; photo DXR, 2016]

4.22 Durham, North Carolina, Duke University, Goodson Chapel, Hartmann-Cox Architects, 2004; tower of Duke Chapel in the background. [Wikimedia Commons; photo Gregw824, 2005]

4.23 Minneapolis, Minnesota, Central Lutheran Church, 1926–1928, bell tower finished 2004–2006. [Wikimedia Commons; photo Farragutful, 2007]

Texas.[64] The steel skeleton construction was accurately clad with pink bricks and shine white on the inside. The model here was not the proven, richly decorated buildings of the High and late Gothic periods, but, at special request of the parish, explicitly a building of the early Gothic period, the Elisabeth Church in Marburg, Germany, in its architecturally modest form [Fig. 4.25].[65] Apparently, a change of style was decided as a demarcation from the neo-Gothic architecture of the 1920 and 1930s. The costs amounted to $36.4 million. According to the architects, the challenge was to reproduce the stone architecture of the model building in a different material.

St. Martin's Church, built in one of the suburbs that emerged after World War II, adds another Gothic landmark to Houston's urban fabric, which is marked downtown by buildings such as the Antioch Missionary Baptist Church (1875, Richard Allen), the Episcopal Christ Church Cathedral (consecrated 1893, J. Arthur Tempest and Silas McBee), and the neo-Romanesque Catholic Annunciation Church (1869, Nicholas Clayton), and in midtown by the Trinity Episcopal Church (1917–1921, Cram and Ferguson).[66] While work on the Trinity Episcopal Church was completed in the 1960s and 1970s with the installation of the final stained glass windows, the simultaneous move of parishioners to the suburbs and the increasing commercialization of the neighborhood ushered in its decline.[67]

The Ave Maria University Oratory in Ave Maria, Florida is the center of a Catholic university city, founded in 2003 by the pizza

64 The church is one of the largest episcopal congregations on the North American continent. Its most prominent members were former U.S. President George Bush and his wife Barbara. Jackson and Ryan also designed Our Lady of Lourdes Catholic Church for the Vietnamese community in neo-Romanesque and neo-Gothic style (around 2010).

4.24 Houston, Texas, St. Martin's Episcopal Church, Jackson & Ryan 2000–2004.
[Wikimedia Commons; photo Farragutful, 2016]

4.25 Marburg, Germany, St. Elizabeth's Church, 1235–1283.
[Wikimedia Commons; photo Megacity01, 2006]

billionaire and missionary Tom Monaghan [Fig. 4.26].[68] The city and the church were built between 2006 and 2008, with an investment of $200 million. The external shape of the church resembles an oversized pointed arch, while buttresses are made of modest steel arches. The main façade, made of prefabricated concrete slabs, was clad with stone slabs in shades of brown and ochre, which form a subtle ornament of intersecting pointed arches. A minimalist rose window and a gallery of figure niches above the three portals are further transformations of Gothic style into modernity. The interior is dominated by the visible steel beams that carry the building.[69]

While new Gothic-style churches are being built, as in Houston, or work is still in progress to complete them, as in St. John the Divine in New York, there are now many abandoned churches, such as St. Peter and Paul Church in Pittsburgh, which was completely renovated by the architect John T. Comès after a fire in 1905. Sometimes another congregation acquires the building and remodels it according to their needs. There are also radical changes of use, for example, St. Helen's Church in Pittsburgh, originally built in 1929–1931 for a Slovak congregation, has been converted into a car showroom.[70]

College and University Churches as Special Construction Task

College and university churches form a special group of sacred buildings, as they operate within a specific functional context: as places of worship of usually interdenominational educational institutions, which also consider the teaching of a social value system as an educational purpose, they are generally open to all denominations for use. It is precisely for this reason that the Gothic stylistic idiom is the style of choice that has been used since the nineteenth century, for

65 See "Matrix Structural Engineers: Award-Winning Projects," <https://web.archive.org/web/20070430121908/http://www.matrixstructural.com/awardwinning.shtml>.

66 "Trinity Episcopal Church, Houston," in: *The Handbook of Texas Online, Texas State Historical Association* (TSHA), online: <https://tshaonline.org/handbook/online/articles/ietan>.

67 Since then, this decline has been offset by new initiatives.

68 Goeßmann, "Uni-Gründung Ave Maria: Campus ohne Sünde," *Der Spiegel*, July 14, 2006.

69 <https://www.screenflex.com/ave-maria-church-naples-fl/>; <http://www.gcatholic.org/churches/usa-14/23408.htm>; <https://www.dailymail.co.uk/news/article-2370041/Welcome-promised...atholic-college-town-built-Dominos-Pizza-millionaire-founder.html>.

70 <http://www.hannacre.com/uploads/media/hlwe-flyers/St_Helens_Church.pdf.>.

4.26 Ave Maria, Florida, Ave Maria University Oratory, interior 2006–2008.
[© Jim West / Alamy Photo Stock]

example, in the Batell Chapel at Yale University (1874–1876), the Evans Memorial Chapel at the University of Denver (1878, 1960 translocation to its present location), the Kirkpatrick Chapel of Rutgers State University (1873), and St. Thomas of Villanova Church on the campus of Villanova University (1883–1887).

The church's position in the overall complex is always prominent: as the center, at the entrance, on a hill. In each case, the church functions as a point of orientation. Since the early twentieth century, the Gothic architectural style on the campus has also served to unify individual buildings, which were constructed in disparate architectural styles. This occurred, for example, with West Point Military Academy Chapel (1906–1910) as part of a comprehensive expansion phase, whose general development plan was drawn up by the Cram, Ferguson, and Goodhue offices.[71] Even under superintendent Major Richard Delafield (1856–1861), numerous buildings were erected in the Gothic style, which he believed to be an appropriate vocabulary for a military academy.[72]

While the Gothic architectural design is mostly used in a formulaic way like a stencil, creating a certain monotony, the chapels are individualized by the iconographic programs. In addition to motifs from the Old and New Testaments, the focus is on other depictions from the entire cultural history as an identification of value systems and educational concepts of the respective colleges.[73] The syncretistic worldviews generated in this way were intended to serve as patterns of action for the young people. Glass windows perform an eminent role as a medium for the visualization of educational ideals. Their interchangeability enables subsequently pictorial modifications to the building if daily political events are to be remembered.[74] Finally, the construction of these chapels allowed numerous benefactors to demonstrate their sense of community. The commitment of the Rockefeller (Rockefeller Chapel, University of Chicago), Heinz (Heinz Memorial Chapel, University of Pittsburgh), and Millar (Millar Chapel University, Northwestern University) families was extraordinary.

Many campus chapels were built after World War I, including St. Andrew's Collegiate Chapel (formerly Main Chapel Divinity Site) Philadelphia Divinity School, Pennsylvania, 1919–1924 by Zantzinger, Borie, and Medary; Rockefeller Chapel, University of Chicago, Illinois, 1918–1928 by Bertram G. Goodhue [Fig. 4.27]; Princeton University Chapel, New Jersey, 1924–1928 by Ralph A. Cram [Fig. 4.28].

A special group are those designed as tower buildings, like the four buildings mentioned here. They tower above the other buildings, which is why they also serve as landmarks on their respective campuses and beyond, in their cities. Examples include the Harkness Memorial Tower, Yale University, New Haven, Connecticut, 1917–1922 by James Gamble Rogers [Fig. 4.29]; the Luther Tower Concordia Seminary, Clayton, Missouri, 1922–1966 by Charles Z. Klauder; and the A.P. Green Chapel, University of Missouri in Columbia, Missouri, 1921–1926 by Jamieson and Spearl.

During and following the Great Depression, several important Gothic university

71 On June 28, 1902, Congress approved the sum of $5,500,000 for the expansion and renovation of the military complex, which had been in existence since 1779; in 1903, a competition was held for a general development plan, which was won by the then renowned office of Goodhue, Cram, and Ferguson with its neo-Gothic buildings.

72 "National Register of Historic Places Inventory – Nomination Form, 2," <https://npgallery.nps.gov/NRHP/GetAsset/NHLS/66000562_text>.

73 For example, Rockefeller Chapel, University of Chicago in Chicago, Illinois (1918–1928, Bertram G. Goodhue) and Princeton University Chapel, Princeton, New Jersey (1924–1928, Ralph Adams Cram).

74 Significant in this context is the Sage Chapel of Cornell University, Ithaca. Built between 1873 and 1875, and extended in three phases until 1940, the original building was added in 1991 with a stained-glass window containing portraits of three activists of the Civil Rights Movement, commemorating their murder by the Ku Klux Klan on the evening of June 16, 1964: Cornell graduate Michael Schwerner; Andrew Goodman, whose parents studied at Cornell University; and James Chaney.

4.27 Chicago, Illinois, University of Chicago Rockefeller Chapel, Bertram G. Goodhue, 1918–1928. [Wikimedia Commons; photo Matthew Bisanz, 2012]

4.28 Princeton, New Jersey, Princeton University Chapel, Ralph Adams Cram, 1924–1928. [© Princeton University]

4.29 New Haven, Connecticut, Yale University, Harkness Memorial Tower, James Gamble Rogers, 1917–1922. [Wikimedia Commons; photo 2007]

4.30 Pittsburgh, Pennsylvania, University of Pittsburgh, Heinz Memorial Chapel, Charles Z. Klauder, 1933–1938. [Wikimedia Commons; photo Dllu, 2015]

chapels were demonstratively donated, including those of Duke University in Durham, North Carolina, 1930–1932 by Julian F. Abele; Trinity College in Hartford, Connecticut, 1932–1933 by Philipp H. Frohman; and Heinz Memorial Chapel at University of Pittsburgh, Pittsburgh, Pennsylvania, 1933–1938 by Charles Z. Klauder [Fig. 4.30].

Like World War I, World War II caused a social and historical break. Above all, the dropping of the two atomic bombs on Hiroshima and Nagasaki marked a turning point that once again fundamentally shattered the faith in the previous value system, which had been laboriously rebuilt in the interwar period. The post-war generation instead aspired to universities rather than to churches,

4.31 Valparaiso, Indiana, University of Valparaiso, Chapel of the Resurrection, Charles Stade & Associates, consecration 1959.
[Wikimedia Commons; photo Hakkun, 2007]

4.32 Colorado Springs, Colorado, United Air Force Academy Chapel, Walter Netsch, 1959–1962.
[Washington, Library of Congress: LC-DIG-highsm-04090; photo Carol M. Highsmith]

because the values of the Christian faith were doubted, as Edward D. Mills noted in 1956 in his book *The Modern Church*.[75] While after World War I, Gothic architecture was apparently used quite deliberately to revive a lost system of values within the educational system, the Gothic style developed in two directions in new buildings after World War II: on the one hand, there was a radical break in the architectural language, and on the other hand, buildings were realized that documented the continuity of traditions. At the same time, there were remarkable syntheses of modernism and neo-Gothicism: an example is the Chapel of the Resurrection of the University of Valparaiso (Valparaiso, Indiana, consecrated in 1959) by the architects Charles Stade and Associates, with its expressive, polygonal chancel with high windows. Models for the Chapel of the Resurrection are the postwar building of Coventry Cathedral for the nave and the ancient Church of the Holy Sepulchre in Jerusalem for the chancel [Fig. 4.31].[76]

The United Air Force Academy Chapel in Colorado Springs (1959–1962), made of aluminum and glass, also appears rather futuristic at first glance [Fig. 4.32]. The basic idea of this building is, however, Gothic in its entirety. The most striking feature of the interdenominational chapel is the forty-six-meter-high "Nurdach" construction with seventeen spires, each of which consists of a steel frame with aluminum cladding.[77] In between, glass surfaces allow light to enter the interior of the Protestant upper church. The glass bands evoke a ribbed vault. The chapels and prayer rooms of other denominations are located in the basement, each with separate entrances. During the planning process, the accountable architect Walter Netsch, employee at the Skidmore, Owings, and Merrill office, was sent to Europe to study Gothic cathedrals, such as Chartres and the Notre-Dame de Paris: "I was really worried because Gordon Bunshaft had sent me to Europe to look at Gothic architecture and Renaissance architecture."[78] Gordon Bunshaft provided the reason for the trip: "Because you're going to do another controversial building, Walter, and you've got to be able to say that you've seen Chartres and Notre-Dame."[79] The building demonstrates both the universal, cross-denominational aspirations of American university chapels, which have persisted into the modern age, and the fact that types and forms of Gothic architecture are still considered binding for this purpose. This paradox of contradictory concepts is ironically broken in the article "Iconic American Buildings Re-Envisioned in the Gothic Revival Style" (2018) by Vasundhra Aggarwal.[80]

75 Mills, *The Modern Church*.
76 Buggeln, 'The Shape of a New Era Valparaiso's Chapel of the Resurrection in Historical Context," 6–14. Buggeln, *The Suburban Church*. Dedication booklet, *Chapel of the Resurrection*, 1959, with list of sponsors.
77 The basic module for the entire campus is based on the number 7 and half of it 3.5. The chapel was built as a tetrahedron in the shape of paper folds in the style of Japanese origami. The design has received many awards: among others The R.S. Reynolds Memorial Award, 1964; Silver Medal of Honor: Design and Craftsmanship, 1965.

Conclusion

Gothic-style building has been successful and widespread in the United States for about two hundred years for two main reasons. First, Gothic architecture is considered a genuine Christian architectural style, and second, it expresses the Christian religiousness of faith deeply rooted in American society. The most significant expression of faith in God is the motto "In God we Trust," which has appeared on U.S. coins since 1864 and on paper money since 1955.[81] The use of Gothic style in sacred architecture has always been associated with traditional constructions and assertions of validity—between the different denominations or on part of the Christian "majority society" toward ethnic and religious minorities.

The Catholic Cathedral of Christ the Light in Oakland, California, by architect Craig W. Hartman illustrates the trends of the twenty-first century in the use of modern building materials and methods, which are due to geological conditions, as well as innovative digital techniques. Planning for the filigree glass architecture began in 2000, and in 2008 the church was consecrated. The relationship between modernism and Gothic is manifested in the depiction of Christ Pantocrator behind the altar similar to Christ in Glory in the Tetramorph (1962) at Coventry Cathedral:[82] the model of the west portal of Chartres Cathedral was transformed into a mosaic of light using digital pyrotechnics on aluminum panels [Fig. 4.33].[83] Gothic as an eternal value could hardly be more innovative and transformed into the future of the twenty-first century.

4.33 Oakland, California, Catholic Cathedral of Christ the Light, Christ in Majesty, Craig W. Hartman, 2000–2008.
[Wikimedia Commons; photo Skier Dude, 2008]

78 Quotation by Netsch, interviewed by Detlef Mertins, 2002: Netsch reported the deep impressions of his European tour, especially about the lighting in the Sainte Chapelle: "Of course, I landed in Paris, and the first building I saw was Notre Dame, and the second was St. Denis, the earlier church in an earlier version of Gothic and Sainte-Chapelle. Sainte-Chapelle made a tremendous impression on me being flooded with colored light, and the fact that it had a chapel on two floors. I also saw St. Francis of Assisi when I got to Italy, and Gordon remembers it as his inspiration on his having decided that the chapel at the Academy should be on two levels. I can remember Gordon and I discussing both buildings. […] But the Gothic form, this soaring form, the complex geometry, was something that was inspiring. How could that be in the final result?"

79 Netsch, interviewed by Detlef Mertins, 2002.

80 Aggarwal, "Iconic American Buildings Re-Envisioned in the Gothic Revival Style".

81 Related to this is a strong "civil religion," but not a "state religion" or the primacy of one denomination, because freedom of religion is anchored in the Constitution of the United States (First Amendment of the Constitution).

82 I thank Bruno Klein for this reference.

83 Alderman, "The Lonely God: Oakland Cathedral in the Light of Tradition."

5
Ecclesiastical Gothic in Twentieth- and Twenty-First-Century Canada

Bettina Marten

Introduction

In Canada, religious architecture in the Gothic stylistic idiom appeared from the early nineteenth century onward—first in the form of isolated elements such as pointed arches, and from about 1840 programmatically in the buildings of the ecclesiological movement. Other congregations started using it immediately, especially the Roman Catholics and the Methodists.[1] Three factors seemed to favor the dissemination: first, the reception of Pugin's True Principles by immigrant architects who received commissions in Canada; second, the disparity of the population structure—descendants of French, British, and Irish colonists, but also numerous indigenous ethnic groups—which was to be unified into a state polity and apparently found a universally accepted architectural style in the Gothic style of architecture; and third, the spread of this building program through architectural treatises on church building with the extension of the railroad developing a national infrastructure even to the most remote areas of the continent.[2]

The image of the "proper" church construction, in other words the Gothic style, conditioned the buildings by the qualities they conveyed, such as beauty, economy, and appropriateness.[3] Important actors in this process were the church building committees, which were composed of the country's elite: influential businessmen, lawyers, and high-ranking members of the clergy. The decision on the architectural style of a new church was in their hands.[4] The prevailing assumption was that with the omnipresence of the Gothic architectural style, the potential for identification with the national feeling would also increase.

In the nineteenth century, churches in the Francophone provinces were based on more French models, in the Anglophone provinces on more British models, recoursing back specifically to A.W.N. Pugin. The Anglican Christ Church Cathedral in Fredericton, New Brunswick, built 1845–1850 to designs by Frank Wills, was adapted from St. Mary's Church in Snettisham, Norfolk, England. The Catholic Saint Patrick's Basilica in Montreal, designed by Pierre-Louis Morin and Father Felix Martin for the Irish community of the city, is obviously based on French Gothic buildings.[5] Work on the Catholic Basilica of Our Lady Immaculate in Guelph, Ontario, built 1876–1888 to plans of the Irish-born architect Joseph Connolly (1840–1904), was not finally completed until 1926, when the two towers on the west façade were added.[6] Connolly designed other important cathedrals, including St. Peter's Basilica in

5.01 Hamilton, Ontario, Cathedral Basilica of Christ, William Russel Souter, 1931–1933.
[Wikimedia Commons; photo Jfvoll, 2018]

1 For the history of sacred architecture from the sixteenth century to around 1760, see Gowans, "Church Architecture in New France". For the role of architecture as a strategy in the formation of national identity see Liscombe, "Introduction. Writing into Canadian Architectural History," 1–33, 13. For an extended bibliography on neo-Gothic architecture in Canada, see The Society for the Study of Architecture in Canada, "Reading List": <https://canada-architecture.org/reading-list/> (September 30, 2020). Gauthier, *Le Devenir de l'Art d'eglise des paroisses catholiques du Québec.*

2 On July 1, 1867, the British North America Act was enacted, unifying the provinces of Ontario, Quebec, New Brunswick, and Nova Scotia into the Dominion of Canada as protection against U.S. annexation. In 1869 the Northwest Territories joined, in 1870 Manitoba, 1871 British Columbia, 1873 also Prince Edward Island. The statute of Westminster of 1931 established Canada's sovereignty, and religious freedom was enshrined in the 1982 Canadian Charter of Rights and Freedoms (Article 2).

3 Magrill, *A commerce of taste.*

4 Ibid., 83–106, 173–174.

5 See the home page of the Directory of Federal Heritage Designations: <https://www.pc.gc.ca/apps/dfhd/page_nhs_eng.aspx?id=658>.

6 Thurlby, "The Church of Our Lady of The Immaculate Conception, at Guelph", 32–40. On Connolly, see Thurlby, "The Roman Catholic Churches of Joseph Connolly (1840–1904). The Adaption of A.W.N. Pugin's 'True Principles' and Aspects of Irish Identity in Ontari", 76–93.

5.02 Vancouver, British Columbia, Cathedral of the Holy Rosary, Thomas E. Julian and H. J. Williams, 1899–1900.
[Wikimedia Commons; photo dronepicr, 2018]

London, Ontario in 1880, and St. Mary's Roman Catholic Church in Toronto in 1881. As in the major U.S. cities, competition in church building between the denominations continues in Canada's cities: in Toronto, St. Michael's Roman Catholic Cathedral Basilica (1845–1890), based on designs by William Thomas, was quickly followed by Anglican Cathedral Church of St. James (1850–1890), on plans by Frederick William Cumberland.[7] The abovementioned churches of the nineteenth century set Gothic landmarks in the major cities for the buildings of the following century. While numerous studies are available on Gothic-styled churches of the nineteenth century, scientifically reliable studies for the twentieth and twenty-first centuries on this subject are rare.[8] The following examples continue the notions that have already been explained in the United States chapter.

Urban Contexts: Vancouver (British Columbia)

The large cities in the east began building cathedrals and churches as early as 1850. In the west, this process only started toward the end of the nineteenth century, when new cities were founded. The Catholic Cathedral of the Holy Rosary, built 1899–1900, was one of the first major construction projects after Vancouver was officially founded in 1886 and following the destruction caused by a devastating fire in the same year [Fig. 5.02].[9] In 1892 the planning and especially the raising of funds began, which remained scarce throughout the construction. The foundation stone was laid in 1899. The architects Thomas Ennor Julian and H. J. Williams were inspired by French models. The pointed arch turned into a continuous motif, also in the pointed barrel vault. The main façade is characterized by two towers of different heights flanking the central nave. The different tower heights may reflect the incompleteness of medieval church towers. In France, this is the result of historical building processes; here, it is a historically adapted *Schauelement* (element of ostentation). In Vancouver's 1898 city map, which depicts the Old Town, the Cathedral of the Holy Rosary is already planned into the urban environment in the immediate vicinity of the First Congregational Church and St. Andrew's Church. Other church buildings are positioned in the nearest neighborhoods. The First Congregational Church and St. Andrew's Church later moved their locations: St. Andrew's Church in 1927, and First Congregational Church in 1950. Thus, the original denominational concentration in downtown was broken up.

First Baptist Church and St. Andrew's-Wesley United Church, located on the main Burrard Street axis and facing each other, form a charming urban ensemble of Gothic style.[10] First Baptist Church was built us-

7 Simmins, *Building the Victorian Dream.*
8 For the nineteenth century, see, for example, the articles of Candace Iron, Peter Coffman, and Malcolm Thurlby in: Brittain-Catlin, De Maeyer, and Bressani, eds. *Gothic Revival Worldwide.*
9 For further information, see the Holy Rosary Cathedral home page: <https://www.holyrosarycathedral.org/architecture/>.
10 See home page: "Canada's Historic Places," <https://www.historicplaces.ca/en/rep-reg/place-lieu.aspx?id=10919>.
11 Kalman and Ward, *Exploring Vancouver: The architectural guide*, 164.
12 For images, see <https://www.glassincanada.org/our-building/canadian-memorial-church-historical-panels-1497-to-1928/>.
13 Kalman and Ward, *Exploring Vancouver: The architectural guide*, 54; Kalman, Phillips, and Ward, *Exploring Vancouver: The Essential Architectural Guide*, 49.

ing traditional masonry techniques from 1911 onward according to plans by Edmund Burke of the Burke, Horwood & White Office. A fire destroyed the building in 1931, but it was rebuilt immediately. St. Andrew's-Wesley United Church, designed by the brothers Robert Percival Twizell and George Sterling Twizell, both proven specialists in the Gothic stylistic idiom, emerged 1927–1933 as a reinforced concrete skeleton construction in perpendicular style [Fig. 5.03]. The chosen architectural language provoked criticism, partly because it was thought to be too pretentious for representation, and partly because it was considered inappropriate to follow Anglican models.[11]

The Canadian Memorial United Church in Vancouver, place of national remembrance to commemorate Canadian soldiers who died in France and Belgium during World War I, originates from a promise made by Father George Fallis, who had provided pastoral care to the soldiers in the field. Built 1927–1928, again on designs of the architects Twizell and Twizell, the memorial appears rather modest and massive in its shape with lancet windows and buttresses as the most prominent features of Gothic style [Fig. 5.04]. The multi-lane windows depict scenes from the history of Canada reflecting an Anglo-centric view of events, with little mention of Canada's indigenous peoples.[12]

St. James Anglican Church in the Japantown neighborhood arose 1935–1937 according to plans by Adrian Gilbert Scott on a property formerly owned by the Canadian Pacific Railway.[13] The reinforced concrete skeleton structure, which is prominently positioned at a road junction, contains Gothic elements such as the stepped portal or lancet windows, which have been transformed into a modern, functional form.

5.03 Vancouver, British Columbia, St. Andrew's-Wesley Church, Twizell and Twizell, 1927–1933. [Wikimedia Commons; photo Joel Mabel, 2010]

The Church as Integrative Place for Immigrants: Miramichi, New Brunswick

In places where different confessional groups with potential conflicts met, from the nineteenth century onward, church buildings in Gothic style were instrumentalized as integrative elements, as in the instance of the Catholic Basilica of St. Michael's in Miramichi, New Brunswick, the episcopal seat of the Roman Catholic Diocese of Chatham from 1860 to 1938 [Fig. 5.05].[14] Built by the Berlinguet Company between 1903 and 1922 on a crest overlooking the Miramichi river, the project originally dated back to Patrick Keely, architect of St. Mary's Basilica in Halifax (1869–1899). He was commis-

14 See Heritage Office, City of Miramichi, Site File #04-07, database Canadas historic places: <https://www.historicplaces.ca/en/rep-reg/place-lieu.aspx?id=2737>. About the strategy of achieving the integration of disparate population groups by using the Gothic style, see Thurlby, "The Roman Catholic Churches of Joseph Connolly (1840–1904)," 78–81.

5.04 Vancouver, British Columbia, Canadian Memorial United Church, stained glass window with historical scenes (Manitoba-Window), 1927–1933.
[© JSMimages / Alamy Photo Stock]

5.05 Miramichi, New Brunswick, St. Michael's Cathedral 1903–1922, on a project of Patrick Keely from 1878.
[© Canadabrian / Alamy Photo Stock]

sioned for the new church after the previous building had been destroyed by fire in 1878.[15] The single tower façade is crowned by a copper roofed spire. A small polygonal west apse (Our Lady's Chapel) was added in 1909 to provide structural security. The exterior is austere, while the interior opens a bright and light, three-aisled church with reticulated vaults. The time-delayed building constructed by using traditional masonry techniques seemed to correspond to the conservative orientation of the parishioners, Irish Catholics, and could thus fulfill an identity-forming function. Irish immigrants arrived in the late eighteenth century in the area that had previously been under French protectorate but fell to the English in the Seven Years' War. The Irish community subsequently had to deal with reprisals. The importance of the building's rank as a cathedral (until 1938) and the fame of the commissioned architect seemed to have supported the parish's integrative aims.[16]

Reception of U.S. Gothic Style in Canada: Hamilton, Ontario

U.S. Gothic style first made its appearance with the small Saint Mary's Anglican Church in Walkerville, Ontario[17] and with the All Saints Anglican Cathedral in Halifax, Nova Scotia, both designed by Ralph Adams Cram and built 1902–1904 and 1907–1910, respectively, using traditional masonry techniques.[18] The Halifax Cathedral features the Gothic stylistic idiom reduced to a minimum.

The Catholic Cathedral Basilica of Christ in Hamilton, Ontario (1931–1933) opens another aspect, because it is an example of the reception of U.S. neo-Gothic in Canada [Fig. 5.01].[19] The building is located prominently on an open space in the city. The staircase in front of it provides additional visual height. The structure is characterized by a rusticated dark masonry, which

15 About Patrick C. Keely see Kervick, *Patrick Charles Keely, Architect: A Record of His Life and Work*. <https://babel.hathitrust.org/cgi/pt?id=mdp.39015064344750&view=1up&seq=8>.
16 See: "History – St. Michaels Basilica," <https://stmichaelsbasilica.com>.
17 I thank Bruno Klein for this reference. See Macdonell, *Haunted by the Gothick*; Macdonell, *Ghost Storeys*.
18 Halifax, "Cathedral of 'All Saints,'" in: *The Canadian Architect & Builder* 22 (1908), 1, 11–14.
19 Wubbenhorst, "America's influence on the Cathedral of Christ the King in Hamilton," 41–50.
20 Hamilton Catholic St. Patrick's Church, built 1875–1876 on plans by Joseph Connolly, already prepared the ground of modernity for St. Michael's Cathedral. See Thurlby, "The Roman Catholic Churches of Joseph Connolly (1840–1904)", 78–81.
21 Glebe originally meant "church land" and is an area within a church community that is used to support a pastor. The land may be owned by the church or its profits may be reserved for the church.

contrasts with the decorative, light elements. The façade flanked by buttresses is given a striking appearance by a double-stepped portal, the blind arcade above, and a deep window niche. The square tower on the right side is transformed into an octagon on the upper floors. It recourses to the Harkness Memorial Tower of Yale University in New Haven (1921, see Fig. 4.29), which in turn cites St. Botolph's in Boston (1425–1430), Lincolnshire in the United Kingdom. The author of the balanced composition of the building was local architect William Russel Souter (1894–1971). Souter had studied architecture at the University of Pennsylvania in Philadelphia from 1914 to 1917. During the planning phase, he traveled to New York in 1931 together with the responsible Bishop McNally and the building contractor Pigott to study the recent churches, especially St. Vincent Ferrer by Bertram G. Goodhue. At Hamilton, Souter created a building that took up the latest trends in Gothic style from the United States.[20]

Sacred Elegance Uptown: Ottawa

The infrastructure of new neighborhoods included the construction of new churches as well, and opened up opportunities for the parishes for better representation through architecture. Well-known architects were appointed to give the new buildings an appropriate form. Two parish churches in Ottawa's Glebe[21] residential area, which has been developed as a suburb since about 1870, are examples of adapted Gothic forms in modest elegance: St. Matthew's Anglican Church (Cecil Burgess, 1929–1930) and Blessed Sacrament Catholic Church (John Gibb Morton, 1931–1933)[Fig. 5.06].[22] Both buildings are steel-framed structures clad with Indiana limestone. The Gothic forms appeared in a modern adapted manner in the traditional basilican buildings. Both churches received colored stained glass windows. The parishes took out loans to finance their churches in difficult economic times. While the faithful of St. Matthew's Anglican Church accepted the modesty of their church, there was protest from the members of the Blessed Sacrament Catholic Church, who considered their church too unadorned.

5.06 Ottawa, Ontario, Blessed Sacrament Catholic Church, John Gibb Morton, 1931–1933. [Wikimedia Commons; photo SimonP, 2006]

Various Types of Continuity: Sherbrooke and Calgary

With long construction periods or new buildings, different kinds of continuities can be observed. Long construction periods lead to changes of plans. New buildings take up design elements from the previous building and adapt them into a contemporary language.

The Catholic Cathédrale Saint-Michel in Sherbrooke, Québec, is based on designs by Louis-Napoléon Audet (1881–1971), one of the most influential architects of the Gothic style.[23] The new church was intended to replace a predecessor building that was oriented north to south. Audet corrected the orientation to east to west, as is custom-

22 See Farr, *Church in the Glebe – St. Matthew's, Ottawa, 1898–1988*. Church home page: <https://www.stmatthewsottawa.ca/index.php/about-us#history>; Coulthart, <https://www.katecoulthart.ca/st-matthew>; <http://www.blessedsacrament.ca/our-community-life/a-history-of-blessed-sacrament/>.

23 Lacroix, "La chapelle de l'évêché de Sherbrooke," 3–34. See also <https://expo.rassas.org/en/cathedral/st-michaels-basilica-cathedral-of-sherbrooke>.

5.07 Sherbrooke, Québec, Cathédrale Saint-Michel, interior. [Wikimedia Commons; photo Libertad-pb, 2011]

5.08 Calgary, Alberta, St. Mary's Cathedral, Maxwell Bates and Alfred Hodges, 1955–1957. [© BenLar137]

ary. Between 1914 and 1916, the foundations were laid, and the southern entrance area was raised. But then construction work stopped until 1956. The resumption of work started with modifications and by 1957, the building had almost been completed. Two towers remain unfinished. There is a discrepancy between outside and inside: while the dark stone material and the Gothic ornamental elements make the façade appear massive and antiquated, the church interior gives a light and dynamic impression, due to the design of the slender pillars and the vaulting [Fig. 5.07].

The previous building of the Catholic St. Mary's Cathedral in Calgary, Alberta, from 1887 to 1892, made of the local red sandstone, was demolished in 1955 in favor of today's cathedral, a reinforced concrete structure clad with red brick [Fig. 5.08].[24] The architects of the new building, Maxwell Bates (1906–1980) and Alfred Hodges, endeavored to create a modern Gothic architectural language with ornamental elements made of light sandstone, which allows the memory of the previous building and the local building tradition to live on. After the elevation to cathedral status in 1912, there were initiatives for the construction of a new church from 1928 onward, which was to begin in the late 1930s. World War II and greatly increased costs delayed the realization of a new building until the 1950s.

Tradition and Adaptation: The National Shrines

One of Canada's most important places of pilgrimage is the Catholic Basilique of Sainte-Anne-de-Beaupré, near Québec [Fig. 5.09].[25] The history of this pilgrimage dates back to the seventeenth century. Several churches had been built since then to venerate the Mother of Mary. The predecessor of today's church was destroyed by a fire in 1922. As early as 1923, work began on the new building designed by Maxime Roisin (1871–1960). In 1924 the steel framework was erected, which was covered with cut stones during the following years. In 1926 the exterior construction was completed. The building is a hybrid in neo-Romanesque and neo-Gothic style, representatively designed as a large five-aisled pilgrimage church based on French models, capable of accommodating more than half a million visitors annually. The construction was supervised by Louis-Napoléon Audet, who attracted attention with his design for the abovementioned

Cathédrale Saint-Michel at Sherbrooke, among others.

The Basilique Notre-Dame-du-Cap in Trois-Rivières, Québec, is another important national pilgrimage site in Canada [Fig. 5.10].[26] In 1954, the predecessor building was demolished in favor of the current complex. According to the ideas of Adrien Dufresne, a central-plan church was constructed 1955–1964. The choir, entrance hall, and six chapels give the impression of an octagonal structure. Dufresne used Gothic style elements in free and modern adaptation, such as pointed arches, rose windows, wimpergs, and an open gallery above the main portal. The dome vault of the interior is supported by mighty crossing parallel arches as found in medieval pilgrimage churches, for example, in Spain (e.g., Torres del Rio, Santa María de Eunate).

24 "Cornerstones: St. Mary's Cathedral [1887–1955]," <https://web.archive.org/web/20040606015451/http://calgarypubliclibrary.com/calgary/historic_tours/corner/stmarys1.htm>; "Cornerstones: St. Mary's Cathedral [1955–]," <https://web.archive.org/web/20040606014939/http://calgarypubliclibrary.com/calgary/historic_tours/corner/stmarys.htm>.

25 Répertoire du patrimoine culturel du Québec, "Basilique de Sainte-Anne-de-Beaupré," <http://www.patrimoine-culturel.gouv.qc.ca/rpcq/detail.do?methode=consulter&id=93392&type=bien#.XTWDJy3qjdQ>.

26 Its history dates back to the seventeenth century. See Martel, "Adrien Dufresne et l'emergence de l'architecture religieuse moderne au Québec (1936–1964)", 86–91.

5.09 Sainte-Anne-de-Beaupré, Québec, place of pilgrimage, Maxime Roisin, 1923–1946.
[Wikimedia Commons; photo Didier Moïse, 2014]

5.10 Trois-Rivière, Québec, Basilique Notre-Dame-du-Cap, Adrien Dufresne, 1955–1964.
[Wikimedia Commons; photo Saffron Blaze, 2009]

5.11 Skatin, British Columbia, Church of the Holy Cross 1895–1906. [Wikimedia Commons; photo Brian Kipp Photography, 2015]

Beyond the Metropolises: Skatin and Inuvik

Even in the remotest regions of Canada, basic Gothic forms such as pointed arches and rose windows were used in church construction; for example, the wooden Church of the Holy Cross in Skatin (British Columbia, 1895–1906) and the wooden Church of Our Lady of Victory Church in Inuvik (Northwest Territories, 1958–1960).[27] The Church of the Holy Cross in the Skatin First Nation area was built 1895–1906 by indigenous tribes after the Fils de Marie Immaculée congregation had established a mission there. It represents a group of wooden churches known as "Carpenter Gothic" or "Wooden Gothic" [Fig. 5.11]. The western façade is estimated to provide an exceptional perspective because of the disposal of the three spires: between the two flanking towers, a third spire rises above the gable, which seems to imitate a crossing tower. But the lateral view reveals its real position only close to the main façade.

The Catholic Our Lady of Victory Church in Inuvik in the Northwest Territories was constructed 1958–1960.[28] The architect, Friar Maurice Larocque, intended for the building to reflect the local culture, which is most evident in the igloo form. The choice of the circular ground plan is due to the ground, because the permafrost soil proved unsuitable for a rectangular church building with a tower. Instead, it required a special foundation, made of a meter-thick gravel bed on which a bowl-shaped concrete slab and a reinforced concrete base were placed. The circular wooden structure with a dome consisting of aluminum panels rises up above. The ogival windows in the wooden wall and in the tambour, as well as the shortened buttresses at the transition from wall to dome, represent the Gothic style.

Conclusion

Based on French or English models, the Gothic stylistic idiom served in Canada from the nineteenth century onward as a vehicle to integrate disparate population groups with different geographical, religious ethnic, or cultural backgrounds for ensuring peaceful coexistence, especially between the various immigrant groups and the local population, even in the most remote areas of the country. In the second half of the twentieth century, the social aspect lost its importance. New churches began to appear as free adaptations of Gothic architecture as well as abstractions, such as the two Catholic churches built in the region of Lac-Saint-Jean: Eglise de Saint-Marc-de-Bagotville at Saguenay, 1955–1956 by plans of Paul-Marie Côté [Fig. 5.12], and the Eglise de Saint-Pierre in Alma, built 1962–1963 according to the designs of Armand Gravel and Loubo Georgiev.[29] Gothic style is apparently of no current importance in Canadian architectural discourse.

5.12 Saguenay, Québec, Église de Saint-Marc-de-Bagotville, Paul-Marie Côté, 1955–1956.
[© Canadian Register of Historic Places, 12461; photo 2009]

27 On Skatin, see Magrill, *A commerce of taste*, 135–137.

28 "Brother LaRocque Designs Arctic Igloo-Shaped Church," *The New London, Conn., Evening Day, Associated Press*, March 5, 1960, 5. See also church home page: <https://olvinuvik.com>.

29 On Eglise de Saint-Marc-de-Bagotville, see: <http://www.patrimoine-culturel.gouv.qc.ca/rpcq/detail.do?methode=consulter&id=105554&type=bien#.X5wWti2X_dQ>; on Eglise de Saint-Pierre, see: <http://www.patrimoine-culturel.gouv.qc.ca/rpcq/detail.do?methode=consulter&id=155166&type=bien#.X5wcci2X_dS>. Bergeron, *L'architecture des églises du Québec: 1940–1985*. See also home page "Les églises du Québec – Chicoutimi" for a general survey of churches in this area, <https://patrimoineduquebec.com/eglisesduquebec/chicoutimi/>.

6
Gothic Down Under

Barbara Borngässer and Bruno Klein

Australia and New Zealand show a number of outstanding neo-Gothic religious buildings from the nineteenth and early twentieth centuries, primarily Anglican and Roman Catholic cathedrals or parish churches. Because both countries are still members of the Commonwealth, they are culturally closely tied to England—a fact that is also reflected in their architecture.[1] Thus, the Gothic Revival, spread by the works of Augustus Welby Northmore Pugin and John Ruskin, has left its mark on both profane and ecclesiastical building as well as in decorative art, with unbroken continuity into the twentieth century, and in part even up to the present day.[2]

However, the main period of neo-Gothic building activity lies in the later nineteenth century, and thus outside the time covered by this book. The neo-Gothic churches in Australia and New Zealand are nevertheless presented here in connection with the region-specific and characteristic phenomena: the long-lasting construction process of those buildings. Many churches Down Under, located in Australia mainly in the southeast of the continent, were begun around the middle of the nineteenth century in the course of the gold rush to replace previous, more modest, buildings. However, they were often only completed after decades of interruption due to economic crises and wars. Towers in particular remained unfinished for a long time—in some cases, these towers remain unfinished still today. The double-towered façades of great cathedrals in Adelaide, Melbourne, Goulburn, Sydney, Newcastle, and Brisbane, for example, only found their final form between 1930 and 2010. That confirms the continuing building practice in neo-Gothic architecture from the nineteenth century on, a routine in which not only old plans were completed but also some new ones were added, defying all modernisms and ruptures in style.

There is a lot of serious scientific literature on nineteenth-century neo-Gothic architecture in Australia and New Zealand.[3] Much attention is also paid to the work of the Pugin family and the worldwide spread "Puginism."[4] However, comprehensive studies on churches of the twentieth and twenty-first centuries in the neo-Gothic tradition are still pending, a fact that also applies to the even restricted number of modern ecclesiastical buildings borrowing motifs from medieval Gothic. Important information about individual cases is provided by local publications and websites as well as by the lists of Australian and New Zealand Heritage; especially the latter contains revealing notices on construction processes, architects, and engineers.

Australia

Façades and Towers: Fields of Experimentation for Moderate Innovation

Gothic Revival transfer from England to Australia and New Zealand was in some instances very direct: building designs for big neo-Gothic churches were sometimes ordered in England and then adapted in Australia by local architects and construction companies;[5] for instance, this happened with St. Peter's in Adelaide (begun in 1868/1869)[6] and St. Paul's Anglican Cathedral in Mel-

6.01 Sydney, St. Mary's Cathedral, Assembly of spires, 2000. [© Brett Costello / Newspix]

1 As outline: <https://www.church-histories.net.au/architecture>.
2 Andrews, "Pugin in Australia."
3 Bremner, *Imperial Gothic*; Andrews, *Australian Gothic*; King and Willis, "The Australian Colonies."
4 Burns, "Global Gothic"; Andrews, *Australian Gothic*; Stiles, *Reading Ruskin*; Randles, *Medievalism and the Gothic in Australian Culture*. Some of these works mainly deal with profane architecture and interiors.
5 For the adaptation of the building plans: Bremner, "Propagating Ideas and Institutions," 18–19.
6 Andrews, *Australian Gothic*, 36–38; Bremner, *Imperial Gothic*; Grant, *St Paul's Cathedral*; also <https://en.wikipedia.org/wiki/St_Paul%27s_Cathedral,_Melbourne >; <https://cathedral.org.au/cathedral/history/> and <https://vhd.heritagecouncil.vic.gov.au/places/815>.

6.02 Adelaide, St. Peter's Cathedral, ca. 1860 (drawn by a clergyman from the design by architect William Butterfield, ca. 1860).
[© State Library of South Australia, Photograph B 1974]

6.03 Adelaide, St. Peter's Cathedral ca. 1930, William Butterfield and Edward John Woods, 1868–1904.
[Wikimedia Commons]

bourne (begun in 1880).[7] In both cases, English architect William Butterfield[8] provided designs in a Victorian Gothic style, and in both cases communication-related delays and disaccords arose, eventually leading to Butterfield's withdrawal. Different opinions about mural surfaces led to disagreement, particularly as polychrome brick masonry was in vogue in England but considered inappropriate in Australia.[9] At St. Peter's [Figs. 6.02 & 6.03], the English plans were acquired, revised, and transformed by the local Australian building contractor Wright, Woods and Hamilton; Edward John Woods, an architect also trained in England and based in Adelaide since 1860, increased the building volume at the request of the bishop and designed a new façade in 1890. In 1899 the nave was completed, and a donation of £10,000 finally enabled the towers to be erected and the apse to be completed. Construction was completed in 1904.

Comparing the various project and construction phases indicates how the building became increasingly more Gothic. In its general design, St. Peter's follows Butterfield's project plan from beginning to end, with double transept, choir tower, and two-towered façade. But the picturesque polychromy of the masonry was abandoned in favor of a more sculptural decoration with pinnacles. The west façade in particular became continuously higher and more dominant. In doing so, it began to look more similar to French Gothic buildings: the towers and the Royal Gallery evoke Notre-Dame in Paris, the rose window is reminiscent of Chartres, and the tower helmets look like those Viollet-le-Duc imagined for his "perfect" Gothic cathedral.

Although the cathedral in Adelaide, which is mainly from the nineteenth century, cannot be in the focus of this study, the constant modification of its towers, away from the original designs, makes it paradigmatic of what was happening in most major neo-Gothic churches in Australia in the twentieth century.

The construction of St. Paul's in Melbourne [Figs. 6.04-6.05-6.06] proceeded in a different way, because the executing architect Joseph Reed largely followed Butterfield's

7 Andrews, *Australian Gothic*, 35–36; Reed, *A history of the cathedral church of St. Peter Adelaide*; Andrews, *Australian Gothic*, 35–36; also <https://en.wikipedia.org/wiki/St_Peter%27s_Cathedral,_Adelaide> and <http://www.stpeters-cathedral.org.au/about/the-building/>.
8 On Butterfield, see: Thompson, *William Butterfield*; Muthesius, *The high Victorian movement in architecture*; on his designs for Australia: Landau, "Butterfield in Australia."
9 Bremner, *Imperial gothic*, 114.

6.04 Melbourne, St. Paul's Cathedral, design of William Butterfield, 1879, Melbourne, State Library of Victoria. [© State Library of Victoria]

6.05 Melbourne, St. Paul's Cathedral in 1907, William Butterfield and Joseph Reed, 1880–ca. 1960. [© State Library of Victoria]

6.06 Melbourne, St. Paul's Cathedral, Façade today (towers completed ca. 1960). [Wikimedia Commons; photo Donaldytong, 2013]

advices.[10] Although Butterfield refused any responsibility for the work after 1884, Reed meticulously copied his designs and used them as a basis for further development. The vividly colored interior complied completely with Butterfield's instructions. St. Paul's was consecrated in 1891, the helmets of the façade towers and the octagonal crossing tower still unfinished. Financial resources to build them weren't found before the 1920s. Then a competition was held, which was won by Sydney architect John Barr, a proven proponent of Victorian architecture.[11] By 1933, he started the construction of the missing towers. Although they were considerably higher than foreseen in the original design – which consequently caused structural problems – notably the likeness of the tower helmets over façade and crossing finally led to an overall harmonization of the upper parts of the entire building.

In addition, the visual importance of the façade was strengthened and the dominance of the cathedral in the cityscape increased. Subsequently, a stylistic change took place from the older lower parts to the newer upper ones: the decorative effect of finely differing wall surfaces by texture and color was given up for a stonework materially more uniform, whereby forms and plasticity became more filigree. In regard to the adapted medieval style, they are "younger" than the lower parts. It is hardly possible to name a specific model for Melbourne. St. Mary in Oxford may be the most likely example, but St. Paul's is actually an original solution, trying to give the rather vague neo-Romanesque-Gothic church a decidedly High

10 McPherson, *That uncomfortable genius*.

11 Grant, *St Paul's Cathedral*, 7.

6.07 Melbourne, St. Patrick's Cathedral, Side view today with towers built 1939. [Wikimedia Commons; photo Donaldytong, 2010]

6.08 Geelong, St. Mary of the Angels, Chancel view. [Wikimedia Commons; photo Marcus Wong, 2007]

Gothic appearance. The Romantic architecture of the nineteenth century was adjusted to formal ideas based on archaeological research, as had happened in Adelaide before.

Almost contemporaneously, St. Patrick's, Melbourne's Roman Catholic Cathedral [Fig. 6.07], also received its spires; a competitive situation immediately comes to mind.[12] St. Patrick's was built between 1858 and 1897 according to plans by William W. Wardell; its forms recall a simple, late thirteenth-century Decorated Style, which has been resumed since Pugin in the Gothic Revival. The building is one of the largest and most important examples of nineteenth-century Australian neo-Gothic.[13] Similar to the other churches, the towers remained unfinished. At least the southwestern façade tower rose with its lower parts above the height of the nave. It was not until 1936 that the entire towers were considered for completion, and in 1937 contracts were signed with W.P. Conolly and G.W. Vanheems, who carried out the work until 1939. Their reinforced concrete construction was based on Wardell's designs and did not introduce any new shapes, though the spires increased considerably in height.

Yet another church in the Melbourne area was completed in neo-Gothic style in the 1930s, St. Mary of the Angels in Geelong, Victoria [Fig. 6.08].[14] Thomas A. Kelly supplied the ambitious plans for this parish church, and the foundation stone was laid in 1854; however, the building in traditional bluestone did not grow beyond foundations before 1871. The following year, the work stopped again, but at least the façade and nave were completed. The crossing, transept, choir with ambulatory, and chapels and towers were constructed by the company Hennessy & Hennessy in Sydney between 1930 and 1937.[15]

Interwar Gothic?

Continuity in the construction of Gothic Revival–style churches during the first half of the twentieth century was not limited to completion. New, commonly called "Interwar-Gothic" buildings were also started.[16] Although this is a correct classification in a chronological sense, the term may not describe an artistic period of its own. Stylistically, buildings of the epoch are not easy to classify. St. George's Church in Parkes, New South Wales [Fig. 6.09] (1926–1956), built in brick by Louis Williams, is characterized by a castle-like exterior with reduced decoration, a feature that also characterizes other smaller buildings of the period. The single-naved Scotch College Chapel in Hawthorn, Victoria

12 On the constructional competition of the confessions in cityscape: <https://www.churchhistories.net.au/architecture>.
13 Boland, *St Patrick's Cathedral: A Life*; Andrews, *Pugin*, 257.
14 Wynd, *A history of St. Mary's Basilica.*
15 On John Francis (Jack) Hennessy: East, *Australia's first international architect.*
16 On the phenomenon of interwar churches in the United Kingdom: Bebbington and Jones, *Evangelicalism and Fundamentalism in the United Kingdom.*

6.09 Parkes, New South Wales, St. George's Church, Louis Williams, 1926–1956.
[Wikimedia Commons; photo Mattinbgn, 2013]

6.10 Hawthorne, Melbourne, Scotch College Chapel, Scarborough, Robertson and Love, 1936.
[Wikimedia Commons; photo Melbanian, 2009]

6.11 Canberra, St. Andrew's, 1929-1970s.
[© Allan Patterson, 2002]

(1936) [Fig. 6.10] is also impressively simple; the architects Scarborough, Robertson, and Love were obviously impressed by the cathedral in Albi in southern France.[17] Melbourne architect Thomas George Payne also took up models of the southern French and Catalan Gothic in his churches and chapels, for example in the Newman College Chapel of the University of Melbourne (1938). As the eminent explorer of Australian neo-Gothic Brian Andrews proves, he fell back on writings on Spanish architecture circulating in the United States.[18]

The orientation toward Mediterranean buildings, however, remains the exception in Australian neo-Gothic. In contrast, St. Andrew's, the church of the Presbyterians in the capital Canberra [Fig. 6.11], which was officially refounded in 1927, remains in a rather traditional English style:[19] besides the neo-Romanesque Roman Catholic Cathedral[20] there, it is the most important ecclesiastical building in the city. Construction started in 1929, and St. Andrew's was consecrated five years later, although not much more than the narthex with the left façade tower was finished. The nave and other parts were added in modern Gothic forms only in the 1970s. St. Andrew's remains completely modest in the cityscape of Canberra. Together with the surrounding small-scale residential buildings, it looks like an old village church, pretending tradition. It presents itself as picturesque, but not as the great transcendental monument of the modern metropolis: this task was finally left to the eclectic Australian War Memorial, opened in 1941, which operates with motifs borrowed from the Gothic, especially in the elaborated glass windows inside.[21]

17 Andrews, *Australian Gothic*, 40. The influence of Albi Cathedral on nineteenth- and twentieth-century British church architecture has been studied by Thomas, "The influence of Albi Cathedral: the use of historic precedent in nineteenth and twentieth century church design."
18 Andrews, *Australian Gothic*, 42–45.
19 Little information is available on this and the following church: <https://www.churchesaustralia.org>.
20 In 1969 it took over completely the function of the previous Gothic Revival Cathedral in Goulburn (built from 1871 to 1890).
21 The project of a large neo-Romanesque cathedral (1928) was not carried out, see East, *Australian Romanesque*, 86.

22 <https://en.wikipedia.org/wiki/St_Francis_Xavier%27s_Cathedral,_Adelaide>; <https://web.archive.org/web/20061015020001/http://www.adelaide.catholic.org.au/StFXCathedral/History/architecture.htm>; Andrews, *Australian Gothic*, 105–106.

23 Martin, *Pugin*, 256–257.

24 The exact building history of the cathedral is difficult to discern. In some cases, the information published on the internet about the planning and construction process does not correspond with the facts that can be obtained from the historical photographs. Above all, in 1923–1926 there must have been a considerable intervention in the existing older building fabric, which was adapted to more modern stylistic ideas.

Long-Lasting Construction Processes

The continuity of neo-Gothic construction sites up to World War II may be considered an obvious, perhaps somewhat tardy, continuation of the Gothic Revival. But the uninterrupted building process beyond this epochal threshold is more illuminating: in the case of the Catholic Cathedral of St. Francis Xavier's in Adelaide [Fig. 6.12], there are 140 years from foundation stone to completion.[22] The church, begun in 1856, was always planned to be built step by step, due to the tight finances of the diocese. The second phase of construction started in 1886 on designs from Peter Paul Pugin.[23] In 1923–1926, the missing sections up to the façade followed, whereby apparently a further change of plans took place: the side aisles received gables, by which the already existing sections were also decorated. The tower, started at the same time, could only be completed in 1996.[24]

The exterior of St. Mary Star of the Sea in Melbourne was planned since 1891 in a style close to French Gothic; with its opulent interior, the parish church is one of the most elaborate of its time.[25] However, the planned high façade tower was abandoned early on, and has remained unfinished to this day (summer 2021).

Like the entire state of Victoria, Bendigo, north of Melbourne, benefited from the gold rush and developed into a prosperous city with remarkable Victorian architecture. Here, with considerable financial support from the German-born priest Henry Backhaus, Sacred Heart Cathedral [Fig. 6.13] was erected, the third largest church building in Australia.[26] The designs for the sophisticated building in Decorated Style were provided by the company Reed, Smart & Tappin. The foundation stone was laid in 1897, and in 1901 the three-aisled nave and the façade with the flanking towers were completed. In 1908, however, the work was stopped due to lack of money. In a second building period, which lasted from 1954 to 1977, the architects Alan Ralton and Frank Turner achieved the east sections with the three-aisled transept, the crossing, the four octagonal chapels, and the high crossing tower; they centered on the original plans by William Tappin, but erected the crossing tower over a steel framework with wall cladding. Disregarding this technical intervention, the entire building presents itself as a uniform monument in the style of English High Gothic, not least for the basilica interior, structured by finely profiled bundled pillars. Stained glass windows and mobile furnishings show the finest Victorian craftsmanship.

6.12 Adelaide, St. Francis Xavier's, planning 1856, 1886–1926 built on designs of Peter Paul Pugin, tower of 1996.
[Wikimedia Commons; photo JohnArmagh, 2012]

6.13 Bendigo, Victoria, Sacred Heart Cathedral, Reed, Smart & Tappin 1897–1908, Alan Ralton and Frank Turner 1954–1977.
[Wikimedia Commons; photo Larry. Ellis, 2011]

St. Saviour's, the cathedral of the Anglican diocese of Goulburn [Fig. 6.14], newly founded in 1861, is still waiting for its spire. The church is the work of the busy master builder Edmund Blacket, Colonial architect of New South Wales, who was especially appreciated for his elaborate tower constructions.[27] It is said that he had drawings brought from England to design the towers of St. Andrew's in Sydney similar to York Minster. But unfortunately, he was unable to see one of his largest churches completed: the cruciform building with the fine "late Gothic" tracery windows was indeed already finished in 1884, but the planned mighty façade tower had barely exceeded the foundations. It was not until one hundred years later, supported by funds from the Bicentennial Commemorative Program, that concrete efforts were made to continue the work. First of all, the existing foundations were examined and strengthened, and at the same time the search for suitable stone began. Old quarries in the region were reopened and material from demolished monuments (Fitzroy Bridge) was requisitioned. For the technical planning of the tower's construction, the team around Peter Freeman & Partners sought the advice of the construction company in Bendigo, which already had experience in this respect. In 1986 the specific work began, whereby stone construction was only minimally reinforced by concrete addition and a steel skeleton completely renounced. In this way, an attempt was made to come as close as possible to the specifications of Edmund Blacket. The top of the tower is currently (2021) still waiting for its completion.

After a fire destroyed Sydney's first Roman Catholic Cathedral, St. Mary's [Fig. 6.15], in 1865, Archbishop John Bede Polding commissioned William Wardell, a student of Augustus Welby Pugin, to design a magnificent new building.[28] Wardell, already distinguished by the construction of St. John's College in Sydney and the plans for St. Patrick's in Melbourne, was given a free hand in the choice of style, so long as everything would be beautiful, grand, and powerful: "Any plan, any style, anything that is beautiful and grand, to the extent of our power."[29] In 1868, the foundation stone was laid for the mighty cathedral, inspired by the Decorated Style of the thirteenth century in England; the façade, however, is strongly influenced by French Gothic—as is St. Peter's in Adelaide. The building presents itself as a cruciform plan with a crossing tower, double towers on the façade, and a long, straight, closed choir. The large tracery window behind the altar resembles that of the Lincoln Cathedral. Work on this demanding project proceeded hesitantly, starting in the north, with the choir and the crossing, which was completed with its tower in 1900. The nave was built between 1913 and 1928, the crypt

6.14 Goulburn, St. Saviour's Cathedral, completed in 1884 with the tower continued since 1986, still expecting its spire. Clearly visible the different stone colors of the ancient and new parts. [Wikimedia Commons; photo Mattinbgn 2013]

6.15 Sydney, St. Mary's Cathedral, begun 1868 on designs of William Wardell, Nave ca. 1928, spires erected 2000. [Wikimedia Commons; photo JohnArmagh, 2012]

25 <https://vhd.heritagecouncil.vic.gov.au/places/1276>.

26 <https://vhd.heritagecouncil.vic.gov.au/places/3311/download-report>; Andrews, *Australian Gothic*, 67.

27 On Blacket: Bremner, *Imperial Gothic*, 258–264.

28 *Kelleher, Saint Mary's Cathedral;* Andrews, *Australian Gothic*, 70–72; <https://www.environment.nsw.gov.au/heritageapp/ViewHeritageItemDetails.aspx?ID=5055071>.

29 <https://en.wikipedia.org/wiki/St_Mary%27s_Cathedral,_Sydney>.

6.16 Newcastle, Christ Church, decisive plans by John Horbury Hunt 1883, towers and transept 1970s. [Wikimedia Commons; photo Adam.J.W.C., 2012]

in the 1960s. The façade with its three portals and the great rose remained unfinished, as the towers were only built in their lower parts. The cathedral did not receive its spires until 2000 [Fig. 6.01]. Formally based on Wardell's design, the spires are supported by a steel framework that was mounted with the help of a Russian helicopter. Thus, after 145 years of construction, St. Mary's finally transmits the sublimity that Archbishop Polding had in mind. Sydney's Roman Catholic Cathedral is considered one of the largest and most important buildings of the worldwide Gothic Revival, despite or perhaps because of its long and continuous construction history.

Christ Church in Newcastle [Fig. 6.16] is a neo-Gothic cathedral that equals in size and equipment the churches of Melbourne and Sydney; it was also constructed over a period of more than one hundred years.[30] It was begun as a monumental brick building according to the designs of John Horbury Hunt in 1883[31]; after several changes of architects and plans, Frederick George Castleden and his successors took over the further construction in 1909. At this time, the nave and crossing were completed, but only provisionally closed. In 1911 or 1912, the gallery and the eastern sections were completed. In 1924 the extension of the also neo-Gothic Warrior's Chapel was finished, shortly before the work came to a standstill in 1928. It was not until the 1970s that the towers and transept were completed, whereby the architects John Sara of Castleden & Sara used Hunt's original plans.

Also in Brisbane, the capital of the newly created federated state of Queensland in Australia, the construction of large churches dragged on for decades. The new building

30 <https://www.environment.nsw.gov.au/heritageapp/ViewHeritageItemDetails.aspx?ID=5061305>.

31 About Hunt: Bremner, *Imperial Gothic*, 265–272.

of St. Stephen's that was founded in the year 1863 could at least be concluded in the year 1922 with a crossing, transept, and sanctuary, but in a much more modest frame than originally planned.[32]

Most remarkable is the case of St. John's, the Anglican Cathedral of Brisbane [Figs. 6.17 & 6.18], which was completed only a few years ago with the emplacement of the statues of the saints on the façade.[33] After laying its foundation stone in 1901, the church, with its mighty apse, was built in three major construction phases, which lasted from 1906-1947, 1965-1969, and 1989-2009. The reference point was and always remained the design by John Loughborough Pearson, which his son Frank adapted to its definitive site after his father's death. During the first phase, the eastern sections, crossing, and transept were built, as well as the first bay of the adjacent nave. In 1947, funds were available to convert the church into a war memorial, and the foundations for two more bays were laid; though the westward expansion was only completed after 1965. Finally, in 1989, construction of the western bays, the façade with its towers, and the crossing tower could begin. As one of the few buildings of the continent, St. John's has stone vaults. The financing of the 40 million Australian dollar project to finish the cathedral was enabled by donations as well as regional and governmental funds. In 2009, the now towered building was consecrated.

6.17 Brisbane, St. John's Cathedral in 2008, John Loughborough Pearson and Frank Loughborough Pearson, begun 1901, towers completed 2009.
[© Bruno Klein, 2008]

6.18 Brisbane, St. John's Cathedral in 2020.
[Wikimedia Commons; photo kgbo, 2020]

32 <https://brisbanecatholic.org.au/about/cathedral-of-st-stephen/#cathedral-story>.

33 <https://apps.des.qld.gov.au/heritage-register/detail/?id=600076>; <https://en.wikipedia.org/wiki/St_John%27s_Cathedral_(Brisbane)>.

6.19 Perth, St. Mary's Cathedral, 1863–2010.
[Wikimedia Commons; photo Michal Lewi, 2014]

6.20 Darwin, St. Mary's Star of the Sea, interior, Ian Ferrier, 1958–1962.
[Wikimedia Commons; photo Torbenbrinker, 2019]

Excursus: Gothicizing Modernity

In contrast to secular buildings, the number of modern churches in Australia and New Zealand is limited, which, as indicated at the beginning, speaks for the special urbanistic role of older Gothic ecclesiastical architecture in Australian cities. Gothic-looking new buildings or extensions are of little importance. The narrow and low neo-Gothic nave of the Roman Catholic Cathedral of St. Mary's in Perth [Fig. 6.19] (1863–2010) was demolished in 2009, because the church was too small. Instead, a new nave was built, the dimensions of which reached those of the choir, which had already been enlarged before. In the angles between the nave and the transept, two spacious new rooms were created over a quarter-circular floor plan. Their outer walls are completely glazed, and the supports between the individual windows are reminiscent of Gothic buttresses. As a counterpart to the existing single tower, a new one was erected, which in terms of cubature and structure completely adapts to its historical model without denying its own modernity.[34]

Darwin, the capital of the Northern Territory, on the other hand, boasts three modern churches that deal with Gothic structures: St. Mary's Star of the Sea Cathedral [Fig. 6.20], 1958–1962) is built over high parabolic arches, Uniting Church (1960) presents itself box-like with an outer structure reminiscent of a supporting framework.

Australian Gothic?

Gothic church building of the twentieth and twenty-first centuries in Australia ties in completely with the Gothic Revival architecture of the nineteenth century in English tradition, and it fundamentally continues this convention. In contrast to Latin America, for example, a dissociation from the architecture of the mother country did not seem to be required, and distancing was no subject of style debates. Rather, the adherence to Victorian patterns promised continuity in the social sphere of the European-dominated communities and served as a self-assurance of "white" Christianity. What is striking is the continuousness in the choice of the stylistic idiom. And so an integration of indigenous elements cannot be noticed; there were anyway only few, probably rather painful, points of contact between the Aborigines in Central Australia and the prospering cities near the coast.[35]

Gothic construction between the world wars was characterized by pragmatism: building forms were continuously applied in a

34 <https://en.wikipedia.org/wiki/St_Mary%27s_Cathedral,_Perth>; <https://web.archive.org/web/20120510074445/http://register.heritage.wa.gov.au/viewplace.html?place_seq=2124&offset=0&view=description>; Wysokowski, "Unusual rebuilding method of historic St Mary's cathedral in the capital of Western Australia."

35 On the expulsion of the Aborigines from the coasts and the ambivalent role of the missions: Brome, *Aboriginal Australians.*

simplified manner, all too costly projects were brought to a temporary conclusion, and modern construction techniques were used for faster and cheaper completion. On the other hand, in the last decades of the twentieth century and in the beginning of the twenty-first century, numerous building projects that formerly had been left behind have been completed. This applies especially to the completion of towers and spires. New technologies now also permit the rapid execution of sophisticated constructions: this may explain why the original designs of the nineteenth century are increasingly used. It would even be worth considering whether the spectacular putting on of spires by helicopters, for example, might more or less unconsciously express the modernity of Gothic churches.

New Zealand

The development of the Gothic Revival in New Zealand, especially in the nineteenth century, doesn't differ much from that in Australia. Although there are less large cathedrals, notably the city of Dunedin on the South Island shows an impressive ensemble of churches in this style.[36] With regard to the topic of this book, among them the Anglican St. Paul's Cathedral [Fig. 6.21] merits special attention, because it was not started until the year 1913, replacing a previous building.[37] The church was consecrated already in the year 1919, but at that time it was far from finished. It was decided not to complete it according to the original plans only in the 1950s. The small old choir was substituted by a new one between 1969 and 1971. The proportions and the tight vertical structure of the choir are in keeping with the neo-Gothic church, but otherwise it is completely modern in style.

In Nelson, on the North Island, a new Anglican cathedral [Fig. 6.22] was begun in 1925 in neo-Gothic forms based on French Rayonnant architecture according to plans by Frank Peck—the wooden preceding church was in danger of collapsing due to earthquake damage. However, construction work was suspended for decades during the Great Depression. It was not until 1954 that a project for a simplified continuation was drawn up, a plan that was apparently highly controversial because of its modernized forms. According to this, the church was completed from 1962 to 1967.[38] While the necessary structural additions to the church interior are architecturally modest, the steeple, which is completely pierced by tracery, is an independent performance of twentieth-century Gothic architecture.

The Anglican Holy Trinity Cathedral of Parnell [Fig. 6.23] shows a similar combination of old and new, but here the choir is the oldest part, and the nave with façade is

36 Hamilton and Hamilton, *Early Churches in and around Dunedin*.

37 <https://en.wikipedia.org/wiki/St_Paul%27s_Cathedral,_Dunedin>; Hamilton and Hamilton, *Early Churches in and around Dunedin*, 22–23.

38 <http://www.theprow.org.nz/places/nelson-s-landmark-cathedral/#.Xr6qIC-nknV>; Baker, "Christchurch Cathedral Nelson," <http://www.theprow.org.nz/assets/files/Helen-Baker-Christ-Church-Cathedral-Nelson-Essay-2.pdf>.

6.21 Dunedin, New Zealand, Saint Paul's Cathedral, begun 1913 after plans of Edmund Harold Sedding, new choir 1969–1971 by McCoy and Wixon.
[Wikimedia Commons; photo Benchill, 2009]

6.22 Nelson, New Zealand, St. Paul's Cathedral, begun 1925 on plans by Frank Peck, completion 1967.
[Archive Bruno Klein]

6.23 Parnell, Auckland, New Zealand, Holy Trinity Cathedral, interior, neo-Gothic chancel 1957–1963 by Richard Toy, modern nave completed 1995. [Wikimedia Commons; photo Andrewrabbott, 2015]

younger. The entire construction period took place during the second half of the twentieth century:[39] the choir was built between 1957 and 1973 [Fig. 6.24], and after an interruption in construction, which was connected to a radical change of plans, the remaining sections were consecrated in 1995. While the older parts show an almost minimalistic Gothic style with large undecorated wall surfaces on the outside, and simply profiled pillars without capitals, arches, and groined vaults, the younger parts break completely with Gothic formal tradition: the nave is an almost square, column-less room. The ancient chancel provides the height and width to dimension the central ceiling section, which descends to the floor to low, sawtooth-like windows at the sides; their proportions and interior design vaguely evoke a 'Gothic' impression. [Fig. 6.25]

These few examples show that in twentieth-century New Zealand, it was still possible to build in Gothic forms, but, unlike in Australia, there exists no stylistically homogeneous persistence of long-term constructions. A lot of different reasons can be established for this, and they vary from building to building. Two of these reasons stand out: first, church building in New Zealand is not as strongly influenced by the Gothic Revival as in Australia. Prominent buildings such as the Catholic cathedrals of Christchurch or Wellington are works of the neo-Renaissance. Their architect was Francis William Petre, who also designed the neo-Gothic Catholic Cathedral of Dunedin and buildings in other styles.[40] Secondly, due to the numerous heavy earthquakes, the churches repeatedly needed to be repaired or renewed completely. So it was hardly possible to achieve an undisturbed continuity of construction once started. But it may also be that the permanent pressure for renewal made the modern earthquake-proof building seem better than the old unstable one. There is no other explanation for the fact that a building such as the neo-Gothic Anglican Cathedral of Christchurch,[41] which was severely damaged by the 2011 earthquake,

was at first to be demolished—a fate that was only to be averted after massive protests in 2017. The aforementioned neo-Renaissance Catholic Cathedral in the same city, however, will be demolished. Even though such measures are no longer possible in most parts of the world today, the example of New Zealand shows that neo-Gothic ecclesiastical architecture does not yet belong to a historically closed epoch and is thus perhaps not worthy of protection. It remains to be seen whether Gothicizing architecture is capable of evoking a greater emphasis than architecture in other historical styles. In any case, on the occasion of the demolition of the Catholic neo-Renaissance cathedral, no discussions comparable to the dispute over the preservation of the neo-Gothic cathedral of Christchurch have been handed down.[42]

6.24 Parnell, Auckland, New Zealand, Holy Trinity Cathedral in 1971. [Archives New Zealand; photo G. Riethmaier]

6.25 Parnell, Auckland, New Zealand, Holy Trinity Cathedral, West window by Robert Ellis and Shane Cotton with christian Polynesian iconography in partly medieval Gothic colors. [Wikimedia Commons; photo Andrewrabbott, 2015]

39 <http://www.holy-trinity.org.nz/discover; https://en.wikipedia.org/wiki/Holy_Trinity_Cathedral,_Auckland> with incorrect dates of construction.

40 With John Cyril Hawes (1876–1956), Australia also had an architect who built large churches in a variety of styles, including the neo-Gothic church of St. Mary in Ara Coeli, Northampton (1936). Andrews, *Australian Gothic*, 30.

41 Between 1864 and 1904, the Anglican Cathedral of Christchurch was built according to Gilbert Scott's original plans, which were modified by the New Zealand architect Benjamin Mountfort during construction: <https://my.christchurchcitylibraries.com/cathedrals-of-christchurch/#ChristChurchCathedral>.

42 <https://en.wikipedia.org/wiki/Cathedral_of_the_Blessed_Sacrament,_Christchurch>.

7
Neo-Gothic in India
Autonomy, Fusion, Exuberance

Peter Scriver, Amit Srivastava, and Pedro Guedes

The Gothic architecture of India is one of the more conspicuous material-cultural legacies of the long and profound entanglement of the subcontinent with the expanding European world, particularly at the height of colonial imperialism in the second half of the nineteenth century. Symbolically, and most emphatically in the case of the religious buildings of the British colonial subculture, Gothic could connote an unapologetic cultural chauvinism; it was an introduced style that represented the ostensibly profound differences in spiritual beliefs, taste, and aesthetics of the colonizers relative to those of the religiously and ethnically diverse subject population. By the early twentieth century, however, a more elemental and almost abstract strain of Gothic characterized some of the earliest propositions of modernism in Indian architecture. Emerging in the final decades of colonial rule, this was a distinct counterpoint to the final Indo-classical turn in the architecture of the British Indian regime. Meanwhile, the perennial renewal and relevance of this constantly evolving mode of architectural expression in contemporary Indian religious culture underscores the fact that Gothic is also—and has always been, throughout its relatively brief intercession in India's architectural history—a medium of intercultural exchange and invention [Fig. 7.01].

7.01 Shivamogga (Shimoga), Karnataka, Sacred Heart Cathedral, 1994–1997. [Wikimedia Commons; photo Primejyothi, 2009]

The Introduction and Evolution of a Gothic Tradition under British Colonial Rule

Gothic Revival, in its initial picturesque version, arrived in India as early as 1820, when work began on the castellated Hampton Court–like buildings of Bishop's College on the banks of the Hooghly River near Calcutta (Kolkata today).[1] But it would be another two decades before the first significant Gothic churches were built. Modeled on the late Gothic perpendicular style of Canterbury Cathedral and York Minster, but fashioned primarily of brick and *chunam* (an indigenous form of polished lime plaster) and vaulted by lightweight iron trusses, St. Paul's Cathedral, Calcutta, 1839–1847, was a resourceful simulacrum of the Gothic by its engineer designer, William Nairn Forbes, that marked a definitive break from the neo-classical precedent of Gibb's St. Martin in the Fields, the model that had hitherto dominated church building across the British colonial world.[2]

Meanwhile, a more principled version of the English Gothic Revival was introduced to India almost simultaneously, on the other side of the subcontinent, with the construction of the Afghan Memorial Church in Bombay (Mumbai) in 1847 [Fig. 7.02]. A shrine to honor the fallen of the First Anglo-Afghan War (1839–1842), the Afghan Memorial Church was designed by another versatile engineer in the service of the East India Company, Henry Conybeare, who had based his design on the guidelines for historically correct Gothic issued a year earlier by the Cambridge Camden Society. In 1846 the

1 Halder and Halder, *Colonial Architecture at Calcutta*, 26.

2 Davies, *Splendours of the Raj*, 149–151.

7.02 Mumbai (Bombay), Maharashtra, Afghan Memorial Church, Bombay, Henry Conybeare, 1847. [Archive Bruno Klein]

7.03 Kanpur (Cawnpore), Uttar Pradesh, Cawnpore Memorial Church, Walter Granville, 1861. [Wikimedia Commons; photo Shivam Maini, 2016]

Society's monthly journal, the *Ecclesiologist*, had outlined its recommendations for the use of the Speluncar or Lombardic Gothic style for British architecture in India. Deviating from the general recommendations for a Middle Pointed style defined by its geometrical tracery, a variant of Lombard was suggested for the southern and tropical regions of the empire as this Italian Gothic tradition was associated with warmer climates and was considered the mother style of medieval architecture.[3] Churches in India ought to be massive and monumental, it was argued, with thick masonry and "almost without windows."[4] With nearly glassless façades, rounded arches, low roofs, and possible polychrome masonry, the "effect was to depend on outline and mass rather than variety and contrast of surface."[5]

A further, assiduously correct response to the guidelines for the proto-Gothic Lombardic style in particular was the design by Walter Granville, Consulting Architect to the Government of Bengal, for the Cawnpore Memorial Church (1861) in Kanpur [Fig. 7.03]. This was another symbolically significant shrine, built to commemorate fallen British soldiers and colonial servants following the bloody suppression of the popular revolt of 1857–1858 that had swept across northern India. A subsequent effort to adapt the more diaphanous higher Gothic features of the thirteenth-century French style to the harsh light of the Gangetic plains in William Emerson's 1871 design for All Saints, Allahabad (Prayagraj) [Fig. 7.04] would be regarded by later commentators as an obvious failure. Writing from South Africa shortly before he was to travel to India to consult on the design of the new imperial capitol complex at New Delhi (1912–1931), Herbert Baker acknowledged the challenge that the Gothic style had posed for his predecessors such as Emerson working as colonial architects in sunny climes:

> Emerson, [...] the introducer of Gothic into India, [...] seems to have at last repented of his error [...] I, for one, am not in favour of throwing overboard all our national traditions in church architecture. I feel, however, that the more sincerely we architects set about our work, the more nearly we shall find ourselves

3 Hershey, "High Victorian Gothic," 75.
4 Scott, "Some notes on the Cathedral of Las Palmas with a Few Thoughts on Tropical Architecture," 40.
5 Webb, "On the Adaptation of Pointed Architecture," as cited in Hershey, "High Victorian Gothic," 76; see also Bremner and Nelson, "Propagating Ideas."

unconsciously approaching the forms of the Romanesque rather than those of the more highly-developed Gothic style.[6]

Smaller churches in more or less orthodox Gothic Revival styles would continue to be built well into the twentieth century as refuges of Englishness and Christian faith in India, along with church-affiliated schools and colleges, particularly in the exclusive highland "hill stations" to which the European colonial community routinely retreated from the heat.[7] However, the primary application and development of the Gothic style in India in the latter half of the nineteenth century was to be in the secular architecture and infrastructure of the modernizing Indian metropolises.

In the aftermath of the revolt of 1857, a call to order within the colonial regime had instigated a sea change in approach to the political management as well as the technical development of the subcontinent. While government was transferred from the East India Company to the direct rule of the British Crown, a new policy of "Peace and Public Works" would literally build bridges and new credibility for the regime, as well as a new architectural face.[8] Distinct from its parochial and backward-looking ecclesiological associations, the novel Gothic Revival style of London's new law courts and railway stations, along with the new Houses of Parliament was a symbolic statement of progress and modernity as well as solidarity in the political context of Britain's global empire. By the time that Queen Victoria had formally assumed the title of Empress of India in 1877, Victorian Gothic Revival was everywhere. As Volwahsen notes, "it was Bombay and not London that developed in the second half of the nineteenth century into the center of Victorian Gothic Revival Style."[9] But this call to order in form and governance had also accelerated a process of technical consolidation and improvement that had been initiated with the establishment of the Public Works Department (PWD) of British India in 1855. Dominated by military engineers, and increasing numbers of their civil and mechanical counterparts—competing modern professionals who far outnumbered qualified architects in the colonial field—the PWD had focused equally on the rationalization of contextually appropriate design and building practices.[10] This had also favored the modish Gothic turn in style.

Neo-Gothic approaches to construction, detailing, and formal composition enabled adventuresome engineer-architects such as

6 Baker, "Plea for English Gothic."
7 For a definitive architectural and cultural-historical survey, see: Bhatt, *Resorts of The Raj*.
8 Scriver and Srivastava, *India*, 25–30.
9 Volwahsen, *Splendours*, 129; see also London, *Bombay Gothic*.
10 Scriver, *Empire-Building*.

7.04 Prayagraj (Allahabad), Uttar Pradesh, All Saints Cathedral (Church of North India), William Emerson, 1871.
[Wikimedia Commons; photo Ojas Tripathi, 2012]

7.05 Karachi, Sindh, Pakistan, Frere Hall, Henry St Clair Wilkins, 1863–1865.
[Wikimedia Commons; photo A. Savin, 2020]

7.06 Chennai (Madras), Tamilnadu, Madras Law Courts, R.F. Chisholm, J.W. Brassington and Henry Irwin, 1882–1892.
[Wikimedia Commons; photo W.A. Cross, *Illustrated Guide to the South Indian Railway*, 1913]

the Royal Engineer, Henry St. Clair Wilkins, and Assistant Engineer Muncherji Cowasji Murzban to innovate with new building types and functions (hospitals, colleges, public halls, markets, railway stations), that had few if any precedents in the solid Georgian neoclassical building tradition of the previous "Company" regime, which had built upon the colonial trading empires and architectures of the French, the Dutch, the Danish, and the Portuguese before them.[11] Wilkins, in particular, exemplified the military engineering cadre of the PWD, and the combination of technological wherewithal and artistic sensibility that defined the Gothic rationale of the public architecture of British India between the 1860s and 1880s [Fig. 7.05].[12] Wilkins's arguments for the suitability of the Venetian Gothic style were subsequently followed by others, including eminent metropolitan architects such as George Gilbert Scott in the designs he sent out from London for the library and senate house of Bombay University.

At the same time, free-style Gothic invention enabled designers to explore the performance and tectonic qualities that local building stones, bricks, and timbers could bring to the style, and how these same materials had been employed in the historical building cultures of the subcontinent. The syncretic eclecticism of later Victorian architecture worldwide found its own particularly flamboyant expression in British India in what would be called the Indo-Saracenic style. In seminal examples such as William Emerson's Muir College in Allahabad, however, and the work of Robert Fellowes Chisholm and PWD colleagues on the major public buildings of Madras (Chennai), culminating in the extraordinary Orientalist fantasy of the Madras Law Courts [Fig. 7.06] built between 1882 and 1892, the inspirations of both the Gothic and the Picturesque were combined in equal measure with the domes, pendentives, and filigree of India's splendid Hindu and Islamic heritage.[13]

By the early twentieth century, however, the question of appropriate architectural style was to be answered with further abrupt turns in fashion and sentiment.

Toward a Gothic-Modern Elementalism

The dawn of the new century was a watershed across the British world. Already in 1899, the Second Boer War had begun to challenge the certainties of the expanding empire in Africa, and by 1901 the Queen-Empress herself was dead, while the former Australian colonies had federated to form a self-governing Commonwealth of their own. Even as the imperial economy was reaching its zenith, growing insecurity about the future cohesion of the empire was heightening nationalist sentiment and driving a renewed search for a recognizable "English" character in the architecture of empire that might help to hold it together.

In India, this question was to be answered unequivocally with the design of the monumental Victoria Memorial Hall in Calcutta in what would be referred to facetiously as the "Edwardian Wrenaissance" manner.[14] As the final major work in India of William Emerson, past president of the Royal Institute of British Architects and the same architect who had designed All Saints Allahabad almost forty years earlier, it marked a seem-

11 Scriver and Srivastava, *India*, 44; for Murzban, see Chopra, *A Joint Enterprise*, 73–115; for the Company style, see Nilsson, *European Architecture in India*.
12 London, "The Prag Mahal."
13 Scriver and Srivastava, *India*, 56–69; for Chisholm, especially, see Jayawardnene-Pillai, *Imperial Conversations*.
14 The 1897 publication of *A History of Renaissance Architecture in England* by Reginal Blomfield, with its characterization of the seventeenth-century architect Christopher Wren as the quintessential English architect, offered a timely solution to the question of national style at this juncture. The deaths of Victoria, followed soon after by King Edward VII in 1910, prompted a flurry of memorial projects in classical revival style across the colonies, which effectively sealed the deal for "Edwardian Wrenaissance" as the new imperial style.

ingly emphatic repudiation of the Gothic Revival from that point forward. When plans to build a new imperial capital at Delhi were announced in 1911, at the coronation of King George V, there was little doubt that it would be fashioned in this same Edwardian neo-Baroque style that was now being employed in colonial architecture across the empire.[15]

Yet, even as Herbert Baker—soon to join Edwin Lutyens on the Imperial Delhi Project—was completing his own neo-Baroque master work for the South African capitol complex at Pretoria, he conceded that to constrain or reduce architecture to the "outward form" of a prescribed style was to misunderstand its more elemental nature and propensity:

> Sympathy will be generally felt with any endeavour to impress on a new colony the stamp of the national characteristics of the architecture of the Mother Country; but a blind and pedantic attempt to achieve this end would only defeat its object; for the impress must be of the spirit, and not of the outward form only. The vitality and adaptability of the parent nation must be expressed in its children's architecture.[16]

When Edwin Lutyens arrived in India in 1912, he was also to struggle to realize the imperial vision of the Edwardian Baroque alongside colonial India's established revivalist tendencies of the Gothic Revival and the Indo-Saracenic. It was not until the end of the next decade, in the work of his protégé, Arthur Shoosmith, that this struggle was reconciled through a rational and ethical approach to materials and form. These were the truest, most elemental principles of architecture, Lutyens believed, which he had learned from his earlier experience building country houses in England in the vernacular and Gothic Revival styles.

Arthur Shoosmith had arrived in India in 1920 as a recent winner of the prestigious Soane Medallion of the Royal Institute of British Architects (RIBA), which had recommended him to Lutyens as a worthy apprentice. Despite several years of work on the Imperial Delhi project, however, Shoosmith had never been entirely comfortable with the unequivocally classical inspiration of its planning and architecture, and had failed to win either of two competitions staged in 1927 for the design of New Delhi's major churches. The winning schemes by his colleague, Henry Medd, for the respective Anglican and Catholic cathedral churches were both variations on the stripped-down manner of Edwardian Baroque in which most of the minor public and commercial buildings of the new capital, along with the official residential quarters for senior British civilian and military officers, were fashioned.

In a series of letters that Lutyens wrote to Shoosmith after the competition, Lutyens had urged Shoosmith to transcend that impasse with style by looking instead at the nobility and sincerity of material, dropping all iconographic sophistication and striving for the essentials.[17] The following year, Lutyens offered his young protégé the additional consolation of the opportunity to design a further significant church that was required for Delhi's new military cantonment.

Shoosmith's Garrison Church of St. Martin (1928–1930) was a resounding response to his mentor's encouragement [Figs. 7.07 & 7.08]. Later described as a "monolith of 31/2 million bricks," it stood in stark contrast to the ornamental stone detailing of Medd's "Wrenaissance revival" cathedrals, offering, as Philip Davies has contended, "the ultimate expression of the form of 20th century Anglo-Indian architecture promulgated by Lutyens and developed by his disciples."[18] Moving away from the sophistry and the iconographic forms and order of late imperial classicism, Shoosmith's church simultaneously seemed to resume the exploration of mass and monumentality that had characterized earlier efforts to introduce and correctly adapt the Gothic Revival to India. The thick masonry and cave-like quality of the Spartan interior with its small round-arched windows, and the glassless façade all aligned with the stylistic requirements of the Spelun-

15 Scriver and Srivatsava, *India*, 73–81.

16 Baker, "Plea for English Gothic."

17 Recommending unadorned brick, Lutyens wrote, "A building of one material is for some strange reason much more noble than one of many." Edwin Lutyens to Arthur Shoosmith, 13 February 1927, quoted in, Irving, *Indian Summer*, 334.

18 Davies, *Splendours*, 241.

7.07 New Cantonment, Delhi, Garrison Church of St. Martin, Arthur Shoosmith, 1928–1930. [© Amit Srivastava]

7.08 New Cantonment, Delhi, Garrison Church of St. Martin, interior, Arthur Shoosmith,1928–1930. [© RIBA Collections]

car style that the Cambridge Camden Society had recommended. Moreover, Shoosmith's adoption of "bare brick" lent the Garrison Church a raw and elemental quality of expression that further echoed the edicts of the Camden Society, which, as Collins notes, "preferred a certain brutal ugliness to the more traditional notions of beauty."[19] This focus on materials, through exposed brick, and the monumental form, which was to depend on outline and mass rather than variety and contrast of surface, set the stage in India for a further reinterpretation and adoption of these principles that was to follow in the second half of the twentieth century with the development of distinctively situated variants of the late modern brutalist style in the secular architecture of independent India. Shoosmith's design also served to connect architectural developments in late imperial India more directly with the questions of modernity that were driving significant new developments in contemporary church building in Britain, most notably the evolving designs by Giles Gilbert Scott for Liverpool Cathedral. [Figs. 3.06 & 3.07]

Another clear echo in India of those developments back home, as well as the more immediate inspiration of Lutyen's elementalist architectonics and Shoosmith's seminal exemplar, were the designs by Walter Sykes George for St. Thomas's Church in the New Delhi suburb of Paharganj (1929–1932) [Fig. 7.09], and his later buildings for St. Stephen's College at the University of Delhi (1939–1952). George had also been a member of the team of resident assistant architects, including Shoosmith and Medd, who developed and realized Lutyens's and Baker's designs for the new capital. However George was to stay on in India for the rest of his career and realize a significant body of work of his own, helping to forge the path toward modernism for the fledgling Indian architectural profession. As George himself explained the enigmatic nature of his style, it could be labeled "Primitive or Egyptian or Greek or Gothic or Renaissance or Hindu or Chinese, but it derives some from all [...] It does not represent anything but pure form, as dictated by the material."[20]

A similar syncretism characterized the designs and teaching of Claude Batley. Another doyen of the modern architectural profession in India in its formative decades, Batley had a profound influence on many young architects of the first generation as the director for almost two decades of India's only professionally accredited school of architecture before the end of colonial rule in 1947. Articulating the Gothic qualities of the historic Bijapuri and Gujarati building styles, for example, Batley encouraged his students to discern common rationalist principles and

19 Collins, *Changing ideals*, 109.
20 RIBA Prints and Drawings Room (V&A Museum), Hope Bagenal papers, BaHo/ 1/3, 8–9: Walter George to Hope Bagenal, January 2, 1959, as cited in Richard Butler, "Anglo-Indian Architect Walter Sykes George."

7.09 Paharganj, Delhi, St Thomas's Church, Walter Sykes George, 1929–1932.
[© RIBA Collections]

7.10 Mumbai (Bombay), Maharashtra, New India Assurance Building, façade detail, Master, Sathe & Bhuta, 1935.
[© Peter Scriver]

tectonic affinities between indigenous and Occidental architectural canons, toward the design development of appropriate architectural responses to the needs of modern India.[21] Such "middling modernist" approaches to what was understood to be the "double-end" of progressive yet necessarily culturally sensitive development in the final years of colonial rule could not, however, thwart the more direct and disjunctive impact of international architecture and design culture in the first half of the twentieth century, and diminutive tributes to Manhattan's corporate Gothic towers and the streamlined forms of Art Deco would compete to redefine the sacred as well as the secular architectures of metropolitan India by midcentury [Fig. 7.10].[22]

Monumental Gothic Churches in the Princely States

Returning to religious architecture, it is notable that many of the largest and newest churches to be built in Gothic style or inspiration in India over the last century are to be found in the peninsular south of the subcontinent, where Christianity made its first bridgehead as early as the first century CE, many centuries before any Europeans reached its shores. Although there is no evidence of direct rivalry, it is also noteworthy that several of the largest and stylistically most authentic of these monumental Gothic churches were built outside the direct aegis of the British colonial system, in the semi-autonomous states of India's former princely rulers.

Medak Cathedral—since 1947, a cathedral of the Church of South India in what is now the state of Telegana [Fig. 7.11]—was built between 1914 and 1924 in the former princely state of the Muslim Nizam of Hyderabad. Akin to some of the most astonishing colonial church projects undertaken elsewhere around the world in the early twentieth century, in the autumn of European imperialism and the last wave of muscular missionary outreach, this stone colossus was raised as a famine relief project under the leadership and zeal of its Wesleyan Methodist founder, Reverend Charles Walker Posnett, in what was the middle of almost nowhere at the time, ninety kilometers outside of the Nizam's capital city.[23]

An even more magnificent and fastidiously correct Gothic pile—the Cathedral of St. Joseph and St. Philomena [Fig. 7.12]—was built a decade later (1933–1936) in the capital of the neighboring Mysore State, with the patronage and blessing of its progressive Hindu Maharaja, Nalvadi Krishnaraja Wodeyar. The towering stone spires and

21 Batley, *Design Development of Indian Architecture*. See also Scriver and Srivastava, *India*, 99–100.
22 For the politics of style in late colonial development in the respective British and French imperial worldviews, see Crinson, *Modern Architecture and the End of Empire*; and Rabinow, *French Modern*. For corporate Gothic in 1930s Bombay, see Scriver and Srivastava, *India*, 106.
23 Ramakotaiah, "Medak Cathedral."

7.11 Medak, Telegana, Medak Cathedral, John Bradshaw Gass, 1914–1924. [Wikimedia Commons; photo Myrtleship, 2011]

7.12 Mysuru (Mysore), Karnataka, Cathedral of St. Joseph and St. Philomena, M. Daly, 1933–1936. [© Peter Scriver]

24 St. Philomena's Cathedral, Mysore.
25 Gregorios et al., "Syrian Orthodox Churches in India," 285–286.
26 Županov, "One Civility, but Multiple Religions."
27 Brockey, "Doubting Thomas."
28 Nasrani Syrian Christian Network (NSC), "History of denominations."
29 Aranha, "From Meliapor to Mylapore"; see also Hosten, *Antiquities from San Thomé and Mylapore*.
30 The author (Guedes) visited the church in 2014 along with other sites related to St. Thomas in greater Chennai.
31 Edward, *Indigenous Church Architecture of Kerala State*; see also: Helder, *Indo-Portuguese Architecture in Cochin and Kerala.*

main façade were modeled reasonably closely on the precedent of Cologne Cathedral, at roughly half-scale.[24] Dedicated to St. Philomena, however, of whom a sacred relic was brought from Italy to Mysore (Mysuru) to be contained beneath its altar, it is not clear why the German cathedral was considered a relevant model. Ongoing conservation work on the cathedral observed as recently as 2017 is progressively overlaying the original stone and brick construction with a thick render of faux stone that favors a homogenized, Disney-esque fantasy impression of the structure over the noble gravitas of the original unadorned stone.

Thus, during the British rule in India there had been a neo-Gothic architecture, which on the one hand, was in the tradition of the English Gothic Revival, and on the other hand, was to correspond with the newly invented architecture of the Indian subcontinent that was actively attempting to fuse the principles and spirit of both Indic and European architectural traditions—Gothic in particular—under the colonial state.

But there were also quite different roots, and routes, through which Christian sacred architecture had been established historically in India. These arose more strongly to the fore after India's independence, becoming relevant and vital drivers again for the construction of new churches in the Gothic style.

Christian Architecture and Gothic Expression in Contemporary Indian Religious Practice

Christianity in India flourished long before most of Europe came under the Cross. It is said that St. Thomas the Apostle brought the Word to the subcontinent in CE 52, founding congregations among the cosmopolitan merchants of Muziris on the Malabar coast, whose trade links extended to Arabia and Alexandria.[25] Much later, in the early sixteenth century, the Portuguese attempted to bring these communities under Rome, contriving to sever their allegiance to the Chaldean church at the Synod of Diamper (1599).[26] After fifty-four years, the community split, with many rejoining the Syrian Orthodoxy in the first of many fragmentations, resulting in a multiplication of distinct Saint Thomas churches.[27] Today, in intensely religious India, competition for congregations has brought a proliferation of churches, pilgrimage sites, and elaborate festivals.[28]

On the east coast of India, in what is now a Chennai suburb, the settlement of Santhome de Mylapore, founded by the Portuguese in the early 1500s, centered around a church over the tomb of St. Thomas, who had been martyred nearby. In the area's diverse trading communities of Eurasians, Armenians, and lower caste Indians, many were attracted by Roman Catholicism.[29] The original Portuguese church was replaced in 1894 by an enormous Gothic basilica designed by a British architect and conventionally planned [Fig. 7.13]. The architecture is a continuous confection of plastered surfaces and moldings, comprising pointed arches, tracery, crockets, tall gables, and a steepled tower.[30] This church indigenized the vocabulary of forms that had gained prestige in colonial Gothic Revival buildings erected by the British throughout India, just as the style was beginning to be replaced by Edwardian baroque. Here, among local Christians, Gothic took on semiotic power, and they made it their own. It was intended to embody the essence of Christianity in a world where religion entered every aspect of people's lives. Gothic offered a recognizable ornamental repertoire that could be applied with intensity and elaboration, setting it apart from those adopted by other religions.

In Kerala—formerly the Princely state of Travancore—toward the end of the nineteenth century, churches across the indigenous spectrum outgrew their original buildings and precincts, many dating from the sixteenth century. Most had been built under the influence of Jesuits who had grafted classical masonry façades onto buildings whose plans and volumetric arrangements had been finely tuned to long-standing liturgical demands.[31] Ornamental programs blended Western classical elements with a vocabulary of forms and moldings originating in Hindu temples and Kerala's unique timber

7.13 Chennai (Madras), Tamilnadu, Santhome de Mylapore, 1894.
[© Pedro Guedes]

7.14 Arthunkal, Kerala, St. Andrew's Basilica, 1910–1967.
[Wikimedia Commons; photo Chaliyan, 2007]

7.15 Vallarpadam Island, Kerala, Our Lady of Ransom. [in.worldorgs.com]

7.16 Edappally, Kerala, St George's Forane Church, Vastushilpalaya, 2015. [© G.V. Balasubramanian]

architecture. Typically, naves were flanked by external verandahs affording protection from torrential rain and the intense tropical sun. Churches were often freestanding in compounds surrounded by walls, similar to Hindu temple precincts with ambulatory elements such as stations of the cross and shrines at intervals in this structured syncretic external ritual space.[32]

The foundation stone of St. Andrew's Basilica at Arthunkal, south of Kochi in Kerala, was laid in 1910 [Fig. 7.14]. Only completed in 1967, "the world's largest shrine of St. Sebastian," is a sparsely ornamented Gothic building. It has walls of brown granite and contrasting tracery in pale buff plaster with a conventional church plan. In comparison to twenty-first century Gothic in Kerala, it is remarkably restrained in its ornament. The church hosts a major pilgrimage site with a festival lasting over two weeks, attracting tens of thousands, including Hindus who attribute miraculous powers to the saint.[33] This Basilica was among the first churches in Kerala to upscale gigantically, but unlike Santhome in Mylapore, the old church was retained as a depository for less popular altars and saints. This trend of building ever larger churches with extravagant pilgrimage programs continues, facilitated by the now universal use of reinforced concrete, where larger spans, taller structures, and massive volumes of building can be completed in record time. The present structure of the Shimoga Sacred Heart Cathedral in Shivamogga, Karnataka, built between 1994 and 1997, is said to be the second largest church in India, covering an area of 18,000 square feet [Fig. 7.01]. Uninhibited plastering to homogenize all elements can be fully enjoyed in the enormous Basilica of Our Lady of Ransom at Vallarpadam [Fig. 7.15].[34] This elaborate confection combines Gothic composition with round arches and attracts over one million visitors every year in a nine-day festival. At night, thanks to multicolored LEDs, new forms emerge with confidence, owing no allegiance to precedent.[35]

St. George's Forane church at Edappally condenses these trends toward gigantic attractiveness in its pilgrimage venue [Fig. 7.16].[36] The building is clothed in an amalgam of recognizable Gothic motifs, homogenized in white plaster, and supplemented by strategic gilding of statues and other parts. Surprisingly, the extremely ornate, domed, octagonal Gothic entry porch effortlessly blends in Corinthian columns with red granite shafts. Two, freestanding, intensely Gothic, three-story bell towers frame this entry.

32 Reitz, "The Cheriapalli in Kottayam."
33 "St. Andrew's Basilica, Arthunkal St. Sebastian's International Pilgrim Centre," <http://www.arthunkalbasilica.com>. The author visited this church in 2014.
34 "National Shrine Basilica of Our Lady of Ransom," <https://www.vallarpadambasilica.com>.
35 The author visited this church in 2014.
36 "St George Forane Church consecration today," *Times of India*, April 19, 2015, <https://timesofindia.indiatimes.com/city/kochi/St-George-Forane-Church-consecration-today/articleshow/46973320.cms>. See also: Pradeep, "Between the old and the new church."
37 Kavi, "Indian cardinal."

The style is proudly described as a "blend of European and Keralite architecture." Most remarkable of all is the plan. Clearly, conventional church forms were inadequate to the task of sheltering congregations of ten thousand pilgrims. A vast octagon provides a huge space with clear spans of forty-three meters, giving an overall area of 8,200 square meters. This interior features an overwhelming diversity of architectural motifs, some of them emerging from known styles, while others spring from pure invention. Everything is held together by a proliferation of color and gilding, doubled in its visual impact by an intensely reflective red marble floor. During its inauguration in 2015, Cardinal Alencherry's lone voice condemned the church's unrestrained extravagance.[37]

The architects, Vastushilpalaya, whose commercial practice is comfortable with a panoply of exuberant modern styles, outline their "Progressive Architecture" design philosophy thus:

> We believe in an Architecture which imbibes the spirit of the past, incorporates the needs of the present and anticipates the hope for the future.[38]

South Indian Gothic is alive, well, and evolving. Its stylistic boundaries are fluid, and in the power of its forms and detail, captures the Christian spirit.[39] Ceremonies, rituals, and the use of space typical of Hinduism and other live religions migrate across what Europeans would perceive as insurmountable boundaries.[40] This is illustrated by the recent practice of erecting *dwajasthambam*, metal flagpoles common to Hindu temples, in church precincts as in the case of St. Joseph's Cathedral in Trivandrum (Thiruvananthapuram), Kerala [Fig. 7.17]. However, the ethos that best illuminates this rich world is encapsulated in the words of the celebrated Hispano-Indian theologian Raimon Panikkar, who describes himself as a "Hindu by Religion and a Catholic by Faith."[41] Christianity has deep roots in India's religions.

7.17 Trivandrum, Kerala, St. Joseph's Cathedral, 1912–1927.
[Wikimedia Commons; photo Carol Nettar, 2012]

38 Vastushilpalaya Consultancy Private Limited, "Mission and Philosophy," <http://www.vastushilpalaya.com/> (consulted 03-10-2020).

39 Olikara, "The Syrian Christian Church."

40 Robinson, "Negotiating Traditions".

41 Quotation from a personal conversation with Raimon Panikkar at a conference workshop at the People and Cities Conference at Coventry Cathedral in 1969. At the time, he was Professor of World Religions at Harvard University. At the conference, he gave a keynote address. See: Panikkar, "People of God."

8
The Persistence of Neo-Gothic Architecture in Twentieth- and Twenty-First-Century South America

Martín M. Checa-Artasu

Introduction[1]

Neo-Gothic architecture had a wide spread in South America between the three last decades of the nineteenth century and the first three of the twentieth, leaving numerous examples: chapels, parish churches, sacral interiors, exterior renovations, funeral elements, civil works, and even great cathedrals. A presence that can be explained, because it became the constructive solution, according to the policy developed by the Catholic Church in those years. Also, although to a lesser extent, it was a building solution for the various Protestant churches that settled in South America. Likewise, this style was felt more in civil works, both in houses and mansions of the economic and political elites, and in other infrastructures such as hospitals, banks, or schools. Here, with other ideological considerations more focused on the representativeness and legitimacy of the power vested by capital management, the exploitation of certain natural resources and the incipient industrialization abounded.[2]

It has been said that the Latin American neo-Gothic is a phenomenon of internationalized and destatalized cultural "neocolonialism."[3] In part, this is an accurate assessment. When it is profoundly investigated, Latin American neo-Gothic is revealed as a style that was mainly dedicated to the service of an institution deeply rooted in the Latin American cultural and social construction: the Catholic Church. This institution, together with architects, builders, religious staff, and devotees, endowed this style with stronger European roots, and with intimately Latin American meanings, which are only observable when studying in detail the many existing examples. The use of indigenous materials such as wood, volcanic stone, marbles, and local quarry; decorations that refer to the flora and fauna of specific countries and the technique itself – sometimes self-taught by those who built – are clear samples that the neo-Gothic in South America was not simply a Europeanizing copy. This style, perhaps like no other, agglutinated that what was imported from Europe, hybridizing it with its own solutions derived from the migratory, cultural, and political dynamics that occurred in the different countries on the continent.

That way, between the decades of 1870 and 1930, the neo-Gothic style was exhibited itself in temples that, in most cases, became spatial symbols of the political and social balance between the Catholic ecclesiastical hierarchy and the national governments. Symbols that reflected the Catholic revival that, toward the end of the nineteenth century, took place throughout the South American continent with different expressions according to each country. Furthermore, those temples were the expression of the social and territorial repositioning by the Catholic hierarchy after decades of wars, conflicts, disposals of assets, and expulsions by many liberal South American governments. The bibliography on the evolution of the Catholic Church in the nineteenth and twentieth centuries on the continent is numerous and allows us to illustrate the different circumstances of the relations between church and state in the different nations.[4] Those were not uniform, because they had their own characteristics according to each country. It even seems to

8.01 Ipiales, Colombia, Sanctuary of Nuestra Señora del Rosario of Las Lajas, design 1911 J. Gualberto Pérez and Abraham Giacometti, redesign Lucindo María Espinosa Medina, late 1920s. [Wikimedia Commons; photo Diego Delso, 2015]

1 This chapter has been translated from Spanish to English by Perla Benítez Domínguez.
2 A first approach to this issue, which is rarely considered, although with a European perspective, is: De Bièvre, "Trade, political coalitions, and neo-Gothic architecture in Europe." In Latin America I have only located one specific paper on this topic: Negro, "El acertijo de la arquitectura neogótica en el Perú," 62–75. Even so, there are numerous small palaces, mansions, and other types of buildings in the main cities of Argentina, Chile, Uruguay, Ecuador, Peru, and Mexico.
3 Niglio, "La cultura eclettica e lo sviluppo del Neogotico," 25–44.
4 On history of the Catholic Church in Latin America, there is a vast bibliography. The book series published by the Commission for the Study of Church History in Latin America stands out; other examples include Krebs, *La Iglesia de América Latina en el siglo XIX* and Luque, *Iglesia en América Latina (siglo XIX)*. Likewise, references abound in Patiño, *La iglesia en América Latina*; Meyer, *Historia de los cristianos en América Latina*; and Ramón, *Más allá de los Andes*.

be that there is a correlation between the degree of tension in church–state relations, the internal ordering processes of the Catholic Church (new dioceses, follow-up of rules of the Holy See, increase of priests and religious orders, and recovery of the functions of the church in teaching and health) and the construction and remodeling of temples and churches. A correlation in which the neo-Gothic is the style to be followed since it allowed recovering the glorious and medieval past of the Church, where its role in society was predominant. This recovery was necessary to create "Catholic societies" as the only path for the development of Latin American countries.

After that period of apparent preponderance of the neo-Gothic, that style survived in Latin America beyond those years. The neo-Gothic tradition persisted by taking different perspectives and by extending its presence in all kinds of buildings, mostly religious, to the present day. The result is that, over 150 years, the neo-Gothic style left nearly one thousand examples in South America, although unevenly distributed if each country is analyzed.[5] In the face of such a number of examples, it is surprising that there has not yet been an appraised study on the diffusion and characteristics of this architectural style.[6] This work shows how the neo-Gothic survived in the twentieth century and how it is perceived today.

First Perspective: The Religious Orders, Diffusers of the Neo-Gothic

From the end of the nineteenth century and until well into the following century, the expansion of religious orders in South America, both new (Salesians, Lazarists, or regular canons of the Immaculate Conception) and of colonial origin that returned to the continent (Carmelites, Jesuits, or Capuchins), was very prominent. Expansion was found to be in unison with the development of social Catholicism and the revival of teaching, health, and social services managed by the Church. Religious orders promoted the internal colonization of many territories of Latin American countries, even well into the twentieth century, creating parishes and chapels in those places, as well as in neighborhoods and in many cities that, over the twentieth century, experienced remarkable population growth. In that context, several religious orders left numerous examples of neo-Gothic architecture in Bolivia, Chile, Colombia, Peru, Ecuador, Venezuela, and Argentina.[7]

Four notable examples of the use of the neo-Gothic during the first half of the twentieth century can be listed by religious orders. The first religious order is that of the Discalced Carmelites in Chile, with churches built in Chillan[8] and inaugurated in 1913; in Santiago de Chile, the temple of the Niño Jesús de Praga, built between 1917 and 1920;[9] the parish of the Virgen del Carmen in Viña del Mar built in 1926; and the similar one erected on the Cerro de Bellavista in Valparaíso between 1926 and 1931.[10] They were designed and built with similar constructions: single-nave temples and hexagonal towers, with façades in brick with reinforced concrete and iron, by the Carmelite architect Rufo de San José between 1910 and 1927.[11] For this order, the Gothic was the style necessary to magnify the cult of the Virgin of El Carmen, a fact that also can be seen in other Carmelite temples in Colombia or Peru.

The second example is the vast activity of the Salesians in Argentina and Colombia, with the outstanding work of two priests of that order, who were also architects: Ernesto Vespignani and his disciple Giovanni Buscaglione,[12] who more or less systematically, used the neo-Gothic throughout their professional lives. The first was the founder of the Central Technical Office of Salesian architecture at the Buenos Aires headquarters, and he made a personal, eclectic, and highly rich formal interpretation of the neo-Gothic that he would show in some of his many projects in Buenos Aires: Basílica María Auxiliadora and San Carlos (1901–1910) [Fig. 8.02],[13] Nuestra Señora de las Mercedes in Belgrano (1914), Basílica de Nuestra

5 The register of completely neo-Gothic buildings, or those with neo-Gothic elements, made by the author of this text, reports the following figures by country. Mexico: 404; Ecuador: 84, Chile: 147, Venezuela: 89; Uruguay: 32, and Argentina: more than one hundred.

6 There are few works that have sought to analyze from a general perspective the diffusion of the neo-Gothic: Checa-Artasu, "The Catholic Church and Neo-Gothic Architecture in Latin America"; Checa-Artasu, "La Iglesia y la expansión del neogótico en Latinoamérica"; Checa-Artasu, "¿Por qué un libro sobre el estilo neogótico," 25–44; Sundt, "The late Gothic to neo-Gothic revival in Latin America," 119–130; Klein, "El estilo gótico global"; Klein, "Globale Gotik," 163–186; Klein, "La arquitectura neogótica en la Península Ibérica y América Latina," 49–60; Caicedo and Carranza, "Factores sociopolíticos y culturales." Regarding the general study by country, we must highlight for Chile: Pallarés, *Templos católicos neogóticos* and for Argentina: Corti et al., *Iglesias católicas neogóticas*, and Corti and Manzi, *Iglesias reformadas neogóticas en Buenos Aires y alrededores*.

7 Checa-Artasu, "The religious orders and the expansion of neo-Gothic architecture in Latin America," 159–170.

8 About the trajectory of this order in Chile, see: De la Asunción, *Historia de la Orden del Carmen Descalzo en Chile*.

9 Pallarés, *Templos católicos neogóticos*, 148–150.

10 This church was completed by the Carmelite José Manuel de Santa Teresa, consecrated on November 8, 1931. De la Asunción, *Historia de la Orden*, I, 493–495.

8.02 Buenos Aires/Argentine, Basílica María Auxiliadora and San Carlos, Ernesto Vespignani 1901–1910. [© Martín Checa-Artasu, March 2012]

Señora de Buenos Aires (1911–1932), chapel of the school of Santa Brígida (1911–1913), and in Córdoba, the church of María Auxiliadora (1925–1971). Buscaglione made of the neo-Gothic a decorative element for many of the more than thirty churches he designed until 1940.[14] Some of his most remarkable works in said style are the church of Nuestra Señora de los Dolores in Puerto Berrio, which began in 1922 and combines brick with the use of wood in floors and columns, and the church Virgen del Carmen in Bogotá, planned in 1927 and inaugurated on May 8, 1938. An almost twin temple to the Basílica of María Auxiliadora and San Carlos in Buenos Aires, Virgen del Carmen was designed by Vespignani, was attached to a Salesian school, and was noted for the intelligent constructive and decorative mixture between the Italian Gothic and Byzantine.[15]

The third example is the work of the German Lazarist Pedro Huberto Brüning (1869–1938) in Ecuador. This friar was a prolific designer and builder of temples – of medieval construction – many of them of neo-Gothic manufacture, throughout Ecuador between 1899 and 1938. His most outstanding examples include the Church of San Felipe in Latacunga [Fig. 8.03], which was built between 1907 and 1933 – a strong temple in gray quarries, with extraordinary resolution in its ribbed vaults and arcades and refers to the German Gothic.[16] The Magdalena church in Quito, built in brick

11 José Rufo de Aldecoa y Leanizbeazkoa was born in Elgueta, Guipuzcoa, Spain in 1860, and died in 1928 in Chile. He arrived in Chile in 1904 and was the architect of the works, including temples, that the Carmelites built in their colonization in the south of the country and in the main cities. Pallarés, *Templos católicos neogóticos*, 48–49.

12 Among the various references on Vespignani, the most comprehensive study is Lázara, *La edad media argentina.*

13 On this temple, see: Vanzini, *Basílica María Auxiliadora y San Carlos.*

14 On Buscaglione's work, see: Rozo, *Giovanni Buscaglione, 1920–1940*; Carrasco, "Vida y obra de dos piamonteses en Colombia," 105–120.

15 Francel and Ojeda, "Arquitectura ecléctica salesiana," 257–258.

16 Cevallos, *Arte, diseño y arquitectura en el Ecuador*, 49.

8.03 Latacunga, Ecuador, Church of San Felipe, Pedro Huberto Brüning 1907–1933.
[© Martín Checa-Artasu, August 2019]

between 1909 and 1933, with three naves, and a whole Gothic apparatus inside is another example.[17] Finally, the church of San José in La Mariscal neighborhood in Quito is similar to the Magdalena church and was built between 1925 and 1934 as a chapel of the school of the order of the Sisters of Saint Mary Ann of Jesus.

The fourth example is certainly a rarity both for its location and construction. It is the Cristo Pobre Chapel in Jauja, located in the Sierra Central of Peru.[18] Initially, this chapel was associated with the neighboring sanatorium, Domingo Olavegoya, for tuberculosis patients, and its construction started in 1920. It was a project inititated by Luisa Mantes, a nun of the Daughters of Charity of Saint Vincent Paul, and it was designed by the French architect and priest Louis Noel Pául Grandín Blattiere (1876–1931), of the order of the regular canons of Saint Augustine of the Congregation of the Immaculate Conception. This order, created in 1871 in France, had started the evangelization of the Chachapoyas region in the Peruvian Amazon in 1905, and gradually settled in other zones of the country.[19] The Cristo Pobre Chapel is a single-nave church built between 1920 and 1945 in an austere neo-Gothic that takes elements from Notre-Dame de Paris, but which were distorted due to the lack of resources. The result is an almost unique example, considering that the neo-Gothic in Peru barely has a presence.

Second Perspective: The Marian Sanctuaries and the Neo-Gothic

The wide spread of the neo-Gothic on the continent and its role beyond architecture had much to do with the presence of renovated and redefined dedications, some used as keys for construction and national reconciliation by certain governments. Thus, some dedications stand out as related to the body of Jesus Christ as a vehicle of forgiveness and atonement – the sacred heart of Jesus being the most significant, to which cities and even nations were consecrated.[20] Other dedications were derived from redefinitions of the calendar of saints' days such as St. Joseph the Worker, or those of religious orders such as the Virgin of Carmen. Some consecrations also reviewed Marian dedications, which then acquired new ecclesiological meanings; the Immaculate Conception is the most outstanding for its universalist character, and many churches were dedicated to it, some of them of neo-Gothic construction.[21]

Another dedication of nineteenth-century creation that can be linked to the neo-Gothic is the one that comes after the apparitions of the Virgin Mary to Bernadette Soubirous (1844–1879), in Lourdes in the French Pyrenees in 1858. The rapid approval that the Church gave to this appearance, added to the healing properties of devotion, would activate a growing Marian veneration in Lourdes, which, moreover, would quickly be linked to the dogma of the Immaculate Conception. This generated, throughout the

17 Cevallos, *Arte, diseño y arquitectura en el Ecuador*, 53.
18 Obregón, "Aporte de la arquitectura neogótica en Jauja," 217–226
19 On the presence of this order in Jauja and its works, see: Aste and Madrid, *Breve historia de Santa Fe de Hatun Xauxa;* Hurtado, *La Iglesia Matriz de Santa Fe y la Capilla de Cristo Pobre de Jauja.*
20 That was the case in Ecuador and Colombia. See: Henríquez, *Imperio y ocaso.*
21 On the outstanding role of this dedication, see: Bastero, "La Inmaculada Concepción en los siglos XIX y XX," 79–104.

Catholic world, a follow-up of the dedication and almost mimetic reproduction of the key elements of Lourdes: the cave and the sanctuaries – that of the Immaculate Conception and of the Rosary, both built in neo-Gothic style.

Some of the best known examples of this in Latin America were constructed in the twentieth century, such as the temple of Nuestra Señora de Lourdes in Chapinero, in Bogotá[22] [Fig. 8.04], designed in 1904 by Julio Lombana to replace a temple built in 1875. In 1917, the effects of an earthquake damaged the church and its rebuild was commissioned to the Colombian architect Arturo Jaramillo Concha.[23] Between 2009 and 2014, it was extensively restored, recovering the play of colors of its quarry and the decoration of its central tower that marks its three large gateways on the façade.[24] Another example of neo-Gothic construction is the Sanctuary of Nuestra Señora de Lourdes, in Los Santos Lugares in the province of Buenos Aires, Argentina, designed by Etienne Quichet. Said sanctuary, seventy-two meters long and thirty-three meters wide, was built between 1922 and 1972 in exposed brick and following the construction scheme of the French temple,[25] with a crypt inside and neo-Gothic elements in its exterior and interior architecture. Finally, the temple to the Virgin of Lourdes, in the Flores neighborhood of Buenos Aires, was promoted by the community of the Bernardine sisters.[26] It was designed by the architects Pablo Pater and Alberto Morea, and was built between 1929 and 1940 by the engineer Rafael Ayerza, who also participated in the construction of the Buenos Aires law school, designed by the engineer Arturo Prins. Nowadays, it is one of the best examples of civil neo-Gothic on the continent. The single-plant Buenos Aires church follows the guidelines of the French Gothic and in its fundamental pieces it imitates the first Basilica of Lourdes, which was built in 1888.[27]

Other Marian dedications of more local character were also reinforced in the first years of the twentieth century throughout the continent.[28] The vast majority had a colonial origin and were built around miraculous apparitions or by the zeal of the friars who evangelized the different territories. Hence, linked to these dedications at the beginning of the twentieth century, sanctuaries were renovated and rebuilt in neo-Gothic style. One of the most outstanding is the Sanctuary of the Virgen de El Cisne, in the homonymous locality of the province of Loja in Ecuador. The German Lazarist Pedro Huberto Brüning designed, between 1916 and 1930, various plans for this temple, which replaced a more modest one built in the eighteenth century.[29] From 1934 to 1978, its construction was carried out – directed by the Chilean architect Hugo Faggioni Marí and the Ecuadorian Ángel Sangucho – following a project of neo-Gothic construction that modified the previous one of Brüning, of the Italian architect Paolo Russo. Its external decoration, combined with the sky blue tones of its walls, as well as its interior full

8.04 Chapinero, Bogotá, Colombia, Temple of Nuestra Señora de Lourdes, designed 1904 by Julio Lombana. Rebuilding 1917 by Arturo Jaramillo Concha, restoration 2009–2014. [© Martín Checa-Artasu, June 2014]

22 Ortega, "Apuntes para la historia de Chapinero," 96.
23 Arango et al., *Bogotá y la Sabana*, 174.
24 The restoration was commissioned to the architects Max Ojeda Gómez and German González Páez and engineer Fernando Pachón Madrigal. See: Madrigal, "Lourdes."
25 López and Petrina, eds., *Patrimonio arquitectónico argentino*, 448; Crama and Ruggerio, "La Virgen de Lourdes y su santuario en Santos Lugares."
26 It is the Congregation of Sisters of Charity and Christian Instruction founded in 1698, also known as the Sisters of Charity of Nevers, or Ladies of Nevers. One of her nuns was Bernadette Soubirous; hence her popular name.
27 Corti, "Iglesia de Nuestra Señora de Lourdes," 91–99.
28 An extensive compilation of the active Marian cult that reached the twentieth century in Latin America, can be found in: Matovelle, *Imágenes y Santuarios*.
29 Cevallos, *Arte, diseño y arquitectura en el Ecuador*, 174–175.

30 A detailed explanation of this temple can be found in: Pasuy and Sánchez Delgado, "Nuestra Señora del Rosario," 161–166.
31 Enríquez et al., *Espinosa y Santacruz.*
32 Echeverry, "Catedral Basílica de Manizales Nuestra Señora del Rosario," 1–26.

of Gothic elements, seek to aggrandize the devotion to a Virgin with great status in the Andean country.

Another dedication of remarkable expansion that must be associated with the neo-Gothic is that which derived from the connection of the Virgin Mary with the mysteries of the Rosary. This would be a dedication of penance and forgiveness, which takes the life of Jesus as a kind of vital transit to be followed by the believer, both in his messages and in his teachings, and which requires a sacred space where this is reflected. Thus, at the beginning of the twentieth century, some temples dedicated to the Virgin of the Rosary in the neo-Gothic style appeared throughout the continent, some of them promoted by religious orders, such as the Dominicans. One of the most notable examples in constructive terms, but also in symbolic terms, is the Sanctuary of Nuestra Señora del Rosario of Las Lajas in Ipiales [Fig. 8.01], Colombia.[30] It was designed in a Romanizing style by the Ecuadorian engineer J. Gualberto Pérez and Italian architect Abraham Giacometti in 1911. Construction was settled on one side of a narrow canyon of the Guaitara River, with a bridge to access the church. At the end of the 1920s, the Colombian architect Lucindo María Espinosa Medina (1871–1945) redesigned the temple in a sort of French Gothic style, in terms of construction technique and decorations,[31] given its peculiar geographical location, with a dreamlike nature. This was necessary for the Sanctuary of Nuestra Señora del Rosario to become a holy pilgrimage sanctuary, because in that place, the Virgin appeared to an indigenous woman, Maria Mueses and her deaf-mute daughter, Rosa, in 1754.

Another outstanding temple to that dedication is the Basílica of Nuestra Señora del Rosario, in Manizales, Colombia. It is a temple made entirely of reinforced concrete, showing the versatility of this material even with Gothic elements. It was designed by French Julien Polti (1877–1953), winner of an international competition for its construction and was built between 1928 and 1939, by the Italian company Papio Bonarda & Co, made up of Angelo Papio and Gian Carlo Bonarda. The austere and forceful resolution of its 2,300 square meters, added to the use of stained glass and a large canopy on the main altar – created by the Portuguese Joaquim Santos – shows the possibilities of the neo-Gothic in its play with architectural modernity.[32]

Likewise, the Sanctuary Nuestra Señora del Rosario de Agua Santa, in Baños, Ecuador [Fig. 8.05] is also remarkable. There, the seated image of a Virgin of the Rosary is located, which, at least from the seventeenth

8.05 Baños, Ecuador, Santuario Nuestra Señora del Rosario de Agua Santa, interior, Thomas Cornelius Halflants, begun 1904.
[© Martín Checa-Artasu, August 2019]

century, has been venerated in the area as protector of the attacks of the nearby volcano Tungurahua as well as to give a curative character to the many sources of the nearby Pastaza River.[33] This sanctuary was built on an austere Gothic model from 1904, according to the plans that Belgian Dominican Thomas Cornelius Halflants (1831-1909) – a priest in the town since 1887 – had ordered in his country.[34] In 1920, the works continues, following a design for the towers by Lazarist Brüning.[35] The church, with a lushly Gothic interior, culminated in 1944, having used volcanic stone from the area for its construction, which makes of it a unique example, and having inside decorations centered on the paintings resembling votive offerings, an idea of Dominican Enrique Mideros, carried out between 1938 and 1940.[36]

Third Perspective: Migration as an Expansion Factor for Neo-Gothic

Among the continuities of the neo-Gothic in the twentieth century are those derived from migration and colonization by population of certain nationalities. In this case, we can differentiate the individual migration of a specific technician who finds possibilities of development in a Latin American country, from the migration associated with organized colonization processes.

In the first instance, examples of architects or engineers that develop neo-Gothic architecture are numerous throughout the continent. A paradigmatic example is the case of Paolo Russo Scuderi (1885–1971), an Italian architect who, together with his brother Antonino, developed an active career first in Quito and later alone in Guayaquil, between 1930 and 1944. There, through projects for the company Compañía Italiana Sociedad General de Construcciones[37] and later for his own company, Compañía de Construcción Ytaly.[38] He knew how to take advantage of the cocoa production boom that fostered the urban growth of Guayaquil.[39] In this city, Russo designed several churches in neo-Gothic style that would be built with concrete. The combination of style with that material results in a scenic Gothicism, devoid of ornamental exuberance. This is observed in the design and construction of the San Pedro cathedral, which was started in 1930 and completed in 1971;[40] on the façade and interior of the La Merced church, built between 1934 and 1936; on the façade, almost a stage, of the church of Nuestra Señora del Carmen or of the Victoria, built between 1935 and 1941, which was built by architect Luigi Fratta and in the Santuario Mariano Arquidiocesano de María Auxiliadora, erected between 1934 and 1936, probably the most elaborate temple of all that he built.[41] This, from 2013, has been beautifully dignified by a main altar with a replica of the Immaculate Conception of Lorenzone, painted by the Ecuadorian artist David Pacurucu.[42]

Concerning the second – migration via colonization processes – a significant case is observed in the series of parish churches of Gothic construction that the German migration left in different places in Latin America. A paradigmatic example is the parish of San Agustín in Puerto Octay [Fig. 8.06], on the shore of Lake Llanquihue in Chile. In this region, an active German colonization developed from the second half of the nineteenth century, with different settlements around the aforementioned lake: Puerto Montt, Chamiza, Frutillar, Puerto Varas, and Puerto Octay. In this region, the German Jesuit missionaries from the last years of the nineteenth century started their proselyt-

33 Vargas, *Nuestra Señora del Rosario en el Ecuador*, 115–116. It should be added that veneration had arisen because Baños was the gateway to the evangelizing mission of Los Canelos, carried out by the Dominicans in eastern Ecuador since the seventeenth century. See: Matovelle, *Imágenes y Santuarios*, 447.

34 Halflants, *Le Père Thomas-Corneille Halflants*, 96.

35 Cevallos, *Arte, diseño y arquitectura en el Ecuador*, 93.

36 This friar, prominent Ecuadorian artist, painted about twenty canvases between 1938 and 1940 on the alleged miracles attributed to the Virgin, which hang on the walls of the temple. These serve as votive offerings in the face of the most diverse problems. See: SA, *Milagros de la Virgen de Agua Santa*. It should be added that the veneration of this Virgin had emerged as Baños was the gateway to the evangelizing mission of Los Canelos carried out by the Dominicans in eastern Ecuador since at least the seventeenth century (Matovelle, *Imágenes y Santuarios*, 447 sqq).

37 This company carried out works such as the Municipal Palace, the Luis Vernaza General Hospital, the Municipal Market, Garages España, and various private residences. Transalpine architects include Francesco Maccaferri, Rocco Queirolo, Luigi Fratta, and Paolo Russo. See: Del Pino, "La presencia italiana en la arquitectura republicana de Ecuador," 37–56.

38 Del Pino et al., *Italianos en la arquitectura de Ecuador*, 156 and 170.

39 Bock, *Guayaquil*, 112 y s.

40 The project was carried out by Paolo Russo, who directed the work until 1941. It was continued by the Catalan architect Joan Orús Madinyá until 1958, who carried out the façade. Finally, Orús, together with the Chilean architect Alamiro González, finished the work in 1970. See: Castillo, *La catedral de Guayaquil*, 95–129; Riofrío, *El Corazón de la ciudad*, 5–10; Lee et al., *Testimonio y memoria de la arquitectura histórica de Guayaquil*, 104–106.

41 Castro and Paredes; *Guayaquil es mi destino para vivir la ruta de la fe*, 32, 52–54; Estrada, *Guía histórica de Guayaquil*, 260 and 345; Castro, *Espacios sagrados y arquitectura religiosa de Guayaquil*, 57 and 72.

42 Mosquera, "María Auxiliadora."

8.06 Puerto Octay, Chile, Parish of San Agustín, interior, Francisco and José Hitschfeld, 1908.
[© Martín Checa-Artasu, March 2019]

izing work. One of them, Jan Mellwig Hanrad (1845–1928) from Westphalia, founded in the little village of Puerto Octay, in March 1904, the first parish, which caught fire three years later. The fire provoked the support of said community to build a new temple, armed by two local carpenters of German origin: Francisco and José Hitschfeld.[43] The result was a church blessed on March 25, 1908, built entirely of larch and laurelwood and covered with foil. Outwardly, the church is very simple, but its interior conists of ribbed vaults and walls, built with a mixture of sheets of wood of different colors and textures, and columns of the same material. The result is one of the most beautiful wooden churches in Latin America. It is one example of the several churches in this region that are built with wood, the result of the presence of German carpenters.[44] These churches were constructed in a neo-Gothic style and collaterally followed the tradition of building churches in this material in the nearby archipelago of Chiloe,[45] where we find the church of San Francisco, in Castro, a magnificent neo-Gothic wooden temple designed by the Italian Eduardo Provasoli in 1910.

In the area around Lake Llanquihue, several neo-Gothic temples were built at the end of the nineteenth century and in the first decades of the twentieth century. The Lutheran churches of Chamiza include Puerto Montt, built in 1891;[46] Puerto Varas, built between 1923 and 1924;[47] and Frutillar, completed in 1929. The Catholic parishes are Maullin, built in 1895, and the Inmaculada Concepción in Frutillar, built in 1939, which is located near the abovementioned of Puerto Octay.[48] The relationship between German migration and the neo-Gothic had a new episode in the Araucanía region from 1937 to 1977, thanks to the constructive work of the German Capuchin Bernabé Gutknecht, who built several wooden churches clearly inspired by the German Gothic;[49] the most notable example is the parish church of Panguipulli.

43 Pape, "13. Parroquia San Agustín," 173.
44 Guarda, *Iglesias de madera Cautin-Llanquihue*, 12.
45 Cherubini, *La escuela de carpinteros alemanes de puerto Montt*.
46 Sánchez, "La iglesia luterana de Puerto Montt."
47 Estudio de arquitectura Puerto Varas, *Expediente Técnico Templo Luterano*.
48 Weil, *Historia de Frutillar*, 71; Berg and Cherubini, *Ocupación, arquitectura y paisaje*, 172 and sqq.
49 Goycolea, *La actividad constructora del R.P. Bernabé Gutknecht*.
50 De la Riestra, "Gótico y neogótico en la arquitectura de la catedral de La Plata," 30–67.

Fourth Perspective: The Great Neo-Gothic Temples in South America

One of the most significant survivals of the neo-Gothic in the twentieth century is the continuation of the great temples started at the end of the nineteenth century and that were not completed until the final years of the twentieth century or even in the present. Although some temples have a significant dedication, they are built in these dimensions for their links with the political construction of a region or country, or because their dedication is associated with the aim to serve the construction of a national identity. In this section, three of the most notable examples on the continent are the cathedral of La Plata [Fig. 8.07], the Basílica de la Virgen de Luján [Figs. 8.08 & 8.09], both in Argentina, and the Basílica del Voto Nacional in Quito, Ecuador [Figs. 8.10 & 8.11].

The La Plata cathedral [Fig. 8.07], dedicated to the Immaculate Conception, is one of the most notable examples of this rereading of the Gothic in Latin America. La Plata is not a copy. It is a readaptation with lots of components derived from the artistic genius that migration and the economy brought together in Argentina in the early years of the twentieth century. De La Riestra illustrates in detail not only the symbiosis of Gothic construction elements from Germany and northern Europe in its construction but also the assortment of the different parts of its ground plan, derived from many other European Gothic churches.[50] This cathedral is framed also in the project of a new capital for the province of Buenos Aires, abetted by the provincial governor of that time, Dardo Rocha, to whom a crypt was built in the temple. The urban design created *ex novo* for the new capital was designed by the surveyor and engineer Pedro Benoit (1836–1897). It is a distribution in checkerboard, with diagonal connection axes having an urban center where the political power – the municipality – and the religious power – the church – were concentrated. These circumstances explain the large dimensions of this temple

8.07 La Plata, Argentine, Cathedral of Immaculate Conception, plan Pedro Benoit, 1885–1999.
[© Martín Checa-Artasu, March 2012]

8.08 & 8.09 Luján, Argentine, Basílica de la Virgen de Luján, interior and exterior Uldéric Courtois (plan), 1890–1935. [Wikimedia Commons; photo Aleksandrs Timofejev, 2013 & Ezarate, 2016]

51 López and Petrina, eds., *Patrimonio arquitectónico argentino*, 442–444.
52 Durán, "Gestiones del Episcopado argentino," 97–132.
53 Durán, "La basílica nacional de Luján," 65–96; Durán, "Río Cuarto asociado a la construcción de la Basílica de Luján," 17–66; Durán, *De la Frontera a la Villa de Luján*, 105–655; Fogelman, "Exvotos y secularización," 167-223.
54 Gazaneo amd Gazaneo, "The Basílica of Our Lady of Luján," 493–540 and Corti, "Origin and development of Neo-Gothic," 304–323.
55 This Basilica is 100 m long, 68.5 m wide at the transept, and 42 m in front. Its two towers are each 106 m tall.

of 5,300 square meters and its 112-meter-high towers, because it must have been a reflection of the new city that was being built.

On April 30, 1884, the first stone of a temple designed by Pedro Benoit was laid, in collaboration with German architect Ernest Meyer and the Frenchman Émile Bonnet Coutaret (1863–1949). The works began in October 1885 and they lasted until 1999. In those 114 years, the work management has been carried out by some of the most renowned Argentine architects: the Salesian Vespignani (1908–1915), Isaac Villamonte, Rafael Ayerza, and Carlos Massa, among others.[51]

As we have already mentioned, in different countries Marian dedications constituted and reinforced, which would be structured as an element to promote national construction. Two very notable examples of this are in Argentina and Ecuador.

In Argentina, the cult of the Virgin of Luján, which originated in the seventeenth century and strengthened over the years, would take its maximum expression with the construction of a huge neo-Gothic sanctuary that came to replace an earlier, much deteriorated, church. This new temple arose thanks to the will of the French Lazarist priest Jorge Maria Salvaire,[52] who knew how to link the great popular devotion to that Virgin, a simple image of the Immaculate Conception, with the political needs of the Argentine Catholic elites and the relationship they had with French Catholicism and the papacy. On May 8, 1887, after the papal approval, the Virgin of Luján was crowned with great solemnity. That act justified the need to erect a great devotional temple [Figs. 8.08 & 8.09]. Three years later, on February 2, 1890, the first stone of a huge French Gothic–designed church was laid by Gallic architect Uldéric Courtois (1843–1914).[53] Courtois, a student of Eugène-Emmanuel Viollet-le-Duc (1814–1879) was clearly influenced by him, especially in the idea of generating environments and architectural elements that assimilated

8.10 & 8.11 Quito, Ecuador, Basílica of Voto Nacional, interior and exterior Joseph Emile Tarlier (plan), 1890–1988. [© Martín Checa-Artasu, August 2019]

a possible idea of the Gothic.[54] In addition, he knew how to justify the larger dimensions[55] of the temple, because he believed that a reinterpretation of the Gothic was the most appropriate for the power and symbolism of the Marian dedication that it should contain.[56] These two aspects explain why various constructive elements intermingle in the building, taken from different examples of French Gothic cathedrals (especially, from Notre-Dame de Paris, and to a lesser extent, from Amiens and Reims) but adapted to the local technical reality. For example, the calculation of the vaults was made by Ernesto Vespignani, who introduces the use of reinforced concrete for its construction.[57] However, the French style of the project is unquestionable: most of the decorative elements such as the stained glass, statuary, and organ are imported from France. In addition, the temple was built between 1890 and 1935 with the participation and work management of numerous technicians, especially French and to a lesser extent, Argentine.[58] Despite its large dimensions, it only took forty-five years to be built, which can be explained by the support of a large amount of filigrees and its capacity to attract capital. It should be remembered that in 1930, the Virgin of Luján becomes the patroness of Argentina, Uruguay, and Paraguay.

Another example of the relationship between a dedication and the will that serves the national construction can be found in Quito, Ecuador, with the long-term construction of the Basílica del Voto Nacional [Figs. 8.10 & 8.11].

This temple is the result of the consecration of the Ecuadorian nation to the Sacred Heart of Jesus on March 25, 1874.[59] This was conducted by the archbishop of Quito, José Ignacio Checa y Barba. The consecration that had been promoted by the very Catholic General Gabriel García Moreno, ruler of the country from 1861 to 1865, and from 1869 to 1875. He saw the consecration as a justification for both his policies and for Ecuador's

56 Courtois, "La Basílica de Luján," 213–230 and Varela, *Breve historia de la Virgen de Luján*.

57 Maurín de Rufino, "Ernesto Vespignani," 49.

58 Over the course of forty-five years of the project management, participated engineers Alfonso Flamand and Rómulo Ayerza; architects Uldéric Courtois, Ernesto Moreau, Francisque Fleury Tronquoy, Fernando Sombrum, Pedro Trouvé and Enrique Laspé, and Jorge J. Cortabarría. See: López and Petrina, eds., *Patrimonio arquitectónico argentino*, 456.

59 Espinosa and Canal. "La memoria transnacional de Gabriel García Moreno," 3–23.

national construction process.[60] His governments were presided by a conservative messianism in which the construction of a Catholic society was the solution for Ecuadorian development. Furthermore, García Moreno had established excellent relations with the Holy See, through a concordat signed in 1863, and had given notable benefits to the clergy and to the Jesuits who were incardinated in the power structures. Likewise, this consecration positioned him as an international champion of political Catholicism in times of a clear confrontation with liberalism in Europe and America.[61]

For these policies, García Moreno was assassinated in 1875 and became a martyr of Catholicism. In 1883, the possibility of building a large temple dedicated to the Sacred Heart was raised, that, in addition, embraced the body of the general and other eminent Catholics. Thus, a group of citizens of Quito, led by the deputy and priest José Julio María Matovelle Maldonado (1852–1929), got government support to cover the purchase of the land and the work. From 1895, Matovelle and the congregation he created, the Oblate Missionaries of the Most Holy Hearts, were in charge of managing the works.

In architectural and artistic terms, this temple is probably the best example of neo-Gothic architecture of South America, because in it, the French influences of the medieval Gothic are concentrated, and the decorative reinterpretation with aspects of Ecuadorian culture is combined with others of contemporary sacred modernity.

The project was commissioned by presidential decree to the architect of the Bourges diocese, Joseph Emile Tarlier (1825–1902), who had constructed and rehabilitated twenty-six neo-Gothic churches in the center of France.[62] He was inspired by the Saint-Étienne de Bourges cathedral for the design of the Quito temple, a project he carried out between 1890 and 1894, and that was sent by ship to Ecuador.[63] The choice of Tarlier, aged sixty-five, can only be explained by the close relations of French Catholics with Ecuadorians, connected thanks to the figure of García Moreno.[64]

This Basílica has some similarities with the temple of Bourges: the plan, the large gateways, the pillars with columns of its interior, and the opening sequence of the towers. The spire of the dome or the lateral façades are taken from other temples. Even in this Basílica there is a chapel in the apse dedicated to the Immaculate Heart of Mary,[65] which refers to the plans of Amiens, or to the neo-Gothic Saint Patrick's Cathedral (1858–1865) in New York. In Quito, the basilica was designed and built by the German architect Franz Schmidt and beautifully decorated by the Lazarist Brüning.[66] This chapel would serve to develop the cult during the first decades of construction.

The foundation stone of the Basílica was laid on July 10, 1892, and it was consecrated on July 12, 1988, after ninety-six years of construction. The work was directed by the Germans Franz Schmidt and Pedro Brüning, and the Italian-Swiss Francisco Durini Cáceres, who introduced the use of concrete versus the quarry. In the 1960s and 1970s, the work was directed by the Ecuadorian engineer Galo Pazmiño and the Ecuadorian architect Virgilio Flores Vallejo.[67]

This temple dedicated to the Sacred Heart also served as the mausoleum for the remains of García Moreno, the archbishop Checa Barba, and the priest Matovelle. This fact promoted the construction of a national cemetery in its basement, where some of the presidents of that country are buried around an enormous sculpture of a Risen Christ, the work of Ecuadorian sculptor América Salazar. The union of politics with the Ecuadorian Church is magnified by forty-eight stained glass windows with the key figures of the Ecuadorian church at the top of the temple. These stained glass windows, together with the twenty-four chapels and the three rosettes, cover 900 square meters and were designed by Mario de Ayala Moya (1932–2011), who was of Spanish origin but had his workshop in Cali, Colombia.[68] This artist knew how to complement the religious

60 Apparently, the person who advised García Moreno for the consecration was Father Manuel Proaño, National Director of the Apostleship of Prayer in Ecuador. See: Pattee, *Gabriel García Moreno y el Ecuador de su tiempo*, 351.

61 Espinosa and Canal, "La memoria transnacional de Gabriel García Moreno," 4–5

62 There are numerous works of both construction and renovation of Emile Tarlier, from Bourges, including the Church of Sainte-Madeleine in Jalognes and the parish church of Saint Armand in Saint-Denis-de Palin. See: Chazelle, *Le patrimoine du canton de Sancerre* and Leniaud, *Répertoire des architectes diocésains du XIXe siècle*.

63 Sigüenza, *Quito: patrimonio de la humanidad*, 78; Medina "Basílica: Entre el gótico y la fe," 251–252.

64 Espinosa and Canal. "La memoria transnacional de Gabriel García Moreno," 8.

65 It is a dedication linked to the Sacred Heart of Jesus.

66 Álvarez, *Estudio iconográfico de la pintura mural*.

67 López Molina, "Basílica del Voto Nacional."

68 On the career of this artist, see: Jaramillo, "Mario de Ayala Moya."

figures in the stained glass windows with backgrounds, showing a variety of orchids, the national flower of Ecuador, manifesting its maximum expression in the main rosette of the temple. Likewise, the reinterpretation of Ecuadorian culture is felt in the gargoyles of the building, which display Ecuador's own fauna, such as iguanas, armadillos, Galapagos tortoises, and condors. The aesthetics of the temple acquired a tone of contemporary sacred art with statuary and doors designed by the Spanish sculptor Agustín de la Herrán Matorras, throughout the 1970s and 1980s.[69] This sculptor designed the gigantic virgin of the Panecillo between 1973 and 1976, promoted by the Oblate priests. This piece, together with the Basílica, gives a distinct Catholic scenery to the landscape of the historic center of Quito.

Fifth Perspective: The New Temples and the Gothic in Architectural Modernity

The construction of new temples in neo-Gothic style, from the 1950s and even until today, has been a constant in South America. The examples, although not as numerous as they were in the past, are of a great variety. Some follow the pattern of Gothic as the abovementioned examples, with modernizing adaptations; others reinterpret it within architectural modernity, and they take only the most fundamental elements of Gothic. Several temples built in Venezuela have a lot to do with the slow process of rebuilding the Church in that country throughout the first half of the twentieth century.[70] During the liberal governments of Antonio Guzmán Blanco (three terms between 1870 and 1888), the Church lost all its properties, and the religious orders were expelled. The church could not recover until the dictatorship of Juan Vicente Gómez Chacón (1908–1935) and the successive governments of mid twentieth century. All this explains the late neo-Gothic in this country. Thus, two churches stand out: the San José church, in San Cristóbal, state of Tachira. It was designed and built between 1945 and 1971 by the foremen Jesús Ramón Manrique and M. Camperos, and it was directed by the Italian engineer Giacomo Moro.[71] This church, promoted by the Augustinian Recollects, is a flamboyant Gothic style that uses reinforced concrete, combined with brick, and stands out for its geometrical, almost Art Deco reading of its three high towers.[72] Another example is the Santa Barbara church, in Rubio, state of Tachira. A temple of remarkable dimensions (it is seventy-four meters long and twenty-eight wide, and it features fifty-meter-high towers), the church was designed by the Spanish B. Gracer following the purposes of the Dominican order. It was started in 1934, and a new design on its façade was made between 1978 and 1980, based on a modern reinterpretation of the Gothic style, exposing the concrete structures combined with brick.[73]

Regarding the second typology, neo-Gothic buildings reinterpreted within architectural modernity, cases in South America occur in several countries. It is worth highlighting at least three examples that show the many possibilities of reinterpretation of the Gothic in the frame of modernity of sacred architecture. The first is the Sanctuary de la Inmaculada Concepción in the city of La Azulita, in the state of Merida in Venezuela. The temple was designed by the Italian Italo de Filippis in 1953.[74] It has a granite façade with a forty-three-meter spire and a monumental statue of the Immaculate Conception on its large gateway. Here, the Gothic is expressed in a façade with aesthetics proper of brutalism, which seems to be inspired by the cathedral of the Sagrado Corazón de Jesús in Casablanca, designed in neo-Gothic with arabesque-looking reminiscences by Paul Tournon in 1930.[75] Inside, the three naves of this church are separated with lancet arches resolved with reinforced concrete. Completing the Gothicism of this church are the painted decorations on the ceilings, and the blue, filtered light through the stained glass – designed by the Ecuadorian artist Guillermo

69 A. de la Herrán. Escultura artística, <http://www.adelaherran.com/folletoEscultura.pdf>.

70 Rodríguez, "La iglesia venezolana entre los siglos XIX–XX," 580–582.

71 Romero et al., "El neogótico en la arquitectura religiosa tachirense," 491–493.

72 Marín et al., "Retrospectiva de las tendencias tecnológicas."

73 Romero et al., "El neogótico en la arquitectura religiosa tachirense," 493–495. Instituto Patrimonio cultural, "Catedral Santa Bárbara de Rubio," 66–69.

74 Instituto Patrimonio cultural, "Iglesia Inmaculada Concepción," 25.

75 See the contribution of Bruno Klein in this book.

8.12 Osorno, Chile, Cathedral of San Marcos, León Prieto Casanova, 1962–1977.
[Wikimedia Commons; photo Diego Delso, 2007]

Vásquez – which spread throughout the temple,[76] and especially the apse, where two 20-meter-high stained glass windows with the image of a Holy Christ endow mysticism inside this interesting temple that combines Gothic aesthetics with enormous modernity.

A second example is the Buen Pastor cathedral in Santo Domingo de los Tsachilas in Ecuador, a work that started in March 2003, and is still in progress today.[77] Like many of the churches mentioned above, its construction is based on the contributions of the parishioners,[78] based on raffles, which follow a grandiose building proposal, in this case, promoted by the second bishop of that diocese, Wilson Moncayo Jalil. The temple has been designed and built by the Ecuadorian architect Jaime William Benavides Revelo, who has generated a reinterpretation of the Gothic based on metal structures and the maximum use of ferro-cement, which is visible in the seven bodies of its two 40-meter height towers, in its large triple gateway, the cover of its only nave, its side chapels, and in the dome on the main altar. This temple is an example of adaptation of the Gothic to materials and structures more typical of other types of constructions.

The third case is the San Marcos Cathedral in Osorno [Figs. 8.12 & 8.13], in the Los Lagos region in Chile.[79] Undoubtedly, it is the best example of the reinterpretation of the Gothic in the frame of architectural modernity, both in the use of materials and the elements of the Gothic. It is a project by León Prieto Casanova,[80] a clearly functionalist Chilean architect who won a contest based on the wishes of the bishop of the diocese of Osorno, the Capuchin Francisco Valdés Subercaseaux for a new cathedral of the diocese.[81] Bishop Valdés, an expert on sacred music and liturgy, wanted a new cathedral marked by austerity and a new spirituality to replace the previous cathedral, destroyed by the 1960 earthquake.[82] The foundation stone was laid on June 10, 1962 and was consecrated in 1977. The design of this church is of great versatility and lightness, framed in architectural modernity but tak-

8.13 Osorno, Chile, Cathedral of San Marcos, interior, León Prieto Casanova, 1962–1977.
[© Martín Checa-Artasu, March 2019]

ing the Gothic as an indispensable element in both decorative and structural terms. The new and the medieval come together through various elements. Outside, a forty-five-meter-high tower made of concrete in a lancet shape symbolizes two hands in prayer; it contains several lancet arches crisscrossed at the top. It has a large gateway formed by eleven concrete lancet arches that in its central part contains a triple set of stained glass windows, with a central Pantocrator, and the Virgin Mary and Saint John at its sides. Those stained glass windows have at their sides a 163-square-meter mosaic in tesserae, with Byzantine aesthetic figures of the twelve apostles distributed in several rows. Both elements – stained glass and mosaic, installed between 2005 and 2013 – were created by Juan Francisco Echenique Celis,[83] one of the most renowned Latin American artists in sacred art. Inside, the Gothic is solved by a sequence of lancet arches of concrete, crisscrossed along the apse and chancel of the temple, and in the separation of the naves. All those arcades are textured simulating wood, a material that covers the gabled roof of the temple. The stained glass windows inside are yellow and white, filtering the light, which gives the ensemble a new majesty, more human, which is closer to the liturgical assumptions of the Latin American church closer to Liberation Theology.

76 Mercado, "Relación luz-color en los vitrales."
77 Redacción, "Catedral con estilo único."
78 Redacción, "La nueva Catedral de Santo Domingo."
79 Pape, "1. Parroquia San Mateo," 144–145.
80 This cathedral is a project outside the usual works of this architect, who is more specialized in housing and university projects. See: Basáez, *150 años de enseñanza de la arquitectura*, 122–123 and Prieto Casanova, *Uyarq*.
81 Valdés, *Fray Francisco Valdés Subercaseaux*, 99–102.
82 Fernández-Cobián, "Catedrales chilenas del siglo XX," 236.
83 Armendáriz, "Mosaicos y vitrales en la catedral de Osorno," and Entrevista personal a Juan Francisco Echenique Celis, March 18, 2019.

9
Neo-Gothic Architecture in Mexico from the Porfiriato to the Present*

Martín M. Checa-Artasu

The Presence of Neo-Gothic Architecture in Mexico: Data

Given the wide ignorance that has existed and still exists concerning neo-Gothic architecture in Mexico, when considering any analysis of it, we must try to quantify its presence in the country. Recently, and based on an exhaustive review of bibliography, image repositories, and intense fieldwork, we have been able to determine, up to now, the existence of 407 examples of the use of the neo-Gothic style in architectural elements (complete buildings, interiors and furniture, towers, external decorations, funerary elements, etc.) in Mexico. These examples can be grouped in terms of typology, temporality, and geographical distribution.

Regarding the typology as shown in Table 1, it is confirmed that the neo-Gothic was an eminently religious style: 64.02 percent of the examples of this style are in churches, temples, and chapels, in new buildings (24.32 percent), in repairs and adaptations of sacred furniture and interiors, and in external elements and in towers (36.85 percent). A small percentage is found in non-Catholic Christian churches (3.69 percent).[1] In Mexico, there are few examples—especially from the second half of the twentieth century—that re-adapt Gothic elements to architectural modernity (2.95 percent).

The use of this style in civil engineering (23.10 percent) is prominent, both in dwellings, large houses, haciendas, and more specific examples such as entrance gates, banks, hospitals, schools, or even police stations. Civilian use was one of the expansion routes of neo-Gothic in the country,[2] alone, or combined with other historicist styles and with eclectic imitations. Its predominant decorative use is reflected in window and door arches, in some exterior decorations and in few cases, integrally in façades or interiors. With similar characteristics, we find it in cemeteries, tombs, mausoleums or cenotaphs (9.09 percent). Yet, it is an aspect that is still to be analyzed in detail.

9.01 León, Guanajuato, Templo Expiatorio del Sagrado Corazón de Jesús, Luis G. Olvera (Project) (1921–1941), Carlos Lazo (1941–1953), Juan Carlos Ituarte (1953–1973), Arturo and Gonzalo Acevedo (1973–1987), José María Méndez Córdoba (1987–2015). [© Martín Checa-Artasu, 2009]

TABLE 1
DISTRIBUTION OF THE NEO-GOTHIC STYLE IN MEXICO (BY TYPOLOGIES)

Typology	No. of examples	% of total
New construction (churches)	99	24.32
Civil building	94	23.10
Furniture and interior decoration	65	15.97
Exterior elements	53	13.02
Funerary elements	37	9.09
Towers and bell towers on temples	32	7.86
Non-Catholic Christian temples	15	3.69
Modern religious architecture (Gothic inspiration)	12	2.95
Total examples	**407**	100.00

Source: Own elaboration

* This chapter has been translated from Spanish to English by Perla Benítez Domínguez.

1 These churches have been studied by San Martín, "Templos protestantes neogóticos e ingenieros civiles."

2 This issue has hardly been studied in Mexico. See: Sánchez Hernández and Hurtado Mireles, "El neogótico y su vínculo al culto en la industria en México," 454–469.

GRAPH 1
PERCENTAGE OF NEO-GOTHIC CONSTRUCTIONS IN MEXICO, BY DECADE (208 EXAMPLES)

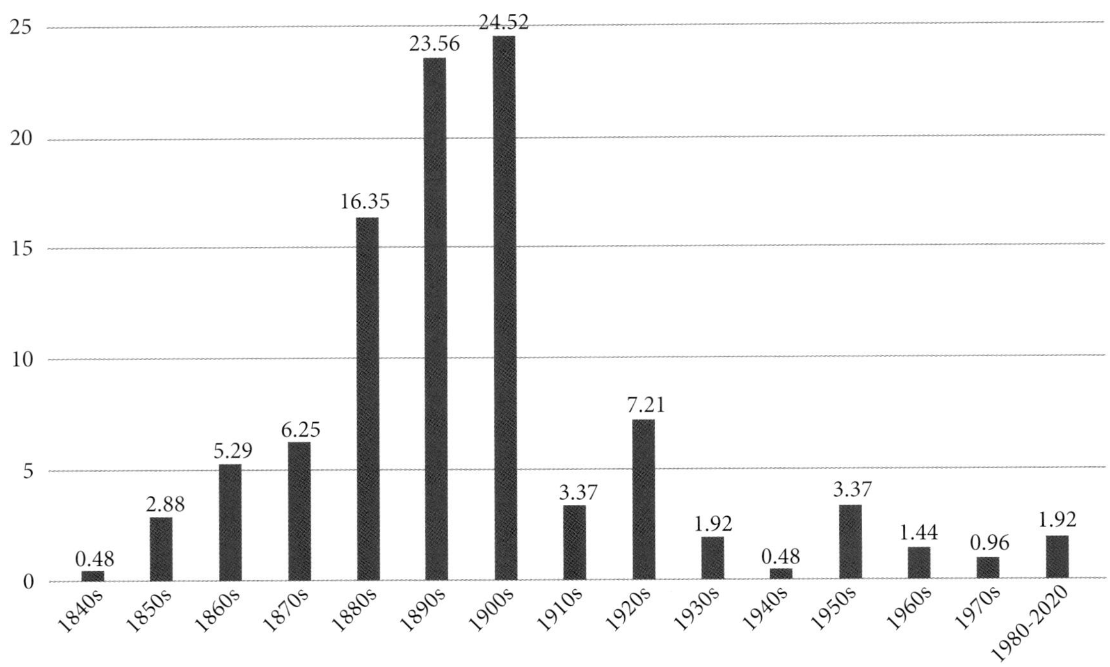

Concerning the chronology of neo-Gothic style in Mexico, in Graph 1, from 208 examples of the types described above that have been dated, we can corroborate data that some other studies had already mentioned.[3] This style had its maximum expansion between 1880 and 1910, where we found 64.42 percent of the examples. This coincides with high numbers in the construction of new churches throughout the country.[4]

Only 14.90 percent of examples were built between 1840 and 1880.[5] This confirms the slow penetration of the style in a context of political conflict between the Church and the different Mexican governments. Despite this, the neo-Gothic appears in the late 1840s and early in the next decade, until it was consolidated forty years later. The first two examples documented of neo-Gothic in Mexico are found one in the city of Aguascalientes: the Church of San Ignacio, known as the *El Conventito* ("The little convent"); its construction began between 1848 and 1850, and it features some neo-Gothic elements on its façade. The second is the reconstruction of the towers of the Guadalajara cathedral, between 1851 and 1854, in a neo-Gothic style following the project of the architect Manuel Gómez Ibarra, who was inspired by European Gothic cathedrals.[6] These towers would later become an urban landmark, imitated throughout Jalisco. They are the initial calls of attention for the expansion of neo-Gothic in Mexico.

For this chapter, it is significant that 20.67 percent of the examples of neo-Gothic in Mexico were begun between 1910 and today. There was a surge in the use of this style in the 1920s, as the result of the situation of recomposition of the Catholicism after the Revolution that eventually deteriorated and derived in an armed conflict: *La Cristiada* (1926–1929). Beyond that regrowth, from the 1930s, the style survives with specific cases, converted, whether in an architectural anachronism, or with some examples of adaptation of the Gothic to modern architecture.

Concerning the geographical distribution, as seen in Table 2 and on the attached map, first, the neo-Gothic style is present throughout the country; second, there are two large concentrations of this style in Mexico. The

3 Checa-Artasu, "La dimensión geográfica de la arquitectura neogótica en México," 327–341.

4 Between 1895 and 1910, 1708 churches were built in Mexico. See: Vargas, *Historia de la arquitectura y el urbanismo mexicanos*, 459.

5 In Mexico there could be two examples prior to 1840 in neo-Gothic style, both with doubtful dates. The first is the tomb of the Baz family in the San Fernando cemetery in Mexico City, built between 1825 and 1828, and used for the first time in those years. This one features Gothic decorations. The subsequent family use and the lack of documentation cast doubt whether this was the first neo-Gothic example in Mexico. Likewise happens with the dating of the Carreón public baths building, popularly known as Los Arquitos in Aguascalientes. Baths were built by municipal initiative in 1821. They were decorated with at least one peristyle with intertwined semicircular arches that generate a series of pointed openings, similar to the access doors to the bathtubs. Among the upper connections of these semicircular arches carved wheels are placed; these are shaped like drops of water. There is no precise dating, because some recent source dates the construction of these elements in the 1830s and another places them at the beginning of the 1850s. See: Gómez and Delgado, "La ciudad de Aguascalientes."

6 García Fernández, "Su construcción, transformaciones y contexto," 15–171 and Moya, "Las torres actuales de la catedral de Guadalajara," 163–196.

TABLE 2
DISTRIBUTION OF THE NEO-GOTHIC STYLE IN MEXICO (BY GEOGRAPHICAL DISTRIBUTION)

State	No. of examples	% of total
Jalisco	84	20.64
Ciudad de México	43	10.57
Guanajuato	27	6.63
Aguascalientes	25	6.14
Michoacán	25	6.14
Zacatecas	24	5.90
Durango	20	4.91
Veracruz	20	4.91
Puebla	16	3.93
Yucatán	14	3.44
Hidalgo	14	3.44
Estado de México	12	2.95
Chihuahua	11	2.70
Tlaxcala	9	2.21
Chiapas	8	1.97
Nuevo León	7	1.72
Coahuila	6	1.47
Tabasco	6	1.47
Oaxaca	5	1.23
Sinaloa	5	1.23
Colima	4	0.98
San Luis Potosí	4	0.98
Tamaulipas	4	0.98
Nayarit	3	0.74
Querétaro	3	0.74
Sonora	3	0.74
Guerrero	2	0.49
Morelos	2	0.49
Baja California Sur	1	0.25
Total: Mexico	**407**	**100.00**

Source: Own elaboration

first is found in the central western states of Mexico (Jalisco, Colima, Guanajuato, Aguascalientes, Michoacán, Nayarit, Querétaro, San Luis Potosí, and Zacatecas) with 48.89 percent of the examples; the second corresponds to Mexico City, with 10.57 percent of the examples. The remaining 40.54 percent of examples are distributed here and there with few examples, both in the north and in the southeast of the country. This particular distribution is the result of several circumstances: the creation of new dioceses in the last decades of the nineteenth century, the presence of both bishops and clergymen, and the eminently combative filigrees in the face of the changes promoted by the liberal governments against the Catholic Church. In addition, in these states, there are important colonial cities that grew and developed during the nineteenth and twentieth centuries.

Finally, what proportion of buildings were built in the neo-Gothic with respect to other styles? According to Katzman, throughout the nineteenth century, about 2,400 religious temples were built in Mexico; of them, 1,500 were initial constructions, that is, 62.5 percent.[7] In relation to the data, which demonstrates that only forty-seven temples were built on a neo-Gothic construction in the nineteenth century, this would indicate that only 3.13 percent of the temples were made

7 Katzman, *Arquitectura del siglo XIX en México*, 156.

ex novo in this style throughout the country. The percentage rises to 22.2 percent if we consider the adaptations and rehabilitations made to already built temples. Additionally, the ninety-six plans of nineteenth-century churches preserved in the Academy of San Carlos show that most were built in the neoclassical style (73 percent); the least common were those made in historicist styles such as neo-Romanesque (12.5 percent) and neo-Gothic (5.2 percent).[8]

The Catholic Church and Neo-Gothic in Mexico

From all these numbers, we can infer that neo-Gothic in Mexico was a style eminently used by the Mexican Church for the construction and renovation of temples. This was developed with great prestige from 1880 to 1910, years that coincide with the ruling terms of General Porfirio Díaz. In addition to this, the use of neo-Gothic was concentrated in the Central Western states of the country and, to a lesser extent, in the Mexican capital.

It was a style that was ideal to respond both constructively and symbolically to the conflictive restoration of the role of the Church in Mexico after the *Guerras de Reforma* and the attacks of radical liberalism promoted by Benito Juárez (1858–1872) and Sebastián Lerdo de Tejada (1872–1876) in the middle of the nineteenth century.[9] The nineteenth-century restoration of the Church in Mexico had at least two specific components. On the one hand, the defensive—intransigent in many cases—positions of the Catholic hierarchy against the anticlericalism of the Mexican state, marked by the separation between the state and the church.[10] On the other hand, there was the relevant extension of Catholicism among the population as an expression of a deeply rooted popular religiosity. In addition, this Catholic restoration was marked by an ambivalent permissiveness of worship and religious expressions by the state. It must be remembered that religion had been relegated to an individual activity, with a significant lack of economic resources, because most of the Church property had been expropriated in the previous decades. Also, in terms of time, this restoration had two moments that coincide with the expansion of neo-Gothic: the first during the *Porfiriato* (1877–1910) and the second after the revolutionary period (1917–1926).[11] The first was a rearrangement of the Catholic hierarchy to the political dictates of Porfirio Díaz, in a kind of *laissez-faire, laissez-passer* by the state.[12] In the second, much more frantic, action, the state gradually showed again an anticlericalism that was answered by the Catholic sectors and that would lead to an armed conflict: *La Cristiada.*

During this restoration, dioceses in the states of Michoacán, Guanajuato, and Jalisco traditionally had the greatest number of believers and practitioners. Said dioceses were the cenacles of the hierarchy that was most refractory and combative to the anticlerical presupposition of the state, capable of using dedications and popular fervor as a form of defense of Catholicism in the territory. That ecclesiastic hierarchy proposed the restoration of the Church by retaking the splendor of it in late medieval times. Hence, the use of neo-Gothic for the construction or renovation of temples was promoted. It should not be forgotten that Gothic architecture had a multipurpose mystical component, because it was associated with the idea of the heavenly Jerusalem; with it, everything incited to a transcendent approach with the sacred. All this was used by those responsible of these dioceses to create symbols linked to that desired social rehabilitation and also was thought as a conciliatory way before the modernization of the country proposed by Porfirio Díaz, but led by the economic and political elites. For many of these dioceses, especially for the most conservative, neo-Gothic would be synonymous of a necessary magnificence attached to a concrete modernity that proposed the return to a glorious past, in which the Church had a pivotal role in society. It should not be forgotten that

8 Utrilla, *La arquitectura religiosa en el siglo XIX*, 90.

9 Blancarte, *Historia de la Iglesia Católica en México*, 120; Galeana, *Las relaciones iglesia-estado durante el Segundo Imperio*, 27.

10 Ceballos, "El clericalismo y el anticlericalismo en México," 39.

11 Romero de Solís, *El aguijón del espíritu*, 60, 295.

12 Ibid., 60–76.

neo-Gothic, perhaps like no other architectural style, hides the desire for a return to a past associated with a certain political ideology, associated with a concrete economic power that now seeks a predominant access to modernity.[13]

After the years of the Mexican Revolution (1910–1917), the development of neo-Gothic acquired a brief impulse, especially marked in the capital of the country, which was curtailed with the start of the *Guerra Cristera* (1926–1929), in which the Catholics of the country rose up in arms against the federal government, which had canceled their rights to exercise their religion. At the end of said conflict and in the following years, the construction of new temples slowed down. The use of historicist styles gradually gave way to the introduction of proposals from the modern architectural movement, especially in the country's great cities. However, neo-Gothic and its modernized derivations will not die. Although there are few examples of a strict stylistic continuity, there still exist some examples of adaptation and reinterpretation of the Gothic in the framework of architectural modernity—even today.

The Great Unfinished Temples: One of the Neo-Gothic Continuities in the Twentieth Century

Concerning architecture, in Mexico there are three large groups of Catholic buildings of neo-Gothic construction that can be distinguished. The first is related to parish churches completed a few years after their initial construction. A second group is that of temples with a colonial or even later past that are now being renovated, or to which neo-Gothic elements are applied. In these two groups, the majority of the buildings are concentrated between 1880 and 1910. These buildings have been analyzed elsewhere.[14]

However, a third group is related to the great temples of neo-Gothic facies, started at the end of the nineteenth century or at the beginning of the twentieth, which due to the lack of economic resources and conflicts such as the Revolution or the *Cristiada*, have been concluded at the end of the twentieth century or still remain under construction today (see Table 3).[15] Among these, four examples stand out: the Santuario Guadalupano in Zamora, Michoacán, designed as a new cathedral by local foreman Jesús Hernández Segura (1896–1914) [Figs. 9.02 & 9.03];[16] in León, Guanajuato, the case of the Templo del Sagrado Corazón de Jesús [Fig. 9.01] is very outstanding;[17] and in Arandas, Jalisco, the temple of San José Obrero [Fig. 9.04][18] and the expiatory temple of Guadalajara [Fig. 9.05].

Undoubtedly, these temples are the most prominent samples of religious neo-Gothic

13 Gil, *El templo del siglo XX*, 24–25.

14 Checa-Artasu, "Revisitando el papel del templo en la ciudad"; "Del neogótico al novogótico"; "La dimensión geográfica de la arquitectura neogótica en México"; "La arquitectura neogótica católica en el norte de México."

15 Checa-Artasu, "Revisitando el papel del templo en la ciudad," 179–206.

16 Checa-Artasu, "El templo y la ciudad," 42–82; Checa-Artasu, "Monumentalidad, símbolo y arquitectura neogótica," 143–194.

17 Checa-Artasu, "Visiones del neogótico mexicano," 90–108.

18 Checa-Artasu, "El templo de San José and Arandas," 11–27; Muñoz and García, *Piedra a piedra,* 2.

9.02 & 9.03 Zamora, Michoacán, Santuario Guadalupano, Jesús Hernández Segura (first project), 1896–1914, Manuel Guzmán Vázquez (1988–1995), Carlos Vargas (1995–2008), Gabriel Chávez de la Mora (interior, 1997–1999).
[Wikimedia Commons; photo Drini, 2010 / Historic Photo; © Jaime Ramos Méndez]

TABLE 3
MAIN CONSTRUCTION DATA OF THE FOUR GREAT NEO-GOTHIC TEMPLES IN MEXICO

Temple and city name Location	Start date	Interruptions	Project author and work management in construction	Dimensions	Current status
San José Obrero Arandas, Jalisco	1902	1908–1920 1926–1937	Unknown (1902–1908) Foreman Teodoro Ortiz Luna (1920–1926) Arch. Ignacio Díaz Morales (1938–1954) Eng. José Luis Amezcua (1954–2000) DEINCONKWI, SA de CV (2006–2010) Arch. Rafael Saucedo Flores (2010–present)	63 meters long, 13.35 meters wide, 28.60 meters crossing 23-meter naves and 43-meter towers	Unfinished
Templo Expiatorio del Santísimo Sacramento Guadalajara, Jalisco	1897	1912–1919	Three initial projects: Eng. Manuel Pérez Gómez (1897), Eng. Salvador Collado (1898), Eng. Adamo Boari (1899) Foremen: Feliciano and Jerónimo García (1901–1912), Eng. Luis Ugarte (1924–1927), Arch. Ignacio Díaz Morales (1927–1972)	Surface: 3,800 m^2 approx. 64.5-meter dome	Completed in 1972
Santuario Guadalupano Zamora, Michoacán	1898	1914–1988	Project of foreman Jesús Hernández Segura (1896–1914) Rebuilding project Arch. Manuel Guzmán Vázquez (1988–1995) Eng. Carlos Vargas Magaña (1995–2008) Arch. Gabriel Chávez de la Mora (interior design and post-concilium Vatican II adaptation) (1997–1999)	Surface: 5,414.58 m^2 Atrium: 6,800 m^2 107.5-meter towers	Unfinished but opened on December 12, 2008. Works inside and minor adjustments are in progress.
Templo Expiatorio del Sagrado Corazón de Jesús León, Guanajuato	1921	1925–1929	Project of Arch. Luis G. Olvera, Eng. Francisco Zamora Martínez, and Arch. Luis G. Olvera (1921–1941) Arch. Carlos Lazo Barreiro (1941–1953) Arch. Juan Carlos Ituarte González (1953–1973) Engs. Arturo and Gonzalo Acevedo Correa (1973–1987) Arch. José María Méndez Córdoba (1987–2010)	Surface: 3,600 m^2 approx. 45-meter dome	Completed in 2010

Sources: Checa-Artasu, "El templo y la ciudad," 42–82; "Monumentalidad, símbolo y arquitectura neogótica,"143–194; "Visiones del neogótico mexicano," 90–108; "El templo de San José en Arandas," 11–27; "El neogótico y el fortalecimiento de la Iglesia en Guadalajara," 40–55; González Escoto, "El templo Expiatorio de Guadalajara"; Casillas, "El Templo Expiatorio de Guadalajara"; Moya, *Arquitectura religiosa en Jalisco*, 207.

architecture in Mexico, because of its long process of construction and their monumentality (see dimensions in Table 3). This is an element inherent in the conversion of a building into a sign determined by the values of a dedication.[19] The architectural structure itself, especially if it is Gothic, enhances that symbolism. Likewise, the long duration of its construction becomes susceptible interpretation. It is enough to recall the symbolism of the stone on which the Christian community was to be built. Stone by stone, these temples culminate with the sustenance and support in the most diverse forms of the community of the faithful.

This monumentality must be associated with the dedications, engines of these constructions not only for their sacred character but for the specific attributes that the Church gives them: both the temple and dedication will be used as an element of that spiritual reconquest. Dedications that take on the figure of Jesus Christ socialized in new and more introspective and profound ways (Sacred Heart of Jesus, Christ the Redeemer or Christ the King) are very useful.[20]

19 Norberg-Schulz, *Los principios de la arquitectura moderna*, 207.

9.04 Arandas, Jalisco, Temple of San José Obrero, unknown designer begun 1902 Teodoro Ortíz (1924), Ignacio Díaz Morales (1937–1954), Julio de la Peña (1954–1956), José Luis Amezcua (1956–1995), Rafael Saucedo (apse and ambulatory, 2008–).
[© Alexis Reynoso, 2007]

9.05 Guadalajara, Jalisco, Templo Expiatorio del Santísimo Sacramento, Adamo Boari and Salvador Collado (Project) (1897–1899), Feliciano y Jerónimo Garcia (1901–1912), Luis Ugarte (1924–1927), Ignacio Díaz Morales 1927–1972.
[© Martín Checa-Artasu, 2012]

In this way, the four aforementioned temples have points in common. On the one hand, the imposition of the invocation for the love toward it of the diocesan bishop or the promoter priest of the temple. On the other hand, devotion to a dedication that due to its characteristics, contemplates the possibility of a large-scale expiation of sins as a resource against attacks on the Catholic religion that the state promoted. Perhaps the clearest example of the above is the strenuous use of the invocation of the Sacred Heart of Jesus to consecrate cities, regions, and even entire nations, all in the same years of the hatching and dissemination of neo-Gothic. In 1856, Pope Pius IX established the liturgical feast of the Sacred Heart; in 1899, Leo XIII consecrated the human race to the Heart of Jesus, explaining this action in the encyclical *Annum Sacrum Pos* (1899).

An example of this in Mexico is the Templo Expiatorio del Sagrado Corazón de Jesús in the city of León. The first stone of this neo-Gothic temple was laid on July 8, 1921, presided over by the Bishop of León Emeterio Valverde Téllez. The temple's design was commissioned to the Mexican architect Luis García Olvera, who had been in charge of repairs at the Catedral Metropolitana and the Parroquia del Divino Rostro in Mexico City. The intellectual promoter was the priest Bernardo Chávez Palacios, who had a strong belief in the gifts and goodness of the Sacred Heart of Jesus. It should be noted that, since January 6, 1914, Mexico had been consecrated to the Sacred Heart of Jesus—a consecration understood by the ecclesiastical authorities as a protective cloak that the Church brought to the country in moments of notable military-political conflict. Not surprisingly, the dedication of the temple to the Sacred Heart and its construction is one of the many consequences of the anticlerical onslaughts of the Mexican Revolution and anticlerical dictates of the Constitution of 1917. It is also one of the many strategies to recover believers and empower the Catholic community.[21] The construction—which would last until 2010—involved the participation of six architects and engineers as construction managers who made a progressive application of contemporary construction techniques.[22] The stone is abandoned to be replaced by artificial marble and concrete. Similarly, the economic costs elongate construction and encourage constructive inven-

20 On this theme, see the work of Díaz Patiño, "Imagen y discurso de la representación religiosa del Sagrado Corazón de Jesús," 86–108.

21 Romero, *El aguijón del espíritu,* 297.

22 Checa-Artasu, "Visiones del neogótico mexicano," 90–108

tive although do not inhibit the expression of artistic magniloquence in the statuary, that is work of two Italians: Adolfo Octavio Ponzanelli (sculpted tympanum in main façade portals) and Bartolomé Gallotti (exterior *Via Crucis*); in the manufacture of temple doors (designed by architect Juan Carlos Ituarte González) and the contemporaneous expression of its stained glasses created by local artists. The Gothic can be seen in its most basic forms (lancet arches, ribbed vaults, tribunes, altars, etc.), immersed in white light, product both of contemporary lighting, and in the color of the building materials.

The long construction of these temples would promote the adequacy of their interiors as a result of the new liturgical guidelines of the Second Vatican Council. This would provide these great churches with an external medieval aspect and an interior that is also medieval but adapted to the new realities that society imposes on the Church. Somehow, this means a subtle transit and a new adaptation of the Gothic to current times. A clear example of this is the Santuario Guadalupano of Zamora, Michoacán, which was designed as a new cathedral by the local foreman Jesús Hernández Segura (1896–1914, Figs. 9.02 & 9.03). The Revolution paralyzed its construction, which was not resumed until 1988, following the project of the Zamoran architect Manuel Guzmán Vázquez, and was completed in 2015.[23] Between 1997 and 1999, the interior, designed by the Benedictine monk and architect Gabriel Chávez de la Mora, was made according to the postconciliar precepts, connected here in a neo-Gothic environment. The result, of sober beauty, renews the liturgical functions of the building and gives new meanings to the dedication of this sanctuary to the Virgin of Guadalupe.[24]

A Paradigmatic Example: Templo Expiatorio del Santísimo Sacramento, Guadalajara

One of the examples of all the above mentioned is the Templo Expiatorio del Santísimo Sacramento in Guadalajara, Jalisco (Fig. 9.05).[25] Its monumentality was designed both to provide a sense of subjugation and of submission, and to become the symbolic exhibitor of the body of Christ, twenty-four hours a day, 365 days a year. Dedicated to the sacrament of the Eucharist, the temple was built to promote forgiveness and atonement for attacks on the Catholic Church by the Mexican state, which had authorized the freedom of worship, allowing the presence in Guadalajara of Protestant groups and had defrocked religious communities. Likewise, the origin of the temple coincides with the creation of a whole series of associations and groups that arise in the Catholic world, where the Eucharist is elevated to the category of dedication and is a means of spiritual dialogue with Jesus Christ. One of them is the Apostolado Expiatorio Eucarístico, created in the diocese of Guadalajara in the late nineteenth century on the initiative of the priest and canon of the Guadalajara cathedral, Pedro Romero Arnaiz. It is precisely around the cult of the sacrament of the Eucharist that a series of devotees gathered, under the leadership of Romero, and constituted a commission that would promote an expiatory temple to the aforementioned cult. This consisted of elderly clerics of antiliberal positions and contrary to the Protestant presence in the country, and secular Catholics who ran the press, education, and advocacy as defense elements of Catholicism.

On August 15, 1897, said commission—supported by the archdiocese—laid the first stone of the expiatory temple.[26] The commission pushed for the execution of the architectural project. There were at least three projects in less than two years. One was from engineer Manuel Pérez Gómez, who had trained at the Jalisco School of Engineering and had done various works for the arch-

23 Checa-Artasu, "El templo y la ciudad," 42–82; Checa-Artasu, "Monumentalidad, símbolo y arquitectura neogótica," 143–194.
24 Checa-Artasu, "Lo neogótico y el Concilio Vaticano II."
25 About this temple, see: Checa-Artasu, "El neogótico y el fortalecimiento de la Iglesia en Guadalajara," 40–55; González Escoto, "El templo Expiatorio de Guadalajara"; Casillas, *El Templo Expiatorio de Guadalajara*; Moya, *Arquitectura religiosa en Jalisco*, 207.
26 Dávila, *Al margen de una polémica*.

diocese. The project was presented in 1897 and nothing is known about it. A surveyor and hydrographer engineer from Jalisco, Salvador Collado Jasso (1859–1909),[27] was requested to work on a second project. He thought of a temple with a baroque dome, somewhat disproportionate and using ribbed vaults made of boulders. This project—which seems to have been of good quality, because it was awarded the second prize and the silver medal at the Jalisco Regional Exposition in 1902—was partially rejected. Thus, in 1899 the archbishopric of Guadalajara commissioned a third project for the temple to the Italian engineer Adamo Boari.[28]

His project had considerable dimensions: 3,800 square meters of surface, three naves, with a bell tower on the left side. It reflects aspects of Italian Gothic with Byzantine reminiscences, with a striking resemblance to the Orvieto cathedral in Italian Umbria that was built in the first decades of the fourteenth century. The only difference that was introduced was a four-body bell tower on the left side of the façade that finished with a large pinnacle and a clock. Once the commission had the architectural projects, it took into consideration the approaches of Boari and, to a lesser extent, those of Collado, to start to build the temple. The foundations were opened and the collection of material—quarry stone—was used to build the first walls. The construction project moved forward from 1901 to 1912, coinciding with the prelature of Archbishop José de Jesús Ortiz y Rodríguez (September 1901 to June 1912) who appointed the canon of the cathedral of Guadalajara, Pedro Romero Arnaiz, for the management of the works. In those years, Feliciano García, an experienced bricklayer, was appointed to be in charge of works. His son, Jerónimo, would continue in the following years with the same work. In 1906, the celebration of the National Eucharistic Congress in Guadalajara would grant the national character to the expiation that was proposed from the temple.

By 1911, the pillars and the sills of the temple were concluded. The next year, due to the revolutionary attacks in Guadalajara, the works were paralyzed until 1919. Although the church was partially constructed—the foundations of the three naves with their walls and columns had been built—the poor conditions of stability and resistance meant that, years later, a series of changes to the original project were needed.

After the revolutionary impasse in which the temple was saved from being dynamited in 1915, the works were resumed, concluding a provisional chapel that would allow the first masses to be held. In February 1924, after the death of Canon Romero, the Archbishop of Guadalajara, Francisco Orozco Jiménez, delegated the management and monitoring of the work to his right hand, the future cardinal José Garibi Rivera, who by that time, was a presbyter. This priest directed the management of the temple with a firm hand, which continued when he became archbishop of Guadalajara. Between 1924 and 1930, he delegated the direction of the construction of the temple to the Jalisco engineer, Luis Ugarte Vizcaíno (1877–1944),[29] a renowned professional with several works in Guadalajara, who built the choir. He was a teacher at the Guadalajara Free School of Engineers, where he would have, as one of his most seasoned students, the architecture intern Ignacio Díaz Morales Álvarez Tostado (1905–1992).[30] Ugarte would invite him to participate in the work of the Expiatorio, assuming the direction of the construction few years later.

Díaz Morales introduced some changes to the draft of Boari and Collado, both structural and imposing stereotomy, the use of stone as the strategy constructive and applying his own conception of the Gothic, influenced by his strong conservative Catholicism and a French vision of it. Thus, Díaz Morales, contrary to historicism, but an obedient Catholic, impregnated the construction of the Expiatorio, from 1927 to 1972, with his particular understanding of Gothic architecture. He made changes to the pillar structure of the temple and to the side walls that were already built, as well as to the ambulatory

27 Salvador Collado was a graduate of the School of Engineers of Jalisco and was the designer of the Arcediano suspension bridge over the canyon of Huentitan, one of the most outstanding works of Mexican engineering in the nineteenth century.

28 Boari had already carried out some works for the archdiocese of Guadalajara (a temple project in Atotonilco Alto) and had participated in the international competition for the Legislative Palace in Mexico City in 1897. A short time later, Boari would design the Postal Palace and the Palace of Fine Arts in Mexico City. See: Checa-Artasu, "De Ferrara a la Ciudad de México"; Checa-Artasu, "Adamo Boari y sus proyectos de arquitectura religiosa en México."

29 About this architect, see: Hermosillo, *Luis Ugarte*.

30 Díaz Morales, "El templo expiatorio," 311–318.

and the inner chapels, building an annex to the temple that would function as an office and hall for night worship. Likewise, he would design and build the main altar, raised above the presbytery between 1960 and 1962. A rectangular platform raised a few centimeters from the ground by six steps, which fits into the main apse of the temple, that allows its front view and also the circulation around it. It is worth noting that the altar designed by Díaz Morales is a design prior to the Second Vatican Council and its norms, but it is a preamble to them in terms of their resolution.[31]

Once the altar was built, the temple was consecrated and dedicated in a ceremony on February 23, 1962, presided over by Cardinal Garibi and the apostolic delegate in Mexico Luigi Raimondi. Ten years later, the temple was concluded, after seventy years of construction. Today it is one of the most outstanding tourist attractions in Guadalajara.

9.06 Mexico City, Church of Nuestra Señora del Rosario, Manuel Torres Torija and Ángel Torres Torija, 1913–1944.
[© Martín Checa-Artasu, 2019]

Neo-Gothic Continuities in the Twentieth Century in Mexico

From the 1920s, religious architecture in neo-Gothic style, after an initial spike, languished as a result of the *Cristero* conflict and the subsequent nationalizations of temples. Certainly, in the following three decades, the Catholic Church built very few temples, and it wasn't until the 1960s that the construction impulse was resumed with the erection of new parishes, largely in the growing cities of the entire country. For this reason, we can hardly document surviving examples of the neo-Gothic style. In Mexico City, we find several examples such as the Parroquia del Divino Rostro, designed and built by architect Luis García Olvera. The foundation stone for this small one-story church with six ribbed vaults was laid on January 1st, 1924.[32] Its construction was the result of a family donation to deposit a chrome image of the Divine Face brought from Rome. Also in the capital, we found the single-nave temple of the Santo Niño de la Paz, which was begun in 1922 on the initiative of Presbyter José María Troncoso. The works were suspended four years later and resumed until 1933 with the help of the city's German Catholic Community; the construction completed in 1942.[33] Another example is that of the isolated temple of Santa Teresita del Niño Jesús in the neighborhood Vista Alegre, built in 1938 in a sober neo-Gothic that in 1993 would be radically transformed.

It is also worth mentioning the church of Nuestra Señora del Rosario [Fig. 9.06], one of the most outstanding examples of neo-Gothic in the city, whose construction began in 1913 at the initiative of the Spanish priest Domingo Fernández, of the Dominican Order of Preachers. The temple was designed

31 Checa-Artasu, "Lo neogótico y el Concilio Vaticano II."
32 "Bienes e Inmuebles Federales. Templos y sus Anexidades," 9 de enero de 1934. Foja 2, Exp. 65/23759, Centro de Documentación en Información del Patrimonio Inmobiliario Federal y Paraestatal, Instituto de Administración y Avalúos de Bienes Nacionales (CDIPIFP-INDAABIN).
33 "Inventario original," October 31, 1937. Exp. 22069, CDIPIFP-INDAABIN.

by architect Manuel Torres Torija and the works were carried out by his brother, the engineer Ángel Torres Torija. The works were suspended on several occasions during the Revolution and during the first post-revolutionary governments and were finally concluded by the engineer Rafael García y Sánchez Facio in 1944.[34] It is a church with a basilica plan without an ambulatory, with three naves—the central one is larger than the lateral ones. The church stands out for the correction of its Gothic forms and some decorative elements such as the stained glass, that were paid for by the parishioners and were commissioned to the Mexican subsidiary of the German company F.X. Zettler,[35] a Munich firm with workshops in various cities in Europe and the Americas. Finally, let us quote the temple of San Pablo El Ermitaño, in the San Pablo neighborhood in Iztapalapa. A church beautifully set at the growing periphery of the city, it is small in size and built in brick on the initiative of a Catholic believer between 1960 and 1972.[36]

Outside the capital are some notable examples in Guadalajara. The church of Nuestra Señora del Rosario [Fig. 9.07],[37] probably one of the best interpretations of the neo-Gothic in Mexico, was built to honor the martyrdom of the priest Daniel Galván during the Revolution. The construction began in 1924, following a project by the Jalisco architect Pedro Castellanos Lambley (1901–1961), with numerous sacred works and who, years later, would take religious habits.

Two years later, due to the *Cristero* conflict and because the foundation had barely been laid, works were paralyzed and did not resume until August 5, 1938, directed by Castellanos until 1957. Engineer Ricardo Agraz Sáinz continued the works until October 30, 1970, when it is consecrated by the Archbishop of Guadalajara. It stands out for its external decoration. Its tower, combined with a slender spire on the main façade, gives the temple a sense of elevation that we must link with the remaining decoration on the façade and, of course, with the dedication of the temple to the Virgin of the Rosary. The decoration in the whole temple focuses on the various mysteries of the Rosary, which we found in the stained glass windows and especially in its large gateway, in which appear, alongside the medieval aesthetic, decorative elements such as mariachis and *Chinas poblanas*.[38]

Also, in Zacatecas, it merits highlighting the temple of Nuestra Señora del Rosario de Fátima.[39] In the final part of Leobardo Reynoso González's term as state governor (1902–1993), the expansion of the city of Zacatecas beyond its colonial-historical center was sought. For this reason, the development of the new Sierra de Álica neighborhood was promoted toward the south of the city, which soon required the construction of a church. While the project was being shaped, the image of the Virgin of the Rosary of Fatima arrived in Zacatecas, which

9.07 Guadalajara, Jalisco, Church of Nuestra Señora del Rosario, Pedro Castellanos Lambley (Project), 1924–1957, Ricardo Agraz 1957–1970.
[© Martín Checa-Artasu, 2015]

34 Calderón, *Del Romanticismo a la modernidad*, 20.

35 About this company, see: Mayer, *Franz Mayer of Munich and F. X. Zettler*.

36 "Relativo a la capilla de San Pablo," July 25, 1967. Foja 1, Exp. 71554, CDIPIFP-INDAABIN.

37 About this temple, see: Checa-Artasu, "Templo de Nuestra Señora del Rosario, Guadalajara."

38 Haro, "La parroquia de Nuestra Señora del Rosario," 127–132; Marcelli, "Una mirada al neogótico mexicano del siglo XX," 750–758.

39 Checa-Artasu, "Del neogótico al novogótico," 35–58.

was brought from Portugal and had begun a tour of visits and processions in Mexico. The arrival of the image and the need for a new church led to the intervention of the Bishop of Zacatecas, Ignacio Placencia Moreira, who proposed the creation of a Comité pro Santuario a la Virgen del Rosario de Fátima for the new neighborhood. In the mid-1950s, the diocese and the pro-sanctuary Committee commissioned the design of the temple to engineer Rutilio Licona, who worked at the Zacatecas City Council and had been designer for the new neighborhood. On October 22, 1950, the first stone of the temple was laid, and the architectural proposal was approved by Bishop Ignacio Placencia Moreira on November 13, 1950. It was a temple with a Latin cross plan with three naves and an enormous tower at its main façade, which is decorated in an exuberant way with pinnacles, gables, tracery, and lancet windows, all designed to be built in stone quarry. The plans alert, on the one hand, the religious fervor that accompanied the commission, expressed in the grandiloquence of the project. On the other hand, they warn that the cost of the work was going to be high and that given the political-economic circumstances, it would not be easy to get the resources to carry it out. Before this circumstance, the pro-sanctuary committee decided to redefine the architectural project by contacting the engineer José Luis Amezcua Sahagún, who at that time was already directing the work of the neo-Gothic temple of San José Obrero, in Arandas, Jalisco, and had a remarkable track record in realization of religious buildings of all kinds.

In September 1954, Amezcua presented two projects, one that, while maintaining the exuberant Gothic decoration, reduced the volume and weight of the tower—defined here as narthex—and a second one, in a more contemporary style, in which the tower lost its Gothic decoration to present itself smoothly, in the form of a belfry, culminating in a square latticework. Apparently, both the pro-construction committee of the temple and the Zacatecan bishopric accepted the first of the projects that maintained the Gothic decoration, but lowered the costs and structural burdens of the temple, an important fact, because it was going to be built on uneven ground. Although Amezcua made some more plans between 1955 and 1956, apparently, he abandoned the project and left the direction of works to the priest Manuel de la Hoz, who was in charge of the new parish. It was he, along with the committee, who put the work in the hands of local foreman Manuel Martínez. Formally, the temple has a Latin cross plan with a central nave and narrow side naves, separated by columns culminating in capitals with vegetal decoration. The work was done in pink quarry brought from Fresnillo and San Cayetano, nearby towns. This work presents different shades of color inside the temple, especially in the ribbed vaults of the central nave and the lateral ones. Such vaults have ribs made of the same quarry stone. The temple's transept is short in its lateral arms and is covered with an octagonal dome above the transept, which interiorly presents windows with Gothic tracery and stained glass windows showing different passages from the Bible, as well as the appearance of the Virgin of Fatima to the shepherds. Outside, the Gothic decoration is collected in the narthex tower, in a sequence with five bodies, marked on the ground by a slender flared gateway, followed by a white stone statue of the Virgin of the Rosary of Fatima located in a large niche and followed by a body with four rosettes, one on each side; in addition, another body with lattice-patterned windows and a pyramidal spire or roof with pinnacles and decorative fleuron at each work joint. On the lateral façades are smaller buttresses and flying buttresses, which suggest that they may have no structural function like many neo-Gothic examples. On May 13, 1966 the temple was erected as a parish, and religious services began to be held on a regular basis. The building process concluded in 2004 with the construction of the crypts, one of which contains the remains of Father Galván.

9.08 Huejotzingo, Puebla, Church of Nuestra Señora del Carmen, begun 1952.
[© Martín Checa-Artasu, 2015]

9.09 León, Guanajuato, Capilla de la Cruz de Cantera, Guillermo Chávez Ochoa, begun 1991.
[© Martín Checa-Artasu, 2020]

Beyond these examples, we can mention a few more, such as the parish of Nuestra Señora de Guadalupe, in Cananea, Sonora.[40] This church is located in a mining settlement and was defrayed by the mining businessman and rancher William C. Greene, owner of The Cananea Consolidated Cooper Company, and his wife Mary Greene Wiswall. It is a simple temple with three naves, with gabled roof and façade, with two truncated towers on each side, and a narthex with three lanceted arches. The works began in 1905 and had several work stoppages, until 1937, when priest Ricardo Monge Valenzuela arrived. It was consecrated on December 24, 1940.

Another one is the Santuario de la Virgen de Guadalupe, in Calvillo, Aguascalientes, whose foundation stone was laid on December 12, 1945.[41] It has a single nave and was built under the direction of the local bricklayers José de la Cruz and Rufino de Loera, in brick with a carved quarry façade, in just twenty years. It features Gothic elements such as a double window with trilobar arches in the manner of a rosette, a triangular pediment with pinnacles and two towers with trilobar windows and pyramidal spires, festooned with pinnacles and trilobar openings. Its interior is painted with filigree and floral motifs in blue and gold tones;[42] it presents three speared arches beneath the chorus, ribbed vaults, and a cupola in its transept, where we find a three-lane altar in pink quarry with Gothic decoration. Apparently, its construction is the consequence of the celebration of a Guadalupan Congress in the diocese of Aguascalientes in 1945, an action that was part of the reconstruction of

40 Morales, *La Parroquia de Nuestra Señora de Guadalupe de Cananea.*

41 Trejo, "Calvillo, Aguascalientes," 303.

42 It seems that the decoration of the walls and especially of the pendentives of the dome with images of the appearance of the Virgin to Juan Diego are works of local painter Miguel Velasco Martínez.

43 Padilla, *Después de la tempestad*, 105.
44 Palafox-Muñoz et al., "Nueva ruralidad y sustentabilidad," 69.
45 This church was restored in 2016 with money contributed by the Huejotzingo city council. Recently, the city council has donated an amount to fix the damage caused by the earthquake in September 2017.
46 All the available information attributes to architect Jesús Corro the design of this temple, data that we have not been able to corroborate. There is surely a mosaic made by him in the mid-1980s at the entrance to the temple and two of his frescoes on the altar. About this artist, see: Montero and Mayer, *Arquitectos e ingenieros poblanos del siglo XX*, 511–521.
47 Checa-Artasu, "Una copia de la Sainte Chapelle en León," 20–22.

the Church in Aguascalientes, promoted by Bishop Jesús López y González.[43] Today, this temple has become one of the tourist attractions of Calvillo, since it was nominated "*Pueblo Mágico*" in 2012.[44]

Another example is the simple parish of Cristo Rey in Papantla, Veracruz, the construction of which started in 1953, with the aim to host the cult of Christ the King, which had been a banner during the *Cristiada* and would be so in the following decades. Here, an austere church would be built in a rereading of neo-Gothic, using concrete and brick laminate, painted in white. Another example, in which the neo-Gothic overflows in a multitude of decorations on the façade, and to a lesser extent inside, is the church of Nuestra Señora del Carmen in Huejotzingo, Puebla [Fig. 9.08]. Apparently, the works started in 1952 by a commission of parishioners devoted to the Virgin of Carmen; this commission obtained donations for the construction of the temple, even for the most recent restorations.[45] This church's decorations were made by the renowned Puebla's sculptor and architect Jesús Corro Ferrer (1933–2016) in the 1980s.[46] A touch of contemporaneity contrasts the excess of gables, lanceted arches, and plaster tracery of this temple.

Finally, we must mention the case of the Capilla de la Cruz de Cantera, in León, Guanajuato [Fig. 9.09]. It is a smaller reinterpretation of the Sainte-Chapelle de Paris,[47] promoted by the parish priest José María de la Torre Correa, who was passionate about the history of sacred architecture. The Capilla de la Cruz de Cantera was designed by architect Guillermo Chávez Ochoa, a great connoisseur of sacred architecture, a self-taught sculptor, and author of numerous elements of sacred architecture in several parishes in León. Works initiated in 1991 and have not been finalized to date, both by the lack of economic resources and because of the complexity of project. Today it can be seen in León as a small temple that takes the forms and aesthetics of the Parisian Sainte-Chapelle both on the outside—with a Gothic elaboration full of pinnacles, gables, statues, tracery—and a Gothic spire imitating that of Notre-Dame de Paris, as in the interior, with a sequence of large windows with stained glass that modestly remind the interior of the Parisian chapel.

TABLE 4
CATHOLIC TEMPLES OF MODERN ARCHITECTURE THAT USE GOTHIC ELEMENTS

Name	Place	Start and end year	Architect author of the project
Iglesia de San Marcos	Balancan, Tabasco	1940s	??
Santuario de la Virgen del Peñón	Jonotla, Cuetzalan, Puebla	1923–1950s	??
Catedral de la Asunción de María	Chilapa, Guerrero	1945–1975	Arch. Federico Mariscal Piña
Capilla San Francisco de Asís	Atlautla, State of México	1950–1952	Arch. Honorato Carrasco Navarrete
Parroquia de Santa María de Guadalupe	Pedro Escobedo, Querétaro	1951–1993	Eng. Enrique Ruiz Merino
Capilla de Ntra. Sra. de Fátima	Xalapa, Veracruz	1951–1953	Eng. Guillermo Samaniego
Parroquia de Nuestra Señora del Refugio	Puerto Vallarta, Jalisco	1960–1975	Arch. Tatiana Borioli Berner and Eng. Marcial Reséndiz Galván
Parroquia de San Antonio de Padua	Nacajuca, Tabasco	1965–1968	??
Templo de Nuestra Señora del Refugio de Cerro Gordo	León, Guanajuato	1972	Foreman: Serafín Ramírez Rodríguez
Capilla de Atotonilco	Rinconada de Atotonilco, Tenancingo de Degollado, State of México	1990s–2000s	Builder: Sergio Mena
Templo de San Juan Bautista	Xicotepec de Juárez, Puebla	1947–1996	Arch. Lionzo Velazco Marañón
Templo Virgen de Guadalupe	Juan Martín, Celaya, Guanajuato	2009–2019	Arch. Antonio Velázquez Serrano

Source: Own elaboration from Cruz, "Semblanza de un gran maestro," 41; Hernández Palacios, *Xalapa de mis recuerdos*, 114; Valderrama, "La Virgen del Peñón, un santuario," 49–56; Baños, "Arquitectura en Puerto Vallarta," 86–87; Reyes, *Un ángel para los pobres*, 115.

Some Examples of the Use of the Neo-Gothic in Architectural Modernity

In the twentieth century, the construction of some temples began that clearly fit in the architectural modernity, taking Gothic elements and applying them in their construction (see Table 4).

Among these, there are at least seven in Mexico. Their characteristics are diverse, including small churches where the Gothic is limited to the use of a pointed roof made of fiber cement or brick. That would be the case of the chapel of San Francisco de Asís, in the Popo Park urbanization, in Atlautla, a first-time work by the architect Honorato Carrasco Navarrete (1926–1992), which was built between 1950 and 1952 and is reminiscent of the small colonial mountain chapels.[48] Another similar example is the modest chapel of Nuestra Señora de Fátima, which was built between 1951 and 1953, according to the project of engineer Guillermo Samaniego in the "Veracruz" residential development of the city of Xalapa, Veracruz.[49] This operation was carried out by the parishioners of said urbanization, similar to the one that took place for the Santuario de la Virgen de Guadalupe, in Jonotla, by the Nahua communities in that area.

One side of the pointed roof rests on the walls of a rock where, in 1922, an appearance of the Guadalupana was left printed on the rock. The construction of the temple began in 1923, and its completion was delayed until at least the mid-1950s.[50] Concerning parishes, three examples are in the state of Tabasco. San Antonio de Padua in Nacajuca [Fig. 9.10] seems to have been built between 1965 and 1968.[51] It is a striking church with many Gothic elements especially on its façade, towers, and dome, built with contemporary materials, creating a colorful chromatic result that reminds us the tradition of painted churches in the area.[52] The new parish dedicated to San Marcos, in Balancan—which was built in the 1950s—also includes many Gothic elements. This example, aligns with the Nacajuca and the temple of the Inmaculada Concepción in Villahermosa—refurbished between 1937 and 1945—and that of Santa María de Guadalupe in Frontera. For this last, the old church only was restored using neo-Gothic elements between 1950 and 1951 by local builder Calixto Morán de la Rosa.[53] All of the above were the result of the building recovery process of churches in Tabasco, which were wildly destroyed during the anticlerical government terms of governor Tomás Garrido Canabal (1923–1934).[54]

Another example of the assimilation of the Gothic by contemporary architecture is the parish of Nuestra Señora del Refugio, in Puerto Vallarta, Jalisco, which was built between 1960 and 1975; it is a temple with a rectangular floor plan, with Gothic decorative elements both outside and inside. It was the first project of a young architect: Tatiana Borioli Berner (1939–),[55] and was modified by the civil engineer Marcial Reséndiz Galván (1924–2018), who was widely known

9.10 Nacajuca, Tabasco, Church of San Antonio de Padua, 1965–1968. [© Martín Checa-Artasu, 2013]

48 Cruz, "Semblanza de un gran maestro," 41.

49 Hernández Palacios, *Xalapa de mis recuerdos*, 114.

50 Valderrama, "La Virgen del Peñón, un santuario," 49–56.

51 Álvarez, *Diccionario enciclopédico de Tabasco*, 455.

52 Gallegos, *Iglesias polícromas de la Chontalpa*.

53 Arciniega, "La casa de la Negra Fojaco."

54 Blanco, "El Tabasco garridista y la movilización de los católicos," 117–168.

55 Cortés, *Recordando un Paraíso*, 230.

9.11 Xicotepec de Juarez, Puebla, Church of San Juan Bautista temple, Lionzo Velazco (Project), 1947–1996. [© Martín Checa-Artasu, 2014]

for his works in this town.[56] This combines elements of the architecture of the "Vallarta style" of those years. On the one hand, the use of brick exposed in its construction refers to the mountain architecture of the area, typical of the town and which in the 1950s, was reinvented through the "Vallarta style" that builders, such as Fernando Romero Escalante, developed for U.S. tourist housing in the Gringo Gulch neighborhood.[57] On the other hand, more modern materials were used, such as the reinforced concrete used in this case for the barrel vault that covers the temple and refers us to some examples of functionalist architecture that were built in Vallarta in the 1940s and 1950s. Another parish example is the San Juan Bautista temple in Xicotepec de Juárez, Puebla [Fig. 9.11], begun in 1947 and consecrated in 1996, which sought to replace a badly damaged parish temple from the eighteenth century.[58] This church was promoted by the local parish priest Francisco Velasco Marañón (1903–1985), who carried out an outstanding work in favor of teaching in this town in the Sierra de Puebla.[59] The project of temple — that has simplistic similarities to the aesthetics of some European Gothic cathedrals — was designed by Lionzo Velazco, brother of the mentioned priest, in a flamboyant Gothicism, which was unlikely to develop given the economic conditions in those years of the diocese of Tulancingo, to which it belongs, and of the parishioners that it was going to host. For this reason, it took several decades to build, and the result is extraordinary in its internal simplicity. Externally, it wants to imitate the forms of Notre-Dame de Paris, achieving it superficially. Despite this, this church has become an urban landmark and a tourist attraction.

Another example brings us closer to the aesthetic possibilities of the Gothic assimilated into other forms that are not inherent to it (the ogival). This is the case of the exuberant cathedral of the Asunción de María, in Chilapa, Guerrero, designed and built by architect Federico Ernesto Mariscal Piña (1881–1971) from 1945 and completed three decades later. Its eclectic forms, at times Art Deco, at times avant le lettre brutalism, tell about the whole series of Gothic elements of any cathedral.[60]

Finally, I want to mention the use of Gothic forms in contemporary architecture proposed by two temples. One is the parish of the Virgin of Guadalupe in Pedro Escobedo, Querétaro. A design by engineer Enrique Ruiz Merino was built over forty years: from 1951 to 1993. It stands out, because of its particular combination of materials such as brick, quarry, ceramic bosses of the cover, and the marble plates of its walls, generating a contemporary rereading of the Gothic, only recognized here by the use of the lancet arch in the façade, the large windows, and its roof. A similar resolution, although simpler, is that of the temple to the Virgin of Guadalupe, in the community of Juan Martin, Celaya, Guanajuato [Fig. 9.12]. It is a single-nave temple that was started in 2009 and was completed in 2018.[61] This is a project by architect Antonio Velázquez Serrano, made in pink quarry and fiber cement. It resembles

56 Pineda, "Marcial Reséndiz Galván."
57 Baños, "Arquitectura en Puerto Vallarta," 86–87.
58 Gómez Salas, *Pláticas de Sobremesa*, 315.
59 Reyes, *Un ángel para los pobres*, 115.
60 Noelle, *Arquitectos mexicanos desconocidos del siglo XX*, 152; Noelle and Schávelzon, "Monumento efímero a los héroes de la Independencia," 166–167; Vargas, *Federico E. Mariscal. Vida y obra.*
61 Moreno, "Casi listo."

a party tent, decorated with twenty stained glass windows embedded in onyx and a mosaic Pantocrator on its main gateway. The result confers a medieval aesthetic in the twenty-first century in the framework of a peri-urban community.

These temples force us to reflect on the reasons why constructive and decorative elements were made to refer us to the Gothic. These reasons are diverse: the attachment of the architect or the priest who initiated the temple with that style, a kind of belief that the constructive ideal of a Catholic temple is anchored in the Gothic, or simply a building proposal that is consistent with the need to generate a symbol that denotes the presence of the Catholic Church in that place.

9.12 Community of Juan Martin, Celaya, Guanajuato, Temple to the Virgin of Guadalupe, Antonio Velázquez Serrano, 2009–2018.
[© Martín Checa-Artasu, 2020]

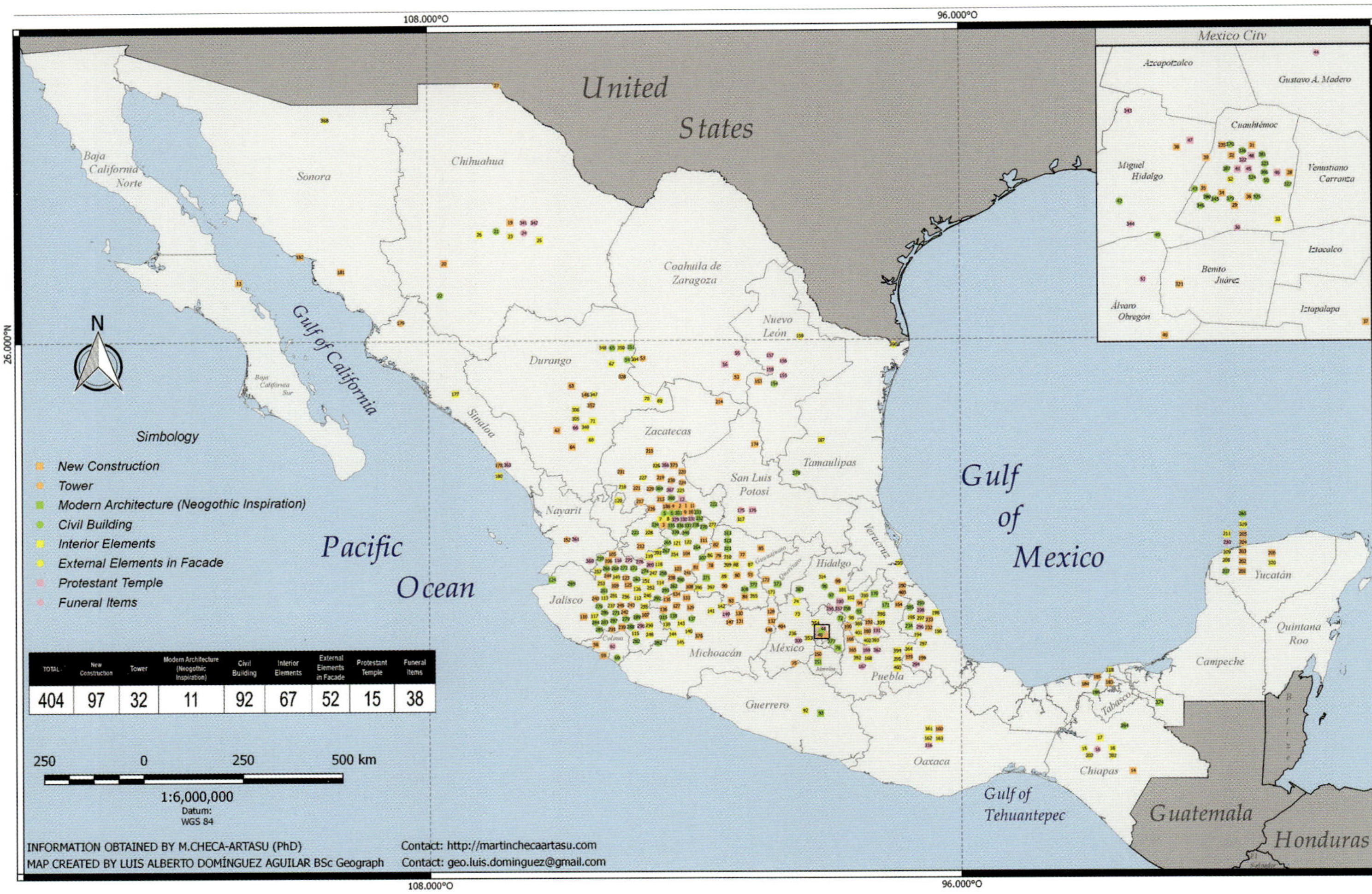

LOCATION OF NEOGOTHIC ARCHITECTURE EXAMPLES IN MEXICO

NEW CONSTRUCTION

1. "Parroquia del Sagrario" (El Conventito), Aguascalientes, Aguascalientes.
2. "Templo de la Purísima Concepción", Aguascalientes, Aguascalientes.
3. "Santuario de la Virgen de Guadalupe", Calvillo, Aguascalientes.
4. "Templo de San Domingo", Aguascalientes, Aguascalientes.
13. "Templo de Santa Barbara", Mulegé, Baja California Sur.
14. "Templo de San José", Comitán de Domínguez, Chiapas.
19. "Templo de la Sagrada Familia", Chihuahua, Chihuahua.
20. "Templo de Cristo Rey", Creel, Chihuahua.
28. "Templo Expiatorio Nacional de San Felipe de Jesús", Cuauhtémoc, CDMX.
29. "Parroquia de Nuestra Señora del Rosario", Cuauhtémoc, CDMX.
31. "Parroquia del Inmaculado y Sagrado Corazón de María", Cuauhtémoc, CDMX.
32. "Parroquia de María Reparadora", Cuauhtémoc, CDMX.
34. "Templo de la Sagrada Familia", Cuauhtémoc, CDMX.
35. "Iglesia del Niño de la Paz", Cuauhtémoc, CDMX.
36. "Instituto Teresiano María Isabel Dónde", Cuauhtémoc, CDMX.
37. "Capilla del San Pablo el Ermitaño", Iztapalapa, CDMX.
38. "Santuario de María Auxiliadora", Miguel Hidalgo, CDMX.
39. "Parroquia del Divino Rostro", Miguel Hidalgo, CDMX.
40. "Capilla Gótica Instituto Cultural Helénico", CDMX.
53. "Santuario de la Virgen de Guadalupe", Saltillo, Coahuila.
58. "Templo del Señor San José", Colima, Colima.
59. "Templo de la Virgen de la Salud", Colima, Colima.
62. "Parroquia del Sagrado Corazón de Jesús", Ciudad Lerdo, Durango.
63. "Iglesia de San Francisco Javier de Lajas", Coneto de Comonfort, Durango.
64. "Capilla de San Martín de Porres, Durango, Durango.
77. "Iglesia de Nuestra Señora de la Asunción" (de la Saleta), Dolores Hidalgo, Guanajuato.
78. "Templo Expiatorio del Sagrado Corazón de Jesús", León, Guanajuato.
79. "Parroquia de Nuestra Señora Del Carmen", León, Guanajuato.
80. "Iglesia de Santa María de la Asunción", Guanajuato, Guanajuato.
81. "Parroquia del Señor de la Misericordia", Jalpa de Cánovas, Guanajuato.
82. "Templo del Inmaculado Corazón de María", León, Guanajuato.
83. "Parroquia de San Juan Bautista", Moroleón, Guanajuato.
84. "Capilla anexa al Santuario de Nuestra Señora de la Luz", Salvatierra, Guanajuato.
85. "Santuario de la Virgen de Guadalupe", San Luis de la Paz, Guanajuato.
94. "Capilla del Apóstol Santiago", Apan, Hidalgo.
103. "San José Obrero", Arandas, Jalisco.
104. "Templo Parroquial del Señor San José de los Sauces" (Los Sauces), Encarnación de Diaz, Jalisco.
105. "Templo Expiatorio del Santísimo Sacramento", Guadalajara, Jalisco.
106. "Templo Nuestra Señora del Refugio", Guadalajara, Jalisco.
107. "Templo de San Antonio de Padua", Ciudad Guzmán, Jalisco.
108. "Iglesia de Santa María de Guadalupe", Degollado, Jalisco.
109. "Parroquia de Nuestra Señora del Rosario o del Padre Galván", Guadalajara, Jalisco.
184. "Catedral Santo Cristo de Esquipulas", Villahermosa, Tabasco.
185. "Iglesia de la Inmaculada Concepción La Conchita", Villahermosa, Tabasco.
188. "Templo de Nuestra Señora del Refugio, capilla Hacienda Cañada Honda", José María Morelos/Cañada Honda, Aguascalientes.
189. "Capilla de la Hacienda La Trinidad", Santa Cruz, Tlaxcala.
190. "Capilla de la Hacienda de Mazapa", San Antonio Mazapa, Tlaxcala.
192. "Parroquia de Nuestra Señora Del Carmen", Santa Ana Chiautempan, Tlaxcala.
193. "Capilla Compañía Industrial de Orizaba, S.A.", Rio Blanco, Veracruz.
200. "Parroquia de Cristo Rey", Papantla, Veracruz.
201. "Iglesia de la Soledad en Hacienda San José Eknakan", Cuzamá, Yucatán.
202. "Capilla de Nuestra Señora del Carmen", Mérida, Yucatán.
203. "Capilla de San José en el Colegio María de Monserrat", Mérida, Yucatán.
204. "Capilla de San Juan Bautista", Municipio de Mérida, Yucatán.
205. "Capilla de Hacienda de San Ignacio Loyola", Progreso, Yucatán.
206. "Capilla de Chenché de las Torres", Temax, Yucatán.
212. "Templo de San José", Nochistlán de Mejía, Zacatecas.
213. "Capilla del Diezmo", Jerez de García Salinas, Zacatecas.
214. "Capilla de Nuestra Señora de Guadalupe" (El Huachito), Concepción del Oro, Zacatecas.
215. "Capilla de Río de Medina", Saín Alto, Zacatecas.
216. "Templo de San Juan Bautista", Tepetongo, Zacatecas.
217. "Kiosco del Jardín Zaragoza", Tepetongo, Zacatecas.
219. "Santuario Diocesano de Nuestra Señora de Guadalupe" (Guadalupito), Zacatecas, Zacatecas.
220. "Templo de la Virgen del Rosario de Fátima", Zacatecas, Zacatecas.
221. "Escuela de la Torre", Jerez de García Salinas, Zacatecas.
232. "Templo Nuestro Señor de El Calvario", Coatepec, Veracruz.
233. "Iglesia de Nuestra Señora de Fátima", Coatepec, Veracruz.
235. "Templo de Nuestra Señora de la Salud", Cuauhtémoc, CDMX.
238. "Capilla de El Calvario", Atotonilco Alto, Jalisco.
239. "Capilla del Sagrado Corazón de Jesús", Zapotiltic, Jalisco.
321. "Capilla Ex Convento Madres Repadoras", Mixcoac, CDMX.
375. "Templo de Nuestra Señora de Loreto", Bañon, Villa de Cos, Zacatecas.
376. "Templo Nuevo", Taretan, Michoacán.

CIVIL BUILDING

5. "Baños Públicos Los Arquitos", Aguascalientes, Aguascalientes.
6. "Capilla Oratorio del Museo Regional de Historia de Aguascalientes", Aguascalientes.
21. "Hospital Central Universitario, Porfirio Díaz", Chihuahua, Chihuahua.
22. "Castillo Sheperd", Batopilas, Chihuahua.
42. "Residencia Privada", CDMX.
43. "Casona El Divino o Casa O'hea/Austin", Ciudad de México.
269. "Casa en Calle Hidalgo, s/n", Mascota, Jalisco.
270. "El Parián", Ojuelos de Jalisco, Jalisco.
271. "Portales Morelos, Zaragoza, Hidalgo y Mina" (El Parián), Sayula, Jalisco.
272. "Palacio de las Vacas o Casa de la Calle San Felipe N°634", Guadalajara, Jalisco.
273. "Casa en Calle Pedro Moreno N°118", Guadalajara, Jalisco.
274. "Casa en Calle Nueva Galicia N°987", Guadalajara, Jalisco.
278. "Portal Casa", Ejutla, Jalisco.
279. "Portal Casa en Calle Degollado", Atoyac, Jalisco.
280. "Decoración Casa Portal Morelos", La Barca, Jalisco.
282. "Portales en Tecalitlán", Tecalitlán, Jalisco.
283. "Portal Zaragoza", San Gabriel, Jalisco.
284. "Portal Corona", San Gabriel, Jalisco.
285. "Portal Ocampo", San Gabriel, Jalisco.
286. "Portal Hermenegildo Galeana", Sayula, Jalisco.
287. "Portal Colón", Sayula, Jalisco.
288. "Casa en Calle Refugio Barragán de Toscano N°32, Casa Diaz, Restaurante Los Portales", Ciudad Guzmán, Jalisco.
289. "Casa de la Calle Primero de Mayo N°58, papelería Alva", Ciudad Guzmán, Jalisco.
292. "Portales y Presidencia Municipal", Jamay, Jalisco.
293. "Ex hacienda Jamay", Jamay, Jalisco.
299. "Antiguo Palacio Episcopal. Museo de San Rafael Guízar y Valencia", Xalapa, Veracruz.
301. "Casa de la Calle Rivero y Gutiérrez N°315, Actual Preparatoria Fco. I. Madero", Aguascalientes, Aguascalientes.
307. "Casino Español", León, Guanajuato.
308. "Casa de la Calle Juárez N°226", Salvatierra, Guanajuato.
311. "Casa de la Calle Positos N°90", Guanajuato, Guanajuato.
312. "Casa de la Calle Cantador N°19", Guanajuato, Guanajuato.
313. "Casa de la Calle Tepetapa N°87b", Guanajuato, Guanajuato.
315. "Casa Calle Benito Juárez N°46", Cotija, Michoacán.
323. "Palacio Postal", CDMX.
324. "Antigua Inspección de Policía", CDMX.
325. "Asilo Ancianos del Buen Retiro, hoy Universidad de Londres", CDMX.
326. "Escuela Primaria Ignacio Manuel Altamirano", CDMX.
327. "Proyecto Apartamentos en Calle Jesús María", CDMX.
332. "Hotel Imperial", Aguascalientes, Aguascalientes.
333. "Casa Julia Pani/Museo Regional de Historia", Aguascalientes, Aguascalientes.
334. "Casa en calle Morelos N° 517", Aguascalientes, Aguascalientes.
335. "Casa Tomás Hernández Ruiz en calle Morelos N° 519", Aguascalientes, Aguascalientes.
336. "Casa en calle José María Chávez N° 444. Sucursal Compartamos Banco", Aguascalientes, Aguascalientes.
337. "Ex Hacienda Cañada Honda", José María Morelos/Cañada Honda, Aguascalientes.

110. "Templo de la Purísima", Autlán de Navarro, Jalisco.
111. "Capilla Hacienda Tlalixcoyan", Lagos de Moreno, Jalisco.
125. "Santuario del Sagrado Corazón", Tonalá, Jalisco.
127. "Santuario Guadalupano", Zamora, Michoacán.
128. "Templo de la Inmaculada Concepción", Angangueo, Michoacán.
129. "Templo de San Francisco de Asís", Ixtlá de los Hervores, Michoacán.
130. "Templo de la Visitación", Morelia, Michoacán.
131. "Iglesia de María Auxiliadora", Morelia, Michoacán.
132. "Parroquia de San Pedro Apóstol", Senguio, Michoacán.
133. "Parroquia del Sagrado Corazón de Jesús", Tocumbo, Michoacán.
134. "Templo Expiatorio del Sagrado Corazón de Jesús", Zamora, Michoacán.
135. "Santuario de Guadalupe", Zamora, Michoacán.
136. "Capilla de la Ex Hacienda El Molino", Vista Hermosa de Negrete, Michoacán.
150. "Templo de Nuestra Señora del Carmen", Cuernavaca, Morelos.
153. "Templo Expiatorio San Luís Gonzaga", Monterrey, Nuevo León.
160. "Iglesia de La Soledad", San Agustín Etla, Oaxaca.
164. "Templo de la Virgen de Guadalupe" (Iglesia de los Jarritos), Cuetzalan, Puebla.
165. "Templo de Nuestra Señora del Carmen", Huejotzingo, Puebla.
166. "Capilla Fábrica de El Carmen", San Martín Texmelucan, Puebla.
172. "Capilla Propiciatoria o de Maximiliano de Habsburgo" (Cerro de las Campanas), Querétaro, Querétaro.
174. "Catedral de la Inmaculada Concepción", Matehuala, San Luis Potosí.
181. "Parroquia Nuestra Señora de Guadalupe", Cócorit, Sonora.
182. "Templo de San Fernando", Guaymás, Sonora.
183. "Iglesia de San Antonio de Padua", Nacajuca, Tabasco.

49. "Capilla Casa Manuel Escandón, hoy Hospital Escandón", CDMX.
50. "Antigua Sede del Banco Agrícola Hipotecario de México" (Hotel City Centro), CDMX.
54. "Teatro Isauro Martínez", Torreón, Coahuila.
60. "Portal Medellín", Colima, Colima.
65. "Monumento a Miguel Hidalgo", Mapimí, Durango.
72. "Casa Principal Hacienda de Zuapayuca", Axapusco, Estado de México.
95. "Anexos de la Hacienda de Zotoluca", Apan, Hidalgo.
96. "Centro Cultural Universitario La Garza", Pachuca, Hidalgo.
97. "Escuela Julián Villagrán", Pachuca, Hidalgo.
137. "Antiguo Edificio del Colegio de La Purísima", Jacona de Plancarte, Michoacán.
138. "Portal Allende", Michoacán.
154. "Casa del Alcalde Gregorio D. Martínez", Monterrey, Nuevo León.
186. "Café del Portal", Villahermosa, Tabasco.
207. "Casa de Peter Schirp", Mérida, Yucatán.
222. "Torre del Reloj", Pinos, Zacatecas.
223. "Kiosco Plaza Principal", Jalpa, Zacatecas.
258. "Portales Jardín de la Presidencia", Tonila, Jalisco.
259. "Hacienda de Santa Ana", Tequila, Jalisco.
261. "Casa en Calle Constitución N°19", Tecolotlán, Jalisco.
262. "Portales Morelos", La Barca, Jalisco.
263. "Preparatoria N°1, UDG", Guadalajara, Jalisco.
264. "Casa en Calle Agustín Rivera s/n", Lagos de Moreno, Jalisco.
265. "Casa en Calle Ramón Corona N°39", Teocaltiche, Jalisco.
266. "Casa en Calle Garibaldi N°755", Guadalajara, Jalisco.
267. "Casa en Calle 5 de mayo s/n", Teocaltiche, Jalisco.
268. "Hospital del Sagrado Corazón de Jesús", Guadalajara, Jalisco.

338. "Casa Ventura Salazar Ramírez en calle Refugio Reyes N°110", Aguascalientes, Aguascalientes.
339. "Hotel Casino El Recreo", Aguascalientes, Aguascalientes.
340. "Casa Familia Leal en calle Venustiano Carranza N° 306", Aguascalientes, Aguascalientes.
345. "Casa Particular", Cuauhtémoc, CDMX.
346. "Casa Torreblanca", CDMX.
351. "Casa Particular en Avenida Benito Juárez con Libertad", Mapimí, Durango.
358. "Hacienda Chavarria", Pachuquilla, Hidalgo.
365. "Hacienda Petechtunich", Acanceh, Yucatán.
368. "Mercado General Jesús González Ortega", Zacatecas, Zacatecas.
369. "Escuela de la Torre", Jérez, Zacatecas.
370. "Casa en calle Dr. Atl N° 125", Santa María la Ribera, CDMX.
377. "La Casa Gótica", Santa Catarina Ayotzingo, Chalco, Estado de México.
378. "Casa Minerva", Tula, Tamaulipas.
379. "Casa Tranquilino Navarro" en calle Guanajuato N° 40, CDMX.
380. "Casa Funeraria Zamudio" en calle Durango N°187, CDMX.
381. "Casa Requena/Legarreta" en calle Santa Veracruz N° 24, colonia Guerrero, CDMX.
382. "Portales Plaza Principal", Tepalcatepec, Michoacán.
383. "Presidencia Municipal", Huichapan, Hidalgo.
384. "Presidencia Municipal", Tumbalá, Chiapas.
385. "Palacio Municipal", Altotonga, Veracruz.
386. "Casa Escandón/Dr.Lavista" en calle Puente de San Francisco N° 31 (Avenida Juárez), CDMX.
387. "Casa Guillermo Landa Escandón" en calle Antonio Caso N°31, CDMX.

PROTESTANT TEMPLE

12. "Iglesia Nacional Presbiteriana Emmanuel", Aguascalientes, Aguascalientes.
41. "Centro Cultural Tudor", Cuauhtémoc, CDMX.
45. "Templo El Mesías, Balderas N°47", CDMX.
46. "Iglesia Metodista La Santísima Trinidad", CDMX.
47. "Iglesia Gethsemaní", CDMX.
48. "Primera Iglesia Bautista", CDMX.
56. "Primera Iglesia Bautista", Saltillo, Coahuila.
100. "Iglesia Metodista del Divino Salvador", Pachuca, Hidalgo.
149. "Primera Iglesia Bautista", Morelia, Michoacán.
158. "Iglesia La Trinidad", Monterrey, Nuevo León.
169. "Iglesia Metodista Episcopal", Puebla, Puebla.
176. "Iglesia Cristiana Central", San Luis Potosí, San Luis Potosí.
191. "Templo El Buen Pastor", Apizaco, Tlaxcala.
260. "Templo Baptista Emanuel", Guadalajara, Jalisco.
298. "Iglesia Nacional Presbiteriana El Divino Salvador", Xalapa, Veracruz.

TOWER

9. "Templo La Merced o El Rosario", Aguascalientes, Aguascalientes.
10. "Templo de San José", Aguascalientes, Aguascalientes.
11. "Templo de Nuestra Señora del Rosario", Aguascalientes, Aguascalientes.
27. "Santuario de San Lorenzo", Ciudad Juárez, Chihuahua.
57. "Iglesia del Perpetuo Socorro", Torreón, Coahuila.
75. "Parroquia Inmaculada Concepción", Zacualpan, Estado de México.
90. "Parroquia de Nuestra Señora de Guadalupe", Irapuato, Guanajuato.
91. "Iglesia de San Miguel Arcángel", San Miguel de Allende, Guanajuato.
99. "Capilla Hacienda de San Miguel Regla", Huasca de Ocampo, Hidalgo.
123. "Catedral de Guadalajara", Guadalajara, Jalisco.
146. "Templo de San Francisco de Asís", San Juan del Río, Durango.
147. "Capilla de Nuestra Señora de la Escalera", Tarímbaro, Michoacán.
148. "Templo de San Simón Celador", Angangueo, Michoacán.
152. "Catedral de la Asunción de María", Tepic, Nayarit.
178. "Catedral Basílica de Inmaculada Concepción", Mazatlán, Sinaloa.
179. "Parroquia del Sagrado Corazón de Jesús", El fuerte, Sinaloa.
199. "Santuario de Santa María de Guadalupe, La Concordia", Orizaba, Veracruz.
224. "Templo de San Juan de Dios", Zacatecas, Zacatecas.
229. "Torre de la Iglesia de El Cargadero", Jerez, Zacatecas.
230. "Torre del Templo de Nuestra Señora de Guadalupe", Guadalupe, Zacatecas.
231. "Capilla de La Purísima", Valparaíso, Zacatecas.
240. "Templo del Sagrado Corazón", Tecolotlán, Jalisco.
241. "Iglesia de Nuestra Señora de la Soledad", Ayotlán, Jalisco.
242. "Iglesia de la Inmaculada Concepción", Sayula, Jalisco.
243. "Parroquia de San Luis de Tolosa", Tuxcueca, Jalisco.
244. "Santuario de Nuestra Señora de Guadalupe", Ahualulco de Mercado, Jalisco.
*245. "Santuario de Nuestra Señora de la Defensa", Juanacatlán, Jalisco.
291. "Parroquia del Cristo de la Misericordia de Amula", San Gabriel, Jalisco.
328. "Iglesia de Nuestra Señora del Refugio", Villa Juárez, Durango.
352. "Iglesia de San Fermín", Pánuco de Coronado, Durango.
403. "Catedral Nuestra Señora de la Asunción", Papantla, Veracruz.
404. "Capilla Hacienda La Providencia", La Providencia, San José del Rincón, Estado de México.

EXTERNAL ELEMENTS IN FACADE

7. "Templo del Ave-María", Aguascalientes, Aguascalientes.
8. "Templo de La Medallita Milagrosa", Aguascalientes, Aguascalientes.
15. "Templo del Calvario", Chiapa de Corzo, Chiapas.
23. "Templo de San Juan Bautista", Chihuahua, Chihuahua.
52. "Iglesia Sagrado Corazón de Jesús", CDMX.
69. "Parroquia de la Virgen de Guadalupe", San Juan de Guadalupe, Durango.
73. "Santuario Virgen de la Piedrita, Canalejas", Jilotepec, Estado de México.
86. "Templo de la Cruz de Cantera", León, Guanajuato.
87. "Iglesia de San Rafael o de la Santa Escuela", San Miguel de Allende, Guanajuato.
92. "Parroquia de Santiago Apóstol", Enrique Neri, Guerrero.
98. "Capilla Hacienda San Diego Tlalayote", Apan, Hidalgo.
112. "Parroquia San Luis Obispo de Tolosa", San Luís Soyatlán, Jalisco.
113. "Templo del Sagrado Corazón de Jesús", Tecolotlán, Jalisco.
114. "Parroquia de San Agustín", Tototltán, Jalisco.
115. "Santuario de Sagrado Corazón", Zapotiltic, Jalisco.
122. "Santuario Jesús, María y José", Encarnación de Diaz, Jalisco.
139. "Parroquia de Nuestra Señora de Guadalupe", Chavinda, Michoacán.
140. "Parroquia de San Agustín", Jacona de Plancarte, Michoacán.
141. "Iglesia de Nuestra Señora del Rosario", Coneo, Michoacán.
142. "Templo del Señor del Perdón", Villa Morelos, Michoacán.
159. "Capilla de Nuestra Señora de Lourdes", Cerralvo, Nuevo León.
173. "Templo de San Pedro Apóstol", Huimilpan, Querétaro.
194. "Templo de Nuestra Señora de Guadalupe", Coatepec, Veracruz.
195. "Capilla Nuestra Señora de la Luz", Coatepec, Veracruz.
196. "Catedral de Xalapa", Xalapa, Veracruz.
197. "Iglesia de Santiaguito", Xalapa, Veracruz.
208. "Casa de la Cristiandad", Mérida, Yucatán.
209. "Parroquia San Rafael Arcángel", Mérida, Yucatán.
218. "Iglesia de la Virgen del Refugio", Valparaíso, Zacatecas.
225. "Templo de San Juan de Dios", Zacatecas, Zacatecas.
226. "Templo de Nuestra Señora de la Purificación", Fresnillo, Zacatecas.
227. "Santuario de la Virgen de la Soledad", Zacatecas, Zacatecas.
236. "Iglesia Virgen de Fátima", Almoloya de Juárez, Estado de México.
*237. "Santuario Nuestra Señora de la Defensa", Juanacatlán, Jalisco.
277. "Santuario de Nuestra Señora del Refugio", Ojuelos de Jalisco, Jalisco.
281. "Iglesia de Guadalupe", Ferrería de Tula, Jalisco.
295. "Catedral de Nuestra Señora de la Asunción", Tuxpan, Veracruz.
302. "Templo de la Asunción de la Virgen. Barrio de los Mexicanos", San Cristóbal de las Casas, Chiapas.
303. "Templo de El Calvario", Tuxtla Gutiérrez, Chiapas.
304. "Iglesia del Perpetuo Socorro", Torreón, Coahuila.
305. "Iglesia de San Juan Bautista de Analco", Durango, Durango.
309. "Capilla Nuestra Señora de Lourdes en Basílica Nuestra Señora De Guanajuato", Guanajuato, Guanajuato.
310. "Templo de los Hospitales", Guanajuato, Guanajuato.
314. "Capilla de la Ex hacienda de San Juan Hueyapan", Huasca de Ocampo, Hidalgo.
318. "Iglesia Santa María De Guadalupe", Frontera, Tabasco.
347. "Santuario Nuestra Señora de Guadalupe", San juan del Rio, Durango.
348. "Templo Santiago Apostol", Mapimí, Durango.
353. "Hacienda Jajalpa", Ocoyoacac, Estado de México.
388. "Parroquia de Nuestra Señora de Guadalupe", Cananea, Sonora.
389. "Templo de Nuestra Señora de Loreto", Españita, Tlaxcala.
390. "Catedral de Nuestra Señora del Refugio", Matamoros, Tamaulipas.
391. "Parroquia de San José", Tlaxcala, Tlaxcala.

INTERIOR ELEMENTS

17. "Iglesia San Jacinto" (Main Altarpiece), San Cristóbal de las Casas, Chiapas.
18. "Iglesia de San Lucia" (Main Altarpiece), San Cristóbal de las Casas, Chiapas.
25. "Parroquia San Pablo Apóstol" (Santa Mónica's Altar), Meoqui, Chihuahua.
26. "Capilla de la Sagrada Familia" (Altar), Cuauhtémoc, Chihuahua.
33. "Templo de Santa Teresita del Niño Jesús", Cuauhtémoc, CDMX.
67. "Catedral Nuestra Señora De Guadalupe" (Altar), Gómez Palacio, Durango.
68. "Templo de Nuestra Señora De los Ángeles" (High Altar), Durango, Durango.
70. "Parroquia de la Virgen de Guadalupe" (High Altar), San Juan de Guadalupe, Durango.
71. "Templo de San Agustín" (Altar), Durango, Durango.
74. "Capilla Ex Hacienda de Arroyozarco" (Main Altar), Aculco, Estado de México.
88. "Templo de Belén" (High Altar and Pulpit), Guanajuato, Guanajuato.
89. "Parroquia de Nuestra Señora de Guadalupe" (Altar), Irapuato, Guanajuato.
101. "Capilla de la Ex Hacienda de San Juan Hueyapan" (Confessional), Huasca de Ocampo, Hidalgo.
102. "Capilla de la Ex Hacienda de San Miguel Regla" (Altarpieces), Huasca de Ocampo, Hidalgo.
117. "Parroquia Santa María de Guadalupe" (High Altar), El Grullo, Jalisco.
118. "Templo de Santa Teresa" (High Altar), Guadalajara, Jalisco.
119. "Parroquia de Nuestra Señora De la Soledad" (High Altar), San Pedro Tlaquepaque, Jalisco.
120. "Templo de San Juan Bautista" (Altar), Mezquitic, Jalisco.
121. "Santuario Jesús, María y José" (Altarpieces and Altars), Encarnación de Diaz, Jalisco.
126. "Templo de San Felipe Apóstol" (High Altar), Tonalá, Jalisco.
143. "Templo de San Francisco" (Altarpieces, Altar), Tarecuato, Michoacán.
144. "Capilla de Jesús", Peribán, Michoacán.
145. "Templo de San Francisco, Capilla Virgen de Guadalupe" (Altar), Ixtlán de los Hervores, Michoacán.
161. "Capilla de Nuestra Señora De Belén, Santuario de Guadalupe" (Main Altar and Side Chapels), Oaxaca, Oaxaca.
162. "Templo de la Compañía de Jesús" (Altars), Oaxaca, Oaxaca.
163. "Iglesia de Nuestra Señora del Patrocinio" (Confessional), Oaxaca, Oaxaca.
168. "Catedral de Puebla" (Chapel), Puebla, Puebla.
177. "Catedral de Nuestra Señora Del Rosario" (Pulpit), Culiacán, Sinaloa.
180. "Catedral Basílica de Inmaculada Concepción" (High Altar), Mazatlán, Sinaloa.
187. "Basílica de Nuestra Señora del Refugio", Ciudad Victoria, Tamaulipas.
198. "Iglesia del Sagrado Corazón" (Altar and Niches), Coatepec, Veracruz.
211. "Oratorio de la Hacienda Yaxcopoil, a San Gerónimo" (Altar, Chapel), Yaxcopoil, Yucatán.
228. "Parroquia del Señor de Jalpa" (High Altar), Jalpa, Zacatecas.
246. "San Francisco de Asís" (High Altar), Tizapán el Alto, Jalisco.
247. "Templo de Nuestra Señora del Rosario" (High Altar), Zapotlanejo, Jalisco.
248. "Parroquia de San Juan Bautista" (High Altar), Tuxpan, Jalisco.
249. "Iglesia de San Juan de Ocotán" (High Altar), Zapopan, Jalisco.
250. "Capilla del Sagrado Corazón de Jesús" (High Altar), Zapotiltic, Jalisco.
251. "Capilla de la Hacienda de Santa Ana" (High Altar), Zapopan, Jalisco.
252. "Capilla Mayor del Hospicio" (High Altar), Cabañas, Jalisco.
253. "Santuario de Nuestra Señora de Guadalupe" (High Altar), Ahualulco de Mercado, Jalisco.
254. "Parroquia Virgen de la Asunción" (Altars), Jalostotitlán, Jalisco.
255. "Parroquia San Miguel Arcángel" (Altar, Chapel), Teocuitatlán de Corona, Jalisco.
256. "Parroquia de San Francisco de Asís" (High Altar), Zacoalco de Torres, Jalisco.
257. "Parroquia de San Marcos", San Marcos, Jalisco.
297. "Templo Expiatorio Sagrado Corazón de Jesús o El Beaterio", Xalapa, Veracruz.
306. "Capilla del Arzobispado" (Altarpiece, High Altar), Durango, Durango.
317. "Catedral Metropolitana de San Luis Rey" (Altarpiece, Altar), San Luís Potosí, San Luís Potosí.
319. "Iglesia de San Juan Bautista" (High Altar), Mérida, Yucatán.
320. "Iglesia de Nuestra Señora de los Remedios", Izamal, Yucatán.
349. "Santuario de la Virgen de Guadalupe" (High Altar), Durango, Durango.
350. "Templo Nuestra Señora de Guadalupe" (Cypress), El Mezquital, Durango.
354. "Capilla Fábrica San Ildefonso" (Windows, Confessional and Pulpit), Villa Nicolás Romero, Estado de México.
355. "Capilla del Oratorio de los Dolores" (High Altar), Salvatierra, Guanajuato.
359. "Capilla Virgen de Guadalupe" (Altarpiece Altar), Acaxochitlán, Hidalgo.
364. "Iglesia de Santa María de los Siervos" (Altar, Chapels), Orizaba, Veracruz.
392. "Parroquia de San Clara de Asís", Ocoyucan, Puebla.
393. "Templo Inmaculada Concepción", Yahualica Jalisco.
394. "Templo de San Francisco", Ciudad Serdan, Puebla.
395. "Templo de Jesús Nazareno", Ciudad Serdán, Puebla.
396. "Templo San Juan de Dios", León, Guanajuato.
397. "Templo San Miguel La Real", León, Guanajuato.
398. "Santa María de la Asunción", Tetela de Ocampo, Puebla.
399. "San Francisco de Asís", Ixtacamaxtitlán, Puebla.
400. "Templo de San Andrés Apóstol", Ciudad Serdán, Puebla.
401. "Parroquia de Santa Ana", Santa Ana Chiautempan, Tlaxcala.
402. "Capilla del Señor Jesús", Santa Ana Chiautempan, Tlaxcala.

FUNERAL ITEMS

16. "Panteón San Cristóbal de las Casas", San Cristóbal de las Casas, Chiapas.
24. "Mausoleo de Francisco Villa", Chihuahua, Chihuahua.
30. "Capilla del Panteón Francés de La Piedad", Cuauhtémoc, CDMX.
44. "Panteón del Tepeyac", CDMX.
51. "Capilla Responso Panteón Guadalupe Mizcoac", CDMX.
55. "Panteón de Saltillo", Saltillo, Coahuila.
61. "Tumba de Manuel Álvarez", Colima, Colima.
66. "Panteón de Oriente o de Durango", Durango, Durango.
116. "Panteón de Belén", Guadalajara, Jalisco.
155. "Capilla Ardiente, Panteón del Carmen", Monterrey, Nuevo León.
156. "Capilla Ardiente y Puerta de Panteón de Dolores", Monterrey, Nuevo León.
157. "Puerta de Panteón del Carmen", Monterrey, Nuevo León.
167. "Panteón Municipal de Puebla", Puebla, Puebla.
175. "Panteón El Saucito", San Luis Potosí, San Luis Potosí.
210. "Mausoleo Vega Ibarra y Castillo en el Cementeric General de Mérida", Mérida, Yucatán.
275. "Panteón de Atemajac del Valle", Zapopán, Jalisco.
276. "Cementerio de Mezquitán", Guadalajara, Jalisco.
290. "Cementerio Miguel Hidalgo", Ciudad Guzmán, Jalisco.
294. "Cementerio de Orizaba", Orizaba, Veracruz.
296. "Panteón 5 de Febrero", Xalapa, Veracruz.
300. "Panteón General La Soledad", Toluca, Estado de México.
316. "Panteón San Miguel", Oaxaca, Oaxaca.
322. "Panteón de San Fernando", CDMX.
329. "Mausoleo Familia Giacinti. Panteón de la Cruz", Aguascalientes, Aguascalientes.
330. "Panteón de los Ángeles", Aguascalientes, Aguascalientes.
331. "Monumento Funeraro, Panteón de la Cruz", Aguascalientes, Aguascalientes.
341. "Cementerio de Dolores", Chihuahua, Chihuahua.
342. "Cementerio de Dolores", Parral, Chihuahua.
343. "Panteón Español", CDMX.
344. "Panteón de Dolores", CDMX.
356. "Panteón Inglés", Real de Monte, Hidalgo.
357. "Panteón Municipal", Pachuca, Hidalgo.
360. "Cementerio Municipal Ixtlán", Ixtlán, Nayarit.
361. "Panteón Cementerio Hidalgo", Tepic, Nayarit.
362. "Cementerio Francés de Puebla", Puebla, Puebla.
363. "Cementerio Ángela Peralta", Mazatlán, Sinaloa.
366. "Cementerio de Santa Teresa", Fresnillo, Zacatecas.
367. "Cementerio La Purísima", Zacatecas, Zacatecas.

MODERN ARCHITECTURE (NEOGOTHIC INSPIRATION)

76. "Capilla San Francisco de Asís", Atlautla, Estado de México.
93. "Catedral de la Asunción de María", Chilapa Guerrero.
124. "Iglesia de Nuestra Señora del Refugio" Puerto Vallarta, Jalisco.
151. "El Chapitel Calvario", Cuernavaca, Morelos.
170. "Templo de San Juan Bautista", Xicotepec de Juárez, Puebla.
171. "Santuario de la Virgen del Peñón", Cuetzalan, Puebla.
234. "Capilla de Nuestra Señora De Fátima", Xalapa, Veracruz.
371. "Templo de Nuestra Señora del Refugio del Cerro Gordo", León, Guanajuato.
372. "Templo Virgen de Guadalupe", Juan Martín, Celaya, Guanajuato.
373. "Parroquia Santa Maria de Guadalupe", Escobedo, Querétaro.
374. "Iglesia de San Marcos", Balancán, Tabasco.

*these examples belong to two or more categories

10
Gótico à brasileira
Gothicizing Church Building between Amazonia and Rio Grande do Sul

Barbara Borngässer

Since the beginning of the twentieth century, far more church buildings in medieval styles have been built in Brazil than modern ones, including monumental cathedrals in the country's metropolises. The *Lista de Catedrais do Brasil* on Wikipedia mentions fourteen neo-Gothic and eight neo-Romanesque new cathedral buildings for the twentieth century alone; another five are classified as "modern" and twelve as "contemporary."[1] The rest fall under the category of neoclassical and eclectic.

This result may come as a surprise, because Brazil's twentieth-century architecture is considered to be exemplary for its modernism, also in ecclesiastical architecture: fine examples are Oscar Niemeyer's chapel of Pampulha, his cathedral of Brasília, the light-flooded Santuário Dom Bosco in the same city, and even Edgar Fonseca's expressive cathedral in Rio de Janeiro.

How to explain these apparent and strong contrasts between the image and the reality of Brazilian ecclesiastical architecture? What might be the motives behind the continuous choice of historicist forms? What significance is attached to the Gothic idiom in particular? Which motifs are adopted and/or assimilated? How do neo-Gothic and modernism get along? Finally, does the Brazilian reception of the Gothic differ from that of other nations?

All these questions, as already noted in the introduction, are new and groundbreaking. Only Martín M. Checa-Artasu and Olimpia Niglio have dealt with those topics in their publications, although they have mainly treated the Spanish-speaking areas of Latin America as well as secular buildings.[2]

An overview, not to speak about an inventory, of neo-Gothic churches of the twentieth and twenty-first centuries doesn't exist by far, neither for Brazil nor elsewhere—most probably as a result of a long-living orthodoxy and normative publication activity on modern architecture.[3] There are only a few individual studies available for Brazil, such as on the buildings of Simon Gramlich in the southern part of the country.[4]

Information is therefore mainly provided by so-called gray literature, which needs to be critically evaluated and classified. Exhaustive research is not to be expected in the following pages, simply because of the mass of such buildings and the lack of published information about them. Thus, only some tiny stones can be provided in the following pages to the more comprehensive great mosaic of the Gothic idiom in modern Brazil architecture.

Prelude: Petrópolis (1884–1969)

The decisive turn away from the long predominant colonial-style architecture and toward the implementation of neo-Gothic is marked by the construction of São Pedro de Alcântara in Petrópolis, Rio de Janeiro [Fig. 10.02].[5] Since 1871, Emperor Pedro II and his daughter Isabel had been planning the new parish church in the *Cidade Imperial* near Rio de Janeiro, the summer residence of the Brazilian imperial family. Planning history is revealing: in 1876, Italian architect Federico Roncetti provided a first project for a neo-Renaissance building echoing St. Peter's in Rome; the foundation stone was laid in

10.01 Santa Cruz do Sul, Rio Grande do Sul, Cathedral of São João Batista, Simon Gramlich, 1928–1977. [Wikimedia Commons; photo Caetano051068, 2015]

1 <https://pt.wikipedia.org/wiki/Lista_de_catedrais_do_Brasil>.

2 Checa-Artasu, "La Iglesia y la expansión del neogótico en Latinoamérica"; Checa-Artasu and Niglio, eds., *El Neogótico en la arquitectura americana*.

3 See the introduction to this volume. Exemplary for the reception of neo-Gothic in the architectural criticism of modernism: Bruand, *A Arquitetura contemporânea no Brasil*, 42: "Deve-se dizer que o resultado deixou muito a desejar: não só é difícil citar um único êxito do ponto de vista estético, como também parece que os arquitetos e contructores rivalizavam-se numa incrível competição de feiúra." ("It must be said that these [medieval and picturesque styles] leave much to be desired: Not only is it difficult to name a single aesthetically successful example, but it seems that their architects and constructors are engaged in an incredible competition for ugliness").

4 Fagundes e Braga, *A trajetória do arquiteto alemão Simão Gramlich em campos cruzados no sul do Brasil*; Fagundes e Braga, "Simon Gramlich and the neo-gothic churches in southern Brazil."

5 The restoration report: *Catedral São Pedro de Alcântara* (pdf). Furthermore, see Netto, *Breve Histórico da Catedral de Petrópolis*.

10.02 Petrópolis, Rio de Janeiro, Cathedral of São Pedro de Alcântara, Francisco Caminhoá, begun 1884. [Wikimedia Commons; photo Jorge Antonio de Oliveira Vincente, 2014]

the same year. However, realization was delayed and in October 1882, a new design, this time in neo-Gothic style, was commissioned to Bahian architect Francisco Caminhoá.[6] Caminhoá proposed a three-nave building with a central façade tower, transept, choir with ambulatory, and main axial chapel. The project, which incorporates a wide variety of French motifs, was approved in February 1883 at the express request of Princess Isabel. It was realized from 1884 onward, albeit with decades of interruption, and it finally completed during the Republican era.[7]

Two common motifs may be mentioned for the change of plans: the alleged inappropriateness of Renaissance for a Brazilian church, and the strong presence of the Germans and Portuguese, who were seemingly supposed to be more familiar with neo-Gothic ecclesiastical buildings than with a work in the antique-classical guise. However, it is obvious that in the 1870 and 1880s, neo-Gothic style became established throughout South America.[8] In the field of ecclesiastical architecture, we should mention San Alfonso in Cuenca, Ecuador (1874); Nuestra Señora de Lourdes in Bogotá (1875); the Santa Capilla in Caracas (1883); and the Argentine cathedrals of Luján (1887–1932) [Figs. 8.08 & 8.09] and La Plata (begun in 1884) [Fig. 8.07].[9] Despite its late completion in 1999, La Plata is the initial work of a qualitatively new reception of Gothic architecture in Latin America, which is based on many different models and is understood as the quintessence of European predecessor buildings. It is no coincidence that its construction went hand in hand with the new foundation of the city, which was to be designed as a cosmopolitan planned city according to the most modern urbanistic criteria.[10]

In La Plata, as in Petrópolis, the choice of a supranational, Gothic language of forms can therefore be interpreted as a conscious rejection of the colonial style, in these cases of the Spanish-Portuguese past and its Baroque or classical style. The romantic topos, according to which the Gothic is to be seen as the only formal language adequate to the

Christianity, was joined here with another interpretation: that of an architectural decoding of the colonial power. The apparent recourse to European architecture of the Middle Ages would thus not be a reference to old Europe, but rather appeared to be a kind of liberation—the neo-Gothic style seems to have established itself as a supranational Christian architectural language.

Belo Horizonte

With the proclamation of the *República dos Estados Unidos do Brasil* on February 24, 1891, a new area of urbanistic development started. The city of Belo Horizonte is representative of this. Designated in 1897 as the new capital of Minas Gerais, the state rich in gold and minerals, it was completely redesigned as a planned city—only a little later than La Plata in Argentina. The foundation was accompanied by the radical demolition of the existing colonial town and the construction of two monumental neo-Gothic churches, the cathedral Nossa Senhora da Boa Viagem [Fig. 10.03][11] (first planning 1894, actually built in 1911–1932) and Nossa Senhora de Lourdes (1916–1922) [Fig. 10.04].[12] They are located not far from each other in the center of the city and are integrated into the chessboard grid of the plan of Aarão Reis.[13] The two churches, very different in detail, take up Gothic motifs in a symbolic way; they captivate by the multitude of their towers and pinnacles, their tracery windows, and in the case of the Lourdes church, by the elaborate "Gothic" support system of the interior. Nevertheless, they are far from being copies of European buildings; rather, they transcend their architectural models.

Admittedly, neo-Gothic churches are also often perceived as unsuitable in the modern urban landscape. For example, the avant-garde musicologist Mário de Andrade rebukes the Gothic style as "the strangest of all styles," but at the same time he admits that cathedrals in particular, as great public buildings, must be Gothic. In contrast, he concedes parish churches must use modest, colonial forms.[14]

6 Francisco Caminhoá knew the French Gothic style from his own experience, because he was able to travel Europe from 1855 as a scholarship holder of the provincial government and to study in Paris at the École des Beaux-Arts, Pereira, "O Ensino da arquitetura e a trajetória dos alunos brasileiros na École des Beaux-Arts em Paris no século XIX."

7 To the history: <https://www.catedraldepetropolis.org.br/matriz-velha/>.

8 See the contribution of Martín Checa-Artasu in this book on neo-Gothic in Latin-America with several illustrations.

9 As one of the few neo-Gothic buildings of South America, the cathedral of La Plata is treated in a monograph, *La Catedral de la Plata*, mainly regarding the dependence of its architecture on Europe models. Cf. the two essays by Riestra, "El gótico posterior a la Edad Media"; Riestra, "Gótico y neogótico en la arquitectura de la Catedral de la Plata." See also Checa-Artasu in this volume and Sundt, "From Late Gothic to Gothic Revival in Latin America," 124.

10 See again Checa-Artasu in this volume.

11 Almeida, *Fé na modernidade e tradição na fé.*

12 Dias, "O século XIX e o neogótico na Arquitetura brasileira."

13 Salgueiro, *Engenheiro Aarão Reis.*

14 Pinheiro, "Neogothic architecture in Rio de Janeiro and in São Paulo," 101–115, specially 111; see also the introduction to this volume.

10.03 Belo Horizonte, Minas Gerais, Cathedral Nossa Senhora da Boa Viagem (Our Lady of Good Voyage), 1911–1932.
[Postcard, archive Bruno Klein]

10.04 Belo Horizonte, Mina Gerais, Nossa Senhora de Lourdes, 1916–1922.
[Foursquare City Guide, Filipe M., 2011]

10.05 & 10.06 São Paulo, Sé (Metropolitan Cathedral), Maximilian Emil Hehl, 1993–1954; towers completed 2002. [dreamstime xxl_48277416 and xxl_146608282; photo Alf Ribeiro]

10.07 São Paulo, Sé (Metropolitan Cathedral), toucans, detail of sculpture. [© Instituto Sao Paulo Antiga]

A Brazilianization of the Gothic: The Cathedral of São Paulo (1913–1954)

Already during the construction of the Petrópolis cathedral voices raised complaints that the neo-Gothic style neither did justice to Brazilian nature nor to civilization.[15] The Sé of São Paulo seems to contradict these accusations on various levels [Figs. 10.05 & 10.06].[16] Its design, according to the plans of the German architect Maximilian Emil Hehl, was approved in 1888. But the foundation stone for the monumental, 111-meter-long domed basilica was not laid until 1913. As in most cases considered here, the construction period stretched over several decades: the church was only consecrated in 1954, but the two 92-meter-high towers could not be completed provisionally before 1969 and finally in 2002. According to Hehl's original plans, a five-aisled cathedral with a nonprojecting transept and double ambulatory at the choir was built; its neo-Gothic architecture was inspired by European cathedral Gothic without referring to special models. A "medieval" lodge, working for decades, was set up to carry out the construction of the brickwork and the surfacing stonework.

Enlightening evidence for the recoding of historical models can be found above all in the field of architectural sculpture. Thus, both on the façade and in the interior, representations of Brazilian flora and fauna alongside biblical motifs are to be found: cocoa and coffee plants, passion fruit, *caju* (cashew), as well as armadillos, herons, lizards, and toucans [Fig. 10.07]. This "actualization" of the animal repertoire was quite common: at the Basílica del Voto Nacional in Quito,[17] gargoyles in the form of native birds (pelicans, etc.) were installed at about the same time. In São Paulo, other typical elements of Gothic churches were interpreted with regard to the Brazilian people, for example, the granite of the walls as a symbol for the strong and fearless *bandeirantes* who once explored the interior of the country.[18] The attempt to popularize and nationalize European neo-Gothic is obvious.

New and inventive is the reinforced concrete dome, reminiscent of Brunelleschi's Florentine cathedral dome, which Alexandre Albuquerque, Hehl's successor, defended against criticism in 1920:

> Brunelesco, the important author of the dome of Santa Maria del Fiore, was also

15 *Jornal do Comércio*, May 1, 1883, see also the restoration report *Catedral São Pedro de Alcântara*, 22–24.

> accused of error, extravagance and absurdity. And although he was attacked, he saw his great idea become reality. Brunelesco designed and built it and thus developed the architectural style further. For him, the great dome shining high above the houses of old Florence was a "vision of art." In São Paulo Cathedral, too, the dome represents the further development of the style, using processes of modern technology. [...] To criticize the existence of the dome in a Gothic cathedral of the age of steel and reinforced concrete would be to impose the simple role of copyist on the impressive architect who created it; it would be to confirm the reproduction of medieval models with applause.[19]

In referring to the Florentine cathedral cupola, Albuquerque alludes with a certain pride to the historic heyday of municipal development that seemed to be approaching São Paulo in the 1920s—not least because of the labor force of hundreds of thousands of Italians working on the coffee plantations and in the factories of the state. But the dome, which was only completed in the 1940s, would soon have to share its radiance with the skyscrapers of the city center.

It is probably no coincidence that this process came at a time when Brazil was redefining itself. In 1922, the Semana de Arte Moderna held in São Paulo triggered a tremendous push toward modernity, while at the same time Brazilian intellectuals such as Mário de Andrade and Oswald de Andrade (not related, despite shared name) demanded the definition of a Brazilian national character, however different it might be.[20] For Oswald, Brazil's strengths lay in its cultural diversity, from indigenous culture to the cosmopolitan avant-garde—an identity that he confidently saw as an export hit, similar to the Brazilian wood, pau brasil.[21] In the "Manifesto Antropófago" published in 1928, Oswald became even clearer: "we must treat European culture anthropophagicly, because we must eat it and digest all that is good in it; then we should bring out all this again in a more superior form, with a great deal of humour and critical spirit."[22]

To devour the foreign, to digest it well, and to create something new out of it with a wink and a reflection can certainly be understood as a leitmotif of Brazilian ecclesiastical architecture.

The Cathedral of Olinda between Neo-Gothic and Neo-Baroque

The cathedral of Olinda, Pernambuco [Figs. 10.08a–e] is an example for multiple experiences in changes of style.[23] Founded in the late sixteenth century, burned down by the Dutch in 1631, and rebuilt in Baroque colonial style from 1656 on, it received a neo-Gothic covering between 1911 and 1920. That was initially celebrated enthusiastically; however, Archbishop D. Miguel de Valverde decided as early as 1930 to renew it again in rich neo-Baroque forms, taking up the style of the churches in nearby Recife. This solution survived for more than forty years, until the Brazilian monument preservation authorities, represented by the local FUNDARPE (Fundação do Patrimônio Histórico e Artístico de Pernambuco) and the national authority SPHAN (Serviço do Patrimônio Histórico e Artístico Nacional), decided to restore the church to its supposed eighteenth-century state (1974–1983). Thus, the Sé presents itself today in a relatively simple baroque garb, with an added second tower and unadorned side walls enclosing the older annexes; all traces of the 1930s and earlier alterations were erased.

16 Albuquerque, *A Catedral de São Paulo*; Santos, "A Catedral metropolitana de São Paulo por Maximilian Emil Hehl (1891–1916)," 4–15; Ramirez and Neto, *De igreja de taipa a catedral*; Albuquerque, "The São Paulo cathedral and its Architect Builder"; Kuhn, *Cidade, arquitetura e religião*; Sundt, "From Late Gothic to Gothic Revival in Latin America," 127–128.

17 Checa-Artasu, "La Iglesia y la expansión del neogótico en Latinoamérica." See also his contribution in this book.

18 Leite, *A Catedral de São Paulo*, 13, quoted after Ramirez and Neto, eds., 195.

19 Albuquerque, *A Catedral de São Paulo*, 35: "Erro, extravagância e absurdo, também foi dito de Brunelesco, o exímio autor da cúpula na Igreja de Santa Maria das Flores. E apesar de perseguido, viu realizada a sua grande ideia. Projetando-a e construindo-a, Brunelesco fez apenas avoluir o estilo e para ele era uma "visão de arte," a grande cúpula brilhando altaneira sobre o casario da velha Florença. Na Catedral de SP, a cúpula é também o evoluir do estilo, lançando mão de processos da técnica moderna. [...] Criticar a existência da cúpula em uma catedral gótica da época de aço e do cimento armado, seria exigir do notável arquiteto que a delineou o simples papel de copista; seria aplaudir reprodução de modelos medievais" (English translation by the author).

20 Documents, videos, and literature on the Semana de Arte Moderna: <http://enciclopedia.itaucultural.org.br/evento84382/semana-de-arte-moderna-1922-sao-paulo-sp>.

21 Andrade, *Manifesto da poesia Pau-Brasil*.

22 Andrade, *Manifesto Antropófago*: "... devemos ser antropofágicos com a cultura europeia, pois devemos comê-la e digerir tudo aquilo que ela tem de bom, devolvendo isso na forma de uma produção superior, com muito senso de humor e crítica ..." (English translation by the author).

23 Silva, "Arquitetura eclética em Pernambuco"; in detail about the last restoration: Cabral, "Entre destruições, achados e invenção" <http://www.scielo.br/scielo.php?script=sci_arttext&pid=S0101-47142016000100181>.

10.08a Olinda, Pernambuco, Cathedral of São Salvador do Mundo, after 1631. Painting (oil on canvas) by Frans Post, 1662.
[Amsterdam, Rijksmuseum]

10.08b Olinda, Pernambuco, Cathedral of São Salvador do Mundo, 19th century.
[sanctuaria.art]

10.08c Olinda, Pernambuco, Cathedral of São Salvador do Mundo, after 1920 (Gothicized).
[Postcard, archive Bruno Klein]

10.08d Olinda, Pernambuco, Cathedral of São Salvador do Mundo, after 1930 (neo-Baroque).
[© IBGE]

10.08e Olinda, Pernambuco, Cathedral of São Salvador do Mundo, today.
[Wikimedia Commons; photo Delma Paz, 2008]

Eclectic Cathedrals in the Middle of the Twentieth Century

Between the 1920s and 1960s, several monumental churches were constructed from Fortaleza, Ceará in the north to Santa Catarina do Sul, Rio Grande do Sul in the south, creatively combining Romanesque and Gothic elements.[24] While the Brazilian state presented itself as a country of modernity with buildings by Oscar Niemeyer, Lúcio Costa, and others, lots of ecclesiastical patrons opted however for churches in a medieval style. Reasons were manifold. In parallel to the avant-garde churches of Pampulha, Brasília, and Rio de Janeiro, basilicas with traditional elements such as twin towers, flying buttresses, Gothic vaults, roses, tracery, and lavish stained glass were slowly but constantly rising. One of them was the Catedral Metropolitana of Fortaleza, among the largest cathedrals in Brazil [Fig. 10.09].[25] With its two 75-meter-high towers, it still dominates the skyline of the city. The three-nave building with transept, polygonal crossing tower, and choir with ambulatory appears consistently Gothic on the outside. Its double-towered façade, with portals and a central rose, seems French. The interior is stylistically dominated by a sober, quite abstract Romanesque-Gothic. The French engineer Georges Mounier, who worked in Recife, provided the plan for the reinforced concrete construction; the foundation stone was laid in 1939, and the building was completed in 1978. The German-born archbishop and cardinal Aloysio Lorscheider played a significant role in its financing.

While little is known about the details of planning and construction of the cathedral of Fortaleza, there is instead a certain group of churches in southern Brazil relatively well documented, allowing a look behind the scenes. These are the enormous neo-Gothic churches by Simon Gramlich[26] (b. 1887 Herbolzheim, Germany, d. 1968), which were built in the states of Rio Grande do Sul and Santa Catarina between 1928 and 1968. Their architecture evokes memories of medieval cathedrals as does their outstanding position in the cityscape. Thus, the construction of the Cathedral of Santa Cruz do Sul, which started in 1928, was one of the biggest churches of its time of South America: it is eighty meters long and the final tower height is eighty-two meters [Figs. 10.01 & 10.10]. But Gramlich's final adoption of neo-Gothic design wasn't the first choice at all: the competition for the new cathedral, which was announced in 1927, was won by Victorino Zani with a neo-Renaissance style project. The execution of Gramlich's design was only accepted after severe protests from the parish, which objected that the hitherto planned building was not "German" enough.[27] The finally realized church is a summa of High and late Gothic architecture, which he translated in a generic way into a sober modern language of forms. Special models can hardly be named, but as in Fortaleza, the enormous

10.09 Fortaleza, Ceará, Cathedral of São José, Georges Mounier, 1939–1978. [Wikimedia Commons; photo Claudio Oliveira Lim, 2007]

24 See *Lista de Catedrais do Brasil*, <https://pt.wikipedia.org/wiki/Lista_de_catedrais_do_Brasil>.
25 Lima, *A Catedral*.
26 For Gramlich, see the thesis of Fagundes e Braga, *A trajetória do arquiteto alemão Simão Gramlich em campos cruzados no sul do Brasil* and the contributions of Fagundes e Braga and Borngässer in: Borngässer and Klein, eds., *Neugotik global – kolonial – postkolonial*, 244–249 and 251–262.
27 <http://iuriaz.blogspot.com/2008/10/um-novo-templo-para-uma-santa-cruz-que_18.html>.

10.10 Santa Cruz do Sul, Rio Grande do Sul, Cathedral of São João Batista, interior, Simon Gramlich, 1928–1977. [Wikimedia Commons; photo Eugenio Hansen, 2009]

10.11 Venâncio Aires, Rio Grande do Sul, São Sebastião Mártir, Simon Gramlich, 1927–1952. [sanctuaria.art]

10.12 Itajaí, Santa Catarina, Paróquia Santíssimo Sacramento, Simon Gramlich, 1940–1955. [Wikimedia Commons; photo Larissa Fraga, 2012]

28 <https://patrimonioespiritual.org/2017/08/02/matriz-de-sao-sebastiao-venancio-aires-rs/>.
29 Vieira, *A Igreja Matriz do Santíssimo Sacramento e a Constituição da Cidade de Itajaí.*

double-towered façade, the deep funnel-shaped portals, the rose window, the filigree architectural decoration, and much more suggest an explicit reference to the European Middle Ages. The three-nave hall-type church, with its hinted transept, is decorated with elaborate star vaults inside. Almost at the same time, Gramlich built the church São Sebastião Mártir in Venâncio Aires; the decision to build took place in 1927, construction began in 1929, and the church was not completed until 1952, when its towers were finished [Fig. 10.11].[28] Only slightly smaller and lower than São João Batista, it has a similar appearance: the interior is dominated by graceful fan vaults.

Gramlich's greatest work in the truest sense of the word is the Igreja Matriz in Itajaí, for which he supplied the first plans in 1940. They show a mighty church building in Romanesque-Gothic cathedral style with façade and transept towers and a huge rose window above the portal zone à la Notre-Dame in Paris [Fig. 10.12]. The planning history is particularly revealing here:[29] the archbishop of the diocese, Dom Joaquim Domingues de Oliveira, didn't agree with the designs. The archbishop thought they were too pompous, too expensive, and too difficult to build in due course; instead, he had in mind a much simpler and more quickly realizable building. Gramlich was therefore initially released from the project, and Dom Joaquim preferred a design by the engineer Felipe Buendgens. But the building commission didn't agree and continued to favor Gramlich's project, because only a unique, monumental church would be appropriate for the emerging city. Supported in this way, Gramlich provided an even larger design, for which the foundation stone was laid immediately.

10.13 Blumenau, Santa Catarina, São Paulo Apóstolo, interior, Dominikus and Gottfried Böhm, 1953–1958. [© dreamstime xxl_75824971]

10.14 Brusque, Santa Catarina, São Luiz Gonzaga, Dominikus and Gottfried Böhm, 1953–1962. [Wikimedia Commons; photo Rodrigo Weber, 2008]

Gothicized Modernity: Churches by Gottfried Böhm[30]

The choice of a retrospective Gothic stylistic idiom was not universally accepted, as is shown for instance by the commissions to the German architects Dominikus and Gottfried Böhm, father and son. In 1937, the former was asked to send designs for the *Heimatsiedlung* of Timbó, Santa Catarina to "counter the lack of style among German immigrants."[31] Gottfried Böhm, for his part, was called to Blumenau, Santa Catarina in 1953, where he supplied and finally executed a modern competing design for one of Gramlich's eclectic projects. Here, as in neighboring Brusque, individual voices advocating for a rationalist

30 On Dominikus and Gottfried Böhm in Brazil, see: Borngässer, "Neugotik und Moderne im Süden Brasiliens."
31 Expression of the chaplain Johannes Beil. See Voigt and Flagge, *Dominikus Böhm 1880–1955*, 155, cat. no 234.

32 At a glance: Hess, *Oscar Niemeyer*.
33 Significantly, there is little information about the Santúario Dom Bosco, but there are many photographs; on the history of Dom Bosco, see: Gama, *Brasília, a terra prometida*.
34 Segre et al., *Um paradoxo patrimonial*; for the history, see: <https://catedral.com.br/>.
35 However, Lúcio Costa situates the Cathedral of Brasília on an open space to the side of the main axis of the Plano Piloto: "numa praça disposta lateralmente, não só por questão de protocolo, uma vez que a Igreja é separada do Estado, como por uma questão de escala," *Relatório do Plano Piloto*, 1957, item 9, s. Lúcio Costa, 289.
36 Studying Brazil: *Santos, Métrica, proporção e luz*.
37 <https://www.gazetadopovo.com.br/haus/arquitetura/brasil-tera-primeira-catedral-indigena-na-amazonia-financiada-pelo-vaticano/>.

ecclesiastical architecture prevailed, not least because of its quicker and cheaper implementation. It is noticeable that in both cases, in São Paulo Apóstolo in Blumenau (1953–1958) and in São Luiz Gonzaga in Brusque (1953–1962), medieval Gothic elements were clearly used—not uncommon in the work of the Böhms [Figs. 10.13 & 10.14]. In Blumenau, the characteristic architectural elements are the filigree concrete pillars with segmental arch arcades that surround the exterior and build the structure of the interior. The east wall is decorated with an abstract rose window. A characteristic feature of the building in Brusque is its formally predominant verticality: protruding concrete struts are staged as a modern implementation of Gothic flying buttresses; filigree framed, light-ground glass windows create a light atmosphere reminiscent of late Gothic church rooms. Perhaps even more decisive than the "Gothic" details might have been—at least in the 1950s—the urbanistic effect of the cathedral, which rises high above the city in an apparently medieval manner.

Gothic Motifs in Brazilian Avant-Garde Architecture

While innumerable "Gothic" churches were being built all over Brazil, there are only few decidedly modern ecclesiastical buildings in Brazil whose images circulated around the world. First, São Francisco de Assis in Pampulha and second, the cathedral of Brasília, both of which were built by Oscar Niemeyer in 1943 and 1958–1970, respectively [Fig. 10.15].[32] Third, the Sanctuary Dom Bosco in Brasília, which was executed by Carlos Alberto Naves in 1963–1970 [Fig. 10.16].[33] And fourth, the cathedral of Rio de Janeiro, built in 1964–1979 according to plans by Edgar Fonseca and Burle Marx.[34] In fact, the chapel of Pampulha—the spiritual center of a leisure area with a provocative architecture of parabolic arches and hangar-like concrete structure—was a daring experiment fiercely opposed at the time, for which it is today all the more admired. It shouldn't be overlooked that this small monument was only partially public.

In contrast, the main ecclesiastical buildings in Brasília—the cathedral and the Santuário Dom Bosco—were constructed as signs of modernity, but at the same time they also used and played with historical motifs. As previously in La Plata and Belo Horizonte, they were integral parts of the modern rational city;[35] as part of the *Plano Piloto* in Brasília, one of the most daring urbanistic projects of the twentieth century, they claimed an exceptional status. These prominent monuments work with Gothic vocabulary: the skeleton construction of the Cathedral of Brasília, the pointed arches of the Santuário Dom Bosco, and the stained glass windows in Brasília and Rio contribute decisively to the overall impression of modern churches. The heavenly verticality of the

10.15 Brasília, Metropolitan Cathedral of Nossa Senhora Aparecida, interior, Oscar Niemeyer, 1958–1970. [Wikimedia Commons; photo Cayambe, 2009]

10.16 Brasília, Sanctuary Dom Bosco, interior, Carlos Alberto Naves, 1963–1970. [Wikimedia Commons; photo Pedro Ventura/Agência Brasília, 2015]

10.17 Project of the Yanomami Cathedral in Amazonia, Creatos Arquitetura 2019. [© Creatos Arquitetura Divulgação]

support systems, the dematerialization of the wall, and the colored light that penetrates the panes are all consciously used retrospective motifs that evoke the meditative atmosphere of the church interior. This is certainly not a Brazilian phenomenon; at least since Auguste Perret's Notre-Dame in Raincy and Le Corbusier's chapel Notre-Dame-du-Haut in Ronchamps, it has become obvious that modern architecture and mysticism can complement each other.[36]

The most recent example of the supposedly timeless nature of Gothic architecture is the project for the Yanomami Catedral Indígena in Amazonia [Fig. 10.17].[37] Staggered pointed arches made of natural materials form a flower-like, abstract church monument. It seems as if an idea of the late eighteenth century is realized here: the combination of the Primitive Hut with Gothic architecture as the incarnation of the Nordic forest.[38]

The "Heralds of the Gospel" and Their Architectural Imaginations

In 2001, the ultraconservative community of the Arautos do Evagelho ("Heralds of the Gospel") founded in Brazil was recognized by Pope John Paul II.[39] Their aim is missionary work and new evangelization, with special devotion to the Virgin Mary of Fatima.[40] Organized in the manner of medieval military orders, the lay brothers and sisters dedicate themselves to the protection of tradition, family, and property; they wear medieval-inspired clothing and maintain strictly ritualized ceremonies. Their churches are also influenced by the Middle Ages: since their foundation, the heralds have been building churches in South America in the style of the European High Gothic, so far three in their home country of Brazil, and others in Peru, Colombia, and Paraguay.[41] The buildings are financed exclusively by donations and thanks to modern technology, are completed in a short time.[42] While from the outside evoking different models, such as the façade of Orvieto Cathedral (Nossa Senhora do Rosário de Fátima in Embu das Artes/SP, Fig. 10.18), their interiors present themselves as light-flooded, colorfully painted glass boxes. They evoke the upper church of Sainte-Chapelle in Paris in its nineteenth-century restored color version, however, without copying it in detail. At Embu, for example, the interior, which in this case has three naves and no transept, has a three-zoned structure and is cross-ribbed vaulted; supporting elements, wall surfaces, and windows shine in the most lavish colors; the vaultings are blue and decorated with golden stars, as in Paris [Fig. 10.19]. Under the key term *materialização da via espiritual* ("materialization of the spiritual path"), this collage of significant elements of European Gothic is extensively justified in circles of the Arautos. Monsignor Giuseppe A. Scotti, the 2015–2016 president of the Joseph Ratzinger Pope Benedict XVI Foundation, summarized the discussion after his stay in Brazil as follows:

38 This parallel setting with Hirschfeld, *Theorie der Gartenkunst*.

39 For information about the now highly controversial Community: <https://pt.wikipedia.org/wiki/Arautos_do_Evangelho> and <http://revistaepoca.globo.com/Revista/Epoca/0,,EDG70724-6014,00-CATOLICISMO+MEDIEVAL.html>. The dissertation by Amaral on the internet presence of the Heralds is instructive: *O Católico ideal*, <https://www.unip.br/presencial/ensino/pos_graduacao/strictosensu/comunicacao/download/comunic_flaviagabrielacramaral.pdf>.

40 On the tradition of the veneration of the Virgin of Fatima in Latin America, see the contribution of Martín Checa-Artasu in this book.

41 Brazil: Embu das Artes/SP, Nossa Senhora do Rosário da Fátima, 2004–2014; Caieras/SP, Nossa Senhora do Rosário, 2006–2008; Nova Friburgo/RJ, Capela Nossa Senhora de Fátima, consecration October 13, 2018; Peru, Nuestra Señora de la Encarnación, consecration March 31, 2008; Colombia, Nuestra Señora de Fatima, consecration August 8, 2015; Paraguay, Ypacaraí, Madre del Buen Consejo, consecration December 16, 2018.

42 Numerous videos on construction and consecration are available on Youtube, s.v. Heraldos del Evangelho or Arautos do Evangelho, currently project for a church in Cuiabá/MT <https://www.youtube.com/watch?v=EsSGlNmXcag>.

10.18 Embu das Artes, São Paulo, Nossa Senhora do Rosário de Fátima, 2004–2014. [Wikimedia Commons; photo Mike Peel, 2017]

I understand the architectural evolution in the history of the Heralds of the Gospel as a materialization of the spiritual path [...]. It is not a return to the past, but a look toward the future. It is not a repetition of the European Gothic. Brazil is giving a fruit that we have only begun to decipher.[43]

The model of "materialization" is adopted more or less faithfully by all South American churches of the Community—in the United States and Canada, however, the Heralds prefer more modern architecture. Nothing is communicated about the builders of these churches. However, as the founder of the Order, João Scognamiglio Clá Dias, said in his message on the occasion of the consecration of the chapel in Nova Friburgo, Rio de Janeiro, the construction would be the work of the angels who worked tirelessly in the design of the plans, in the shaping and in the choice of colors.[44] Once again, a pseudo-medieval topos is taken up here, that of anonymous, divinely inspired architecture.

The abovementioned examples lead to a heterogeneous picture of modern neo-Gothic ecclesiastical architecture in Brazil. The panorama ranges from a rather vague adoption of European models over eclectic mixed styles to rationalist and avant-garde interpretations of Gothic building forms. The motives that led to the choice of a Gothic language of form appear at least as diverse, reaching from the progressive national spirit of awakening of the early twentieth century to pragmatic considerations and the conservative backward-looking attitude of the Heralds of the Gospel.

Despite these divergences, a number of constants can be named that are possibly valid beyond Brazil's borders:

- The Gothic idiom of the twentieth and twenty-first centuries is understood as an alternative to modernity or as its enrichment. It gains new qualities from the tension between tradition and modernity and distances itself from the traditional neo-Gothic style of the nineteenth century.
- The Brazilian or Latin American neo-Gothic style does not tie in with a practical colonial-historical tradition, as is the case in North America, but rather presents itself as a new beginning and rejection of the former's, in this case that of the Spanish-Portuguese, hegemony.
- With its *grandiosidade*,[45] the neo-Gothic reflects the economic rise of the cities. It thus parallels the supposed heyday of the Old World. The Gothic cathedral crowns the cityscape as it once did and is intended to create identity, a motif that carries weight in the booming metropolises of South America.
- Neo-Gothic architecture references the

43 "Entendo a evolução arquitetônica na história dos Arautos do Evangelho como uma materialização da via espiritual [...]. Não é um retorno para o passado, mas um olhar para o futuro. Não é uma repetição do gótico europeu. O Brasil está dando um fruto que nós apenas começamos a decifrar." <https://sanctuaria.art/2018/09/19/igrejas-arautos-do-evangelho/>.

home countries of the numerous New Brazilians. On the other hand, *Gótico à brasileira* enables pragmatic adaptation to regional requirements and the integration of folkloric Brazilian motifs.

- There are no formal differences between the Catholic and the (few) Protestant churches.
- Due to political upheavals, most neo-Gothic cathedrals are only completed after decades of construction, some only in the late twentieth century. The latter may also have benefited from the boom of postmodernism. The long construction period and the adherence to the original plan are not seen as problematic, but rather as continuity and divine providence.
- European models are not quoted literally. Motifs such as the double-towered façade, choir with ambulatory, ribbed vaults, tracery, etc. are sufficient as a reference to the great cathedrals of Cologne, Paris, or Chartres.
- Gothic structures and modern building techniques are not contradictory: reinforced concrete construction in particular allows for new interpretations of skeleton construction and is regarded as an ideal complement to traditional techniques. The architects are often anonymous engineers trained in Europe; they guarantee a fast and cost-effective construction, which academic architects do not necessarily provide.[46]
- In some cases, Gothic enthusiasm was entangled with the rejection of Baroque and classicism, perceived as colonial and inappropriate to modern Brazil. The consequences included the demolition and neglect of several Baroque churches.

The overarching question remains whether concrete expectations are associated with the Gothic idiom. Among others we might assume that neo-Gothic forms in multi-ethnic and multicultural Brazil could be a sign of building identity—not only in defiance of modernity, but almost in competition with it: both claim universal validity.

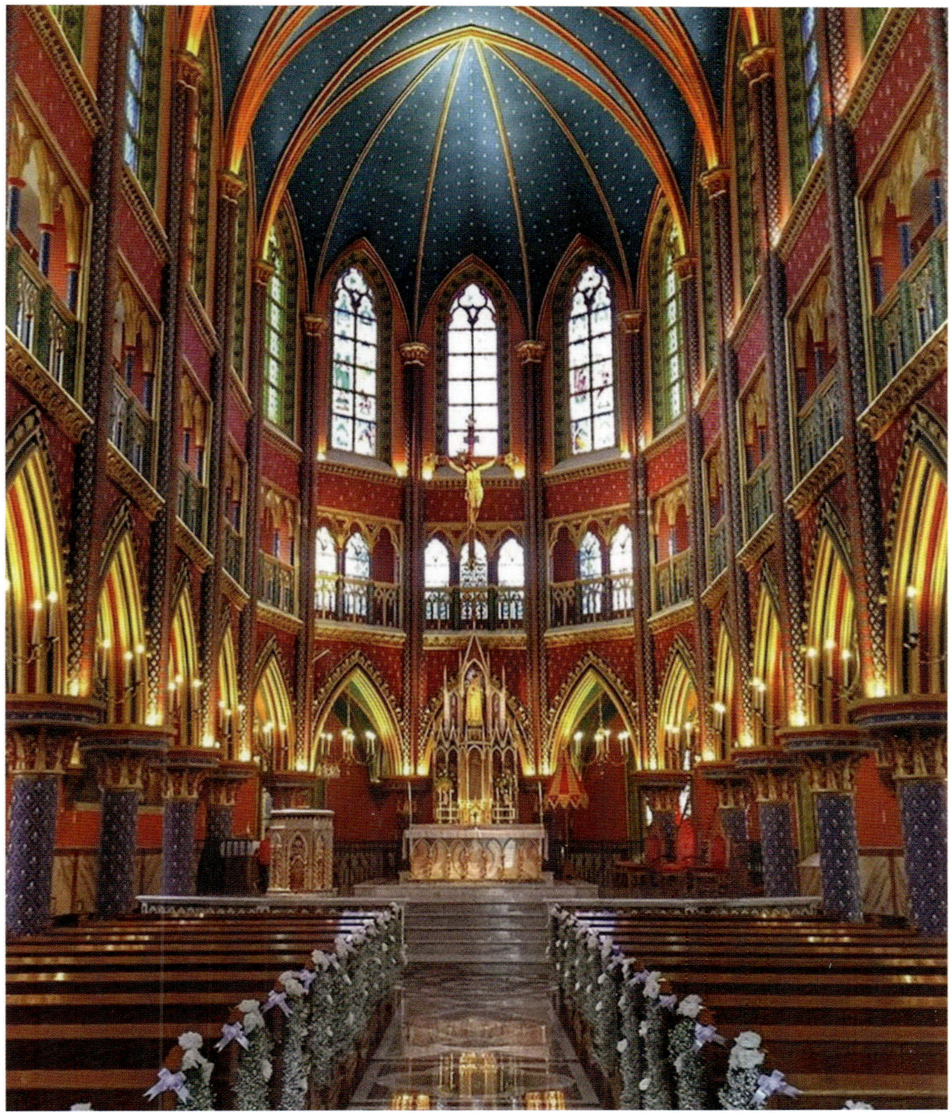

10.19 Embu das Artes, São Paulo, Nossa Senhora do Rosário de Fátima, interior, 2004–2014. [© Renato Moraes, São Paulo]

44 "Se os olhos de todos pudessem comprovar de maneira sensível a assistência celeste que acompanhou cada passo do empreendimento, certamente veriam quanto os Anjos atuaram com incansável perseverança orientando o traçado dos planos, inspirando o desenho das formas, a escolha das cores, a execução de todas as etapas." <https://arautosfriburgo.com/inauguracao-da-capela-de-nossa-senhora-de-fatima-em-nova-friburgo/>. It is certainly not surprising that the pictorial program of the churches imitates in motifs and style the works of Fra Angelico.

45 For the characterization of Simon Gramlich's monumental style, see Borngässer, "Neugotik und Moderne im Süden Brasiliens."

46 See Fagundes e Braga, *A trajetória do arquiteto alemão Simão Gramlich em campos cruzados no sul dc Brasil*; Vermeersch, "A construção da Catedral da Sé"; Borngässer, "Neugotik und Monderne im Süden Brasiliens."

11
Gothic Architecture in Africa from Colonial to Postcolonial
An Attempt

Bruno Klein

11.01 Ouagadougou, Burkina Faso, Cathedral of the Immaculate Conception, 1934–1936.
[Wikimedia Commons; photo Sputniktilt]

Research, Problems, and Perspectives

Until now, there has been no detailed overview of historicist, especially ecclesiastical, architecture in Africa.[1] For other continents, too, this applies all the more to the neo-Gothic style of the twentieth and twenty-first centuries and the modernist architecture derived from it. Nevertheless, the situation here is even more complicated, mainly due to the great historical, cultural, and religious differences on the continent and the heterogeneous colonization and decolonization. In fact, the differences are so enormous that any attempt at a unifying summary is not only doomed to failure, but must be regarded as abusive. The following considerations are therefore a spectrum of ideas, but in no way a synthesis. Nevertheless, some basic structures are visible.

Thus, the respective African buildings were predominantly constructed during a colonial period. This is comparable to China, but distinguishes these buildings from those on the American continents, where neo-Gothic churches of the same time date from the postcolonial era. In the African colonies, on the other hand, they served not only as isolated symbols of presumed superiority of European culture in general,[2] but they were also important tools to distribute and to stabilize it.[3] Traditional European ideas of urban planning were transported with them, and they structured their surrounding areas. First of all, they were the main centers for the spread of Christianity, with which the area was religiously and ritually deeply permeated, especially because the affinity between religious mission and political colonization was ideologically and structurally similar.[4]

On the other hand, those churches were not only unambiguous symbols of certain political intentions, because they could also become signs of resistance, especially in times when political colonialism was increasingly criticized. Moreover, the main protagonists of European colonization did not always and continuously behave in the same way and for example, were occasionally able to deal respectfully with the culture they found.[5] And not least, African colonies were places of refuge for many European emigrants, in particular during World War II. For example, during the German occupation of France, Brazzaville in the French Congo and Algiers were both capitals of *France libre* between 1940 and 1944.

As already indicated, a geographical distinction must also be made between several cultural areas of the religions. Thus, for a long time, hardly any new churches were built in the Islamic countries, except some smaller functional buildings for the Europeans. In this regard, Egypt is a special case, where churches were erected for the Coptic Christians, particularly after the country's independence.[6]

The situation was again different in areas that were traditionally Islamic. But colonies were transformed into provinces of the Christian "motherland," as for example in Algeria, whose coastal region was, since 1881, part of France and was divided into three departments. A lot of buildings there, from the nineteenth and the first half of the twentieth centuries, are stylistically close to the contemporaneous architecture in France,

1 With the exception of single countries. See: Demissie, ed., *Colonial architecture and urbanism in Africa*. With several contributions: Jackson and Uduku, "Sub-Saharan Africa." Architectural history about Africa seems to concentrate mainly on "traditional" or modern architecture.
2 Very impressively, but subjectively described in: Amutabi, "Buildings as Symbols of Colonial Hegemony."
3 For example, the cathedral of Likoma [Figs. 11.20 & 11.21] was built under European direction by local people, and its construction was staged as a kind of service, because it began with morning prayers and songs. Winspear, "A short history of the universities mission to Central Africa," 32.
4 Bremner, "Pro Fide et Patria," 262–263.
5 See, e.g.: Radoin, "French Territoriality and Urbanism."
6 Tadros, "Vicissitudes in the Entente between the Coptic Orthodox Church and the State in Egypt (1952–2007)."

sometimes with elements borrowed from Gothic. In central and southern Africa, developments were again different. First, smaller churches were built in the coastal towns and regions, and with the accelerated colonization also of the hinterland or in central Africa, starting in the late nineteenth century, missions were founded. Especially in South Africa, administrative church structures were quickly created, which required the building of parish churches and cathedrals. In central Africa, this happened slightly later, mainly in the twentieth century. After many initially provisional buildings, permanent churches were finally built there, on which work was carried out well into the twentieth century. They are often located in missions that follow their own urbanistic rules,[7] or in cities that hardly correspond to European ideas of urban structures when they grew in the wake of colonialism—not chaotic, but in a contradictory way to systematic planning ideas. In those environments, the latter churches often appear paradoxical: on the one hand, their construction results from the desire to implement traditional European values and ideas of order in the colonies by means of architecture; on the other hand, together with their urban environment, they form a new kind of urban structure.[8]

In the following remarks, an attempt will be made to arrange a small exemplary selection from a rich architectural inventory, by means of comparative analysis of building style and typology. There's no question that such a first attempt will contain errors. It is equally clear that abstract criteria are applied here, which often cannot do justice to every individual case. The in-depth contextual research that is actually necessary and which this contribution would like to encourage, was hardly possible.[9] From a European perspective, for example, it remains to be examined what role national churches such as the Anglican and also the heterogeneous Catholic missionary congregations have attributed to the choice of their architectural stylistic means and what expectations they have associated with it.[10] Research and literature on African mission history remain quite silent on this. But this does not necessarily have internal reasons. Because in contrast to historicist buildings from early colonialism up to the beginning of the twentieth century which have meanwhile found their way into the history of architecture,[11] those of the period from the First World War to the 1960s remain largely disregarded. While one can almost guess an inner urge to raise an architectural voice in that critical phase of colonialism, the written sources about that for this are not open yet—they are silent.[12] This only changes with the global phenomenon of postmodernism.

Disparate Beginnings

Before the examination of ecclesiastical architecture in Africa of the twentieth and twenty-first centuries built in Gothic forms, it is useful to take a short look at the time before the epochal threshold of World War I, because the continent was systematically colonized in the second quarter of the nineteenth century.[13] From then on, a few more years passed before the newly founded missions or cities could build permanent churches, replacing the first provisional ones. This process began, with few exceptions, shortly before 1900. So, in comparison with Europe, America, and Australia, neo-Gothic or Gothic Revival architecture arrived very late in Africa, but about the same time as in India, Japan, and China. Therefore, no regional distinct stylistic building tradition existed from which the architecture of new churches, built in Gothic forms during the twentieth century, could start from. As a consequence, the short epoch before the First World War and the longer one afterward, which lasted until decolonization, was a unity in the sense of architectural history, much more than elsewhere. It may even be said that neo-Gothic as a style with coherent features only emerged in Africa in the twentieth century. If the same architecture can be defined elsewhere as a late phase of neo-

7 Cleys and De Meulder, "Imagining a Christian Territory."
8 Van Reybrouck, *Kongo*, 200–201.
9 In general, the methodological problem must be noted that the art historical view of the theme of continuous neo-Gothic does not reflect "the voices and agency of the disarticulated." (Juneja, "'A very civil idea…,'" 467.) In this respect, the literature does not meet traditional scientific standards. But it is developing dynamically.
10 For the English "Universities' Mission to Central Africa (UMCA)," see: Bremner, "Pro Fide et Patria," 265–272. On the diverse initiatives in former Belgian Congo: Kineth, *Licht in die Finsternis*, 25–31. On the missions of Scheut: Cleys and De Meulder, "Imagining a Christian Territory" and the contribution of Thomas Coomans in this book. About the similar role of missionaries and religious orders in Latin America, see: Checa-Artasu, "Religious orders and the expansion of Neo-Gothic architecture in Latin America."
11 Bremner, *Imperial Gothic*; Brittain-Catlin et al., *Gothic Revival Worldwide*.
12 On the problems of colonial archives: Stoler, "Colonial archives and the arts of governance."
13 Keywords for that earlier period are the "Race for Africa" and the Berlin Congress of 1885, which led to a de facto division of the continent among European powers.
14 <https://de.wikipedia.org/wiki/Carl_Otto_Hager>. Ritter, "Hager, Carl Otto".

11.02 Malabo, Equatorial Guinea, Cathedral Santa Isabel, Luis Sagarra Llauradó, 1897–1916, towers 1924. [Wikimedia Comons; photo Denis Barthel]

11.03 & 11.04 Lomé, Togo, Cathedral Sacre-Cœur, exterior, plans by Brother Johannes (Franz Hopfer), begun 1901/1902. [© Ulrich Münstermann]

Gothic or Gothic Revival, in Africa its focus is actually only in this period. This is shown by a look at the inconsistent beginnings. Only in South Africa, where the first quite densely European-populated areas were located, has there been a relatively homogeneous neo-Gothic building culture since the middle of the nineteenth century. One of the protagonists was the Saxon-born architect and painter Karl Otto Hager (1813–1898),[14] who built several small churches there in a romantic neo-Gothic architectural style, which remained, however, largely without direct architectural succession.

The earliest major Gothic cathedrals, built around 1900, are solitary in their form, such as the one in Malabo, the capital of Equatorial Guinea on the Atlantic island of Bioko, a Spanish colony at the time [Fig. 11.02]. This three-nave hall church with a double-tower façade in relatively simple forms, except for the spires, was built between 1897 and 1916 according to plans by Luis Sagarra Llauradó. The upper stories of the towers followed in

1924.[15] Together with San Juan Bautista in Arucas on Gran Canaria,[16] it is the only neo-Gothic Spanish church in Africa.

Approximately at the same time, in 1901–1902, a large neo-Gothic church was also built in Lomé in the then German colony of Togo [Figs. 11.03 & 11.04], cathedral of the archbishopric of Lomé since 1955. It was constructed according to plans by Brother Johannes (civil name: Franz Hopfer) of the Steyler Missionaries.[17] In 1914, galleries were added above the side aisles to the original basilica so that its outline today is of much more compact shape than in the origin. Conversely, in 1940 the formerly massive tower helmets were replaced by open-tracery spires.

Neo-Romanesque: No Detour

Late Romanesque and High Gothic styles are simultaneously present in the exterior of Lomé Cathedral—the younger style, surprisingly, in its lower parts, and the older in the upper ones. This is a characteristic phenomenon, because in the colonial ecclesiastical architecture of Africa, the historic recourse was less closely targeted to Gothic than on other continents. Neo-Romanesque there continued well into the twentieth century, otherwhere apparently unusual: for example, there are neo-Romanesque churches in the former German colonies, such as in Bagamoyo, capital from 1888 to 1891 of the former German East Africa,[18] or St. Mary's Cathedral in Windhoek the capital of the then German Southwest Africa, built from 1906 to 1908.[19]

Neo-Romanesque churches were built with preference in the former Italian colonies, even after the end of the colonial period.[20] In Eritrea, Christian but not Catholic, the Basilica of the Rosary was built in Asmara [Fig. 11.05] from 1921 to 1923 according to plans by Oreste Scanavini from Milan—a church that stylistically does not follow Italian Gothic but closely resembles Lombard Romanesque of the twelfth century.[21]

The Italian architect Antonio Vandone was responsible for the plans of the neo-Romanesque cathedral of Mogadishu in Somalia, then Italian Somaliland [Fig. 11.06]. It was similar to the cathedral of Cefalù in Sicily.[22] Built between 1923 and 1928, it was destroyed in the Somali civil war in 2008—reconstruction is under discussion. Even after the Second World War, a large church in forms unmistakably based on Romanesque models was built in Adigrat in Ethiopia.[23]

15 Obama Avine, *Evolución de la construcción en Guinea Ecuatorial*, 34–37; Andruet, "La catedral de Santa Isabel en Malabo," with further literature. Supervision of the construction from a distance by Antoni Gaudí, or at least a review of the plans by him, is repeatedly brought into play, but cannot be proven; above all, it must be considered improbable for stylistic reasons.

16 About Arucas, see my contribution on Europe in this book.

17 <https://fr.wikipedia.org/wiki/Cathédrale_du_Sacré-Cœur_de_Lomé#cite_note-3>. The sacristy and choir section of the cathedral were damaged by fire on January 2, 2017. <https://africa.la-croix.com/incendie-a-ravage-sacristie-de-cathedrale-de-lome/>. Another, smaller neo-Gothic church of this time, also built by the Steyler Missionaries, stands in Kpalimé. <https://de.wikipedia.org/wiki/Kathedrale des Heiligen Geistes (Kpalimé)>. In Togo, the Catholic Steyler Missionaries competed with the Protestant Bremen Mission, which also built churches, such as a large neo-Lombard one also in Lomé. Illustration in: Gayibor, ed., *Histoire des Togolais. Vol. 4: Le refus de l'ordre colonial*, 42.

18 Watson, "Areas of concern."

19 <https://de.wikipedia.org/wiki/St.-Marien-Kathedrale_(Windhoek)>. A systematic publication with an extensive bibliography on German colonial urban planning and architecture appeared just as this book was going to press, but it could not be included here: Zentralinstitut für Kunstgeschichte in München, ed. *Kunstchronik. Themenheft 'Globale Räume des deutschen Kolonialismus'.*

20 However, on the Dodecanese archipelago in the eastern Mediterranean, which was first annexed by Italy and then granted to it by the League of Nations (1912–1943), a neo-Gothic cathedral was built in the capital Rhodes in 1924–1925. The island, which in the Middle Ages belonged to the Order of St. John from 1310, was considered a historical Italian Christian outpost against the Ottoman Empire, only recently defeated. Therefore, old buildings were restored, and new ones were erected to reconstruct an imaginary situation of the fourteenth century. Martinoli and Perotti, *Architettura coloniale italiana nel Dodecaneso 1912–1943*, 374–379.

21 <https://it.wikipedia.org/wiki/Chiesa_della_Beata_Vergine_del_Rosario_(Asmara)>. To modern Asmara in general, see: Volgger, *Architecture in Asmara*, and Bader, *Moderne in Afrika*.

22 <https://en.wikipedia.org/wiki/Mogadishu_Cathedral>.

23 <https://en.wikipedia.org/wiki/Cathedral_of_the_Holy_Saviour,_Adigrat>.

24 For an introduction into the Italian colonization of Libya, see: Capresi, "Architectural Transfer, Italian Colonial Architecture in Libya," especially 34–38. About the Sacred Heart Cathedral: <https://en.wikipedia.org/wiki/Tripoli_Cathedral>.

25 In fact, even in the 1930s, at the time of Italian colonial rule, there had already been thoughts of giving the cathedral, located in a central square of the new town, a new façade. Capresi, *The new Face of Tripoli (Libya)*, 102–103.

11.05 Asmara, Eritrea, Basilica of Our Lady of the Rosary, Oreste Scanavini, 1921–1923.
[Wikimedia Commons; photo Sailko, 2015]

11.06 Mogadishu, Somalia, Roman Catholic Cathedral (1923–1928) in 1936.
[© MARKA / Alamy Stock Photo, RKRPE8]

11.07 Tripoli, Libya, former Roman Catholic Sacred Heart Cathedral, Saffo Panteri, 1923–1928.
[Public domain]

11.08 Tripoli, Libya, former Roman Catholic Sacred Heart Cathedral, converted in Gamal Abdel Nasser Mosque in the 1970s.
[Wikimedia Commons; photo Abdul-Jawad Elhusuni]

In Tripoli, in the former Italian Libya, seized from the Ottoman Empire shortly before the First World War, the Sacred Heart Cathedral [Fig. 11.07] was built between 1923 and about 1928 according to designs by Saffo Panteri.[24] Its original architecture in the Lombard Romanesque underwent remarkable changes: after the church was converted into the Gamal Abdul Nasser Mosque in the 1970s, a formal Islamization took place: the façade was given a neo-Moorish appearance, and the campanile was transformed into a minaret [Fig. 11.08].[25]

The role of neo-Romanesque architecture in the sub-Saharan zone is to be assessed quite differently, because here the choice of

11.09 Lubumbashi, Congo, Roman Catholic cathedral, begun in the 1920s. [© KADOC-KU Leuven]

11.10 Cape Town, South Africa, Anglican St. George's Cathedral, interior, Herbert Baker, 1904–1936. [Wikimedia Commons; photo Nkansahrexford, 2014]

style was not primarily made for political reasons. Rather, the High Gothic style of classical models such as Paris, Westminster or Cologne, was considered unsuitable there in view of the natural conditions. For such light-flooded churches would have been too bright and would also have heated up too much. Much more suitable, therefore, seemed an architecture between late Romanesque and early Gothic, with large wall surfaces and small windows. It corresponded both to the ideologically aspired Gothic ideal and to local requirements.[26] As an example, the cathedral of Lubumbashi (former Elisabethville, Congo, Fig. 11.09),[27] may be mentioned, which was probably begun in the 1920s. It even shows echoes of early Christian architecture.[28]

Neo-Gothic

In South Africa, the spread of Gothic Revival in ecclesiastical architecture was only accelerated in the late nineteenth century in the course of systematic colonialism. It started in the settlement centers of British rule.[29] After the foundation of a first diocese in Cape Town (South Africa had previously belonged to the Province of Calcutta of the Anglican Church) and then other suffragan dioceses, cathedrals and other churches were needed. As elsewhere in the Empire, their designs were the work of English architects. Thus, the oldest parts of the cathedral of the diocese of Grahamstown were designed by the prominent architect George Gilbert Scott.[30] The most important of those churches in the twentieth century is the Anglican St. George's Cathedral in Cape Town, built approximately

26 Baker, *Plea for English Gothic*, 36. I thank Pedro d'Alpoim Guedes for this important hint.

27 <https://en.wikipedia.org/wiki/Sts._Peter_and_Paul_Cathedral,_Lubumbashi>.

28 Finally, also neo-Byzantine buildings such as the cathedral of Dakar (Senegal), consecrated in 1938, should not be overlooked.

29 To summarize this and the following: Elphick, *Christianity in South Africa*, 330–336; Bremner. "Pro Fide et Patria," 239–275.

30 Tower, 1874–1879; Bremner, *Imperial Gothic*, 97–100; Bremner, "Pro Fide et Patria," 256–257.

31 The foundation stone was laid as early as 1901, but the start of construction was later. <https://en.wikipedia.org/wiki/St._George%27s_Cathedral,_Cape_Town>.

32 Baker had studied with the prominent neo-Gothic architect George F. Bodley, who was also involved in the early construction phase of Liverpool Cathedral and had supplied plans for Washington Cathedral. Frank, "Baker, Herbert (1862)".

33 <https://www.chronicle.co.zw/st-marys-cathedral-basilica-the-jewel-of-matland/>; <https://www.bulawayoarchdiocese.org/cathedralbasilica>.

from 1904 to 1936 [Fig. 11.10].[31] The unfinished church shows a severe Gothic style of strongly reduced forms as the approximately simultaneous Liverpool Cathedral [Fig. 3.07]. The architect, Herbert Baker, was also responsible for a number of other South African churches from the first third of the twentieth century in a similar stylistic idiom.[32]

In the former Jesuit Mission of Bulawayo in Zimbabwe, then the British colony of Southern Rhodesia, a new church grew up from 1903 onward [Figs. 11.11 & 11.12].[33] It is a cathedral since 1955. The three-aisled basilica, without a transept, with a lateral tower at the façade, was built from local granite.

11.11 Bulawayo, Zimbabwe, Roman Catholic St. Mary's Cathedral, begun 1903.
[© Aleksandr Doubeikovsky]

11.13 Harare, Zimbabwe, Catholic Sacred Heart of Jesus Cathedral, 1924/1925.
[© Inner City Deanery, Harare]

11.12 Bulawayo, Zimbabwe, Roman Catholic St Mary's Cathedral, begun 1903.
[Wikimedia Commons; photo BigSugarDaddy, 2017]

11.14 Nairobi, Kenya, Anglican All Saints' Cathedral, 1917–1952.
[© Images of Africa Photobank / Alamy Stock Photo, A45AFP]

11.15 Kampala, Uganda, Namirembe, Anglican Cathedral of the Sacred Heart of Jesus, Arthur Beresford Pite, 1914–1920.
[© Barbara Gonget / Alamy Stock Photo, AXBYDF]

11.16 Dar es Salaam, Tanzania, Catholic cathedral, 1897–1902.
[Wikimedia Commons; photo 2009]

11.17 Dar es Salaam, Tanzania, Protestant Church, Friedrich Gurlitt, 1898–1899.
[Wikimedia Commons; photo 2016]

This gives a relatively rough surface on the outside, as was common in Europe from the Gothic Revival in England and to the so-called *Reformarchitektur* in Germany in the early twentieth century.

The Catholic cathedral in the capital Harare [Fig. 11.13], dating from about 1925, with a double-towered façade, also displays these stylistic features, which were also characteristic of English Arts and Crafts architecture.[34] In Nairobi, the Anglican All Saints' Cathedral [Fig. 11.14] (1917 to 1952)[35] was successively enlarged by several architects, who gave each section its own character.[36]

The Anglican Namirembe Cathedral near Kampala, Uganda [Fig. 11.15],[37] built from about 1914 to 1920 according to plans by Arthur Beresford Pite,[38] also shows a picturesque style. It was preceded by three buildings destroyed by natural disasters: already unusual in its disposition, the brick building largely dispenses with applied ornamentation; instead, the architecture is given rhythm by ogival blind niches in the outer walls and a vivid roof shape.

Namirembe Cathedral in Kampala is particularly close to several churches from around 1900, such as for example, in Dar es Salaam [Figs. 11.16 & 11.17]—not, however, in the strict formal sense, but in terms of its stylistic habitus. In the capital of the then German colony East Africa, a Catholic cathedral with many elements from Romanesque to late Gothic was built between 1897 and 1902,[39] together at about the same time (1898–1899) with the Azania Front Lutheran Church. The architect of the latter was Friedrich Gurlitt.[40] In their eclecticism, but above all because of their deliberately picturesque silhouette, both churches could have stood in the Berlin suburbs. They represent the *Heimatstil*, which was widespread in Germany at the time and was part of the great international movement of Arts and Crafts, Art Nouveau, Jugendstil, and modernism.[41]

Two buildings in Lagos, Nigeria, British protectorate since 1862 and Crown Colony from 1886, are difficult to locate in the international stylistic context. The Catholic Holy Cross Church (cathedral since 1950), consecrated in 1881, was built by and for the important group of former slaves who had returned mainly from Brazil.[42] In the place of this first church, which showed relatively simple Gothic forms, a new building was constructed between 1934 and 1939 in a "classical" Rayonnant style [Fig. 11.18].[43] Apparently, the previous building was gradually replaced, so that parts of it may still be found in the present church.

The extent to which Catholics and Anglicans staked their claims by means of archi-

11.18 Lagos, Nigeria, Roman Catholic Cathedral, 1934–1939. [Wikimedia Commons; photo Kelechinaba, 2017]

11.19 Lagos, Nigeria, Anglican Cathedral, Bagan Benjamin, 1924–1946. [Wikimedia Commons; photo Ayodele Yusuf, 2017]

34 Jackson, *Historic Buildings of Harare*. <http://zimfieldguide.com/harare/harare's-historic-buildings—-avenues>.
35 <https://www.allsaintsnairobi.org/about/>.
36 Near the cathedral, a large community center has been built in recent years, consisting of several buildings that reflect its Gothic style. <https://www.miprojects.co.ke/project-portfolio/all-saints-cathedral-ctc/>.
37 <https://www.monitor.co.ug/News/National/-making-of-Namirembe-Cathedral-Bishop-Hannington--Mwanga/688334-5271116-s84w7f/index.html>.
38 Mesecke, "Pite, Arthur Beresford".
39 <https://de.wikipedia.org/wiki/Kathedrale_St._Josef_(Daressalam)>.
40 Partsch, "Gurlitt, Friedrich".
41 A good visual impression of the urbanistic function of these churches is provided by the numerous historical postcards, compiled by Hofmann, "Deutsche Kolonialarchitektur."
42 Architects were Lázaro Borges da Silva and Francisco Nobre. Strickrodt, "The Brazilian Diaspora to West Africa in the Nineteenth Century," 62.
43 <https://fr.wikipedia.org/wiki/Cathédrale_de_la_Sainte-Croix_de_Lagos>; <http://gregnwoko.blogspot.com/2014/11/history-of-holy-cross-cathedral-lagos.html>.

11.20 Likoma, Malawi, Anglican St. Peter's Cathedral, exterior, 1903–1911. [Postcard, archive Bruno Klein]

11.21 Likoma, Malawi, St. Peter's, interior, 1903–1911. [© Babatin/worldpress.com]

tecture is shown by the fact that, in Lagos, an Anglican one was built parallel to the new Catholic cathedral [Fig. 11.19].[44] Also here, the new building of the twentieth century replaces an older one: the foundation stone of the first church, dedicated to Christ, was laid in 1867, while the enlarged replacement was constructed between 1924 and 1946.[45] Stylistically, it is based on historical Gothic building forms, but combines them, especially on the outside, in a completely unhistorical way. The Catholic cathedral, on the other hand, adheres quite close to medieval forms that can be dated precisely into the late thirteenth century.

Between these two poles of, on the one hand, particularly precise and, on the other hand, very liberal recourse to Gothic architecture and Gothic stylistic elements, there is a whole series of West and Central African churches: most of them are built of adobe or brick, often with several naves and no vaulting, always with a double-towered façade—even if that often remained unfinished—and stylistically often classified between Romanesque and Gothic.[46] Although spread over a wide area, they form a homogeneous group in formal terms. Some of them were carried out by Protestant missionaries, such as the British University Missions or the Church of Scotland, others by Catholic missionaries, such as the Belgian missionaries of Scheut,[47] or of the Société des missionnaires d'Afrique, which started from France or Algeria. One of the earliest buildings of this type is an Anglican church, St. Peter's Cathedral on Likoma island in Lake Malawi (1903 to 1911) [Figs. 11.20 & 11.21].[48]

This building shows the very characteristics of those churches: they are large in order to receive many people and to be recognizable as the center of a mission or diocese. Their forms are not too elaborate, which on the one hand makes it difficult to identify an exact medieval style as exemplary—hence, their ambiguity with regard to Romanesque or Gothic. On the other hand, it was possible to build them with relatively simple means. As far as is known, they were often designed by European lay architects and—importantly—constructed by the inhabitants themselves, not only to complete the church but also to create a Christian community. In this way, a special African ecclesiastical architecture arose, which was based on popular ideas of medieval European architecture.

After Likoma, another early (1914 to 1925) church of this type is that of the former mission, today the Catholic cathedral of Rubaga [Fig. 11.22].[49] Like nearby Namirembe Cathedral [Fig. 11.15], it is situated close to the city center of Kampala, Uganda. Between 1926 and 1936, an equally large brick church was built in Kisantu [Fig. 11.23] in the then Belgian colony of Congo, with five naves, a double-towered façade, a three-nave transept, and an ambulatory with chapels.[50] It was impossible to find out the background for the construction of the huge, vaulted church of Maboma in the northeast of the

44 Similar phenomena are to be observed elsewhere. For China, for example: Coomans, "The 'Sino-Christian Style,'" 204–205.
45 Jackson and Uduku, "Sub-Saharan Africa"; <https://en.wikipedia.org/wiki/Cathedral_Church_of_Christ,_Lagos>.
46 On the phenomenon of widespread Romanesque reception, see above.
47 Cleys and De Meulder, "Imagining a Christian Territory."
48 Winspear, "A short history of the universities mission to Central Africa," 23 and 32; Bremner, "Pro Fide et Patria," 272–273; <https://en.wikipedia.org/wiki/Likoma,_Malawi>. The inspiration for the construction of this church could have been the Saint Michael and All Angels Church in Blantyre, Malawi, dating from 1889–1891. Walker, "A survey of early buildings in Nyasaland."
49 <https://fr.wikipedia.org/wiki/Cathédrale_Sainte-Marie_de_Kampala>.
50 <https://en.wikipedia.org/wiki/Our_Lady_of_Seven_Sorrows_Cathedral,_Kisantu>.

Congo [Figs. 1.01 & 11.24]. In Duala in Cameroon, a large neo-Romanesque church, cathedral since 1951, was built from 1933 to 1936.[51]

The obviously unfinished cathedral of Ouagadougou [Fig. 11.01], the capital of Burkina Faso, the former French colony Upper Volta, was constructed mainly between 1934 and 1936.[52] It is relatively modest in terms of architectural decoration, due to the fact that it was built with adobe bricks. Nevertheless, structural elements such as buttresses and a three-portal structure crowned with ornamental gables clearly refer to early or High Gothic models. At about the same time—exact dates cannot be ascertained—the Basilica of the Rosary in Mbalmayo in Cameroon [Fig. 11.25] arose, also in bricks with some Gothic elements such as ogival windows.

Modernized Gothic

Ecclesiastical architecture in the former French departments south of the Mediterranean Sea, such as Algeria, or the Protectorate of French Morocco could look very different from that of the Central African colonies. Here, it was apparently no longer a question of constructing local cultural identity through historicist forms, but rather of seeking a direct connection at eye level with the modern architecture of the so-called French

51 <https://de.wikipedia.org/wiki/Peter-und-Paul-Kathedrale_(Duala)>.

52 <https://fr.wikipedia.org/wiki/Cathédrale_de_l%27Immaculée-Conception_de_Ouagadougou?uselang=de>.

11.22 Kampala, Uganda, Rugaba, Catholic Cathedral, 1914–1925. [Wikimedia Commons; photo Philipp Jakob]

11.23 Kisantu, Congo, Roman Catholic Cathedral of Our Lady of Seven Sorrows, 1926–1936. [© KADOC-KU Leuven]

11.24 Maboma, Congo, Church, 1930s, aerial view 1. [© LuAnn Cadd]

11.25 Mbalmayo, Cameroon, Roman Catholic Cathedral of Our Lady of the Rosary, 1934. [Wikimedia Commons; photo Wikiilya, 2009]

11.26 Annaba (Bône), Algeria, former Church of Sainte-Thérèse, 1934–1935. [Postcard, archive Bruno Klein]

11.27 Casablanca, Morocco, former Church of Sacré Cœur, Paul Tournon, begun 1930, under construction (1952). [Fontainebleau, Archives nationales DAPAANS, 377 AP 209; photo Gillot]

motherland. It was rather a coincidence that this architecture occasionally took up Gothic motifs and structural elements. In Annaba (in French 'Bône' 1830–1962), the ancient Hippo, where the Church Father Augustine had been bishop, there is the church of Ste-Thérèse (1934–1935),[53] [Fig. 11.26] a building in certain succession of Notre-Dame-du-Raincy by Auguste Perret.[54]

Stylistically similar, but heightened to monumental proportions, is Sacré Cœur Basilica in Casablanca [Fig. 11.27],[55] begun in 1930 by the French architect Paul Tournon[56] in the then Protectorate of French Morocco. Compared to these buildings in Northwest Africa, which integrate themselves completely into the modern French architecture, Nossa Senhora da Conceição [Fig. 11.28], the Cathedral of Maputo, appears rather isolated at first glance. This church in Mozambique, then Portuguese colony in the southeast of the continent, shows an evident reception of contemporary French architecture such as Notre-Dame-du-Raincy, especially by its tower.[57] However, the structure and forms of its nave and its interior deviate strongly from this model and show little affinity with Gothic architecture—apart from the windows in concrete tracery, which became a trademark of buildings in the Perret succession. The church, built between 1936 and 1944 according to the plans of the Portuguese architect Marcial Freitas e Costa, is in fact not only oriented on the famous French model, but also stands in a Portuguese tradition. An example of this is the Igreja de Nossa Senhora de Fátima in Lisbon, built between 1933 and 1938 by Porfírio Pardal Monteiro,[58] who was closely associated with the French architectural scene of the time and was a student of the eclecticist and neo-Gothicist José Luís Monteiro. Also related to the

53 *L'Algérie Catholique*, 11 (November 1937), article by J. Coureau. According to this, the church was built by the otherwise unknown architects Naz and Butgieg. Quoted after <http://www.seybouse.info/seybouse/infos_diverses/mise_a_jour/maj25.html>. The church has meanwhile been converted into a mosque: <http://diaressaada.alger.free.fr/ka-eglises-seules-CP/Eglises-9B-9C-9D.html>.

11.28 Maputo, Mozambique, Cathedral Nossa Senhora da Conceição, Marcial Freitas e Costa, 1936–1944. [Wikimedia Commons; photo Claus Wonnemann, 2019]

11.29 Pointe Noire, Congo, Notre-Dame-de-l'Assomption, cathedral since 1975, Jules Alazard, 1952/1953. [Wikimedia Commons; photo Loris-Romito, 2008]

French modernist tradition is Notre-Dame-de-l'Assomption in Pointe-Noire, Republic of the Congo [Fig. 11.29], begun in 1952–1953 to the plans of the French architect Jules Alazard.[59] The church displays at the façade a large rose window and the typical concrete tracery windows, but combined with a neo-Romanesque campanile.

Finally, with regard to the specific historical conditions as well as its style, Sainte-Anne-du-Congo in Brazzaville plays a special role [Figs. 11.30 & 11.31 a & b].[60] After long preliminary planning, construction began in 1943, and consecration of the still unfinished building was in 1949. Due to damage during the civil war in 1997, the church was restored in 2010–2011, including the completion of the tower helmet, which had been missing until then. The planning and the first construction period of the church took place when Brazzaville was the capital of the *France libre*. Charles De Gaulle committed himself personally to the construction of the church, which thus has a distinctly French-national character. It is therefore not surprising that this building, designed by the architect Erell (pseudonym for Roger Lelièvre), is also highly emphatic in style: it

54 In the second quarter of the twentieth century, that church played a nearly global role as a model for a modernized Gothic architecture. See e.g. the contribution of Martín Checa-Artasu on South-America in this book.

55 <https://fr.wikipedia.org/wiki/Église_du_Sacré-Cœur_de_Casablanca>. After the independence of Morocco, the church was transformed into a cultural center.

56 Mesecke, "Tournon, Paul". On Tournon, see also the chapter on Europe in this book. [Fig. 3.34]

57 Furtado, *A Catedral de Nossa Senhora da Conceição de Lourenço Marques.*

58 Mesecke, "Pardal Monteiro, Porfírio".

59 <https://fr.wikipedia.org/wiki/Église_Notre-Dame-de-l'Assomption_de_Pointe-Noire_(république_du_Congo)>.

60 <https://fr.wikipedia.org/wiki/Basilique_Sainte-Anne-du-Congo_de_Brazzaville>.

11.30 Brazzaville, Congo, Sainte-Anne-du-Congo, exterior.
[Postcard, archive Bruno Klein]

11.31 Postcard and back of postcard.
[Archive Bruno Klein]

SAINTE ANNE DU CONGO

SANCTUAIRE SOUVENIR DE L'A.E.F.

Brazzaville - Missions des PP. du Saint-Esprit

Le Sanctuaire Souvenir de l'A.E.F. dédié à Sainte Anne du Congo, sera un monument édifié à la gloire des pionniers français de l'A.E.F. A la gloire, aussi de l'Epopée de la France LIBRE (1940 - 1944) dont BRAZZAVILLE fut la Capitale.

Monument grandiose aux lignes à la fois élégantes et originales, long de 85 m., large à la croisée du transept, de 45 m., et surmonté d'une flèche vertigineuse de 60 m. Il sera l'église indispensable à une chrétienté de plus de 50.000 âmes, et le symbole de ce que la France a voulu apporter aux peuples de l'Afrique noire, en idéal de civilisation et de beauté.

CHRETIENS ! Aidez-nous à édifier Sainte Anne du Congo. Adhérez à l'Association " Les Amis du Sanctuaire Souvenir de l'A.E.F. " dont le siège se trouve : 30, Rue Lhomond, PARIS (Ve).

Les dons pourront être versés à l'adresse suivante :

ASSOCIATION SPIRITUS, 30, Rue Lhomond, PARIS

C.C.P. Paris 4540-94, en indiquant au talon du chèque : Sainte Anne du Congo, Brazzaville.

is particularly close to expressionist architecture and, astonishingly enough, especially to its German variant [Fig. 11.32].[61] However, it cannot be ruled out that the architect was also inspired by African models, such as the so-called *Cases obus*, or Musgum mud huts, in the north of Cameroon,[62] especially since an imitation of such buildings was on display at the *Exposition coloniale internationale* in Paris in 1931. Yet both potential stimuli do not even have to exclude each other, precisely because of expressionism's general affinity with the "art of the primitives." And so, Sainte-Anne's work brings together abstracted Gothic, imagined African elements in an architectural language that is perceived as supranational.

On the opposite bank of the Congo river, in the capital Kinshasa (Léopoldville) of the then Belgian colony, the cathedral Notre-Dame du Congo was built from 1947 onward. It also shows parabolic arches inside, but the overall design echoes only few citations from Gothic architecture, in general much less expressive than Sainte-Anne-du-Congo in Brazzaville.[63]

Postmodern Echoes of Ecclesiastical Gothic Architecture

In the postcolonial period, ecclesiastical buildings with reminiscences of Gothic architecture were built continuously, but rarely. In Egypt, however, churches were constructed for Coptic Christians. The aim of this rather discreet, postmodern adoption of the stylistic idiom may have been to demonstrate a certain religious tolerance of the country, both externally and internally.[64]

In this regard, the Coptic Church of the Virgin Mary on the Nile island El Zamalek in Cairo, designed by Ramses Wissa Wassef in 1957, is a modernist precursor.[65] At first glance, the building is by no means Gothic in style, but the short-rhythmed bay division of the nave with narrow, high windows and buttress-like, towering intermediate walls are certainly reminiscent of Gothic elements.

11.32 Berlin, Germany, Kirche am Hohenzollernplatz, Fritz Höger, 1930–1933.
[Wikimedia Commons; photo Silva Hahn]

61 In this context, it is particularly worth thinking of the church at Hohenzollernplatz by Fritz Höger in Berlin (1930–1933).

62 <http://voyage-congo.over-blog.com/article-brazzaville-construction-basilique-sainte-anne-congo-80192453.html>. At that time, Cameroon was still part of the colony French Equatorial Africa (Afrique-Équatoriale française), whose capital was Brazzaville.

63 <https://en.wikipedia.org/wiki/Our_Lady_of_the_Congo_Cathedral>. Because of the large rose-window of the façade in a flat concrete wall, but also with the filigree concrete columns inside, the building shows affinities to the simultaneous churches of Gottfried Böhm in Brazil. The cathedral of Lubango, Angola, as a relatively strict variant of this style, is also comparable. In contrast, the Holy Cross Cathedral in Lusaka, Zambia is a more filigree alternative, which is relatively close to the buildings of Böhm in Brazil. For both buildings, only pictures but no further information could be found. See the article on Brazil by Barbara Borngässer in this book.

64 Tadros, "Vicissitudes in the Entente between the Coptic Orthodox Church and the State in Egypt (1952–2007)," 272.

65 Wissa Wassef had studied at the École des Beaux Arts in Paris in the 1930s. Drawings of the church under: <http://digitalcollections.aucegypt.edu/cdm/compoundobject/collection/p15795coll5/id/198/rec/1>.

11.33 Cairo, Egypt, Saint Marc's Coptic Cathedral, façade, Michel Bakhoum, consecrated 1969.
[Wikimedia Commons; photo Roland Unger, 2010]

11.34 Aswan, Egypt, Coptic Cathedral, consecrated 2006.
[Wikimedia Commons; photo Marc Ryckaert, 2012]

The slender tower with its reinforced edges and recesses in the upper part is related to Notre-Dame-du-Raincy by Perret.

The most important and at the same time largest monument of this style is the Coptic St. Marc's Cathedral in Cairo [Fig. 11.33], designed by the engineer architect Michel Bakhoum and consecrated in 1969 in the presence of the Egyptian head of state Gamal Abdel Nasser and the Ethiopian Emperor Haile Selassie. The building itself is difficult to classify with regard to the use of certain architectural references: the ogival windows and vaults are certainly not intended to refer to European Gothic, but to early Arabic architecture;[66] the building type, however, is vaguely reminiscent of Byzantine. On the other hand, the dimensions and structure of the building as well as the high bell tower also clearly evoke the architecture of Auguste Perret, while the window tracery with figural stained glass is reminiscent of historical Gothic, especially if seen from the interior. The most recent building in this series is the Coptic Michael's Cathedral in Aswan [Fig. 11.34], consecrated in 2006.[67] In addition to the already known elements, the divided windows there should be mentioned, which appear like Gothic tracery formations and have no historical models in regional architecture.[68]

African Gothic?

Even if Gothicizing architecture of the twentieth century shows itself to be heterogeneous in the African regions and countries, it still produces a uniform picture when viewed against the background of developments in Europe. Obviously, in the colonies a modern or "international" style was seldom considered capable of conveying a European marked religious identity or even superiority. This helped historicism to survive when building churches until the end of the colonial period. In this context, the adobe and brick buildings in central and West Africa are an hybrid achievement in their own right, which responds to the conditions of material and climate and has led to a continuous development of Gothic reception. In this respect, in particular the churches in the former Belgian colonies are really to be discovered. What has been presented in this chapter is only a small part of it. In contrast, the Gothic variant, which was widespread in the early twentieth century, especially in the English colonies and closely based on Arts and Crafts architecture, does not differ fundamentally from what was built at the same time in the "mother" country. This also applies to the modernist Gothic adaptations in the former French regions from the southern coast of the Mediterranean to Portuguese Mozambique. The Coptic churches in Egypt,

66 Not to forget that in earlier times there were specific Gothic revival motives in colonial mosque architecture. See: Cantone, "The Point of Pointed Architecture."
67 Gabra and Takla, eds., *Christianity and Monasticism in Upper Egypt*; Gabra and Takla, eds., *Christianity and Monasticism in Aswan and Nubia.*
68 Stylistically comparable are also some churches in the Gulf region, such as the Catholic cathedral in Abu Dhabi or the church in Jebel Ali Village in Dubai.

11.35 Abuja, Nigeria, National Ecumenical Church, 1989–2005, interior. [Wikimedia Commons; photo Kritzolina, 2019]

11.36 Abuja, Nigeria, National Ecumenical Church, 1989–2005, exterior. [Wikimedia Commons; photo Moises.on]

which are in style related indirectly to these examples, are by contrast the result of a self-confident national architecture.

A few decades ago, structures and elements of the Gothic style were adopted by the ecumenical center—or rather the ecumenical national church—in Abuja, the new Nigerian capital in the interior of the country.[69] Beside this building for different Christian confessions, Abuja also has a national mosque and an Anglican cathedral; the Catholic cathedral is still under construction. Except the neo-Islamic mosque, they all show some rather unspecific modern forms. Only the national church, built between 1989 and 2004, with a long interruption,[70] has a lot of Gothic motifs such as ogival portals or windows, and also ribs that evoke a vault but actually directly support the roof (Figs. 11.35 and 11.36). An open buttress system enhances the general impression that Gothic was deliberately evoked here. Perhaps, because it was regarded as style common to all Christian confessions, but also for being considered capable to embody the national belief in progress inherent in the new capital, especially in its modern technical form. In any case, Gothic architecture seems no longer to be colonial. Thus, there are signs of a transformation and hybridization of the formerly imposed style into something of its own.

69 <https://en.wikipedia.org/wiki/Christian_Association_of_Nigeria>; <https://en.wikipedia.org/wiki/National_Christian_Centre>.

70 Constructed by the Italian company Gitto Costruzioni Generali, the information regarding the Nigerian design architect(s) are contradictory: either the building was designed by the Nigerian architectural firm Darchiwork Group (Wikipedia) or the architects from the Oaky Wall Group, led by Wale (<https://web.archive.org/web/20110628200304/http://www.anglican-nig.org/ecum%20centre.htm>).

12
Western, Modern and Postmodern Gothic Churches in Twentieth-Century China: Styles, Identities, and Memories

Thomas Coomans

Twentieth-century China, like no other country in the world, went through a succession of changes of political regimes, revolutions, and wars that deeply impacted the society, including its religious component. Christianity, a foreign religion brought to China by Western missionaries, remained a marginal and fragmented phenomenon despite a certain growth in the last decade of the Qing Dynasty (1900–1911) and during the Republic (1912–1949).[1] The Christian missions in China were a mosaic of dozens of Catholic national and international missionary societies coordinated from the Holy See; Protestants from several different American, British, and other northern European denominations; and Russian Orthodox in northeast China.[2] Tens of thousands of churches, chapels, and mission stations were built throughout China in a great diversity of Western, Chinese, and hybrid types and styles according to the identity of the missionaries and the reception of their projects by Chinese Christians. Gothic was one of these styles. Different regional forms of Gothic were mostly but not exclusively promoted by French, German, and Belgian Catholics, as well as by Anglican, Lutheran, and American Protestant missions.

Many churches were damaged or demolished during the Sino-Japanese War (1937–1945) and the Civil War between Nationalists and Communists (1945–1949). In the early 1950s, the People's Republic of China expelled all foreign missionaries and created two state-sanctioned Churches: the Protestant Three-Self Church and the Chinese Patriotic Catholic Church.[3] From 1949 to the early 1980s, few churches were built in mainland China, and demolition or recycling of old churches continued, especially during the Cultural Revolution (1966–1976). From the early 1980s on, Christian communities of the state-sanctioned Churches gradually recovered their buildings and were challenged to restore surviving old churches and erect new churches. The growth of the Chinese economy and wealth in the last decade of the twentieth century and the early twenty-first century stimulated increasingly ambitious church construction projects, which include postmodern Gothic design, both by Catholic and other Christian congregations.

In this chapter, I will neither trace the origins of Gothic architecture nor map the geography of Gothic (*Kunstlandschaft*) in nineteenth-century China, which I have already done in other publications;[4] instead, I will try to understand the seeming paradoxes of church architecture in twentieth-century China, by developing an approach based on architectural iconology and visual culture.[5] This method, applied to many churches that I visited during fieldwork in different parts of China from 2011 to 2019, allows me to structure this chapter around five questions. Firstly, why could a number of important Gothic and other Western-style churches be built in China after 1900 and strongly contribute both to Christian identity building and informal colonization? Secondly, why did some missionary societies continue to promote nineteenth-century Gothic patterns after the First World War, neither following the evolution of church architecture in Europe, nor accepting the indiginized Chinese

12.01 The North Cathedral (Beitang) in Beijing was built in 1887–1888 in a Gothic style that mixes French, Italian and German influences. After the siege of the Boxers in 1900, it became the symbol of Catholic resistance in the capital of the Qing Empire and two towers were raised on the side bays of the façade. The two Chinese pavilions on the front terrace date from 1888 and protect steles on which are carved the imperial edicts regarding the transfer of the cathedral to the present site. This dialogue between imperial Chinese and Catholic Gothic styles is unique. [© THOC, September 2018]

1 Tiedeman, *Handbook of Christianity*, 214–277, 564–652; statistics: 958–970, 997–1004.
2 Tiedeman, *Reference Guide*.
3 Chan, "Chinese Churches and Communist State."
4 Coomans, "Die Kunstlandschaft der Gotik in China"; Id., "Gothique ou chinoise."
5 Brandl, Ranft, and Waschbüsch, *Architektur als Zitat*; Coomans, "Architectural Iconology and Visual Culture."

Christian style that Rome tried to promote from the 1920s? Why did these missionary societies pretend that Chinese Christians preferred Gothic and other Western styles? Thirdly, modern Gothic churches with reinforced concrete structures were built in Shanghai, Hong Kong, and other big cities in the 1920s and 1930s. Did Protestants and Catholics develop different modern Gothic building types? Fourthly, several Gothic-style churches built at the time of the foreign missions are today protected as key cultural relics of the People's Republic of China. When did the heritagization process of Catholic and Christian churches in China develop and how should it be understood? Fifthly, why do many new churches built in China from the late 1980s continue to use Gothic forms inherited from and referring to the time of the mission? Why do Gothic references still contribute to the architectural representation of Christianity in twenty-first-century China?

12.02 The Sacred Heart Cathedral of Guangzhou, built 1860–1879, refers to thirteenth-century French Gothic style and benefited from Viollet-le-Duc's advice. This ashlar construction introduced forms, techniques and structures into China which were totally unknown and required the training of hundreds of specialized workers. [© THOC, September 2017]

The Breakthrough of Triumphant Gothic after 1900

The year 1900 marks a turn in the history of Christianity and church architecture in China. During the Boxer Uprising (1899–1901), thousands of Chinese Christians and dozens of Western missionaries were massacred, and hundreds of churches were destroyed.[6] The two-month siege by the Boxers of about 3,300 Chinese and seventy-one foreign Catholics who had taken refuge in the compound of the Gothic cathedral of Saint Saviour in Beijing (北堂 *Beitang* at Xishikou 西什库) [Fig. 12.01], as well as the resistance of the French Bishop Alphonse Favier C.M. (樊国梁 1837–1905) and a handful soldiers, was a dramatic, symbolic moment.[7] After the victory of the Eight-Nations Alliance forces and the signature of the Boxer Protocol on September 7, 1901, the Western nations reached their maximum power in China and kept it until the end of the First World War, despite the fall of the Qing dynasty in 1911 and the birth of the Republic in 1912. During that period, Catholic and Christian communities grew significantly.

The Boxer Protocol imposed large and humiliating reparations on the Chinese state, which would have to pay, among other things, for the reconstruction of destroyed churches and the erection of memorials at the sites of the martyrs. Triumphant Gothic-style cathedrals and churches, often with high spires, were erected throughout the country in prominent places, especially by French missionaries belonging to the Society of Jesus (S.J., Provinces of Paris and Champagne), the Congregation of the Mission (C.M., Lazarists or Vincentians) and the Foreign Missions of Paris (M.E.P.) as well as the Congregation of the Immaculate Heart of Mary (C.I.C.M., Belgian Scheut Fathers). Very visible in the public space, these new buildings expressed not only the memory of the massacres but also the Western triumph

6 Tiedemann, *Handbook of Christianity*, 338–343 (with bibliography).

7 Clark, *China Gothic*, 117–124.

of the Catholic missions. They reinforced the informal colonial character of the Church in China and contributed to exacerbate frustration and xenophobic feelings.

Gothic, however, was not totally unknown in China before 1900. Together with other Western styles, it had reached Hong Kong and the Treaty Ports after the First Opium War (1839–1842) and penetrated into China after the Second Opium War (1856–1860) when foreign missionaries were allowed to evangelize and build throughout the country. Most churches from that time have been demolished since, but photographs show diverse hybridized Chinese-Western types, structures, and styles according to the complex modes of interactions between missionaries and local craftsmen.[8] Gothic pointed arches, traceries, pinnacles, rose windows, and plaster rib vaults as well as European construction techniques, notably brickwork and roof trusses, were translated into the secular regional building traditions and appropriated by Chinese as expressions of both a foreign religion and modern novelty. Contrasting with this slow crossbreeding process, "pure" Western buildings, including Gothic churches, were erected in the Treaty Ports where, as in any nineteenth-century colonial hub, foreign architects, engineers, and militaries could realize great works and import construction materials. The Resurrection Chapel of the Anglican cemetery in Hong Kong (1845) and the Anglican Saint John's Cathedral in Hong Kong (1848–1853) are considered the two oldest Gothic-style places of worship in China.[9] In Shanghai, British Anglicans commissioned the famous architect George Gilbert Scott (1811–1878) to send plans to China for the Holy Trinity Cathedral, which was built from 1866 to 1869. Similar grand Victorian Gothic churches were to be found throughout the British Empire.[10] On Catholic side, thirteenth-century French Gothic, rediscovered and promoted by Eugène Viollet-le-Duc (1814–1879) as a new national style, entered China in the wake of a military expedition and the destructive 1857 Battle of Canton.

12.03 The Nanguan Cathedral in Shenyang was rebuilt in 1907–1911 as a French Gothic memorial to the 1900 massacre of missionaries and Chinese Catholics by the Boxers. [© Institut de recherche France-Asie / M.E.P.]

The cathedral of Guangzhou (广州 Guangdong), built by Bishop Zéphyrin Guillemin M.E.P. (名稽埒 1814–1886) from 1860 to 1879, is a remarkable case of export of a huge Gothic church building that included Western foundations, two high spires, a big rose window, portals with sculpted voussoirs, real rib vaults, and flying buttresses [Fig. 12.02].[11] Entirely made of carved stone in a then wooden city, the cathedral was nicknamed the "stone house of the foreign devils" (石室番鬼) by the Chinese and considered a "political, religious and cultural clash" by many.[12] In 1903, the French missionaries of the same apostolic vicariate built the Gothic

8 Coomans, "East Meets West on the Construction Site."
9 Wolfendale, *Imperial to International.*
10 Bremner, *Imperial Gothic.*
11 Masson, "Guangzhou shengxin dajiaotang de sheji he jianzao."
12 Wiest, "The Building of the Cathedral of Canton."

church of Xiashan in Zhangjiang (霞山, 湛江 Guangdong), which is a simplified and reduced version of the cathedral of Guangzhou.

Thanks to state indemnity and growing Christian congregations, the breakthrough of Gothic in post-Boxer China resulted in the building of Gothic cathedrals and churches on memorial places of massacres. In Beijing, the two towers of the façade of the North Cathedral were raised by one floor to be more visible in the skyline, including from the Forbidden City; until that time Empress Dowager Cixi (慈禧太后 1835–1908) had firmly refused to allow such heightening of the building [Fig. 12.01].[13] In Tianjin (天津), the Boxers had burned down the second Wanghailou church (望海楼, Our Lady of the Victory) that had been built after the Tientsin Massacre of 1870 and the destruction of the first Wanghailou church. In 1901–1904, the Gothic church was rebuilt for the third time, higher, larger, and longer, by Bishop Alphonse Favier C.M.[14] In Shenyang (沈阳 Liaoning) the historic capital of Manchuria and the then ruling imperial Qing Dynasty, the Boxers had massacred the French Bishop Laurent Guillon M.E.P. (纪隆 1854–1900) and assembled many Chinese Catholics into Nanguan Cathedral before burning the building. A grand Gothic cathedral with two 40-meter-high towers, designed by Father Henry Lamasse M.E.P. (梁四 1869–1952), was soon built by the Foreign Mission of Paris with the compensation money from the Chinese state [Fig. 12.03]. The use of Chinese blue bricks and the feng shui south–north orientation instead of the traditional Catholic east–west orientation are the two most significant Chinese characters of this French Gothic memorial, which was built 1907–1911 and received five big bells, which were cast in France and shipped to Manchuria.[15] In Jinan (济南, Shandong), the Hongjialou Cathedral was built 1901–1905 after plans by the Tyrolian Franciscan brother Korbinian Paugger O.F.M. (庞会襄 1855–1949). This exceptional Gothic stone and brick building has real brick domical vaults and flying buttresses as well as a rich architectonic stone carved decoration realized by several hundred stone carvers and masons led by the local master mason Lu Licheng (卢立成 dates unknown) [Figs. 12.04 & 12.05]. In 1905–1910, the French Jesuits of Shanghai built the church of Saint Ignatius in the Catholic district of Xujiahui (徐家汇 *Zikawei*), which is said to be the largest Catholic church in East Asia.[16] Designed by the Shanghai-based Scottish architect William Dowdall (道达尔 1842–1928) in thirteenth-century French cathedral Gothic style, this church became a cathedral when the apostolic vicariate of Shanghai was created in 1933. The outer walls made of red bricks and the two high spires enhance its Western character. In the same district of Xujiahui, the Christian art school of Tushanwan (土山湾 *Tou-Sè-Wè*) opened its doors in 1864 and trained orphans among other things in oil painting, stained glass, sculpture, printing, woodcraft, and liturgical furniture, which supplied the huge church market in China and other East Asian countries.[17] Not only were Chinese craftsmen trained in French Gothic and Romanesque styles, but their local work avoided costly imports from Europe. From the early twentieth century, the orphanage started to produce Chinese-decorated Western furniture and objects for the Western market and for expats in Shanghai.[18]

Several churches in French apostolic vicariates were dedicated to Our Lady of Lourdes, and their silhouettes were inspired by that of the Basilica of Lourdes (1862–1871), one of the most popular icons of French Gothic Revival. With its tapered central spire and the two characteristic turrets at the corner of the aisles, the cathedral of the Sacred Heart in Jilin (吉林 Jilin) built in 1917–1919 after plans by Father Henry Lamasse M.E.P., and the church of Our Lady of Daming (大名 Hebei) built by French Jesuits following the same plans in 1918–1921, show the reception in China of a French archetype nearly half a century later.[19] What were the reasons for such architectural "quotes": mimesis, nostalgia, or ideology? This can

13 The comparison of pictures before and after 1900 shows how the towers were made taller. The author climbed in the towers and compared the brick formats, which clearly distinguish the two building phases (April 29, 2013).
14 Sweeten, *China's Old Churches*, 182–207; Clark, *China Gothic*, 117–124.
15 These bronze bells with Gothic decoration wear inscriptions mentioning the date (1911), foundry (Paccard at Annecy-le-Vieux, Haute-Savoie), and names of the bells (Maria-Laurentia, Maria-Felicia, Maria-Henrica, Maria-Natalis and Maria-Camilla). Author's field notes, March 15, 2019 (courtesy Prof. Lü Haiping 吕海平).
16 Guillen-Nuñez, "The Gothic Revival."
17 de La Servière, *L'orphelinat de T'ou-Sè-Wè*.
18 Ma, *Pedagogy, Display, and Sympathy*.
19 Coomans and Xu, *Building Churches in Northern China*, 33–35, 306–318.
20 Coomans and Luo, "Mimesis, Nostalgia and Ideology."
21 Coomans, "East Meets West on the Construction Site."
22 Coomans and Luo, "Missionary-Builders."
23 Van Hecken, "Alphonse Frédéric De Moerloose"; Coomans, "Sint-Lucasneogotiek in Noord-China"; Luo, *Transmission and Transformation*, 120–195; Coomans and Xu, *Building Churches in Northern China*, 38–44.

only be answered with a precise contextualization on a case-by-case basis.[20] Non-French missionaries also built in other Western styles than the Gothic. For example, Italianate Renaissance style was used by Italian Franciscans for the cathedrals of Chengdu (成都 Sichuan), rebuilt in 1904, and Taiyuan (太原 Shanxi), rebuilt in 1905, as well as by the Salesians of Don Bosco for the Cathedral Chaozhou (潮州 Guangdong) in 1908. The cathedral of Kaifeng (开封 Henan), built 1917–1919 by other Italian Franciscans, refers to thirteenth-century Gothic mendicant churches from northern Italy [Fig. 12.06] and has a campanile like that of the Frari in Venice. Dutch Franciscans also opted for Gothic when they built the cathedral of Lu'an (潞安, Changzhi 长治, Shanxi, destroyed) in 1904.

If erecting Western-style cathedrals in the major cities of China was possible, the situation was very different in medium towns, small towns, and villages. Despite the financial compensations paid by the state, it was still hard to find Western architects willing to design elaborate Gothic churches for the China mission and Chinese workers able to read plans sent from Europe and understand Western construction techniques and styles.[21] Until the early 1920s, there were no Chinese architects who had graduated from Western universities. The missionary societies therefore sent their own missionary-builders to China, generally brother carpenters and creative handymen in charge of all issues related to construction.[22] When a grand cathedral had to be designed, it was often the bishop himself or a father who had some knowledge of styles and church architecture who sketched the project. The construction site was supervised on a daily basis by a brother builder.

Missionary-architects with a real architectural education, however, were highly exceptional. The Belgian Father Alphonse De Moerloose C.I.C.M. (和羹柏 1856–1932) is the best known and has been extensively studied.[23] He had been trained as an architect at the Saint Luke School in Ghent and was

12.04 The Sacred Heart or Hongjialou Cathedral in Jinan, built 1901–1905, expresses the triumph of the post-Boxers Catholic Church. Its traceried windows, forest of pinnacles, flying buttresses and spires gives it an overstated Gothic appearance.
[© THOC, June 2018]

12.05 The Sacred Heart or Hongjialou Cathedral in Jinan, built 1901–1905, has a rich decorated interior and domical Gothic vaults, which are a technical prowess.
[© THOC, June 2018]

12.06 The Sacred Heart Cathedral in Kaifeng, built 1917–1919 by Italian Franciscans, refers to the thirteenth-century brick architecture of the Mendicants from North Italy.
[© THOC, June 2013]

fed with the theories of Augustus W. N. Pugin (1812–1852) and the belief that Gothic was the only style suitable for the Universal Catholic Church. Even though he was in China since 1885, he began architectural work in 1899–1900 as a consequence of the Boxers' destructions and the state reparations, which gave him the opportunity to carry out considerable architectural activity in northern China. Active until 1929, he worked not only for the Belgian Scheut Fathers but also for the French Lazarists in North Hebei, the French Trappist abbey of Yangjiaping (杨家坪 Hebei), and the French Jesuits of South Hebei and Shanghai. This is how the "true principles" of Pugin's Christian Gothic, translated into the Flemish Gothic style of the Saint Luke Schools, spread in a universal civilizing perspective until the plains and mountains of northern China and Inner Mongolia.[24] Foreign to local traditions and poorly adapted to climatic conditions, De Moerloose's architecture could be qualified as "pure export" if it had not been realized by a Chinese workforce with local materials.[25] Another missionary architect is the Portuguese Father Francisco Diniz S.J. (葉肇昌 1869–1943), who entered the Society of Jesus in 1896 in Shanghai after having learned architecture in the office of William Dowdall. As soon he was ordained a priest in 1905, the Jesuits entrusted him with the daily supervision of the construction of the Gothic church of Saint Ignatius in Xujiahui from 1906 to 1910 [Fig. 12.07]. Thereafter, he was sent to Europe for one year to follow architecture courses at the École des Beaux-Arts in Paris and an internship in a construction firm, before returning to Shanghai in 1913 and becoming the "architect of the Mission."[26]

Christian population increased noticeably in China after 1900 and the missionaries, whose numbers were also increasing, organized new Marian pilgrimages to places of memory that had resisted the Boxers and other threats. Unlike the Anglicans and Protestants, the Catholics possessed with Marian pilgrimages a tool of evangelization of their own. Several missionary societies promoted pilgrimages and colonized hilltops with churches and chapels overlooking vast landscapes, sometimes even on sites of former Buddhist temples.[27] The two most important pilgrimages were south of Beijing and near Shanghai. After the resistance of the Catholic village of Donglü (东闾 Hebei) against the Boxers, the French Lazarists promoted a Marian shrine and built a great Gothic church to Our Lady of China (1901, destroyed in 1941).[28] From 1870, after having made a vow to Mary, the French Jesuits developed the shrine of Our Lady of Sheshan (佘山 *Zo-cè*) in the outskirts of Shanghai. When, in 1918, the project of a new pilgrimage church was discussed, the issue of its style became central. Father De Moerloose designed a Saint Luke Gothic style project [Fig. 12.08], which was rejected in 1919 by the French Jesuits who wanted Romanesque style. The missionary-architect obeyed his patrons and made a second project for the greatest pilgrimage church of China, which was built from 1921 to 1936 [Fig. 12.09].[29] Other cathedrals and great churches from

24 Coomans, "Pugin Worldwide."
25 De Moerloose's most significant and best preserved church is the church of Xuanhua (宣化 Hebei): Coomans and Luo, "Exporting Flemish Gothic," 237–245.
26 About Father Diniz: Coomans, *Sheshan Marian Shrine in Shanghai*, chapter 7.1.
27 Coomans, "Islands on the Mainland."
28 Trémorin, "Autour de Notre Dame de Tong-lu."
29 Coomans, *Sheshan Marian Shrine in Shanghai*, chapters 5 and 6; Coomans, "Notre-Dame de Sheshan."

12.07 The Cathedral of Saint Ignatius in the Xujiahui district of Shanghai, built 1905–1910, is said to be the largest Catholic church of East Asia. It expresses the success of the French Jesuit Mission in Shanghai and hosted the first plenary council of the Catholic Church of China in 1924.
[© Archives de la Province d'Europe occidentale francophone des Jésuites, FCh, E3]

12.08 The first project for the new basilica of Mary Help of Christians on top of Sheshan Hill near Shanghai, dated 1920, was designed in Sint Luke Gothic style by Father De Moerloose. The French Jesuits rejected it in favor of another Western style.
[© KADOC - KU Leuven, Archives C.I.C.M., De Moerloose]

12.09 The second project for the new basilica of Mary Help of Christians on top of Sheshan Hill near Shanghai, completed in 1923, was designed in eclectic Romanesque style by Father De Moerloose. The construction works lasted from 1923 to 1936.
[© Archives de la Province d'Europe occidentale francophone des Jésuites, FCh, C4]

the late 1910s and early 1920s also adopted Romanesque forms, which, in the eyes of the Chinese, did not present any significant difference compared to Gothic, because both were Western. In the 1920s, however, the stylistic debate would shift and oppose all the foreign styles to the Chinese style.

Gothic in China: An Error of Style?

The great upheavals that agitated the world during the 1910s also had consequences for the Christian churches and missions in China. On the one hand, the fall of the Empire and the birth of the Republic in 1912 accelerated the "search for modern China."[30] On the other hand, the First World War altered the balance of power between Western nations worldwide, including in the concessions of the Chinese treaty ports. Missionary congregations were not immune to these tensions and to the complex entangled political, religious, and national interests. Chinese nationalist and xenophobic sentiments, exacerbated by the May Fourth Movement in 1919, would inevitably turn against the missions of the various Christian churches.

After the First World War, the Catholic Church realized that the Western colonial model would quickly become counterproductive for the evangelization of peoples. The Holy See defined a new strategy, which aimed to replace the Western model and promote true local churches with native bishops and priests. This movement is called "indigenization," that is to say "the rooting and integration of the Christian faith in a particular culture," contrary to the colonial and Eurocentric worldview of the "civilizing mission."[31] Pope Benedict XV (1914–1922) initiated this new dynamic with his Apostolical Letter *Maximum illud* of November 30, 1919, confirmed on February 28, 1926 by the Encyclical Letter *Rerum Ecclesiae* of Pius XI (1922–1939), the "Pope of the Missions." In 1922, Pius XI sent Monsignor Celso Costantini (刚恒毅 1876–1958) to China as Apostolic Delegate with the mission of implementing the process of indigenization.[32] He called the first plenary council of the Roman Catholic Church of China that brought together in Shanghai the vicars apostolic and the provincials of the missionary congregations of China (May 15–June 12, 1924). Two years later, on October 28, 1926, Pius XI consecrated the first six Chinese bishops in Rome.[33] However, Mgr. Costantini faced opposition from several vicars apostolic and missionaries, especially the French, because they lost their dominant position following the end of the colonial system of the French religious Protectorate in 1922 and the rise of a local church.[34]

Christian art and architecture were important components of the Apostolic Delegate's strategy for "Sinicizing Christianity," that is redefining Christianity for the Chinese context.[35] He considered promoting a Sino-Christian style as a major tool for architectural indigenization. Because this has been developed in other recent publications,[36] I will focus here on Costantini's polarizing dialectic related with Gothic. Catholics should abandon all Western styles as soon as possible and Sinicize their architecture, like the Protestants had been doing for more than a decade.[37] Mgr. Costantini used "Gothic" as a metonymy for all Western styles, but by doing so he pointed especially the French missionaries—the major promotors of Gothic, as we have seen—and spared the Italians. His first text, entitled "Proper Style of Church Architecture for the Chinese Mission" was a letter dated April 23, 1923, addressed to two future vicars apostolic to China and published in *The Ecclesiastical Review* of September 1923.[38] The two addressees belonged to the wave of postwar new missionary societies sent to China in order to contribute to indigenization more zealously than the conservative French missionaries.[39] Mgr. Costantini's letter was later revised, translated, and published in several journals as a reference text.[40]

The Apostolic Delegate rejected Gothic and Western Christian art and architecture as the genuine and universal art of the Church:

30 Spence, *The Search for Modern China*, 269–434.
31 Koschorke, "Indigenization"; Standaert, *Inculturation*, 99.
32 *Cardinal Celso Costantini and the Chinese Catholic Church*; Ticozzi, "Celso Costantini's Contribution."
33 Carbonneau, "The Catholic Church in China."
34 Young, *Ecclesiastical Colony*; Soetens, *L'Église catholique en Chine*, 101–109.
35 Zheng, *Sinicizing Christianity*.
36 Coomans, "The Sino-Christian Style"; Coomans, "Indigenizing Catholic Architecture."
37 Cody, "Striking a Harmonious Chord."
38 Costantini, "Proper Style of Church Architecture."
39 James Edward Walsh (华理住 1891–1981), from the Catholic Foreign Mission Society of America (Maryknol), vicar apostolic of Jiangmen (江门 Kongmoon, Guangdong); Edward J. Galvin (高尔文 1882–1956), from the Irish Missionary Society of Saint Columban, vicar apostolic of Hanyang (汉阳, Wuhan 武汉, Hubei).
40 Costantini, "The Need of Developing a Sino-Christian Architecture"; Costantini, "L'universalité de l'art chrétien."

> Speaking of Gothic, the roofs of this style are steep to precipitate the snow; and the spires of Gothic towers harmonize magnificently with the landscapes of Northern Europe; but one cannot say the same of the Gothic towers one sees among the luxuriant palm trees in China.[41]

> Occidental art in China is tantamount to an error of style. [...] Hence it is an artistic blunder to import into this country the Roman[esque] and Gothic styles of Europe. [...] Underlying the practice of importing foreign architecture into China is the question of a faulty method of religious propaganda. [...] We must know how to enter into the spirit of Chinese architecture and enliven it with new Christian life.[42]

> Medieval Christian art [...] is absolutely not a kind of artistic Latin that can be passed off as a form of artistic-Catholic universality. No, definitely not...[43]

Mgr. Costantini appointed Father Adelbert Gresnigt O.S.B. (葛利斯 1877–1956), a Dutch Benedictine monk from the Belgian Gothic Revival abbey of Maredsous, to come to China and create Sino-Christian architecture—which he did during his short stay from March 1927 to January 1932.[44] As soon as he landed in China, the latter was asked by Father Vincent Lebbe C.M. (雷鸣远 1877–1940), the "apostle of inculturation in China," to Sinicize his parish church in Zhaojiazhuang (赵家装 Hebei). This was a small Gothic church about which Father Lebbe said: "God does not seem to be at home in China; he is still living in a foreign house."[45] Eventually, this metamorphosis from Gothic to Chinese did not happen, and Father Gresnigt's plans were used in 1929 to build the neighboring Chinese-style cathedral of Anguo (安国 Hebei) for Mgr. Melchior Sun Dezhen C.M. (孙德祯 1869–1951), one of the six Chinese bishops consecrated in 1926.[46] Despite Mgr. Costantini's respect for the Gothic architect Father De Moerloose, their divergence of opinions about architecture was total. In a letter to a friend, the latter wrote:

> Monseigneur the Delegate especially dislikes Gothic; as all the Italians, his reference is Saint John of Lateran. All the right thinking missionaries and bishops I have seen [understand: the French bishops] think that there is no question of building Chinese churches, this is not practical.[47]

Eventually, the old missionary-architect returned to Belgium in 1929 after having spent forty-four years in China.[48]

The architectural debate, however, was never clearly conducted within the Catholic mission to China. Rome wanted to impose a style that it believed suited its policy of indigenization, but encountered opposition on the field, both from missionaries and Chinese believers. On the one hand, many missionaries and bishops, regretting the days of the French religious Protectorate, boycotted Mgr. Costantini's work by not promoting the emergence of a local clergy and by opposing Sino-Christian architecture. In 1926, Father Paul Jung S.J. (雍居敬 1863–1943) from the French Jesuit mission of Daming anonymously published a handbook offering practical advice and plans for building solid, safe, and economical churches in northern China.[49] Despite the technical character of this book and the author's refusal to deal with questions related to style, a critic of the Chinese style and construction is developed in a long note that refers to articles of two other French missionaries who continued to plead for Western architecture.[50] They argued that Gothic is a real architecture, not a style made of unnecessary ornament and expensive decoration like Chinese architecture. Furthermore, most of the churches given as type models in the plates of the handbook are in Gothic style [Fig. 12.10] and most decorative details come from the Gothic church of Daming, built 1918–1921.[51]

On the other hand, it seems that some Chinese Christians were not happy with the change of style, which in their eyes, created

41 Costantini, "Proper Style of Church Architecture," 290.
42 Costantini, "The Need of Developing a Sino-Christian Architecture," 9–10.
43 Costantini, *L'art chrétien dans les missions*, 92.
44 His most important work was the Catholic University of Peking (辅仁大学 Fu Jen University). See: Coomans, "La création d'un style"; Id., "Unexpected Connections," 281-288.
45 Coomans, "The Sino-Christian Style," 211–212.
46 Wiest, "Le père Lebbe et son église."
47 Leuven, KADOC, C.I.C.M. Archives, T.I.a.14.3.2: letter of A. De Moerloose to K. Van de Vyvere C.I.C.M., August 28, 1924 (translated from Dutch).
48 Coomans, "Unexpected Connections," 275-281.
49 [Jung], *Le missionnaire constructeur, conseils – plans*. Study and edition in: Coomans and Xu, *Building Churches in Northern China*.
50 D.G., "Quelques idées sur l'art chinois"; Doutreligne, "Causerie sur l'art chinois."
51 Coomans, "A Pragmatic Approach to Church Construction."

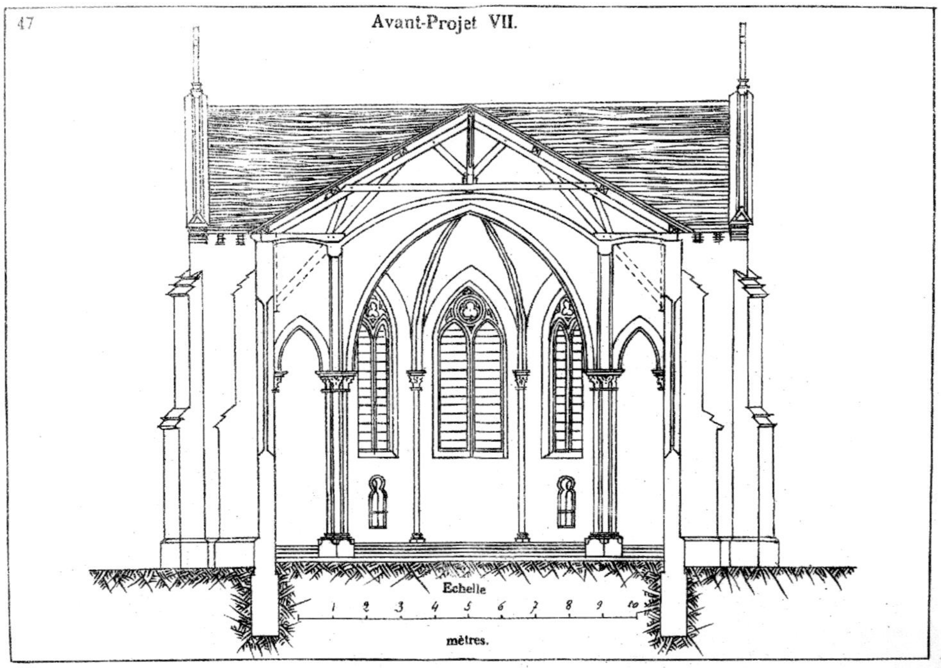

12.10 French Jesuits continued to promote Gothic architecture in the 1920s and 1930s as proves the handbook *Le Missionnaire-Constructeur. Conseils-Plans* published in Xianxian in 1926 and reprinted in 1935, which includes model plans of several types and sizes of Gothic churches.
[© Québec, Université Laval, Bibliothèque des sciences humaines et sociales, NA 6045 M678 1935]

identity confusion. Specific sources on this point are scarce, but both promoters and opponents of the Sino-Christian style refer to the attitude of their parishioners.[52] Conservative missionaries argued that Chinese Catholics refused to worship in churches that looked like pagodas and found Western styles in accordance with the foreign character of Christianity and their Catholic identity. Other Chinese argued that as long God would live in a foreign house, he would not be at home in China—which was Father Lebbe's above mentioned point of view.

The second half of the 1930s was no longer conducive to major projects and the construction of churches. Growing insecurity, political instability, the economic crisis, and the Japanese invasion from 1937 were shaking up China's domestic situation. In Europe, the Holy See was facing the rise of fascist and communist totalitarianisms, and no longer made the missionary question its priority. Indigenization materialized above all in the liturgical furniture and Sinicized iconography that replaced Gothic altars and Western paintings of Mary and saints.

Modern Gothic Churches with Reinforced Concrete Structures

After the First World War, the Gothic paradigm was soon abandoned in Europe in favor of either Romanesque, Byzantine, or early Christian references, in the perspective of the Liturgical Movement that aimed at better participation of the faithful in Catholic liturgy. The Liturgical Movement had been launched in Malines at the National Belgian Congress of Catholic Works in September 1909 and was supported by Pope Pius X (1903–1914). After the First World War, the use of reinforced concrete made possible the construction of a new generation of churches with vast spaces, as required by the Liturgical Movement. Geometric forms and reduced ornamentation, often combined with monumental proportions, characterize interwar Western Christian architecture.[53] At the same time, reinforced concrete developed its own aesthetic devoid of any reference to historic styles. Notre-Dame du Raincy, built near Paris in 1922–1923 by architect Auguste Perret (1874–1954) is an iconic milestone on the path to modern church architecture and innovation.[54]

In China, too, from the early 1920s, many new Christian churches were no longer Gothic but remained Western with explicit national references. Except the shift from Gothic to Romanesque style that occurred in 1919–1921 at the pilgrimage church of Our Lady of Sheshan near Shanghai, earlier discussed, other examples are the cathedral of Hohhot (呼和浩特 Inner Mongolia), built by Belgian Scheut Fathers in 1922–1924, referring to the abbey of Villers in Brabant;[55] the cathedral of Saint Michael at Qingdao (青岛 Shandong) built by German missionaries of the Society of the Divine Word in 1930–1933 in Rhenish Romanesque style [Fig. 12.11];[56] the church of Qiaoergou in Yan'an (桥儿沟, 延安 Shaanxi) built by Spanish Franciscans in 1934 with Spanish references; and Saint Teresa Church in Kowloon (九龙 Hong Kong), built by an Italian bishop and a Portuguese parish in 1930–

52 X, "Objections."
53 McNamara, *Catholic Church Architecture*, 171–185; *L'Artisan Liturgique*, vol. 1–14.
54 Le Bas, "Notre-Dame du Raincy."
55 Coomans and Luo, "Mimesis, Nostalgia and Ideology," 507–508, 520.
56 Faber, "Und trotzte allen Zeiten."

1932, in a modern Romanesque style with a campanile that refers explicitly to that of San Marco in Venice.[57] However, as we have seen, the debate on Sino-Christian style was a paradigm shift for Catholic church architecture from the mid-1920s.

From the 1920s, some Protestant denominations developed various forms of "modern Gothic," clearly identifiable with English Anglican, German Lutheran, or Evangelical, Methodist, and American Presbyterian churches. Modern Gothic was limited to large cities and treaty ports, where modern architecture and reinforced concrete constructions flourished. On the Anglican side, Gothic continued to be the reference style for churches until the mid-1930s and then shifted to Chinese style in Hong Kong.[58] Among other churches, the Anglican Saint Saviour's Cathedral in Anqing (安庆 Anhui), 1900–1903; Saint Paul's Church, 1922–1923, in Nanjing (南京 Jiangsu); Kowloon Union Church in Hong Kong, 1930; and the Presbyterian Mochou Lu Church, 1936, in Nanjing are typical examples of English Gothic characterized by the use of some Tudor style elements such as doors and windows, spireless towers, and open timber roof trusses.

English Gothic was also used as a reference for several chapels of the thirteen universities the Protestants founded in early twentieth century China.[59] In the middle of the campus of Shandong Christian University (齐鲁大学 *Cheeloo University*), founded by American Presbyterians, English Baptists, and Anglicans in Jinan (济南 Shandong), stood Kumler Memorial Chapel, a stone church with a massive tower on the crossing [Fig. 12.12]. It was the only Gothic-style building on the campus designed by the Chicago firm of Perkins, Fellows, and Hamilton and erected in 1923 (since demolished).[60] Another early twentieth-century chapel built by the American Presbyterians can be seen on the campus of the former Hangchow University (之江大学 *Zhijiang University*) at Hangzhou.

Multistory Protestant churches are a special building type that superposes a low chapel for daily use and other rooms on the ground floor, a large congregation hall without pillars on the first floor, and a gallery on the second floor, with two staircases and landings located in the corners of the first bay between the façade and the nave. Catholics never built such churches, because their naves for the assembly as well as the choir had to be established on the ground and thus

12.11 The Saint Michael's Catholic Cathedral in Qingdao was built in Rhineland Romanesque style from 1930 to 1933.
[© Tam Lun, 2011]

57 Coomans and Ho, "Architectural Styles and Identities in Hong Kong."
58 Ellis, "Anglican Indigenization."
59 Cody, "American Geometries."
60 *Educational Buildings by Perkins, Fellows and Hamilton.*

12.12 The Kumler Memorial Chapel at Cheeloo University in Jinan, built 1923 (demolished), looked like an English medieval parish church, with a typical Latin cross plan and crossing tower. Only the roofs of the entrance lobbies had Chinese upturned eaves.
[© Yale Divinity Library Special Collections YDS/RG011/414/5873/4837 / Wikimedia Commons]

could not have any undercroft with profane use. Multistory Protestant churches are urban and offer more usable surface on a small parcel of land. Their forms and cement-cast decoration are of different styles,[61] including Gothic such as Li Xian Hui Church 禮賢會堂 and school in Hong Kong built in 1913–1914 by the Lutheran Rhenish Mission, Kau Yan Tsung Tsin Church in Hong Kong 基督教香港崇真會救恩堂 built in 1931–1932 by the Basel Evangelical Missionary Society [Fig. 12.13], and Rongguang Church 荣光堂 or John Griffith's Church in Wuhan (武汉 Hubei) built in 1931 by the London Missionary Society [Fig. 12.14]. Some modern Gothic churches of the "auditorium type," consisting of an assembly hall with a stage and a U-shaped gallery, were built in China. Dongshan Church 东山堂 in Guangzhou, built by the Baptist in 1923, has geometricized Tudor windows and a Gothic tower.

The most original modern Gothic churches are in Shanghai and were designed by Ladislav Hudec (邬达克 1893–1958), a Slovak Hungarian modernist architect active in China from 1918 to 1945.[62] He designed all kinds of modern buildings in Shanghai, including the iconic Park Hotel and Grand Theatre, both from 1931–1933, as well as buildings, schools, and churches for Western communities of different Christians denominations; these buildings include the paired Art Deco buildings of the China Baptist Publication and China Christian Literature Society, both from 1930–1932. The German Evangelical Church, built 1930–1932 (demolished), with its stepped gables, buttresses, and a massive red brick tower referred to late medieval Gothic brick architecture from northern Germany. The Moore Memorial Methodist Church (Mu'en Church 沐恩堂) was built 1929–1931 on a very visible site at a corner facing Shanghai's racecourse, presently People's Park, and included a Gothic vaulted main auditorium with galleries that could host 1,200 faithful—said to be the largest Protestant church in East Asia—reading rooms for men and women, a kindergarten with a nursery, offices of the board, and other rooms for congregational life [Fig. 12.15]. The whole complex echoed in Shanghai the interwar American modern Gothic architecture that combines reinforced concrete structures, red brick masonry, and stone framed windows of different Gothic types (cross window, oriels, and pointed arch windows with traceries), crenellation, buttresses, and a high spireless tower. In 1929, Hudec made a study trip to the United States, from San Francisco to New York, and certainly became acquainted with modern American Gothic churches. Due to the dramatic changes of Shanghai's skyline, the tower of Moore Memorial Church no longer emerges, and its visual competition with the 1901 spire of the neighboring Anglican Holy Trinity Cathedral, both in the International Concession, could no longer be understood.

Even though he was a Lutheran, Hudec also worked for Catholics whose schools competed with those of the Protestant in attracting children of the Chinese elite with modern facilities and educational programs.[63] Contrasting with these school buildings, the chapel of the Westerners' Cemetery on Rubicon road, today known as Xi Yan Tang (息焉堂 *Sieh Yih* chapel), presents an original blend of modern Byzantine and Gothic styles characterized by a copper-clad concrete dome and a campanile. The chapel was built 1929–1931 in a cemetery on the outskirts of Shanghai with funds raised by Joseph Ma Xiangbo (马相伯 1840–1939), a famous Chinese educator and former Jesuit, and other Catholics. Assisted by the Catholic Chinese architect Francis Xavier Pan Shiyi (潘世义 1890–1948), Hudec designed a cubic volume with a dome and apse, of which all the arches are pointed. The inner space is rhythmed by four slender pillars and a set of pointed arches which support the dome [Fig. 12.16]. The tension of the main lines of the structure is stressed by moldings which raise the gaze toward the crown of small windows and the lightness groined dome. This "expressive" architecture was in all likelihood influenced by Czech Cubism,

an avant-garde movement from the time Hudec studied architecture.

However, pure modernist churches, without any reference to Western and Chinese historic styles, were extremely rare in China. One the one hand, cement, steel bars, and skilled workers were expensive and could only be found in big cities, harbor towns, and places along railway lines. On the other hand, Catholics and Protestants, both Chinese and Western, expressed the sacredness of their places of worship by referring to historical styles or at least including cement-cast elements of these styles in buildings with concrete structures. The modernism of Notre-Dame du Raincy, for instance, had very limited impact in China, even in Shanghai, Tianjin, Nanjing, Wuhan, Guangzhou, Hong Kong, Shenyang, and Harbin, the eight cities that were the most open to international modernity in the 1920–1930s.

12.13 The Kau Yan Tsung Tsing Church of the Basel Evangelical Missionary Society in Hong Kong, built 1931–1932, is a multistory church which takes advantage of the sloping topography. The assembly hall with a gallery occupies the two upper floors, while the lancet windows, buttresses, Tudor-arched porch and spired tower give the reinforced concrete building a Gothic touch. [© THOC, April 2014]

12.14 The assembly hall on the upper floor of Rongguang Church or John Griffith's Church, London Missionary Society, built 1931 in Wuhan, is a warm and enlightened space rhythmed with "tiers-point" arches and covered with a wooden polygonal barrel vault. [© THCC, September 2017]

12.15 The Moore Memorial Methodist Church or Mu'en Church, built 1929–1931, is a masterpiece of Ladislav Hudec in Shanghai. The slender red brick tower, traceried windows and inner auditorium-type space belong to the modern Gothic American church architecture of the interwar. [https://www.virtualshanghai.net/Data/Buildings?ID=679]

61 Other examples of urban Protestant churches with two floors, reinforced concrete, but in modern Chinese style: Presbyterian Si Chang Church 思澄堂 in Hangzhou, 1927; Presbyterian Hong De Church 鸿德堂 in Shanghai, 1928; Hong De Church 洪德堂 in Guangzhou, 1934–1935; Anglican Saint Mary's Church 聖公會聖馬利亞堂 in Hong Kong, 1937.

62 Hua, Qiao, Kató, and Boglárka, *Shanghai Hudec*; Lai, Wu, and Xu, *Zhongguo jindai jianzhu shi*, vol. 4, 29–38.

63 Hudec designed the Sacred Heart Vocational College for Girls (1936), the Aurora College for Women (1937–1939), the Chinese School of the Convent of the Sacred Heart (1938), and the Russian Catholic School Hostel for Boys (1941).

12.16 The Xi Yan Tang Chapel of the Catholic cemetery in Shanghai, built in 1929–1931 after plans by Ladislav Hudec, combines a Byzantine domed space with Gothic arches and reinforced concrete structure. [© THOC, September 2017]

Heritagizing Gothic Churches

From the late 1930s to the early 1980s, architectural activity in church building was virtually nonexistent in China. The Second Sino-Japanese War, the Chinese Civil War, the expulsion of all foreign missionaries from China, and the Cultural Revolution had dire consequences for Christian architecture. Many churches have been demolished or recycled for all kinds of secular uses. Red Guards systematically defaced churches by pulling down their towers and burned all interior furnishings, whatever their style.

In the 1980s and 1990s, most church buildings that had stood the test of time were returned by the government to Christian congregations, who tried their best to restore the sacred function of their places of worship. The surviving churches were generally in poor condition, and the congregations had little or no financial means. Often it took years to congregations to relocate the households that lived in the churches. Re-erecting towers and spires topped with crosses was an important step in restoring the face of the churches in the public space. However, because churches were not yet heritagized and no skills were available for proper conservation, the renovation of many churches has caused irreversible damage to historic buildings. Old churches were also sometimes demolished and replaced with new ones. Some congregations were so shrunken that they no longer needed the buildings the government returned to them and therefore retained the recycled function—which at least generated rent—or could not do nothing but preserve the ruin. When the country's economy began to develop and well-located land increased in value, bishops sometimes sold old churches to real estate developers and used the capital to build new churches at other sites. In all these operations, the powerful State Administration for Construction was involved as the key player.

Only heritage protection could have prevented speculation, but it took some time before churches began to be heritagized, especially because of conflicts of interest between the State Administration for Cultural Heritage and the State Administration for Construction. The State Administration for Religious Affairs is not involved in real estate and heritage issues but controls the activities of congregations, which include the use of buildings. Over the past few decades, the government made considerable efforts to promote heritage, including modern heritage, the category to which belong the churches built from the 1840s to the 1940s.[64] Churches that had been poorly renovated in the 1980s were again and better renovated after having been declared municipal or provincial heritage. Gradually, some Gothic churches have been declared key cultural relics of the People's Republic of China (see Table 1). Paradoxically, the history and style of the first two of them are linked to clashes with French Catholic imperialism. First, Wanghailou church in Tianjin, the memorial church of Tientsin Massacre, twice demolished and three times rebuilt, became national heritage in 1988. Second, the cathedral of Guangzhou, the architectural archetype of French Gothic, erected on the site of the former viceroy's palace, became national heritage in 1996 [Fig. 12.02]. Ten years later, in 2006, two Gothic cathedrals

64 ICOMOS China, *Principles for the Conservation.*

TABLE 1
GOTHIC-STYLE CATHEDRALS, CHURCHES, AND CHAPELS LISTED AS "KEY CULTURAL RELICS" OF THE PEOPLE'S REPUBLIC OF CHINA, BATCHES 3 (1988) TO 8 (2019). CHURCHES THAT ARE PART OF A COMPLEX ARE MARKED WITH (*). COURTESY CUI JINZE 崔金泽.

BATCH YEAR	CITY	PROVINCE	NAME	DENOMI-NATION	BUILT IN
3 - 1988	Tianjin		Wanghailou Church	Catholic	1869 / 1897 / 1904
4 - 1996	Guangzhou	Guangdong	Holy Heart Cathedral	Catholic	1860–1879
5 - 2001	Weizhou	Guangxi	Chengzai Church (*)	Catholic	1880
6 - 2006	Beijing		Xishiku Cathedral / Beitang	Catholic	1887–1888 / 1901
	Ningbo	Zhejiang	Jiangbei Cathedral	Catholic	1872
	Jinan	Shandong	Hongjialou Cathedral	Catholic	1901–1905
	Gulangyu	Fujian	Church (*)	Catholic	1917
	Hangzhou	Zhejiang	Tooker Memorial Chapel on campus Zhijiang University (*)	Presbyterian	1917
7 - 2013	Shanghai		Xujiahui Cathedral	Catholic	1905–1910
	Daming	Hebei	Church	Catholic	1918–1921
	Hohhot	Inner Mongolia	Cathedral	Catholic	1922–1924
	Shenyang	Liaoning	Cathedral	Catholic	1907–1911
	Jilin	Jilin	Cathedral	Catholic	1918–1919
	Jiaxing	Zhejiang	Church and seminary	Catholic	1917–1930
	Wuhu	Anhui	Cathedral	Catholic	1882–1889 / 1895
	Jining	Shandong	Yanzhou Cathedral	Catholic	1897–1899
	Jinan	Shandong	Chapel in Cheeloo University	Baptist / Presbyterian	1923
	Xinyang	Henan	Chapel on Mount Jigong (*)	Protestant	
	Yiyang	Hunan	Wumafang Church	Lutheran	1908
8 - 2019	Beijing		Saint Michael's Church	Catholic	1904–1905
	Shanghai		Holy Trinity Cathedral	Anglican	1866–1869 / 1901
	Shanghai		White Chapel, University of Shanghai (Hujiang University)	Baptist	1937
	Hangzhou	Zhejiang	Chapel of Holy Heart Hospital (*)	Catholic	1920s

that are historically directly connected with the Boxer Uprising were upgraded to key cultural relics: Xishikou Cathedral in Beijing and Hongjalu Cathedral in Jinan, both earlier discussed [Figs. 12.01 and 12.04]. The 2013 batch included the largest number of Gothic churches, dominantly Catholic. In several cases, churches and chapels are part of protected building complexes such as university campuses, colonial settlements, or hospitals (see Table 1). At last, the historic international settlement of Gulangyu Island (鼓浪屿 *Kulangsu*, Fujian) was inscribed on the World Heritage list in 2017. It includes several churches, among which the Catholic church built by Spanish Dominicans in 1917 is the only Gothic one.[65]

However, the heritage issue remains sensitive insofar as the historical and technical knowledge on Western churches in general and Gothic in particular remains limited. The development of research in partnership should improve this situation.[66] The case of the ruined Gothic church of Jiaxing (嘉兴 Zhejiang), a historic city located halfway between Shanghai and Hangzhou, is a good illustration of the complex heritagization of churches [Fig. 12.17].[67] Jiaxing's church was built from 1917 to 1930 by the French Lazarists, under the supervision of the Italian father Ange Asinelli C.M. (韩日禄 1871–1945), on a traditional Latin cross plan with a chancel, transept, nave, aisles, and façade with two high towers. The outer walls are made of brick, but the main structure of

65 Kulangsu, a Historic International Settlement, includes the Protestant Union Church (1911) and Trinity Church (1934), but they are not Gothic.

66 Coomans and Xu, "Built Together, Heritagized Together."

67 With thanks to Prof. Zhang Hui 张晖 and Dr. Shen Ling 沈灵 (Zhejiang University) for site visits and discussions in 2018–2019, and Prof. Lu Yongyi 卢永毅 (Tongji University) for sharing reflections on the restoration project in 2020.

12.17 The Gothic church of the Miraculous Medal in Jiaxing, built 1917–1930, was used as a factory before being returned in 1982 to the Catholic parish which was not in state to stop the ruin process.
[© THOC, September 2018]

12.18 The Gothic church of the Miraculous Medal in Jiaxing, built 1917–1930, was divided in two floors and used as a factory for thirty years. View on the ruined nave before the recent renovation works, which withdrew the inner division and reconstructed the original clerestory, vaults, and roof.
[© THOC, September 2018]

reinforced concrete is hidden behind fake lath and plaster pointed arches, capitals, and rib vaults, which make the Gothic appearance inside a pure decoration. The building was damaged during Japanese bombing in August 1937 and secularized by the local government in the 1950s.

Over thirty years, the former church was used as a factory to bear metal: the ateliers were in the nave, while the chancel and transept hosted the workers' refectory. Because the vibrations of the mechanical presses threatened the roof of the nave to collapse, the upper part of the nave was demolished and a new roof established much lower. In the early 1960s, the nave was divided into two floors and the upper one was used as temporary hospital during an epidemic of bilharzia. When the church was returned to the Catholics in 1982, the congregation used the upper floor of the nave for worship but had no need for the other parts, which quickly degraded. After the collapse of the roofs of the chancel and transept in the late 1990s, the old church became a ruin [Fig. 12.17]. The heritagization of the church and the neighboring former residence of the missionaries began in 2001 with their protection as a Jiaxing city monument, continued with their upgrade as a Zhejiang Province monument in 2005 and a key cultural relic of the People's Republic of China in 2013. In the meantime, the ruin was deteriorating rapidly and measures had to be taken to prevent collapse [Fig. 12.18]. Disagreement on the future use of the church as museum or place for worship caused new delays. Eventually a restoration and reconstruction of the original state was decided and realized in 2020–2021 as part of the redevelopment of Jiaxing's small city archaeologic area. During this process, about seventy years long, China's society and perception of its past changed profoundly.

In Hong Kong, the heritage policy and protection system is quite different. Only one cathedral, one church, and one chapel in the Gothic style are "declared monuments," in other words, receiving the highest degree of protection, while seven other are classified as Grade I historic buildings (see Table 2). Due to the important Anglican and Catholic presence in the British colony, many churches built before the Second World War are Gothic [Fig. 12.19]. In Macao, inversely, most churches are in Portuguese colonial style, except the Gothic chapel of Saint Michael's Cemetery (1874–1875). The latter is not part of the World Heritage area, which includes seven churches.[68]

68 Historic Centre of Macao, UNESCO World Heritage.

12.19 Hop Yat Church, Church of Christ in China, built 1922–1926, is one of the several Gothic-style churches to be a historic building of Hong Kong.
[© THOC, April 2014]

TABLE 2
GOTHIC-STYLE CATHEDRALS, CHURCHES, AND CHAPELS LISTED AS "DECLARED MONUMENTS" AND GRADE I HISTORIC BUILDINGS IN HONG KONG

YEAR	NAME	DENOMINATION	DISTRICT	BUILT IN
DECLARED MONUMENTS OF HONG KONG				
1996	Saint John the Evangelist's Cathedral	Anglican	Central	1846–1849
2013	Bethanie M.E.P. sanatorium and chapel	Catholic	Pokfulam	1873–1875
2017	Kowloon Union Church	Interdenominational	Kowloon	1930–1931
GRADE I HISTORC BUILDINGS OF HONG KONG				
2009	Saint Paul's Church	Anglican	Central	1911 /1934
2009	Hong Kong Cemetery's Resurrection Chapel	Anglican	Wan Chai	1845
2010	Cathedral of the Immaculate Conception	Catholic	Central	1881–1888
2010	Rosary Church	Catholic	Kowloon	1904–1905
2011	Hop Yat Church	Church of Christ in China	Midlevels	1922–1926
2011	Kau Yan Tsung Tsin Church	Basel Evangelical Missionary Society	Western	1931–1932
2019	Saint Andrew's Church	Anglican	Kowloon	1904–1910

69 Bokser, *Original Copies*; Hassenpflug, "European Urban Fictions in China."

70 Henriot and Minost, "Thames Town, an English Cliché."

71 Coomans, "The Sino-Christian Style," 224–227.

Postmodern Gothic: Re-establishing the Face

Today, more or less skilled reproductions of buildings from all over Europe are flourishing in every big city of China. Scholars have analyzed this postmodern phenomenon of featuring Western-style architecture and creating urban fictions. They have interpreted it in the light of the Chinese definition of the concepts of copy and originality.[69] Copied buildings include Gothic churches, such as "Thames Town" (泰晤士小镇 *Taiwushi*, 2006) on the outskirts of Shanghai, where a replica of an English Gothic Revival church in a suburb of Bristol—Christ Church in Clifton (1841–1885)—is pompously called "cathedral."[70] I will not pay attention to these copycats but to another phenomenon that has been developing since the 1980s and requires specific keys to understanding.

After the surviving old churches were returned to Christian and Catholic congregations in the 1980s and 1990s, a wave of construction gradually developed parallel with the growth of China's economy and wealth. Hundreds of new rural and urban churches were built throughout the country by congregations that had been disconnected from the world for thirty years and were ignorant of the religious, architectural, and liturgical changes that occurred during the fifties, sixties, and seventies. The Catholics of mainland China, for instance, completely missed the *aggiornamento* of the Second Vatican Council (1962–1965) as well as the evolution of postwar modern church architecture, while the Catholics of Hong Kong, Macao, and Taiwan followed the evolution of the universal Church.[71]

The architecture of many new churches built in mainland China from the 1980s might surprise, because they integrate pointed arches, high spires, rose windows, pinnacles, and other elements from the Gothic vocabulary into massive frame constructions in reinforced concrete [Figs. 12.20 & 12.21]. They are no copies of Western models, but postmodern Gothic buildings that combine monumental façades and functional inner spaces. One might be surprised that the new churches do not adopt the Sino-Christian

12.20 In 1923–1926, the Scheut Fathers built a large Romanesque style cathedral in Xiwanzi (Chongli), a village that resisted the Boxers in 1900. The cathedral was bombed during the Civil War in 1946. A new cathedral with a reinforced concrete structure was erected in 2010–2015. [© Jean-Marc de Moerloose, May 2011]

12.21 The new cathedral of Xiwanzi (Chongli), built 2010–2015, has a grandiose Gothic-style façade. [© Ferdinand Verbiest Institute, Leuven]

style promoted by the Holy See in the 1920s and 1930s. Mgr. Costantini's architectural legacy seems particularly insignificant in view of his efforts to promote a local church. Was the Roman project of architectural indigenization nothing other than a Western ideal shared by a few Chinese?

Most Chinese Christians thus rejected the Sino-Christian style from the 1920–1930s as well as more recent modern church architecture—without reference to any historical style—and explicitly referred to Western styles, in particular Gothic. It is obvious that post-1980 Christianity in China, both Catholic and Protestant, identifies with a religion coming from Europe and the United States, having survived the Cultural Revolution, and searching for its place in the changing Chinese society. In this complex context, architecture plays an essential role both in energizing congregations around projects and in affirming its existence in the society. Churches are the face of the congregations, and façades with high towers are the face of the churches. This phenomenon may be compared with the triumphant Gothic churches built after the Boxer Uprising, but in a different historical context and with a significance enriched with several more layers. Four examples from different provinces illustrate four patterns of re-establishment. In all cases, the main façade plays the most important visual and symbolic role.

The case of the Sacred Heart Church of Bengbu (蚌埠 Anhui) shows the brutal transformations of a church site and how a congregation with little financial means re-established its place of worship.[72] In 1925, French and Italian Jesuits built a large urban church, which was elevated to the rank of cathedral in 1929 when Bengbu became the seat of a new apostolic vicariate. The façade was an original Gothic-style composition: two crenellated towers with buttresses, portals, and lancet windows flanked the middle part, whose main portal was enhanced with a stretched triangular gable, statues in niches, and lancets [Fig. 12.22]. In the early 1950s, the cathedral was razed and a two-storied entertainment hall erected on the same foundations for Soviet engineers who were contributing to China's modernization by constructing waterworks in the area. That building had a reinforced concrete structure and a monumental granito staircase leading to a dance hall on the upper floor. In the early 1980s, the land was returned to Bengbu's Catholic congregation, which converted the entertainment building into a church by erecting a new façade and transforming the dance hall into a place of worship. The congregation had no archival documents about

72 Based on the author's field notes, August 24, 2016 (courtesy Wang Ziwei 王紫微 and Zhao Dongxu 赵东旭).

12.22 The Gothic cathedral of Bengbu, built 1925, was demolished and replaced in the 1950s by an entertainment hall built on the same foundations.
[© Archives de la Province d'Europe occidentale francophone des Jésuites, FCh]

12.23 In the 1980s, the entertainment hall that had been built on the site of the former cathedral of Bengbu was given to the Catholic parish, which uses it as a church after having erected a new façade.
[© THOC, August 2016]

12.24 The new cathedral of the Sacred Heart in Harbin, built 2003, is a postmodern high rise building with a Gothic façade.
[© THOC, April 2017]

the old church that would have allowed a more accurate reconstruction. The new façade is architecturally poor but recalls more or less the shape of the original façade—not its style—and gives the building the face of a re-established church [Fig. 12.23]. The interior, however, remains the modern concrete construction from the 1950s with nicely designed staircase and ceilings.

The cathedral of Harbin (哈尔滨 Heilongjiang) was erected in 2003 by Bishop Yue Fusheng (岳福生 1964–) along Dongdazhijie, one of the main boulevards of the provincial capital city, surrounded by high-rise buildings and facing a small Orthodox church from 1930 and a Lutheran church from 1916.[73] The postmodern Gothic façade with two tapered towers and spires, a rose window, lancets, and three portals [Fig. 12.24] is in line with the traditional silhouette of medieval and Gothic Revival cathedrals like that of Guangzhou [Fig. 12.02]. Behind the façade, however, the rupture with tradition is complete: instead of a high and deep nave flanked by aisles, there is a seven-story building with a complex program [Fig. 12.25]. The cathedral building contains meeting rooms, the bishop's offices and residence, the diocesan administration, and premises for retreats. The large worship hall is not located on the ground floor but occupies part of the three upper levels. The multistory church type—which Protestants adopted from the 1920s but Catholics rejected for liturgical reasons, as earlier discussed—became one of the most usual types of recent urban churches both for Protestants and Catholics.[74] Especially in the urban context, multistory churches benefit from high-rise regulations and land speculation. Furthermore, such buildings can be megachurches and contribute to the re-establishment of the face of congregations that have long been oppressed.[75]

A third pattern of re-establishment is when a new church refers to an older one by copying more or less accurately its façade or quoting a specific motive in a way that is clearly identifiable and has a significance. We have noticed this phenomenon during fieldwork but have no precise information about the context and reasons of such references. The church of the Holy Cross of Xuanhua (宣化 Hebei), designed by Father De Moerloose C.I.C.M. and built in 1903–1906, became a cathedral when the apostolic vicariate of Xuanhua was created in 1926 and given to one of the six first Chinese bishops, has a façade with two characteristic small round towers and three Gothic traceried windows. The tops of the towers were decapitated during the Cultural Revolution and reconstruct-

73 Based on the author's field notes, April 14, 2017 (courtesy Guo Wei 郭威 and Prof. Liu Daping 刘大平).

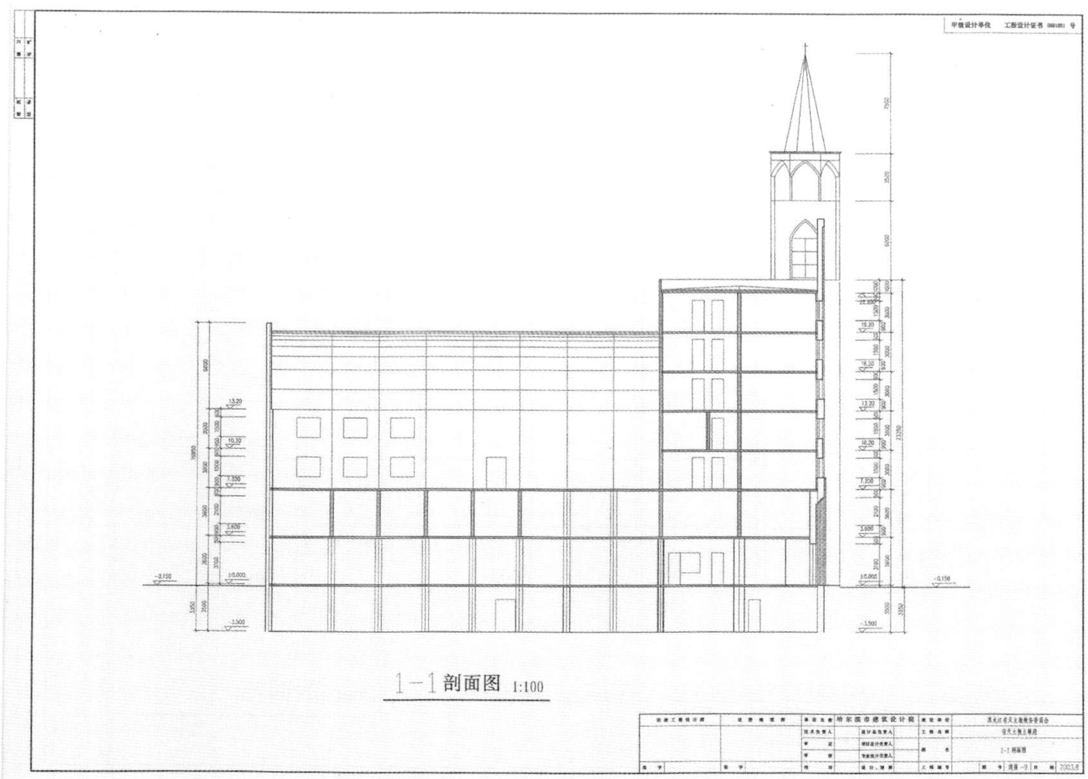

12.25 The section of the cathedral of the Sacred Heart in Harbin, built 2003, shows a seven-story building which includes a worship hall on the back side's upper floor.
[© KADOC-KU Leuven, Archives brother-architect Paul Dequeker CICM]

ed in the 1980s. Later, these tops appeared at least on four new churches in the diocese of Zhangjiakou (张家口 *Kalgan*, Hebei), as if they were a symbol of the re-established Church and its continuity in relation to the former vicariate of Xuanhua.[76] The Gothic façade of the Saint Anthony's Cathedral of Xinjiang (新绛 Shanxi), built by Dutch Franciscans in 1936–1940, mutilated by the Red Guards and restored in the 1980s, is another case in a different context [Fig. 12.26].[77] This façade has inspired several new churches, among which Saint Anthony's Church in Pingtangyu Village (坪塘峪, Taiyuan City), built 1995-1996 [Fig. 12.27].

The fourth pattern is the construction of postmodern Gothic churches on the site of old Gothic churches, which have been damaged or razed several times during the twentieth century and each time rebuilt. These sites are places of memory where reference to Gothic style is a strong statement of Christian identity and continuity. Because of the growth of congregations, each new church is different and larger than the previous. Allan Sweeten has described this phenomenon in Beijing, Tianjin, and Hebei province, where rural areas have a relatively high density of Catholics and churches commemorate destruction and martyrs from the Boxer Upraising to the Cultural Revolution.[78] Such places of memory with grand postmodern Gothic churches that were rebuilt after several destructions include the third cathedral of Xiwanzi (西弯子, *Congli*), rebuilt in 2010–2015 [Fig. 12.21]; the second cathedral of Xianxian (献县, *Zhangjia*), rebuilt in 2000–2003 [Fig. 12.28]; the second Marian shrine of Donglü (东闾), rebuilt in 1989–1992; and many secondary places such as the third church of Xiaohan village (小韩村, Wuqing district of Tianjin), rebuilt in 2004–2005, and the fourth church of Jiahoutan village (嘉后疃, Tongzhou district of Beijing), rebuilt in 2007.[79] This phenomenon is not limited to Hebei province.[80]

Postmodern Gothic churches are easy to identify stylistically, but their significance and perception both by Christians and non-Christians are not as straightforward to

74 Example of a Protestant church: Changchun Siwumalu Church (长春基督教会, Jilin), built 1996–1998, with a seating capacity of 6,000.
75 From 2014, several Christian and Catholic megachurches have been demolished by the government in Zhejiang, Henan, Shanxi and other provinces, because they were "violating land agreements and building codes." Many have a hybrid program and are "not registered with the state for religious activity."
76 The churches of the villages of Shenjingzhen (深井镇, Yu County) and Shangyingzhuang (上营庄, Lijiazhuang Town, Yu County) have similar elevations; the church of Nanlingluo Village (南凌罗, Yu County) is less elaborated but has the same silhouette, while the church of Dongcheng Town (东城镇, Yangyuan County) has three towers. <https://freewechat.com/a/MzAwNzE3MjM4Ng==/2210735722/1>.
77 Coomans, Xu and Zhang, "Imposing ad Provocative."
78 Sweeten, *China's Old Churches*, 18–20, 330–333.
79 Sweeten, *China's Old Churches*, 161–168 (Jiahoutuan), 223–225 (Xiaohan), 237–248 (Xiwanzi), 269–273 (Xianxian), 333–342 (Donglü).
80 For example: Our Lady of the Assumption Cathedral, Ningbo, 1995–2000.

12.26 The cathedral of Saint Anthony in Xinjiang was built by Dutch Franciscans in 1936–1940.
[© Het Utrechts Archief, Nederlandse Minderbroeders, 1224, 291/43]

12.27 The façade of Saint Anthony's church in Pingtangyu Village, built 1995-1996, refers to that of Saint Anthony's Cathedral in Xinjiang.
[© THOC, June 2019]

discern. Architectural historians have not yet analyzed the design processes of these churches, which include the role of the architects and the State Administration for Construction, as well as the debates between bishop, parish priests, congregations, and sponsors. After an interruption of thirty years, Catholic and Protestant congregations were able to re-establish their face in the public space and develop different ways to reconnect with an architectural tradition rooted in style and place.

Gothic Churches and Architectural Representation of Christianity in China

Gothic churches have marked the architectural landscape of China throughout the twentieth century, exhibiting a wide stylistic diversity and partly following major trends in international development, from different European expressions of national Gothic Revival to modern Gothic and postmodern Gothic. In many cases, especially before 1900, Gothic hybridized with local Chinese architectural traditions and then became eclectic by blending with other Western styles. It was also questioned in the 1920–1930s by missionaries themselves who wanted to indiginize Christianity in China, notably by Sinicizing architecture, an effort which met resistance from other missionaries and was ultimately aborted because of the war.

In 1941, the French Jesuit Albert Ghesquières S.J. (蓋斯傑 1901–1978) and the French architect Paul Muller (保罗. 慕乐 1891–?) published in Beijing an important article entitled "How shall we build dispensaries, schools, Catholic missions, chapels, seminaries and religious communities in China?"[81] It was a question of defining, once and for all, what would be the architectural representation of Christianity in China after the war. The article aimed to convince the missionary that doing quality work is a moral duty and that the very condition for building well is to have recourse to professionals, especially architects. The central question of that article, however, is style: "Currently, there has been a happy turnaround in the minds of missionaries, who appreciate the Chinese style and wish to adopt it in their constructions."[82] The use of reinforced concrete and Western roof frames helped to rationalize construction while retaining the shape of Chinese roofs and traditional decoration. The article mentions neither modern Gothic style nor modernism, which would

81 Ghesquières and Muller, "Comment-bâtirons nous?"
82 Ibid., 6.

12.28 An eclectic style Sacred Heart Cathedral of Xianxian (Zhangjia) was built by French Jesuits in the late nineteenth century. It was burned in 1976 and replaced by a new Gothic cathedral in 2000–2003. View on the back side: sacristy, apse and transept. [© Wu Zhong, 2013]

12.29 Fundraising flyer for the construction of a Gothic Catholic church in Wuhai, Inner Mongolia, 2019. [Author's collection]

develop elsewhere in the world after the war. In Father Ghesquières's eyes, Christian architecture in China should be professional, Chinese, and rational, forming a unity between style and construction, as an extension of the Sino-Christian architecture promoted in the 1920s.[83]

This did not happen because the war lasted until 1949, and no churches were built in China until the 1980s. For Chinese Christians, after the expulsion of foreign missionaries and the creation of patriotic Churches, these three decades were a rupture and total isolation, which culminated with the Cultural Revolution. It was not until the 1980s and 1990s that the question of the architectural representation of Christianity arose again, in quite different terms, without the intervention of foreigners and within fully Sinicized Christian denominations. Contrary to what Westerners might have imagined, the congregations rejected the Sino-Christian style—with few exceptions—and opted for postmodern Gothic. This paradigm shift was not a paradox, because Gothic referred to the large churches built after the Boxer Uprising and to the Western roots of a universal religion. Postmodern churches with domes referring to Saint Peter in Rome are rather exceptional, as are also the few cases of postmodern Sino-Christian churches in Shanxi and the campus of the National Seminary of the Catholic Church in China, built in Beijing from the mid-1990s to around 2005.[84]

The Chinese congregations, in their specific contexts and divisions, have cautiously reconnected with the world. Rooted in the memory of their history, they tried to reestablish their identity in the public space by contributing to the heritagization of the old churches from the missionaries' time and by erecting new, larger, and more visible postmodern Gothic churches. This architectural interaction between past, present, and future gives the Gothic churches of China, in their diversity and evolution, a unique meaning.

For many contemporary average Chinese people, Gothic churches, whatever their stylistic origin and religious, cultural and historical significance, are part of the architectural landscape and little more than romantic decors for wedding pictures. It seems that only Chinese Catholics and Protestants whose families survived persecution in rural areas traditionally identify themselves with the Gothic style brought by missionaries and will continue to propagate it into the twenty-first century [12.29].

83 Coomans, "Une utopie missionnaire?" Professionalization was a trend in Europe too; see: Coomans and De Maeyer, "Prêtres et architectes."

84 Weimar, "The 'Sinicized' National Seminary of Beijing."

13
Gothic Revival in Japan in the Early Period of the Occidentalizing

Experiences between Religious and Civil Architecture

Olimpia Niglio

13.01 Nagasaki Prefecture, Oura Cathedral, interior, 1863–1864. [© Olimpia Niglio]

Introduction

> The revolution of the nineteenth century, which was caused by the introduction of Western architecture, began to give place to brick or stone construction and consequently, the trabeated style had to give place to the new arcuated style. We can divide the history of Japanese architecture into two periods by this revolution; it may be said the Japanese architecture had developed continuously without its style being changed before this revolution and since then it has developed into modern architecture under the strong influence of the West. It is, therefore, very important for us to solve the following two problems: (1) When and by whom was the Western style introduced into Japan? (2) How has the new style developed into the modern style? On the second problem, suffice introduced into our country early in the twentieth century and since then the new problem of the relation between construction and design in the modern sense of the word has come to the front.[1]

With this introduction in 1954, Kimimasa Abe, a professor in Aesthetics at the National University of Yokohama, had analyzed a period of Japanese architecture, because the country from 1603 until 1867, during Edo period, had interrupted all international relations. In fact, with the domination of Tokugawa's family, only Dutch merchants were admitted to some Japanese ports. Before this period, the Japanese culture had a short influence from the Occident with the religious missions arrived in Kyushu, the most southwestern of Japan's main islands at Nagasaki prefecture. However, the history of these missions was incredibly sad but left important traces about this first dialogue between Occidental and Far East culture.

Only with the end of the Edo period, the return of imperial family, and the first years of the Meiji Period (1868–1912) did Japan enter a revolution era; many Western merchants and missionaries arrived in the Japanese archipelago to start business activities and to realize new diplomatic agreements. Above all, English and German people were called to improve many sectors as the education, the public administration, international law, and diplomacy, but also the new image of cities. Surely the topic of architecture and of art was fundamental to begin a process of renovation important to establish a dialogue between Japan and the countries with the advanced process of modernization.

It is no coincidence that the first scholars of Japanese architecture were the British and then the Americans, who introduced the first Occidental styles. Japanese architecture had intrigued Western observers since the second half of the nineteenth century, and the early publications by Christopher Dresser (*Japan: Its Architecture*, London, 1882), Edward S. Morse (*Japanese Homes and Their Surroundings*, Salem, Massachusetts, 1886), and F. Baltzer (*Das Japanische Haus*, Berlin, 1903) are all examples that attest to the genuine interest that even contributed to the renewal of Western architecture.[2] In Japan, English culture had favorited the realization of new architecture with revival styles. To the questions of Kimimasa Abe, when and how the new style was developed, now was possible to replay because the meeting with English and German culture had introduced

1 Abe, "Early Western Architecture in Japan," 13.

2 Niglio, *Avvicinamento alla storia dell'architettura giapponese*, 51–77.

3 Hill, *God's architect: Pugin and the building of romantic Britain*, 23.

4 Niglio, "La fortuna critica di John Ruskin in Giappone nella prima metà del Novecento," 270–271.

5 Kikuchi, *Japanese Modernisation and Mingei Theory. Cultural Nationalism and Oriental Orientalism*, 64–85.

6 Sadler, *Japanese Architecture. A short History.*

7 Niglio, *Paesaggio sacro e architettura cristiana nella prefettura di Nagasaki*, 105–135.

a style that before was unknown: the Gothic Revival.

In the first instance, the development of this style was diffused through documents and books: the theories of Augustus Welby Northmore Pugin (1812–1852),[3] famous for the pioneering role in the Gothic Revival of architecture and the studies on John Ruskin (1819–1900),[4] art critic and philosopher, that had influenced the movement "art of the people" promoted by Soetsu Yanagi, Japanese philosopher and lover of the traditional craft.[5] Following these theoretical approaches, the new ideas on the architectural styles had also begun to appear on a practical and operational level with the first brick and stone constructions and according to the Gothic Revival.

The tradition of Japanese architecture from 1868 to after World War II again demonstrates the continuity even in those events in which the traditional forms were purposefully destroyed. The process of the introduction of Occidental architecture in Japan, during the first years of the Meiji Revolution, was very hard, and the new styles had found applications above all in the construction of factories, churches, office buildings, and houses realized by foreign and Japanese architects who had only remotely attempted to use the Japanese architectural vocabularies.[6]

13.02 Nagasaki Prefecture, Oura Cathedral, exterior, 1863–1864. [© Olimpia Niglio]

The Religious Heritage and the Gothic Revival in Japan

With the resumption of international relations, many religious missions came back to Japan. These missions had to leave the territory at the beginning of the seventeenth century due to the restrictions imposed by the Tokugawa shogunate. At the end of the nineteenth century, the first religious missions were those of the Jesuits, Franciscans, and the Protestant community (both English and German).

The presence of these communities facilitated the construction of the first Christian churches on the coasts of Kyushu's island and its archipelago. These missions re-established contacts that had been cut off at the beginning of the seventeenth century. History, however, has taught us that although the laws within Japan did not authorize the spread of foreign religions, Christian culture had taken root and continued its hidden journey. With the reopening of international relations, the first important examples of Gothic Revival architecture were found on the islands and southern coasts of Japan, especially in Nagasaki prefecture.

Many original architectures have been destroyed by earthquakes or the Second World War. However, the Kyushu island preserves an important religious heritage, realized between the end of the nineteenth century and the first decades of the twentieth century, that from June 2018 is also World Cultural Heritage.[7]

13.03 Naru Island, Egami Church, interior, 1918.
[Higurashi Yuichi / Nagasaki Prefectural World Heritage Division]

The first famous church in Gothic Revival is Oura Cathedral, built in 1863 and opened in 1864, located on a hill facing the Port of Nagasaki in the south of the Nagasaki region. This cathedral was designed in 1933 National Treasure by the National Government [Figs. 13.01 & 13.02].

In 1862, Father Furet of the Paris Foreign Missions Society selected the location to construct the church for use as the base of the society's mission in Nagasaki. Oura Cathedral was built in 1864 by missionaries who had come back to Japan after the opening of the nation's ports to foreign trade in the middle of the nineteenth century. It was dedicated to the twenty-six Saints who had been martyred in Nagasaki in the sixteenth century. A group of Hidden Christians in the suburbs of Nagasaki secretly visited Oura Cathedral soon after its completion to reveal their faith to the missionaries. This event was known as the "Discovery of Hidden Christians." Subsequent contact with the missionaries at Oura Cathedral by Hidden Christian leaders throughout the Nagasaki region brought about a new phase of history in the Hidden Christian communities in Japan.[8]

In the south of Japan, there are currently over 130 Catholic churches, and the majority are in the Gothic Revival style. Each of these churches' recounts to us a local history of Christian faith, but many churches have been rebuilt or restored after earthquakes, war events, or for damages for natural reasons. Another interesting example of the Gothic Revival is the Egami Church on Naru Island [Fig. 13.03]. As some documents record the existence of Japanese Catholics on Naru Island in the early seventeenth century, it is highly possible that Catholicism was introduced there between the late sixteenth and early seventeenth centuries. The Egami Church was built in 1918 on a small strip of terraced land in the valley, as was characteristic in the Egami area, with funds gathered from fishing for *kibinago* herring. The Egami Church is the best example of the Gothic Revival in terms of design and structure among the wooden church buildings constructed in the Nagasaki region from the nineteenth century onward.

Certainly, most Christian churches are in Nagasaki prefecture; however, there are also examples of Gothic Revival–style churches built in the center and in the north of Japan. On Honshu Island, in the Yokohama prefecture, in Yamate-cho, there is Christ Church in Gothic Revival [Fig. 13.04]. After the opening of the port of Yokohama in June 1859, Anglicans in the foreign community

8 Nagasaki City, *Survey Report on Oura Cathedral and Related Facilities*, 31.

13.04 Yokohama, Christ Church, founded 1862, present building consecrated 1955.
[© Olimpia Niglio]

13.05 Otaru, Tomioko Cathedral, 1929. [Wikimedia Commons; photo 山本昂左衛門, 2017]

gathered for worship services in the British consul's residence. With the support of the Anglican community, Christ Church was founded in 1862 when Yokohama City became the most important port in Japan.[9] In this same period was started the construction of Yamate-cho, a neighborhood famous, also today, as having been a foreign residential area. Still in Yamate-cho, St. Andrew's Church congregation first gathered at a rented house in 1885. Since 1885, St. Andrew's Church has moved to several locations in Yokohama, and the church buildings were lost twice, in the Kanto Earthquake of 1923 and in the Yokohama Air Raid of May 1945. The present building was consecrated in 1955.

In Tokyo, Nagano, Nagoya, and Kyoto, there are interesting examples of churches in Gothic Revival. In the ancient capital of Japan, Kyoto, is a particularly interesting example: St. Agnes Cathedral [Figs. 13.06 & 13.07]. This church was built, as was the Holy Trinity Church, in 1898. It was erected on the campus of Heian Women's University and changed its name to St. Agnes Church in 1923. This Gothic Revival church was designed by James McDonald Gardiner, an American architect. This construction is one of the oldest Christian churches in Kyoto and from 1985, was designated as the cultural heritage of the city.[10]

In the north, on Hokkaido Island, many Western-style buildings are preserved in the port city of Otaru. The Tomioka cathedral, built in 1929, is the best example of Gothic Revival preserved on the island [Fig. 13.05].

After the Second World War, with the affirmation of Christian missions also in the educational sector, there was the realization of numerous modern churches with references to the Gothic Revival. There have been many stylistic revisions, also adopted in the construction of newer structures not intended for religious services but only for folklore events. In fact, in Japan it is common, even today, to use references to Western culture in both architectural design and artistic production. Therefore, it is essential to know the history of Japanese architecture in-depth in order not to run into errors.

Especially in the port metropolitan cities, where the Western presence has always been particularly dominant, there are numerous cases of small chapels inside hotels that frame ceremonies and events even at marriage.[11] These are only examples that are intended to echo Western styles and forms that many Japanese consider more modern and adapted to great occasions.

9 Sachs, *The Transformation of Anglicanism.*
10 Takeda, "Public and Private Church," 422.
11 On wedding chapels, see the contribution of Barbara Borngässer in this book.

13.06 & 13.07 Kyoto, St. Agnes Church, James McDonald Gardiner, 1898. [© Olimpia Niglio]

Educational and Residential Constructions in Gothic Revival in Japan

While the "authentic" Gothic Revival religious architecture is mainly found in southern Japan and in some important port cities, this style is differently applied to architecture for education or civil architecture in many cities. Even today, contemporary architecture projects echo this style that came from the West at the end of the nineteenth century. The attention paid to Japan by the scholars of the Gothic Revival might seem unexpected, yet by the end of the nineteenth century, this style had found many applications in the Japanese archipelago.

Robert Treat Paine and Alexander Soper in an interesting book realized, in the first edition, in 1955 about the art and architecture of Japan,[12] had analyzed the development of the historical and traditional style of the architecture in wood and earth, until the meeting with Western style and the first example in Gothic Revival or also in other eclectic styles. In Tokyo, as in Kyoto and in the principal cities in Japan, it is common for banks, museums, schools, and institutional offices to be realized in neoclassical style.

In their architectural survey Robert Treat Paine and Alexander Soper had studied the hard transformation of the main cities in Japan analyzing the specific form of the city, the transportation buildings and markets, high-density areas, neighborhoods, and the city as a living environment, the articulation of leisure activities in the amusement parks, pilgrimage centers, and, finally, the image of the city. This image to the end of the nineteenth century was modified with

12 Treat Paine and Soper, *The Art and Architecture of Japan.*

13 Checkland, *Japan and Britain after 1859: creating cultural bridges*, 79–92.
14 Finn, "Josiah Conder (1852–1920) and Meiji Architecture," 86–93; Fujimori, *Nihon no kindai kenchiku (Modern Architecture of Japan)*, 97–102; Fujimori, "Josiah Conder and Japan," 19.
15 Today, Tokyo University.
16 Niglio and Kuwakino, *Giappone. Tutela e conservazione di antiche tradizioni*, 22.
17 Pedlar, *The imported pioneers: Westerners who helped build modern Japan*, 139–143.
18 On Gothic Revival university chapels see also the contribution of Bettina Marten in this book.

the introduction of the new styles and new forms. Dominating this transitional period was the architect Hermann Gustav Louis Ende (1829–1907), designer of the Justice Department in Tokyo with Wilhelm Böckmann (1832–1902)[13] from Germany and Josiah Conder (1852–1920)[14] from England. Conder also had an important influence as a teacher at the Technical College in Tokyo,[15] founded in 1877. Among the first Japanese architects who built important structures adapting the foreign style of architecture were Kingo Tatsuno (1854–1919) and Yoshikazu Uchida (1885–1972) who designed many buildings in the Hongo Campus at the University of Tokyo.[16]

Uchida, architect and structural engineer, was one of five 1907 graduates from the Department of Architecture of Tokyo Imperial University. He was a designer of the important buildings realized on the Hongo campus and Komaba campus of the University of Tokyo. In 1923 during the Kanto earthquake, the Japanese capital was destroyed, and many neighborhoods were canceled and with them the new architectures realized in the Meiji Period. After this earthquake, the English and German heritage, introduced at the end of the nineteenth century, was in ruins. The works of the reconstruction have favored this Occidental heritage and some ruins have been preserved in new constructions.[17] An interesting example was realized by Yoshikazu Uchida in Hongo Campus at the Tokyo University for Yasuda Auditorium, with the Faculty of Science Building [Fig. 13.08]. Here the ancient ruin in Gothic Revival, of the original building realized by Josiah Conder, has been recovered and integrated into the new project.

13.08 Tokyo, Hongo Campus, Tokyo University, Yasuda Auditorium, 1925. [© Olimpia Niglio]

In Tokyo, another important educational Anglican campus is located at Rikkyo University. The origins of this university date from the founding of St. Paul's School for boys in 1874 by Channing Moore Williams, a missionary of the Episcopal Church, and an important personality in the establishment of the Anglican Church in Japan. Also, on this campus the original buildings were built in Gothic Revival.

In 1875, in Kyoto, the St. Agnes School was founded to favorite the education of women. From 1950, this private Anglican school has been an important university in the center of Kyoto City and the name is Heian Woman's University. The original buildings are in the Gothic Revival.

In the same year, also in Kyoto, the protestant educator Niijima Jo, also known as Joseph Hardy Neesima, founded the most prestigious university of Japan. Doshisha University was founded as Doshisha English School and today the Imadegawa campus preserves many original buildings as the Clark Memorial Hall. Five buildings in the Imadegawa campus have been designated as Important Cultural Properties of Japan, including Doshisha Chapel [Fig. 13.09] and Clark Memorial Hall, built between 1875 and 1880.[18]

The circulation of the Gothic Revival style in the Far East is also interesting in other neighboring countries and above all in Korea. By the beginning of the twentieth century, important Anglican missions had also been established in this country. In this context, Japanese colonization should also not be forgotten. The Japanese occupation of

Korea began in 1910 and ended at the end of World War II in 1945. Today there are numerous religious complexes and educational campuses in Korea that are supported by Anglican communities, which have introduced the Gothic Revival.[19]

With the arrival of the British and German people, there was also the construction of neighborhoods exclusively inhabited by foreigners. In the city of Yokohama at the end of the nineteenth century, in a hilly area, the Yamate-cho district was founded, home to important diplomatic buildings but also of many private houses built according to the Western styles of the countries of origin.

This Western colonization had fostered the entry of new artistic and architectural styles that had transformed the image of many neighborhoods of the major Japanese cities. An eclecticism interesting and that still finds its own specific characterization even in more contemporary buildings. In the case of Tokyo, many of these buildings have been rebuilt because of the damage of the Kanto earthquake in 1923.[20]

13.09 Kyoto, Doshisha University, Imadegawa Campus, Doshisha Chapel, 1875–1880.
[© Olimpia Niglio]

Conclusions

Although little known, the culture of Gothic Revival in Japan is particularly important and testifies to precisely that dialogue that had been established, already at the end of the nineteenth century, between Japanese institutions and religious and commercial missions from the West. Of course, with the Meiji period began a program of Occidental heritagization that still lasts to this day.

However, throughout the twentieth century, the attention of historians and architectural scholars in Japan gave little importance to this period of the Gothic Revival without implying that it is precisely from this historical moment that begins a new cultural paradigm that has strongly influenced the whole language of modern and contemporary Japanese architecture.

With the new millennium there was an appreciation in Japan for the architecture realized during the Meiji period (1868–1912) and mainly during the long period Showa (1926–1989), and there were the projects that favored the reconstruction also in the Gothic style of many architectural complexes of English and German origin.

In an interview published in the *Architects' Journal* in February 2014, Japanese architect Kengo Kuma stated that Gothic architecture was not consciously perceived in Japan, but the study of this style had a strong impact on his projects as well as the installation at the Royal Academy of Arts in London (2014) and for the new project Amanpuri Retail Pavilion inaugurated at the beginning of 2020 in Thailand.

19 Strong, *The Oxford History of Anglicanism*, 331–332.
20 Cortazzi, *Introduction – Richard Henry Brunton: Building Japan (1868–1874)*.

14
Gothic and Event Culture
Wedding Chapels

Barbara Borngässer

14.01 Okinawa, Japan, Lazor Garden Alivila Cristea Church Wedding Chapel, twenty-first century. [nipponweddings.com]

Wedding chapels, particularly popular in East Asia, offer a dazzling picture of contemporary reinterpretation of Gothic architecture. The commercially conceived, usually nonreligious affiliated "churches" have largely lost their originally ecclesiastical functions, but still play with the aura of the Christian cult space and in particular with the radiance of the Gothic style.

The appearance of wedding chapels ranges from rededicated church rooms to festive halls of global hotel chains and idyllic new buildings in the open countryside. Their task is to frame, with an exalting architectural setting, the "most beautiful day in life." To perfect this romantic dream, a lucrative market has developed, which advises and equips the wedding guests. Thus, packages are offered that organize the journey, stay, celebration, and ceremonies for the bridal couples. Great importance is given to the visual staging of the wedding couple posing in front of a fairytale backdrop. This has an effect on the architecture, which from the outset, is designed with scenography and visuals in mind.

The Little Church of the West in Las Vegas, which opened in 1942, is considered the ancestor of the wedding chapels.[1] It owed its existence to the liberal legislation of the state of Nevada, which allowed quick and uncomplicated marriages—a circumstance that made Las Vegas a wedding and divorce paradise. The modest pinewood building was modeled on the nineteenth-century neo-Gothic churches of Californian mining towns.[2] Originally part of the Last Frontier Hotel, The Little Church moved several times, and it now belongs to the Mandalay Bay Hotel. During the following decades, all larger Las Vegas Hotels afforded themselves with increasingly noble wedding chapels. The wedding chapel of the Hotel Excalibur deserves a special mention in this context: opened in 1990, its ceiling is decorated by voluminous fan vaults imitating medieval models from England [Fig. 14.02].

From Las Vegas, the trend of marrying in a pseudo-sacral and -historical ambience spread worldwide with continuously growing popularity: thus, since 2017, a entrepreneurial German couple in Saxony could offer the construction of private wedding chapels under the motto "My car – my yacht – my private chapel"—including "original antique" altar and complete church furnishings![3]

Wedding Chapels in the Asian Region

Western-style wedding ceremonies, regardless of religion, confession or even approved rituals of civil marriage, play an progressively major role in many Asian countries, especially in Japan. From 1982 to 1996, the number of marriages according to the Christian model rose from 5 percent to almost 50 percent, compared to the Shinto ritual.[4] Obviously, the pictorial culture of the new media sets a new global standard of glamourous staging, and young couples may also feel restricted by the strictly regulated Shinto ceremony. However, religious reasons apparently don't play any role, as most bridal couples have no connection to Christianity. The celebrating "priest" in such ceremonies acts primarily as a coordinator of wedding

1 <https://littlechurchofthewest.com/about-us/>.
2 <https://de.wikipedia.org/wiki/The_Little_Church_of_the_West>.
3 <https://www.hochzeitskapelle-callenberg.de/privat-kapelle>; <https://www.bild.de/regional/dresden/hochzeit/wir-bauen-uns-eine-hochzeits-kapelle-50932760.bild.html>.
4 Here and in the following: Fisch, "The Rise of Chapel Wedding in Japan". The writer, who himself worked as a "priest" in Japanese wedding tourism, provides a revealing analysis of "Christian Style Weddings" in modern Japan.

14.02 Las Vegas, United States, Hotel Excalibur, Wedding Chapel, 1942. [MGM Resorts International]

14.03 Nagoya, Japan, Glastonia Wedding Chapel, Fumio Eba, ca. 1990. [ebadesignlabel.jp]

choreography. The impression and aura of a Christian, possibly still medieval, church serves as a mental correspondent for lasting love and faithfulness.[5]

The variety of Japanese wedding chapels ranges stylistically from traditional to avant-garde, from medieval to futuristic.[6] Tadao Ando has contributed some spectacular modern, world-renowned buildings.[7] The number of Gothicizing wedding chapels is remarkable! They may consist of entire neo-Gothic churches, architectures with some Gothic elements, historicizing interiors, or even constructions with only seemingly reference motifs such as pointed arches, stained glass windows, towers, or ridge turrets.

One of the most popular wedding chapels in Japan is the Glastonia (St. Carbonek) Wedding Chapel in Nagoya, built on behalf of the Global Wedding Company [Fig. 14.03].[8] It is the work of Fumio Eba and the Eba Design Label Corporation & Edward First Class Architectural Design Office, a company specialized, among other things, in event architecture.[9] Glastonia Chapel is part of a large hotel complex built in a mostly English Georgian style. The wedding chapel, on the other hand, presents itself as a two-storied chapel of the Sainte-Chapelle type in Paris. One reaches the upper single-naved banqueting hall via a representative stair, which is ideal for photo shoots: it first leads into an vaulted anteroom with three pointed arches and gables above. Behind, the façade of the actual chapel rises up with a Gothic rose window and gable above. A thirty-one-meter-high ridge turret crowns the building in a very picturesque way. The interior shows a three-storied elevation. Rib vaults span the nave, and multicolored glass windows bathe the room in a bright, festive atmosphere.

If the architecture in Nagoya can only be classified as Gothic or late Gothic in a general sense, the exterior of St. Grace's Cathedral in Tokyo is in fact clearly inspired by a particular monument, the Cathedral in Barcelona [Figs.14.04a & 14.04b].[10] Despite its high-sounding name, the Japanese building is a pure event space, which is not only advertised with the "authenticity" of its rooms, but also with the culinary delicacies that are served in it. In fact, St. Grace's conjures up a touch of the Mediterranean Middle Ages atmosphere in the surrounding landscape of high-rise buildings. As at the Seu of Barcelona, its façade is character-

5 Löffler, *Fremd und Eigen*; Löffler, "Geborgte Heiligkeit, gebaute Romantik." On the history of the Christian Church in Japan, see the contribution of Olimpia Niglio in this volume.
6 A selection at <https://www.jpwedding.hk>.
7 Löffler, *Fremd und Eigen*; Löffler, "Geborgte Heiligkeit, gebaute Romantik."
8 <http://www.ebadesignlabel-edward.co.jp/works/bridal/glastonia>.
9 <http://www.ebadesignlabel-edward.co.jp>.
10 <http://www.ebadesignlabel-edward.co.jp/works/bridal/st-grace-aoyama>.

14.04a Tokyo, St. Grace's Cathedral Wedding Chapel, Fumio Eba, ca. 2000. [Wikimedia Commons; photo Rs1421, 2010]

14.04b Barcelona, Spain, Cathedral Santa Creu I Santa Eulàlia, façade, Josep Oriol Mestres and August Font, late nineteenth century. [Wikimedia Commons; photo Bengt Nyman, 2013]

ized by the deep stepped portal crowned by a high gable, behind which rises the mighty octagonal façade tower with its open-tracery spire. Filigree tracery also covers the wall surfaces and the wide window openings. The consistent recourse to the Catalan church prospectus, which was essentially a work of the late nineteenth and early twentieth centuries, seems to be significant: it is precisely a historicist monument that displays particular picturesque and urbanistic qualities.[11] The interior of the Tokyo chapel, on the other hand, is English in style, with imaginative decorations inspired by the fan vaults of Peterborough Cathedral. St. Grace's and the chapel in Nagoya are both works by Fumio Eba, thus demonstrating the diversity of his reinterpretation of Gothic architecture.

The subtropical archipelago of Okinawa, with its natural beauty, is recommended for honeymoons. Several companies here have specialized in so-called resort weddings, and the number of wedding chapels alone has risen to over two dozen in recent years. Almost all of them were erected on exposed coastal locations together with the adjacent hotel complexes. The "apses" of the wedding chapels open as a glass room with the blue sea in the background. Sometimes, the wedding altar is placed so that it seems to float above the water. The architectural models of those romantic staffage buildings are usually provided by the Gothic, for example in the Lazor Garden Alivila Cristea Church [Fig. 14.01], which is praised as "A church and banquet rooms designed on the basis of the concept of ultimate satisfaction."[12] As described and well illustrated by advertising images, the white rooms, decorated with pointed arches, pinnacles, high spires, and rib vaults, are not determined in a religious sense, but open to all those "who are simply in love with the idea of romantic church weddings."[13] If necessary, any pictorial elements reminiscent of Christianity can be removed. For Japanese bridal couples, the large bell is of course available for the traditional bell-ringing ceremony.

Outside Japan, too, Christian-style weddings are gaining more and more followers, but the number of new buildings there is significantly lower. This is probably related to the fact that in other regions of Asia, there are historically more "real" churches available that can be used as wedding locations. Such is the case, for example, with

11 On the façade of the Cathedral of Barcelona, see: Urbano, "Neo-Gothic controversial cases in Catalonia in the nineteenth Century."

12 <https://www.visitokinawa.jp/wedding/okinawa-chapel-list>. The website provides further examples of Gothic wedding chapels on Okinawa.

13 <https://www.thestar.com.my/travel/asia/2014/03/15/okinawa-isle-of-perfect-nuptial-bliss>.

14.05 Singapore, Chijmes Hall, 1898, 1996 opening as event center. [singaporebride.com]

14.06 Hong Kong, Bethany Chapel, 1873/2006. [© The Hong Kong Academy of Performing Arts]

14.07 Da Nang, Vietnam, Bà Nà Resort, general view, ca. 2020. [© Mercure Danang French Village Bana Hills]

14.08 Tokyo, Hotel Sheraton Grande Tokyo Bay, Glass Chapel, late 20th or early 21st century. [© Hotel Sheraton Grande Tokyo Bay]

Chijmes Hall in Singapore [Fig. 14.05]:[14] the neo-Gothic building, which was built in 1898 as the second chapel of the convent of the Holy Infant Jesus and decorated with Belgian stained glass windows, was deconsecrated in 1983. In 1990 it was declared a listed landmark. Shortly after the Watabe Wedding Group took over the former convent, it opened in 1996 an event center with wedding chapel, restaurant, and shops.[15]

The Bethany Chapel (George C. Tso Memorial Chapel, Fig. 14.06) in Hong Kong also originally served as the church room of the Sanatorium for Tropical Diseases, founded in 1873.[16] After numerous conversions, decay, and restoration, the complex now houses a film school; since 2006, its chapel is used again for devotions and other religious ceremonies, especially weddings. The opulent historicist furnishings have been largely restored or reconstructed.[17] One of the most recent examples of neo-Gothic event architecture has opened 2015 with the Bà Nà Hill Resort west of Da Nang, Vietnam.[18] The replica of a French town includes hotels, restaurants, and the small, but exquisite "Gothic" church with its elegant bundled pillars and lush decorative sculpture [Fig. 14.07].

Finally, a few wedding chapels whose contemporary architecture plays ostentatiously with Gothic impressions should be exemplarily mentioned, such as the Laguna Wedding Chapel in Guam.[19] The Sheraton Grande Tokyo Bay Hotel can even afford two wedding chapels at once: the Crystal Chapel, which is built directly into the sea, and the Glass Chapel, with its filigree steel pointed arches in a "tropical forest" [Fig. 14.08].[20] Models for this special form of Gothic reception may be found in American modernism, for example in the single-naved buildings of Frank Lloyd Wright's follower E. Fay Jones, the Thorncrown Chapel in Eureka Springs (1980)[21] or the Mildred B. Cooper Memorial Chapel in Bella Vista (1988, Fig. 4.19),[22] both in Arkansas—they are also used as wedding chapels. Often, as in the Laguna Chapel [Fig. 14.09], the chapel space is reduced to the roof, with tightly spaced pointed arches rising directly from the floor or pool area. The so-called A-frame building is reminiscent of the impressive United States Air Force Academy Cadet Chapel in Colorado Springs, a 1960s campus chapel open to various denominations (Skidmore, Owings & Merrill) [Fig. 4.32].[23]

Wedding chapels serve the need for romance and spirituality without specific religious ties. They are transnational and despite their Western origins, globally accepted. Gothic architecture, with its historically developed ability for transcendence, has proven to be particularly effective, so that a large number of wedding chapels make use of complete spatial structures or "Gothic" elements. Even the reduction to a few significant features, such as pointed arches and glass, seems sufficient to evoke the suggestive effect of the church interior, which has developed over centuries. Gothic, successful now also in the commercial ambience of the twenty-first century, proves once again to have become a universally applicable architectural style.

14.09 Guam, United States, Laguna Wedding Chapel, twenty-first century. [www.wheniplan.com]

14 <https://singaporebrides.com/d/chijmes-hall-singapore/chijmes-hall/23339/>.

15 The former church building received a high-tech equipment: "The chapel also features magnificent chandeliers, integrated AV equipment with sophisticated AV system, wall-mounted plasma TV, Wi-Fi System with natural skylight is perfect to comfortably accommodate up to 300 guests for a sit-down banquet." <https://singaporebrides.com/d/chijmes-hall-singapore/>.

16 <https://en.wikipedia.org/wiki/Béthanie_(Hong_Kong)>.

17 <http://www.emmanuel.org.hk/bethanie-restoration/>.

18 <https://vneconomictimes.com/article/biz-traveler/french-village-atop-ba-na-hill>. The picturesque mountain resort flanks an abandoned holiday colony founded in 1919 for French tourists. <https://en.wikipedia.org/wiki/Bà_Nà_Hills>.

19 <https://www.wheniplan.com/detail.php?id=24>.

20 <https://www.sheratontokyo-bay.co.jp/wedding_en/chapel/index.html>.

21 <https://thorncrown.com>.

22 <http://beautifulbellavista.com/chapel.htm>.

23 On other U.S. buildings see the contribution of Bettina Marten in this book.

BIBLIOGRAPHY

Abe, Kimimasa. "Early Western Architecture in Japan". *Journal of the Society of Architectural Historians*, 13 (1954) 2, 13-18.

Abrecht, Birgit. *Architektúr á Islandi – leidarvísir. Architectural Guide to Iceland*. Reykjavik, 2000, German edition: Stuttgart-Munich: Deutsche Verlags-Anstalt, 2000.

Aggarwal, Vasundhra. "Iconic American Buildings Re-Envisioned in the Gothic Revival Style". ArchDaily, 12 December 2018. <https://www.archdaily.com/906896/iconic-americanbuildings-re-envisioned-in-the-gothic-revival-style/> (10 October 2020).

Albertsen, August. *Fører for Nidaros Domkirke, Nidaros Domkirkes Restaurieringsarbeider*. Oslo, 1939; German edition: *Der Dom zu Drontheim*. Oslo: Verlag Nidaros Domkirkes Restaurierings-arbeider, 1942.

Albuquerque, Alexandre. *A Catedral de São Paulo*. São Paulo: Melhoramentos, 1929.

Albuquerque, Maria Beatriz Portugal. "The São Paulo cathedral and its Architect Builder", in: Martín M. Checa-Artasu and Olimpia Niglio, eds. *El Neogótico en la arquitectura americana. Historia, restauración, reinterpretaciones y reflexiones*. Rome: Aracne editrice, 2016, 116-123.

Alderman, Matthew. "The Lonely God: Oakland Cathedral in the Light of Tradition", in: *The Institute for Sacred Architecture*, 2020. <https://www.sacredarchitecture.org/articles/the_lonely_god_oakland_cathedral_in_the_light_of_tradition> (10 October 2020).

Alemán Hernández, Saro and Martín Hernández, Manuel. *Guía del patrimonio arquitectónico de Arucas*. Arucas: Ayuntamiento de Arucas, 1994.

Allsopp, Bruce. "Urban Planning for Delight". *Journal of the American Institute of Architects*, 12 (949) 2, 54-55.

Almeida, Marcelina das Graças. *Fé na modernidade e tradição na fé*. Belo Horizonte: Universidade Federal de Minas Gerais, 1993 (pdf).

Álvarez, José Rogelio. *Diccionario enciclopédico de Tabasco*, vol. 2. Villahermosa: Gobierno del Estado de Tabasco, ICT, 1994.

Álvarez Salvador, Virginia Gabriela. *Estudio iconográfico de la pintura mural y vitrales de la capilla del Corazón de María Basílica del Voto Nacional, Quito*. Thesis (Bsc Arts), Universidad Tecnológica Equinoccial, 2006.

Amaral, Flávia Gabriela da Costa Rosa. *O Católico ideal: Cultura do imaterial e estética no portal dos Arautos do Evangelho*. São Paulo: UNIP, 2013.

Amic, Sylvain; Le Men, Segolène and Coudert, Marie-Claude, eds. *Cathédrales 1789-1914, un mythe modern*. Paris: Somogy Éditions d'Art, 2014.

Amutabi, Maurice. "Buildings as Symbols of Colonial Hegemony: Interrogating Colonial Buildings and Architecture in Kenya's Urban Spaces", in: Fassil Demissie, ed. *Colonial Architecture and Urbanism in Africa: Intertwined and Contested Histories*. Farnham-Burlington: Ashgate, 2012, 325-343.

Anderson, Jocelyn. "Views of political geography in the Seven Years' War: military artists' prints and British consumers". *The Oxford Art Journal*, 41 (2018) 1, 19-38, 141.

Andrade, Oswaldo de. *Manifesto da poesia Pau-Brasil*. Rio de Janeiro, 1924, published in: *Correio da Manhã*, 18 March 1924.

Andrade, Oswaldo de. *Manifesto Antropófago*, *Revista de Antropofagia*, 1 (primeira dentição). São Paulo, 1928.

Andrews, Brian. "Pugin in Australia", in: Paul Atterbury and Clive Wrainwright. *Pugin. A Gothic Passion*. New Haven-London: Yale University Press, 1994, 247-257.

Andrews, Brian. *Australian Gothic. The Gothic Revival in Australian Architecture from the 1840s to the 1950s*. Melbourne: University Press, 2001.

Andrews, Wayne. *American Gothic: It's Origins, Its Trials. Its Triumphs*. New York: Random House, 1975.

Andruet, Mario. "La Catedral de Santa Isabel en Malabo. Una posible intervención de Gaudí en Guinea Ecuatorial". <https://fundacionantoniogaudi.org/Publicaciones/la-catedral-de-santa-isabel-en-malabo-una-posible-intervencion-de-gaudi-en-guinea-ecuatorial.pdf> (5 May 2020).

Annuaire de l'Eglise catholique en République Démocratique du Congo 2012-2013. Kinshasa: Mediaspaul, 2013.

Apers, J. "L'abbaye 'Sainte-Marie de la Pierre-qui-Vire'. Projet de Jean Cosse. Collaboratrice Brigitte De Groof", in: *Dossier ciment 3 'Murs'* (November 1994). <https://www.febelcem.be/fileadmin/user_upload/dossiers-ciment-94-08/fr/3_fr.pdf>.

Apperly, Richard; Irving, Robert and Reynolds, Peter. *A Pictoral Guide to Identifying Australian Architecture: Styles and Terms from 1788 to the Present*. Sydney: Angus & Robertson, 1995.

Arango, Silvia et al. *Bogotá y la Sabana: guía de arquitectura y paisaje*. Bogotá: Universidad Nacional de Colombia; Sevilla: Junta de Andalucía, 2012.

Aranha, Paolo. "From Meliapor to Mylapore 1662-1749: The Portuguese presence in São Tomé between the Qutb Shahi conquest and its incorporation into British Madras", in: Laura Jarnagin, ed. *The Making of the Luso-Asian World: Intricacies of Engagement*. Singapore: Institute of Southeast Asian Studies, 2011, 67-82.

architectura. Zeitschrift für Geschichte der Baukunst, 46 (2016) 2.

Arciniega Ávila, Hugo. "La casa de la Negra Fojaco". *Revista electrónica Imágenes del Instituto de investigaciones Estéticas*, 2016. <http://www.revistaimagenes.esteticas.unam.mx/la_casa_de_la_negra_fojaco>.

Armendáriz, M. "Mosaicos y vitrales en la catedral de Osorno". *El Mercurio*, 22 January 2012.

Aste Müller, Victoria and Madrid De Solís, Ida. *Breve historia de Santa Fe de Hatun Xauxa*. Jauja: Halckon Editores, 1997.

Bader, Vera Simone. *Moderne in Afrika. Asmara-die Konstruktion einer italienischen Kolonialstadt 1889-1941*. Berlin: Gebr. Mann Verlag, 2016.

Baker, Herbert. "Plea for English Gothic". *The African Architect. Journal of the Association of Transvaal Architects*, 26 (July 1911), 36.

Bal, Barnabas Crist, ed. *Chapel of the Resurrection*. Valparaiso: Cede Publishing, 2012.

Baños Francia, José Alfonso. "Arquitectura en Puerto Vallarta. Del imaginario de 'pueblito' a un proyecto de modernidad inacabada", in: Daniel González Romero, ed. *Puerto Vallarta en el imaginario. Procesos de su desarrollo*. Guadalajara: Universidad de Guadalajara Centro Universitario de Arte, Arquitectura y Diseño Centro Universitario de la Costa, 2010, 85-97.

Barry, Helen and Nichols, Cheryl. *The Arkansas Designs of E. Fay Jones 1956-1997*. Little Rock, Arkansas: Arkansas Historic Preservation Program. 63-66. <https://web.archive.org/web/20120529174432/http://www.arkansaspreservation.com/pdf/publications/Faye_Jones.pdf> (PDF) (10 October 2020), archived from the original <http://www.arkansaspreservation.com/pdf/publications/faye_jones.pdf> (PDF) on 29 May 2012.

Basáez Yau, P., ed. *150 años de enseñanza de la arquitectura en la Universidad de Chile, 1849-1999*. Santiago: Universidad de Chile, 1999.

Bastero, J. L. "La Inmaculada Concepción en los siglos XIX y XX". *Anuario de historia de la Iglesia*, 13 (2004), 79-104.

Batley, Claude. *The Design Development of Indian Architecture*. Bombay: J. Tirant. & Company, 1934.

Bayless, Les. "Three who gave their lives: Remembering the martyrs of Mississippi Freedom Summer, 1964". *People's Weekly World*, 25 May 1996 <http://www.hartford-hwp.com/archives/45a/046.html> (10 October 2020).

Bebbington, David W. and Jones, David Ceri. *Evangelicalism and Fundamentalism in the United Kingdom during the Twentieth Century.* Oxford: Online, 2013. <DOI:10.1093/acprof:oso/9780199664832.001.0001>.

Bellenger, Aidan. *Downside Abbey. An Architectural History*. London: Merrell Publishers, 2011.

Berg Costa, Lorenzo and Cherubini, Gian P. *Ocupación, arquitectura y paisaje: Región de Los Lagos.* Santiago de Chile: Universidad de Chile, 2008.

Bergeron, Angelle. "Centennial Completion". *Constructor* (Arlington: McGraw-Hill Construction for Associated General Contractors of America), 93 (September-October 2011) 5, 15-16.

Bergeron, Claude. *L'architecture des églises du Québec: 1940-1985.* Québec: PUL, 1987.

Betsky, Aaron et al. *James Gamble Rogers and the Architecture of Pragmatism*. Cambridge (Mass.): MIT Press, 1994.

Betsky, Aaron. *Architecture Matters*. London: Thames & Hudson, 2017.

Bhatt, Vikram. *Resorts of the Raj: Hill Stations of India*. Ahmedabad: Mapin/Grantha, 1998.

Blancarte, Roberto. *Historia de la Iglesia Católica en México.* Mexico City: Colegio Mexiquense y Fondo de Cultura Económica, 1992.

Blanco Velasco, Isabel. "El Tabasco garridista y la movilización de los católicos por la reanudación del culto en 1938", in: Rubén Aguilar and Guillermo Zermeno, eds. *Religion, politica y sociedad. El sinarquismo y la Iglesia en Mexico: nueve ensayos*. Mexico: Universidad Iberoamericana, 1992, 117-169.

Bock, Marie Sophie. *Guayaquil: Arquitectura, espacio y sociedad, 1900-1940*. Lima: Institut français d'études andines, 2014.

Boland, Thomas Patrick. *St Patrick's Cathedral: A Life*. Melbourne: Polding Press, 1997.

Bonet i Armengol, Jordi, ed. *La Sagrada Familia de Gaudí. El templo expiatorio desde sus orígenes hasta hoy*. Barcelona-Madrid: Lunwerg editores, 2010.

Borger, Hugo, ed. *Der Kölner Dom im Jahrhundert seiner Vollendung*. Vol. 2. Cologne: Museen der Stadt Köln, 1980.

Borger-Keweloh, Nikola. "Mittelalterliche Dome als Nationaldenkmäler", in: Günter Donath and Matthias Donath, eds. *Himmelszeichen. 100 Jahre Meissner Domtürme*. Meissen: Edition Sächsische Zeitung, 2008, 28-46.

Borngässer, Barbara. "Neugotik und Moderne im Süden Brasiliens: Die Kirchenbauten Gottfried Böhms", in: Barbara Borngässer and Bruno Klein, eds. *Neugotik global - kolonial - postkolonial. Gotisierende Sakralarchitektur auf der Iberischen Halbinsel und in Lateinamerika vom 19. bis zum 21. Jahrhundert*. Frankfurt a.M. - Madrid: Vervuert, 2020, 251-262.

Borngässer, Barbara and Klein, Bruno, eds. *Neugotik global - kolonial - postkolonial. Gotisierende Sakralarchitektur auf der Iberischen Halbinsel und in Lateinamerika vom 19. bis zum 21. Jahrhundert. Neogótico global - colonial - postcolonial. Arquitectura sagrada neogótica en la Peninsula Ibérica y América Latina del siglo XIX al XX*. Frankfurt-Madrid: Vervuert, 2020.

Bosker, Bianca. *Original Copies: Architectural Mimicry in Contemporary China*. Spatial Habitus: Making and Meaning in Asia's Architectura. Hononulu: University of Hawai'i Press, 2013.

Brandl, Heiko; Ranft, Andreas and Waschbüsch, Andreas, eds. *Architektur als Zitat: Formen, Motive und Strategien der Vergegenwärtigung*. More Romano, 4. Regensburg: Schnell & Steiner, 2014.

Brandt, Sigrid and Meier, Hans Rudolf, eds. *Stadtbild und Denkmalpflege. Konstruktion und Rezeption von Bildern der Stadt*. Stadtentwicklung und Denkmalpflege, 11. Berlin: Jovis, 2008.

Bremner, G. Alex. "Pro Fide et Patria. Anglicanism and Ecclesiastical Architecture in Southern and Central Africa", in: Fassil Demissie, ed. *Colonial Architecture and Urbanism in Africa: Intertwined and Contested Histories*. Farnham-Burlington: Ashgate, 2012, 239-275.

Bremner, G. Alex, *Imperial Gothic. Religious Architecture and High Anglican Culture in the British Empire, 1840-1870*. New Haven: Yale University Press, 2013.

Bremner, G. Alex, ed. *Architecture and Urbanism in the British Empire*. Oxford: Oxford Scholarship online, 2016.

Bremner, G. Alex and Nelson, Louis P. "Propagating Ideas and Institutions", in: G. Alex Bremner, ed. *Architecture and Urbanism in the British Empire*. Oxford: Oxford Scholarship online, 2016, 1-40.

Bremner, G. Alex and Nelson, Louis P. "Propagating Ideas and Institutions: Religious and Educational Architecture", in: G. Alex Bremner, ed. *Architecture and Urbanism in the British Empire*. Oxford: Oxford University Press, 2016, 159-197.

Brittain-Catlin, Timothy; De Maeyer, Jan and Bressani, Martin, eds. *Gothic Revival Worldwide: A.W.N. Pugin's Global Influence*. KADOC Artes 16. Leuven: Leuven University Press, 2016.

Brockey, Liam Matthew. "Doubting Thomas: The Apostle and the Portuguese Empire in Early Modern Asia", in: Katherine Van Liere, Simon Ditchfield and Howard Louthan, eds. *Sacred History: Uses of the Christian Past in the Renaissance World*. Oxford: Oxford University Press, 2012, 231-250.

Broderick, Robert C. *Historic Churches of the United States*. New York: Wilfred Funk, 1958.

Brome, Richard. *Aboriginal Australians. Black Responses to white Dominance, 1788-2001*. Crows Nest: Allen & Unwin, 2002[3].

Brook, Chris. *Gothic Revival*. London: Phaidon Press, 1999.

"Brother LaRocque Designs Arctic Igloo-Shaped Church". *The New London, Conn., Evening Day* (Associated Press), 5 March 1960, 5.

Brown, H. Miles. *The Story of Truro Cathedral*. Penryn: Tor Marks Press, 1991.

Bruand, Yves. *A Arquitetura contemporânea no Brasil*. São Paulo: Perspectiva, 1991[2].

Buchner, Laura N. "R. Guastavino Co: five decades of construction at the cathedral church of Saint John the Divine", in: Brian Bowen et al., ed. *Proceedings of the Fifth International Congress of Construction History*. Chicago: Construction History Society of America, 2015, 255-265.

Buggeln, Gretchen. "The Shape of a New Era Valparaiso's Chapel of the Resurrection in Historical Context". *The Cresset*, 73 (Lent 2010) 3, 6-14. <https://web.archive.org/web/20131209230549/http://thecresset.org/2010/Lent/Buggeln_L10.html> (10 October 2020).

Buggeln, Gretchen. *Townsend. The Suburban Church: Modernism and Community in Postwar America*. Minneapolis-London: University of Minnesota Press, 2015.

Burns, Karen. "Global Gothic", in: Timothy Brittain-Catlin, Jan De Maeyer and Martin Bressani, eds. *Gothic Revival Worldwide: A.W.N. Pugin's Global Influence*. KADOC Artes 16. Leuven: Leuven University Press, 2016, 131-141.

Bushart, Magdalena. *Der Geist der Gotik und die expressionistische Kunst. Kunstgeschichte und Kunsttheorie 1911-1925*. Munich: Schreiber, 1990.

Butler, Richard. "The Anglo-Indian Architect Walter Sykes George (1881-1962): a Modernist Follower of Lutyens". *Architectural History*, 55 (2012), 237-268.

Cabral, Renata. "Entre destruições, achados e invenção: a restauração da Sé de Olinda no âmbito do Programa Integrado de Reconstrução das Cidades Históricas do Nordeste". *Anais do Museu Paulista: História e Cultural Material*, 24 (2016) 1 (online)

Caicedo-Orozco, A.J. and Carranza-Cely, F.H. "Factores sociopolíticos y culturales que gestaron el estilo neogótico en los países latinoamericanos". *Revista Semilleros*, 2 (2016) 1, 2-10.

Calderón, José. *Del Romanticismo a la modernidad. La parroquia del Rosario en la Ciudad de México*. Thesis (Msc), Universidad Nacional Autónoma de México, 2018.

Campbell, Louise. *Coventry Cathedral: Art and Architecture in Post-War Britain*. Clarendon Studies in the History of Art, 16. Oxford: Clarendon Press, 1996.

Cantone, Cleo. "The Point of Pointed Architecture: Its Revival in Europe and its Appearance in 'Colonial' Mosques", in: Fassil Demissie, ed. *Colonial Architecture and Urbanism in Africa. Intertwined and Contested Histories*. Farnham-Burlington: Ashgate, 2012, 85-106.

Capresi, Vittoria. "The new Face of Tripoli (Libya) in the Thirties". *architectura. Zeitschrift für Geschichte der Baukunst – Journal of the History of Architecture*, 237 (2001), 95-115.

Capresi, Vittoria. "Architectural Transfer, Italian Colonial Architecture in Libya: 'Libyan Rationalisms' and the Concept of 'Mediterraneity', 1926-1942", in: Fassil Demissie, ed. *Colonial Architecture and Urbanism in Africa: Intertwined and Contested Histories*. Farnham-Burlington: Ashgate, 2012, 33-65.

Carbonneau, Robert E. "The Catholic Church in China 1900-1949", in: R. Gary Tiedemann, ed. *Handbook of Christianity in China*. Vol. 2: *1800 to Present*. Leiden-Boston: Brill, 2010, 516-525.

Cardinal Celso Costantini and the Chinese Catholic Church. Thematic issue of the journal *Tripod*, 28 (2008) 148, Hong Kong. <http://www.hsstudyc.org.hk/en/tripod_en/en_tripod_148.html>.

Carrasco Zaldúa, Fernando. "Vida y obra de dos piamonteses en Colombia", in: Rubén Hernández Molina and Olimpia Niglio, eds. *Ingenieros y arquitectos italianos en Colombia*. Ariccia: Ermes. Servizi editoriali integrati, 105-120.

Carson, Clayborne. *In Struggle: SNCC and the Black Awakening of the 1960s*. Cambridge: Harvard University Press, 1981.

Casillas Navarro, Francisco. *El Templo Expiatorio de Guadalajara*. Zapopan: Amate Editorial, 2005.

Castillo Pino, Eduardo. *La catedral de Guayaquil: El espíritu, la historia, la piedra, la luz*. Guayaquil: Arquidiócesis de Guayaquil, 2009.

Castro Barrera, María del Carmen. "Eugène Emmanuel Viollet-le-Duc: una relectura desde México". *Revista Conservación*, 3 (2017), 139-162.

Castro, Parsival. *Espacios sagrados y arquitectura religiosa de Guayaquil*. Guayaquil: Melvin Hoyos Galarza, 2014.

Castro Pita, Pársival and Paredes Cazar, Aurelio. *Guayaquil es mi destino para vivir la ruta de la fe*. Guayaquil: Dirección de Turismo y Promoción Cívica del Municipio de Guayaquil, 2014.

Catedral São Pedro de Alcântara – Relatório Técnico Mapa de Danos & Recomendações de Restauro para o Projeto da Revitalização da Catedral Imperial de Petrópolis e Implantação da Galeria de Arte Auto Expositiva. Petrópolis, 2016 (pdf).

Cathedral Church of Saint Luke (Orlando, Florida). *Centennial Book of the Cathedral Church of St. Luke. Orlando, Florida, 1874-1974*. Orlando (Florida): Cathedral Church of St. Luke, 1974.

Cathedral Church of St. Luke (Orlando, Florida; Episcopal). *Church Records and History, 1900-1992*. Salt Lake City, Utah: Filmed by the Genealogical Society of Utah, 1993.

"Cathedral of 'All Saints,' Halifax, N.S." *The Canadian Architect & Builder*, 22 (1908) 1, 11-14.

Ceballos Rodríguez, Manuel. "El clericalismo y el anticlericalismo en México. Dos caras de la misma moneda", in: Franco Savarino and Andrea Mutolo, eds. *El anticlericalismo en México*. Mexico City: LX Legislatura H. Cámara de Diputados; Instituto Tecnológico de Estudios Superiores de Monterrey; Miguel Ángel Porrúa Editores, 2008, 39-52.

Cevallos, A. *Arte, diseño y arquitectura en el Ecuador. La obra del Padre Brüning (1899-1938)*. Quito: Ediciones del Banco Central del Ecuador; Ediciones Abya Yala, 1994.

Chan Kim-Kwong 陳劍光. "Chinese Churches and Communist State: The 'Patriotic' Churches", in: R. Gary Tiedeman, ed. *Handbook of Christianity in China*. Vol. 2: *1800 to Present*. Leiden-Boston: Brill, 2010, 867-881.

Chazelle, Annie, ed. *Le patrimoine du canton de Sancerre*. Bourges: Conseil général du Cher, 2008. <https://sancerre.cg18.fr/jalognes/index.html>.

Checa-Artasu, Martín. "Monumentalidad, símbolo y arquitectura neogótica. El Santuario Guadalupano de Zamora, Michoacán", in: Octavio Augusto Montes Vega and Octavio Martin González Santana, eds. *Estudios Michoacanos*, XIV. Mexico: El Colegio de Michoacán, 2011, 143-194.

Checa-Artasu, Martín. "Revisitando el papel del templo en la ciudad: los grandes templos neogóticos del Occidente de México". *Religião e Sociedade*, 31 (2011) 2, 179-206.

Checa-Artasu, Martín. "Visiones del neogótico mexicano: el templo del Sagrado Corazón de Jesús en León, Guanajuato (1921-2009)". *Boletín de monumentos históricos*, 21 (January-April 2011), 90-108.

Checa-Artasu, Martín. "El templo de San José en Arandas, Jalisco: un ejemplo del neogótico mexicano inconcluso y monumental (1879-2011)". *Revista Academia*, 22 (2012) 3 (2), 11-27.

Checa-Artasu, Martín M. "La Iglesia y la expansión del neogótico en Latinoamérica: Una aproximación desde la geografía de la religión". *Naveg@mérica. Revista electrónica por la Asociación de Americanistas*, 11 (2013). 1-21.

Checa-Artasu, Martín. "De Ferrara a la Ciudad de México pasando por Chicago: la trayectoria arquitectónica de Adamo Boari (1863-1904)". *Biblio 3W. Revista Bibliográfica de Geografía y Ciencias Sociales*, 1111 (2015). <www.ub.edu/geocrit/b3w-1111.htm>.

Checa-Artasu, Martín. "Del neogótico al novogótico. Algunos ejemplos de arquitecturas religiosas en Zacatecas", in: Martín M. Checa-Artasu, J. Jesús García López and María Cristina Valerdi Nochebuena. *Territorialidad y arquitecturas de lo sagrado en el México contemporáneo*. Aguascalientes: Universidad Autónoma de Aguascalientes, 2015, 35-58.

Checa-Artasu, Martín. "El neogótico y el fortalecimiento de la Iglesia en Guadalajara: El templo Expiatorio". *Estudios Jaliscienses*, 100 (May 2015), 40-55.

Checa-Artasu, Martín. "Lo neogótico y el Concilio Vaticano II en la arquitectura religiosa de México. Los reacomodos de una anomalía". *Actas del Congreso Internacional de Arquitectura Religiosa Contemporánea*, 4 (2015) <http://www.arquitecturareligiosa.es/index.php/AR/issue/view/5>.

Checa-Artasu, Martín M. "The Catholic Church and Neo-Gothic Architecture in Latin America: Scales for Their Analysis", in: Stanley Brunn, eds. *The Changing World Religion Map*. Dordrecht: Springer, 2015, 2437-2451.

Checa-Artasu, Martín. "La dimensión geográfica de la arquitectura neogótica en México", in: Martín Checa-Artasu and Olimpia Niglio, eds. *El neogótico en la arquitectura americana. Historia, restauración, reinterpretaciones y reflexiones*. Rome: Aracne Editrice, 2016, 327-341.

Checa-Artasu, Martín M. "¿Por qué un libro sobre el estilo neogótico en la arquitectura americana?", in: Martín M. Checa-Artasu and Olimpia Niglio, eds. *El neogótico en la arquitectura americana. Historia, restauración, reinterpretaciones y reflexiones*. Rome: Aracne editrice, 2016, 25-44.

Checa-Artasu, Martín. "El templo y la ciudad: los diversos papeles del Santuario Guadalupano de Zamora, Michoacán", in: María Cristina Valerdi Nochebuena, ed. *Santuarios contemporáneos o expresión arquitectónica de una sociedad*. Puebla: Benemérita Universidad Autónoma de Puebla, 2017, 42-82.

Checa-Artasu, Martín. "La arquitectura neogótica católica en el norte de México. Algunos ejemplos", in: María Cristina Valerdi and María Diéguez, eds. *Diseño y método de creación del espacio religioso contemporáneo en Iberoamérica*. Puebla: Benemérita Universidad Autónoma de Puebla - Lodz: Instytut Historii Sztuki, Uniwersytet Lodsky, 2018, 95-128.

Checa-Artasu, Martín. "Adamo Boari y sus proyectos de arquitectura religiosa en México (1897-1902)" in: Martín Checa-Artasu and Olimpia Niglio, eds. *Italianos en México. Arquitectos, ingenieros, artistas entre los siglos XIX y XX*. Rome: Aracne editrice, 2019, 85-106.

Checa-Artasu, Martín. "Religious orders and the expansion of Neo-Gothic architecture in Latin America" in: Barbara Borngässer and Bruno Klein, eds. *Neugotik global – kolonial – postkolonial. Gotisierende Sakralarchitektur auf der Iberischen Halbinsel und in Lateinamerika vom 19. bis zum 21. Jahrhundert / Neogótico global – colonial – postcolonial. Arquitectura sagrada neogótica en la Península Ibérica y América Latina del siglo XIX al XXI*. Madrid: Vervuert Iberoamericana, 2020, 159-170.

Checa-Artasu, Martín M. "Templo de Nuestra Señora del Rosario, Guadalajara", in: Martín M. Checa-Artasu. *El neogótico tapatío. Guía básica para la apreciación del entorno cultural edificado*. Guadalajara: Arquitónica Editorial, 2020.

Checa-Artasu, Martín. "Una copia de la Sainte-Chapelle en León, Guanajuato. La capilla de la Cruz de Cantera". *Revista Ínsula Barataria*, 41 (May 2020), 20-22.

Checa-Artasu, Martín. "Una reinterpretación mexicana del neogótico: la torre parroquial de San Miguel de Allende, Guanajuato", in: Bruno Klein, Barbara Borngässer and Bettina Marten, eds. *Gothic Global – Colonial – Postcolonial. Gothic Sacral Architecture in the Iberian Peninsula and Latin America from the 19th to the 21st century*. Frankfurt-Madrid: Veuvert Verlag/ Iberoaméricana, 2020, 185-198.

Checa-Artasu, Martín M. and Niglio, Olimpia, eds. *El Neogótico en la arquitectura americana. Historia, restauración, reinterpretaciones y reflexiones*. Rome: Aracne editrice, 2016.

Checkland, Olive. *Japan and Britain after 1859: Creating Cultural Bridges*. London: Routledge, 2002.

Cheng, Irene; Davis, Charles L. and Wilson, Mabel O., eds. *Race and Modern Architecture: A Critical History from the Enlightenment to the Present*. Pittsburg: University of Pittsburgh Press, 2020.

Cherubini Zanetel, Gian Piero. *La escuela de carpinteros alemanes de puerto Montt, su formación e influencia más allá de las fronteras*. Santiago de Chile: Editorial Universitaria, 2019.

Chopra, Preeti. *A Joint Enterprise: Indian Elites and the Making of British Bombay*. Minneapolis-London: University of Minnesota Press, 2011.

(Church of England in Canada, ed.) *The Official Report of the Opening of All Saints' Cathedral at Halifax, N. S. The Canadian Church Congress and Other Proceedings at Halifax, Windsor and Annapolis Royal, N. S., in connection with the Bicentenary Commemoration of the Church of England in Canada, 1710-1910*. Halifax, N. S.: Chronicle Print Co., 1911.

Cianciolo Cosentino, Gabriella. "Francesco Saverio Cavallari (1810-1896). Architetto, archeologo, professore e disegnatore", in: Martín M. Checa-Artasu and Olimpia Niglio, eds. *Italianos en México. Arquitectos, ingenieros, artistas entre los siglos XIX y XX*. Rome: Aracne editrice, 2019, 159-176.

Clark, Anthony E. *China Gothic: The Bishop of Beijing and His Cathedral*. Seattle: University of Washington Press, 2019.

Cleys, Bram and De Meulder, Bruno. "Imagining a Christian Territory: Changing Spatial Strategies in the Missionary Outposts of Scheut (Kasai, Congo, 1891-1940)", in: Fassil Demissie, ed. *Colonial Architecture and Urbanism in Africa: Intertwined and Contested Histories*. Farnham-Burlington: Ashgate, 2012, 201-238.

Cody, Jeffrey W. "Striking a Harmonious Chord: Foreign Missionaries and Chinese-style Buildings, 1911-1949". *Architronic*, 5 (1996) 3.

Cody, Jeffrey W. "American Geometries and the Architecture of Christian Campuses in China", in: Daniel H. Bays and Ellen Widmer, eds. *China's Christian Colleges: Cross-Cultural Connections, 1900-1950*. Stanford: Stanford University Press, 2009, 27-56.

Collins, Peter. *Changing Ideals in Modern Architecture 1750-1950*. Montreal-Kingston-London-Ithaca: Mc Gill-Queen's University Press, 1998.

Collum, Marla O.; Krueger, Barbara E. and Kostuch, Dorothy, eds. *Detroit's Historic Places of Worship*. Detroit: Wayne State University Press, 2012.

Connick, Charles Jay. *Adventures in Light and Color: An Introduction to the Stained Glass Craft*. London: Harrap, 1937.

Cook, John Wesley. "A Christian Vision of Unity: An Architectural History of the Riverside Church", in: Peter J. Paris et al. *The History of the Riverside Church in the City of New York*. New York-London: New York University Press, 2004, 137-178.

Coomans, Thomas. "La création d'un style architectural sino-chrétien. L'œuvre d'Adelbert Gresnigt, moine-artiste bénédictin en Chine (1927-1932)". *Revue Bénédictine*, 123 (2013), 128-170.

Coomans. Thomas. "Sint-Lucasneogotiek in Noord-China: Alphonse De Moerloose, missionaris en architect". *M&L. Monumenten, landschappen en archeologie*, 32 (2013) 5, 6-33.

Coomans Thomas. "A Pragmatic Approach to Church Construction in Northern China at the Time of Christian Inculturation: The Handbook '*Le missionnaire constructeur*, 1926'". *Frontiers of Architectural Research*, 3 (2014) 2, 89-107.

Coomans, Thomas. "Die Kunstlandschaft der Gotik in China. Eine Enzyklopädie von importierten, hybridisierten und postmodernen Zitaten", in: Heiko Brandl, Andreas Ranft and Andreas Waschbüsch, eds. *Architektur als Zitat. Formen, Motive und Strategien der Vergegenwärtigung*. More Romano. Schriften des Europäischen Romanik Zentrums 4. Regensburg: Verlag Schnell & Steiner, 2014, 133-161.

Coomans, Thomas. "Indigenizing Catholic Architecture in China: From Western-Gothic to Sino-Christian Design, 1900-1940", in: Cindy Chu Yik-yi 朱益宜, ed. *Catholicism in China, 1900-Present. The Development of the Chinese Church*. New York: Palgrave and Macmillan, 2014, 125-144.

Coomans, Thomas. "Gothique ou chinoise, missionnaire ou inculturée? Les paradoxes de l'architecture catholique française en Chine au XXe siècle". *Revue de l'Art*, 189 (2015), 11-21.

Coomans Thomas. "Une utopie missionnaire? Construire des églises, des séminaires et des écoles catholiques dans la Chine en pleine tourmente (1941)", in: Alexandre Tsung-ming Chen 陳聰铭, ed. *Le Christianisme en Chine aux XIXe et XXe siècles. Figures, événements et missions-œuvres*. Leuven Chinese Studies 31. Leuven: Ferdinand Verbiest Institute, 2015, 45-79.

Coomans. Thomas. "Pugin Worldwide: From *Les Vrais Principes* and the Belgian St Luke Schools to Northern China and Inner Mongolia", in: Timothy Brittain-Catlin, Jan De Maeyer and Mario Bressani, eds. *Gothic Revival Worldwide: A.W.N. Pugin's Global Influence*. KADOC Artes 16. Leuven: Leuven University Press, 2016, 156-171.

Coomans Thomas. "The 'Sino-Christian Style': A Major Tool for Architectural Indigenization", in: Yangwen Zheng 鄭揚文, ed. *Sinicizing Christianity*. Studies in Christian Mission 49. Leiden-Boston: Brill, 2017, 197-232.

Coomans, Thomas. "East Meets West on the Construction Site. Churches in China, 1840s-1930s". *Construction History*, 33 (2018) 2, 63-84.

Coomans, Thomas. "Notre-Dame de Sheshan à Shanghai, basilique des Jésuites français en Chine, 1867-1936". *Bulletin monumental*, 176 (2018) 2, 129-156.

Coomans. Thomas. "Unexpected Connections: The Benedictine Abbey of Maredsous and Christian Architecture in China, 1900-1930s". *Revue Bénédictine*, 131 (2021) 1, 264-299.

Coomans, Thomas. "Islands on the Mainland: Catholic Missions and Spatial Strategies in China, 1840s-1940s", in: Bram Cleys, Bruno De Meulder, Jan De Maeyer and Allen M. Howard, eds. *Missionary Places, 1850-1950: Imagining, Building, Contesting Christianities*. KADOC-Artes 17. Leuven: Leuven University Press, 2021 (forthcoming).

Coomans, Thomas 高曼士. *Sheshan Marian Shrine in Shanghai: Architecture, Space and Symbolism / Sheshan jiaotang jian zao de lishi xun zong* 佘山教堂建遭的历史寻踪. Shanghai: Tongji University Press, 2022 (forthcoming).

Coomans, Thomas and De Maeyer, Jan. "Prêtres et architectes: une leçon de morale", in: Florence Descamps, Frédéric Chappey, Philippe Plagnieux and Sabine Frommel, eds. *Un bretteur au service du patrimoine. Mélanges en l'honneur de Jean-Michel Leniaud*. Paris: Mare et Martin, 2020, 313-323.

Coomans, Thomas and Ho Puay-peng Ho 何培斌. "Architectural Styles and Identities in Hong Kong: The Chinese and Western Designs for St Teresa's Church in Kowloon Tong, 1928-32". *Journal of the Royal Asiatic Society Hong Kong Branch* 香港皇家亞洲學會學報, 58 (2018), 81-109.

Coomans, Thomas and Luo Wei 罗薇. "Exporting Flemish Gothic Architecture to China: Meaning and Context of the Churches of Shebiya (Inner Mongolia) and Xuanhua (Hebei) built by Missionary-Architect Alphonse De Moerloose in 1903-1906". *Relicta. Heritage Research in Flanders*, 9 (2012), 219-262.

Coomans, Thomas and Luo Wei 罗薇. "Mimesis, Nostalgia and Ideology: The Scheut Fathers and home-country-based church design in China", in: *History of the Catholic Church in China from its Beginning to the Scheut Fathers and 20th Century*. Leuven Chinese Studies 29. Leuven: Leuven University Press, 2015, 495-522.

Coomans, Thomas and Luo Wei 罗薇. "Missionary-Builders: Scheut Fathers as Church Designers and Constructors in Northern China", in: Alexandre Tsung-ming Chen 陳聰铭, ed. *Catholicism's Encounters with China. 17th to 20th Century*. Leuven Chinese Studies 39. Leuven: Ferdinand Verbiest Institute, 2018, 333-364.

Coomans, Thomas 高曼士 and Xu Yitao 徐怡涛. *Bolai yu bentu – 1926 nian faguo chuanjiao shi suo zhuan zhongguo beifang jiaotang yingzao zhi yanjiu* 舶来与本土 – 1926年法国传教士所撰中国北方教堂营造之研究 / *Building Churches in Northern China: A 1926 Handbook in Context*. Beijing: Intellectual Property Rights Publishing House, 2016.

Coomans, Thomas 高曼士 and Xu Yitao 徐怡涛. "Built Together, Heritagized Together: Using Building Archaeology for Safeguarding Early Modern Churches in China", in: Joaquim Rodrigues dos Santos, ed. *Preserving Transcultural Heritage: Your Way or My Way? Questions on Authenticity, Identity and Patrimonial Proceedings in the Safeguarding of Architectural Heritage Created in the Meeting of Cultures*. Lisbon: Caleidoscópio – Edição e Artes Gráficas, 2017, 197-206.

Coomans, Thomas; Xu, Yitao 徐怡涛 and Zhang, Jianwei 张剑葳. "'Imposing and Provocative': The Design, Style, Construction and Significance of Saint Anthony's Cathedral, Xinjiang (Shanxi, China), 1936-40", in: João Mascarenhas-Mateus and Ana Paula Pires, eds. *History of Construction Cultures. Proceedings of the 7th International Congress on Construction History (7ICCH 2021), July 12-16, 2021, Lisbon, Portugal*. London-Leiden: CRC Press - Balkema, 2021, 85-92.

Cordes, Karen. "Encore Delivered with Strength and Delicacy: Cooper Chapel, Arkansas: Fay Jones & Maurice Jennings". *Architecture: The AIA Journal*, 77 (October 1988) 10, 52-57.

"Cordonnier, Louis-Marie", in: *Allgemeines Künstlerlexikon. Die Bildenden Künstler aller Zeiten und Völker*, vol. 21. Munich-Leipzig, 1999, 195.

Cornerstones: St. Mary's Cathedral [1887-1955]. <https://web.archive.org/web/20040606015451/http://calgarypubliclibrary.com/calgary/historic_tours/corner/stmarys1.htm> (17 October 2020).

Cornerstones: St. Mary's Cathedral [1955-]. <https://web.archive.org/web/20040606014939/http://calgarypubliclibrary.com/calgary/historic_tours/corner/stmarys.htm> (17 October 2020).

Cortazzi, Hugh. *Introduction – Richard Henry Brunton: Building Japan (1868-1874)*. Tokyo: Japan Library, 1991.

Cortés Lugo de Torres, Josefina. *Recordando un Paraíso*. Puerto Vallarta: Universidad de Guadalajara, 2010.

Corti, Francisco. "Iglesia de Nuestra Señora de Lourdes", in: Francisco Corti, Patricia Grau Dieckmann and Ofelia Manzi. *Iglesias católicas neogóticas*. Buenos Aires: Universidad de Buenos Aires, 2012, 91-99.

Corti, Francisco. "Origin and development of Neo-Gothic in the Catholic churches of the city and province of Buenos Aires". *Postmedieval: A Journal of Medieval Cultural Studies*, 6 (2015) 3, 304-323.

Corti, Francisco; Grau Dieckmann, Patricia and Manzi, Ofelia. *Iglesias católicas neogóticas*. Buenos Aires: Universidad de Buenos Aires, 2012.

Corti, Francisco and Manzi, Ofelia. *Iglesias reformadas neogóticas en Buenos Aires y alrededores*. Buenos Aires: Universidad de Buenos Aires, 2002.

Costantini, Celso. "Proper Style of Church Architecture for the Chinese Mission (letter of the Apostolic Delegate to China Addressed to the American and Irish Missionaries)". *The Ecclesiastical Review*, 69 (September 1923) 3, 288-293.

Costantini, Celso. "The Need of Developing a Sino-Christian Architecture for our Catholic Missions (A letter addressed by His Excellency the Apostolic Delegate in China to the Rt. Rev. Msgrs. James E. Walsh and Edward J. Galvin)". *Bulletin of the Catholic University of Peking*, 3 (1927), 7-15.

Costantini, Celso. "L'universalité de l'art chrétien. Lettre adressée par Mgr. le Délégué apostolique à deux supérieurs de missions". *Dossiers de la Commission synodale / Digest of the Synodal Commission*, 5 (May 1932) 5, 410-417.

Costantini, Celso. *L'art chrétien dans les missions. Manuel d'art pour les missionnaires*. Paris-Bruges: Desclée De Brouwer, 1949.

Courtois, Ulrico. "La Basílica de Luján". *La Biblioteca*, 2 (1896), 213-230.
Cram, Ralph Adams. *Church Building: A Study of the Principles of Architecture in Their Relation to the Church*. Boston: Small, Maynard, 1901.
Cram, Ralph Adams. *The Ministry of Art*. Boston: Houghton Mifflin, 1914.
Cram, Ralph Adams. *The Substance of Gothic: 6 Lectures on the Development of Architecture from Charlemagne to Henry VIII given at the Lowell Institute, Boston, in November and December 1916*. Boston: Jones, 1925.
Cram, Ralph Adams. "Some architectural and spiritual aspects of the chapel". *The Princeton Alumni Weekly*, 28 (26 May 1928) 32, 987-989, 1028.
Crama, Josefina and Ruggerio, María Florencia. "La Virgen de Lourdes y su santuario en Santos Lugares. Del símbolo y el espacio sagrado". *Quintas jornadas de Jóvenes Investigadores*. Buenos Aires: Instituto Gino Germani, 2009.
Crinson, Mark. *Modern Architecture and the End of Empire*. Aldershot: Ashgate, 2003.
Cruz González Franco, Lourdes. "Semblanza de un gran maestro: Honorato Carrasco Navarrete". *Bitácora Arquitectura*, 6 (2011), 38-45.

Danbolt, Gunnar. *Nidarosdomen fra kristkirke til nasjonalmonument*. Oslo: Andresen & Butenschøn, 1997.
Daprato Statuary Company in Chicago, ed. *Creations in ecclesiastical art. Daprato Statuary Company, Pontifical Institute of Christian Art, Chicago, New York altars famous for quality of workmanship; studios*. Chicago, Ill. - Pietrasanta, Italy: Daprato Statuary Company in Chicago, 1916.
Davies, Philip. *Splendours of the Raj: British Architecture in India, 1160-1947*. London: Penguin, 1987.
Dávila Garibi, José Ignacio Paulino, ed. *Al margen de una polémica: documentación referente a la bendición y colocación de la primera piedra del templo Expiatorio Eucarístico, que el M.I. Sr. Maestrescuelas Dr. D. Pedro Romero Arnaiz está construyendo en la ciudad de Guadalajara, seguida de algunos comentarios*. S.l., s.d.
De Bièvre, Dirk. "Trade, political coalitions, and neo-Gothic architecture in Europe". *European Review*, 27 (December 2018) 2.
Dedication booklet, Chapel of the Resurrection. Valparaiso, University of Valparaiso, Sunday, September 27, 1959. <https://www.valpo.edu/chapel/files/2016/11/1959-Sept-27-Dedication-booklet-Chapel.pdf> (10 October 2020).
De la Asunción, Lázaro O.C.D. *Historia de la Orden del Carmen Descalzo en Chile, 1899-1935*. 3 vols. Santiago: Imprenta Chile, 1936.
De la Riestra, Pablo. "Gótico y neogótico en la arquitectura de la catedral de La Plata", in: *La catedral de La Plata. El mayor templo neogótico del siglo XX*. Buenos Aires: MZ ediciones, 2000.
de La Servière, Joseph, *L'orphelinat de T'ou-Sè-Wè. Son histoire. Son état présent*. Shanghai-Xujiahui: T'ou-sè-wè, 1914.
Del Pino Martínez, Inés. "La presencia italiana en la arquitectura republicana de Ecuador", in: Mario Sartor, ed. *América Latina y la cultura artística italiana. Un balance en el Bicentenario de la Independencia Latinoamericana*. Buenos Aires: Istituto Italiano di Cultura, 2011, 37-56.
Del Pino Martínez, Inés; Cepeda Astudillo, Franklin and Compte Guerrero, Florencio. *Italianos en la arquitectura de Ecuador*. Quito: Pontificia Universidad Católica del Ecuador, 2012.
De Maeyer, Jan, ed. *De St. Lucasscholen en de neogotiek 1862-1914*. Leuven: Leuven University Press, 1988.
De Maeyer, Jan. "Pro Arte Christiana. Catholic Art Guilds, Gothic Revival and the Cultural Identity of the Rhine-Meuse Region", in: Wolfgang Cortjaens, Jan De Maeyer and Tom Verschaffel, eds. *Historism and Cultural Identity in the Rhine-Meuse Region. Tensions between Nationalism and Regionalism in the Nineteenth Century*. KADOC Artes 10. Leuven: Leuven University Press, 2008, 159-171.
Demissie, Fassil. "Imperial legacies and postcolonial predicaments: an introduction". *African Identities*, 5 (2007) 2, 155-165. <https://doi-org.wwwdb.dbod.de/10.1080/14725840701403317>.
Demissie, Fassil, ed. *Colonial Architecture and Urbanism in Africa: Intertwined and Contested Histories*. Farnham-Burlington: Ashgate, 2012.
Demissie, Fassil. "Colonial Architecture and Urbanism in Africa: An Introduction", in: Fassil Demissie, ed. *Colonial Architecture and Urbanism in Africa: Intertwined and Contested Histories*. Farnham: Ashgate, 2012, 1-8.
D.G. "Quelques idées sur l'art chinois". *Bulletin catholique de* Pékin, 11 (1924), 127-130, 177-183, 218-221.
Dias, Pollyanna d'Avila. "O século XIX e o neogótico na Arquitetura brasileira: um estudo de caracterização". *Revista Ohun*, 4 (2008), 100-115.
Díaz Morales, Ignacio. "El templo expiatorio", in: Ramón Mata Torres. *Iglesias y edificios antiguos de Guadalajara*. Guadalajara: Cámara de comercio de Guadalajara y Ayuntamiento de Guadalajara, 1984, 311-318.
Díaz Patiño, Gabriela. "Imagen y discurso de la representación religiosa del Sagrado Corazón de Jesús". *Plura. Revista de Estudos de Religião*, 1 (2010), 86-108.
Donnelly, Lu; Brumble IV, H. David and Toker, Franklin. *Buildings of Pennsylvania: Pittsburgh and Western Pennsylvania*. Buildings of the United States. Charlottesville: University of Virginia Press, 2010.
Doutreligne, Denis-Donat. "Causerie sur l'art chinois: Peut-on adopter indifféremment dans nos églises certains détails d'ornementation". *Bulletin de la Société des Missions Étrangères de Paris*, 42 (June 1925), 341-357.
Dunlap, David W. *From Abyssinian to Zion: A Guide to Manhattan's Houses of Worship*. New York: Columbia University Press, 2004.
Dunmur, Juliet. *Edward Maufe. Architect and Cathedral Builder*. London: Moyhill Publishing, 2019.
Durán, Juan Guillermo. "Gestiones del Episcopado argentino ante la Santa Sede en favor del Santuario de Luján (1886). El P. Jorge María Salvaire comisionado oficial". *Teología: revista de la Facultad de Teología de la Pontificia Universidad Católica Argentina*, 89 (2006), 97-132.
Durán, Juan Guillermo. *De la Frontera a la Villa de Luján. Los comienzos de la gran Basílica. Jorge María Salvaire CM (1890-1899)*. Buenos Aires: Bouquet – Facultad de Teología de la Pontificia Universidad Católica Argentina, 2009.
Durán, Juan Guillermo. "La basílica nacional de Luján. El proyecto de su construcción (1887-1890)". *Revista Teología*, 49 (December 2012) 109, 65-96.
Durán, Juan Guillermo. "Río Cuarto asociado a la construcción de la Basílica de Luján y a la gran lámpara votiva", in: D.A. *El discipulado y la configuración con Cristo en la formación inicial. V jornada de estudios, Agosto 2017*. Río Cuarto: Ediciones Diocesanas de la Concepción del Río Cuarto, 2017, 7-63.

East, John W. *Australia's first international architect. A sketch of Life and Career of Jack. F. Hennessy junior* (pdf). St Lucia QLD, Australia, 2013 (accessed 14 April 2020).
East, John W. *Australian Romanesque. A History of Romanesque-Inspired Architecture in Australia* (pdf). Brisbane: The University of Queensland, 2016 (online).
Echeverry, Kevin Alexander. "Catedral Basílica de Manizales Nuestra Señora del Rosario construcción única en su género, Manizales Colombia". *EdA Esempi di Architettura*, August 2019, 1-26.

Educational Buildings by Perkins, Fellows and Hamilton, Architects-Engineers, Chicago. Chicago: E.E. Cortright, 1925.

Ellis, James. "Anglican Indigenization and Contextualization in Colonial Hong Kong: Comparative Case Studies of St. John's Cathedral and St. Mary's Church". *Mission Studies*, 36 (2019), 219-246.

Elphick, Richard. *Christianity in South Africa: A Political, Social, and Cultural History.* Berkeley: University of California Press, 1997.

Enríquez Guerrero, M.L. et al. *Espinosa y Santacruz. Dos arquitectos, dos épocas. Reseña histórica y documentación gráfica de la vida y obra de dos representantes de la arquitectura repúblicana y moderna nariñense: Lucindo María Espinosa Medina y Carlos Alberto Santacruz Burbano.* Pasto: Institución universitaria CESMAG, 2009.

Espinosa Fernández de Córdova, C. R. and Canal, Jordi. "La memoria transnacional de Gabriel García Moreno: la imagen póstuma del caudillo católico en Ecuador, Francia y Roma (1875-1921)". *Historia Crítica*, 75 (2020), 3-23.

Estrada, Julio. *Guía histórica de Guayaquil.* Vol. 2. Guayaquil: Imprenta Poligráfica, 1966.

Estudio de arquitectura Puerto Varas. *Expediente Técnico Templo Luterano. Diagnóstico de intervención de la zona típica y catastro de monumentos nacionales de Puerto Varas etapa 1: registro patrimonial,* July 2011. <http://www.zonatipicapuertovaras.cl/wp-content/plano/fichas/Ficha-MH09-TEMPLO_LUTERANO.pdf>.

Faber, Annette. "Und trotzte allen Zeiten: Neuromanik im Fernen Osten. Bauuntersuchung an St. Michael in Qingdao, eine bayerisch-chinesische Zusammenarbeit". *Denkmalpflege Informationen* (Bayerisches Landesamt für Denkmalpflege), 144 (November 2009), 71-75.

Faber, Tobias. "1904-1929 A Time of Transition", in: Martin Keiding, ed. *Danish Architecture since 1754.* Copenhagen: Danish Architectural Press, 2007, 157-191.

Fagundes e Braga, Thayse. *A trajetória do arquiteto alemão Simão Gramlich em campos cruzados no sul do Brasil: arquitetônico, religioso e político.* Thesis. Florianópolis, 2020.

Fagundes e Braga, Thayse. "Simon Gramlich and the Neo-Gothic Churches in Southern Brazil", in: Barbara Borngässer and Bruno Klein, eds. *Neugotik global - kolonial - postkolonial. Gotisierende Sakralarchitektur auf der Iberischen Halbinsel und in Lateinamerika vom 19. bis zum 21. Jahrhundert.* Frankfurt a.M. - Madrid: Vervuert, 2020, 243-249.

Farr, David. *Church in the Glebe - St. Matthew's, Ottawa, 1898-1988.* Ottawa: St. Matthew's Anglican Church, 1988.

Fernández-Cobián, Esteban. "Catedrales chilenas del siglo XX. Arquitectura, naturaleza y sociedad", in: María Cristina Valerdi and María Diéguez, eds. *Diseño y Método de creación del espacio religioso contemporáneo en Iberoamérica.* Puebla: Benemérita Universidad Autónoma de Puebla - Lodz: Instytut Historii Sztuki, Uniwersytet Lodsky, 2018, 217-245.

Ficher (Fischer), Sylvia. *Os arquitetos da Poli: ensino e profissão em São Paulo.* São Paulo: Edusp, 2005.

Fils, Alexander. *Brasilia. Moderne Architektur in Brasilien.* Düsseldorf: Beton-Verlag, 1988.

Finn, Dallas. "Josiah Conder (1852-1920) and Meiji Architecture", in: Hugh Cortazzi and Gordon Daniels, eds. *Britain & Japan: Themes and Personalities.* London: Routledge, 1991, 86-93.

Fisch, Michael. "The Rise of the Chapel Wedding in Japan. Simulation and Performance". *Japanese Journal of Religious Studies*, 28 (2001) 1-2, 57-76.

Fischer, Gerhard. *Domkirken i Trondheim. Kirkebygget i Middelalteren.* Vol. 2. [Oslo]: Forlaget Land og Kirke, 1965.

Flanagan, Bernard A. *Cathedral of the Sacred Heart.* Newark: Newark Public Library, 1989.

Fogelman, Patricia Alejandra. "Exvotos y secularización: libro y santuario de la Virgen de Luján, fines del s. XIX". ANPUH - *Revista Brasileira de História das Religiões*, 11 (May 2008) 31, 167-202.

Forman, Henry Chandlee. *The Architecture of the Old South: The Medieval Style, 1585-1850.* Cambridge, Mass.: Harvard Univ. Press, 1948.

Francel, Andrés and Ojeda, José Alejandro. "Arquitectura ecléctica salesiana como consecuencia material del contexto político republicano en Ibagué (Colombia), 1904". *Historelo. Revista de Historia regional y local*, 8 (January-June 2016) 15, 238-269.

Frank, Kristiane. "Baker, Herbert (1862)", in: *Allgemeines Künstlerlexikon*, vol. 6. Berlin-Boston: K. G. Saur, 1992, 353-354.

Frank, Marie Ann. "The Theory of Pure Design and American Architectural Education in the Early Twentieth Century". *Journal of the Society of Architectural Historians*, 67 (2008) 2, 248-273.

Frémaux, Céline. "1999, la cathédrale enfin achevée", in: Laurent Ulrich, ed. *Lille: la Treille, lumière du Nord. La grâce d'une cathédrale.* Vol. 10. Strasbourg: La Nuée Bleue, 2014, 130-145.

French, Robert Dudley. *The Memorial Quadrangle - A book about Yale.* New Haven: Yale University Press, 1929.

Fujimori, Terunobu. *Nihon no kindai kenchiku (Modern Architecture of Japan).* Tokyo: Iwanami Shoten, 1993.

Fujimori, Terunobu. "Josiah Conder and Japan", in: Suzuki Hiroyuki. *Josiah Conder: A Victorian Architect in Japan.* Toyko: Bijutsu Shuppan, 1997.

Furtado, Ana. *A Catedral de Nossa Senhora da Conceição de Lourenço Marques: cópia ou inovação do seuarquitecto?* Lisbon: Universidade de Lisboa, Facultade de Lettras, 2016.

Gabory, Emile. *Sainte-Anne d'Auray.* Paris: Plon, 1935.

Gabra, Gawdat and Takla, Hany N., eds. *Christianity and Monasticism in Upper Egypt.* Vol. 2. Cairo-New York: American University in Cairo Press, 2010.

Gabra, Gawdat and Takla, Hany N., eds. *Christianity and Monasticism in Aswan and Nubia.* Vol. 5. Oxford: Oxford University Press, 2013.

Gaehtgens, Thomas W. *Die brennende Kathedrale. Eine Geschichte aus dem Ersten Weltkrieg.* Munich: C.H. Beck, 2018.

Galeana De Valadés, Patricia. *Las relaciones iglesia-estado durante el Segundo Imperio.* Mexico City: Instituto de Investigaciones Históricas, Universidad Nacional Autónoma de México, 1991.

Gallegos Gómora, Miriam. *Iglesias policromas de la Chontalpa.* Mexico City: Instituto Nacional de Antropología e Historia, 2001.

Gama, James Borralho. *Brasília, a terra prometida: turismo místico e religioso na capital do país.* Brasília, 2009.

García Fernández, Estrellita. "Su construcción, transformaciones y contexto", in: Juan Arturo Camacho Becerra, ed. *La catedral de Guadalajara: historia y significados.* Vol. 2. Zapopan: El Colegio de Jalisco, A.C., 2012, 15-171.

García-Gutierrez Mosteiro, Javier, ed. *Las bóvedas de Guastavino en América: libro publicado con ocasión de la exposicion: Guastavino Co. (1885-1962); la reinvencion de la bóveda.* Madrid: Instituto Juan de Herrera, 2001.

Gaul, Joan. *Heinz Memorial Chapel.* Pittsburgh, 1995.

Gauthier, Richard. *Le Devenir de l'Art d'église des paroisses catholiques du Québec. Architecture, arts, pratiques patrimoine (1965-2002).* Thesis (D Phil). Québec, 2004.

Gayibor, Nicoué, ed. *Histoire des Togolais. Des origines aux années 1960.* Vol. 4: *Le refus de l'ordre colonial.* Paris: Karthala Editions, 2011.

Gazaneo, Jorge A. and Gazaneo, Jorge O. "The Basilica of Our Lady of Lujan: transculturation to the pampas of romantic sensibility and Neo-Gothic theory". *Journal of Architecture*, 17 (2011), 493-540.

Germann, Georg. *Gothic Revival in Europe and Britain: Sources, Influences and Ideas*. London: Lund Humphries, 1972.

Germann, Georg. "Bauhütte und Bauhaus. Nachwirkende Ideen der Neugotik". *Kölner Domblatt*, 38/39 (1974), 7-12.

Germann, Georg. *Neugotik. Geschichte ihrer Architekturtheorie*. Stuttgart: Deutsche Verlagsanstalt, 1974.

Germann, Georg. "Der Kölner Dom als Nationaldenkmal", in: Hugo Borger, ed. *Der Kölner Dom im Jahrhundert seiner Vollendung*. Vol. 2. Cologne: Kölnische Verlagsdruckerei, 1980, 161-167.

Ghesquières, Albert and Muller, Paul. "Comment-bâtirons nous dispensaires, écoles, missions catholiques, chapelles, séminaires, communautés religieuses, en Chine?". *Collectanea Commissionis Synodalis*, 14 (February 1941) 2, 1-80.

Gil, Paloma. *El templo del siglo XX*. Barcelona: Editorial Serbal; Col.legi d'arquitectes de Catalunya, 1999.

Gillwald, Katrin. *Ein Primus der Sinnstiftung: Die Riverside Church. Wie eine amerikanische Kirche arbeitet und wirtschaftet*. Berlin: Wissenschaftszentrum Berlin für Sozialforschung (WZB), 2004.

Goeßmann, David. "Uni-Gründung Ave Maria: Campus ohne Sünde". *Der Spiegel*, 14 July 2006. <https://www.spiegel.de/lebenundlernen/uni/uni-gruendung-ave-maria-campus-ohne-suende-a-425043.html> (10 October 2020).

Gómez Salas, Esperanza. *Pláticas de Sobremesa*. Bloomington: Xlibris Corporation, 2017.

Gómez Serrano, Jesús and Delgado Aguilar, Francisco Javier. "La ciudad de Aguascalientes, sus aguas termales y la higiene pública. Los baños de Los Arquitos, 1821-1994". *Investigación y Ciencia*, 25 (2017) 72, 93-117. <https://www.redalyc.org/jatsRepo/674/67453654011/html/index.html>.

González Escoto, Armando. *El templo Expiatorio de Guadalajara*. Zapopan: Universidad del Valle de Atemajac, Amate Editorial, 2006.

Goodyear, W.H. *The memorial quadrangle and the Harkness memorial tower at Yale, James Gamble Rogers, architect*. S.l.: Architectural and Building Press, 1921.

Gowans, Alan. *Church Architecture in New France*. Toronto: University of Toronto Press, 1955.

Goycolea Infante, Roberto. *La actividad constructora del R.P. Bernabé Gutknecht en el vicariato de la Araucania*. Chillán: Facultad de Arquitectura y construcción, Universidad del Bio Bio, [1984].

Grace, John. *Faithful Catholics. Blessed Sacrament Parish A History*. <http://www.blessedsacrament.ca/our-community-life/a-history-of-blessed-sacrament/> (20 October 2020).

Graham, Wade. *Dream Cities: Seven Urban Ideas that Shape the World*. New York: Harper Collins Publishers, 2016.

Grant, James. *St Paul's Cathedral. Melbourne Australia. Guide*. Melbourne: Express Printers Bendigo, 2001.

Gregorios, Paulos and Roberson, Ronald G. "Syrian Orthodox Churches in India", in: Erwin Fahlbusch, Jan Lochman et al., eds. *The Encyclopedia of Christianity*, vol. 5. Leiden: Brill, 2008, 285-286.

Guarda, Gabriel. *Iglesias de madera Cautin-Llanquihue, 1850-1919*. Santiago: Ediciones Universidad Catolica de Chile, 1983.

Guastavino, Rafael. *Escritos sobre la construcción cohesiva y su función en la arquitectura*. Textos sobre teoría e historia de las construcciones. Madrid: Instituto Juan de Herrera, 2006.

Guillen-Nuñez, César. "The Gothic Revival and the Architecture of the New Society of Jesus in Macao and China", in: Robert A. Maryks and Jonathan Wright, eds. *Jesuit Survival and Restoration: A Global History 1773-1900*. Studies in the History of Christian Traditions 178. Leiden-Boston: Brill, 2015, 280-300.

Hadley, Homer M. "Gothic Design. A Gem in Concrete". *The Architect and Engineer*, 119 (December 1934) 3, 13-22.

Halder, Sibabrata and Halder, Manju. *Colonial Architecture at Calcutta: Brick Buildings of Bengal Engineering College*. Howrah: Abhishek Halder, 1999.

Halflants, E. *Le Père Thomas-Corneille Halflants, o.p. (1831-1909). Missionnaire dominicain en Equateur*. Typoscript. S.l., 2006.

Hall, Michael. *George Frederick Bodley and the Later Gothic Revival in Britain and America*. New Haven-London: Yale University Press, 2014.

Hamilton, Judith and Hamilton, Derek. *Early Churches in and around Dunedin*. [Christchurch, N.Z.: J. and D. Hamilton], 2009.

Haro Llamas, Rafael. "La parroquia de Nuestra Señora del Rosario", in: Ramón Mata Torres. *Iglesias y edificios antiguos de Guadalajara*. Guadalajara: Cámara de comercio de Guadalajara y Ayuntamiento de Guadalajara, 1985, 127-132.

Hassenpflug, Dieter. "European Urban Fictions in China: On Urban Travesties, Parodies, and Mimetic transpositions". *EspacesTemps.net* [online], Works, 2008. <https://www.espacestemps.net/en/articles/european-urban-fictions-china/> (1 November 2020).

Hautcoeur, Edouard. *Histoire de Notre-Dame de la Treille dans l'ancienne collégiale de Saint-Pierre et dans la nouvelle basilique érigée en cathédrale par sa Sainteté Pie X le 25 octobre 1913*. Lille: Société Saint-Augustin, 1920.

Hayward, Roger. *Reproduced illustration of an architectural proposal for the National Presbyterian Church of Washington, D.C.* Special Collections & Archives Research Center. <http://scarc.library.oregonstate.edu/omeka-2.0.4/items/show/3481> (10 October 2020).

Helder, Carita. *Indo-Portuguese Architecture in Cochin and Kerala*. New Delhi: Transbooks, 2009.

Henriot, Carine and Minost, Martin. "Thames Town, an English Cliché. The Urban Production and Social Construction of a District Featuring Western-style Architecture in Shanghai". *China Perspective: Urban Planning in China*, (2017) 1, 79-86.

Henríquez, Cecilia. *Imperio y ocaso del Sagrado Corazón en Colombia*. Bogotá: Altamir, 1996.

Herklotz, Ingo. "Review of Gaehtgens, Die brennende Kathedrale". *21: Inquiries into Art, History, and the Visual – Beiträge zur Kunstgeschichte und visuellen Kultur*, 1 (2020), 219-226. <DOI: https://doi.org/10.11588/xxi.2020.1.73145>.

Hermosillo Bagwell, Alison. *Luis Ugarte*. Guadalajara: Secretaria de Cultura, Gobierno del Estado de Jalisco, 2010.

Hernández Palacios, Aureliano. *Xalapa de mis recuerdos*. Xalapa: Universidad Veracruzana, 1986.

Hershey, George L. *High Victorian Gothic*. Baltimore-London: Johns Hopkins University Press, 1972.

Hess, Alan. *Oscar Niemeyer. Bauten für die Öffentlichkeit*. Munich: DVA, 2009.

Higginbotham, Sylvia. *Marvelous Old Mansions: And Other Southern Treasures*. Winston-Salem: Blair, 2000.

Hill, Eric J.; Gallagher, John and American Institute of Architects. *The American Institute of Architects Guide to Detroit Architecture*. Detroit: Wayne State University Press, 2003.

Hill, Rosemary. *God's Architect: Pugin and the Building of Romantic Britain*. Bristol: Allen Lane, 2007.

Hirschfeld, Christian Cay Lorenz. *Theorie der Gartenkunst*. 5 vols. Leipzig: Weidmann, 1779-1785.

Historic Centre of Macao. UNESCO World Heritage, 2005. <https://whc.unesco.org/en/list/1110> (11 November 2020).

Hobart, Lewis P. "Cathedral". *The Architect and Engineer*, 119 (December 1934) 3, 11-12.

Hofmann, Michael. *Deutsche Kolonialarchitektur und Siedlungen in Afrika*. Petersberg: Michael Imhof Verlag, 2013.

Horst, Gertraud. "Ein neuer Kirchenturm für die katholische Pfarrkirche St. Maria Magdalena in Goch". *Das Münster*, 49 (1996), 48-50.

Hosten, Rev. H., SJ. *Antiquities from San Thomé and Mylapore*. Madras: The Diocese of Mylapore, 1936.

Hua, Xiahong 华霞虹, Qiao, Michelle 乔争月; Siegfried, Kató 齐斐然 and Lukács, Boglárka 卢恺琦. *Shanghai Hudec Architecture / 上海邬达克建筑地图*. Shanghai: Tongji University Press, 2013.

Hubertsson Seelow, Atli Magnus. *The Modern Architecture in Iceland in the First Half of the 20th Century: Transfer Processes between Adaptation and Autonomy*. Nuremberg: Verlag für Moderne Kunst, 2011.

Huerta, Santiago. "The Cathedral of Palma de Mallorca, a Wonder of Equilibrium, Rubió i Bellver's Equilibrium Analysis of 1912", in: Paula Fuentes and Anke Wunderwald, eds. *Art of Vaulting: Design and Construction in the Mediterranean Gothic*. Basel: Birkhäuser, 2019, 165-202.

Hurtado Ames, Carlos. *La Iglesia Matriz de Santa Fe y la Capilla de Cristo Pobre de Jauja – Estudios y Documentos*. Huancayo: Imprenta 'Gráfica Palomino', 2010.

Hutchinson, Tara D. "Creating an Architectural Archive: Preservationists puzzle over missing information on the construction of Heinz Chapel", in: *Pitt Campaign Chronicle*. Pittsburgh, PA: University of Pittsburgh Office of News & Information. <https://web.archive.org/web/20100713133254/http://www.chronicle.pitt.edu/media/pcc020107/heinzchap.html.> (10 October 2020).

ICOMOS China (with the approval of the State Administration of Cultural Heritage). *Principles for the Conservation of Heritage Sites in China* 中国文物古迹保护准则. Los Angeles: The Getty Conservation Institute, 2000; revised version, 2015.

Instituto Patrimonio cultural. "Iglesia Inmaculada Concepción", in: *Catálogo del Patrimonio Cultural venezolano. Municipio Andrés Bello, estado Mérida. 2004-2007*. Caracas: Instituto Patrimonio cultural, 2007, 25.

Instituto Patrimonio cultural. "Catedral Santa Bárbara de Rubio", in: *Catálogo del Patrimonio Cultural venezolano. Municipio Junín. 2004-2007*. Caracas: Instituto Patrimonio cultural, 2008, 66-69.

Irving, Robert Grant. *Indian Summer: Lutyens, Baker, and Imperial Delhi*. New Haven-London: Yale University Press, 1989.

Jackson, Iain and Uduku, Ola. "Sub-Saharan Africa", in: G.A. Bremner, ed. *Architecture and Urbanism in the British Empire*. Oxford: Oxford University Press, 2016, 393-421.

Jackson, Peter. *Historic Buildings of Harare*. Harare: Quest Publishing, 1986.

James, Ellen. "Ostell, John", in: *Dictionary of Canadian Biography*, vol. 12. Toronto: University of Toronto / Université Laval, 2003. <http://www.biographi.ca/en/bio/ostell_john_12E.html> (20 October 2020).

James, Jean-Paul, ed. *Nantes*. La grâce d'une cathédrale 9. Strasbourg: La Nuée Bleue, 2013.

Jaramillo Rivera, Juan Pablo and Arango E., Vicente Fernán. "Mario de Ayala Moya. Maestro vitralista". *Revista Civismo*, 447 (April-June 2011). <smpmanizales.blogspot.com/2011/07/revista-civismo-n-447-abril-junio-de.html 1/5>.

Jayawardnene-Pillai, Shanti. *Imperial Conversations: Indo Britons and the Architecture of South India*. New Delhi: Yoda-Press, 2007.

Jensen, Thomas Bo. *P. V. Jensen-Klint: The Headstrong Master Builder*. London: Routledge, 2009.

Jornal do Comércio, 1 May 1883.

Juneja, Monica. "'A very civil idea…' Art History, Transculturation, and World-Making – With and Beyond the Nation". *Zeitschrift für Kunstgeschichte*, 81 (2018) 4, 461-485.

[Jung, Paul]. *Le missionnaire constructeur, conseils – plans. Par des missionnaires de la Chine du Nord*. Xian-xian: Imprimerie de Sien-Hsien, 1926 (reprint, 1935).

Kalman, Harold. *A History of Canadian Architecture*. Vol. 1. Toronto-New York-Oxford: Oxford University Press, 1994.

Kalman, Harold D.; Phillips, Ron and Ward, Robin. *Exploring Vancouver: The Essential Architectural Guide*. Vancouver: University of British Columbia Press, 1993.

Kalman, Harold and Roaf, John. *Exploring Ottawa: An Architectural Guide to the Nation's Capital*. Toronto: University of Toronto Press, 1983.

Kalman, Harold and Ward, Robin. *Exploring Vancouver: The Architectural Guide*. Vancouver-Toronto-Berkeley: Douglas & McIntyre, 2012.

Kappel, Kai. *Memento 1945? Kirchenbau aus Kriegsruinen und Trümmersteinen in den Westzonen und in der Bundesrepublik Deutschland*. Kunstwissenschaftliche Studien 145. Munich-Berlin: Deutscher Kunstverlag, 2008.

Kappel, Kai, ed. *Geschichtsbilder und Erinnerungskultur in der Architektur des 20. und 21. Jahrhunderts*. Regensburg: Schnell & Steiner, 2014.

Katzman, Israel. *Arquitectura del siglo XIX en México*. Mexico City: Fondo Editorial Trillas, 1993 (2nd ed.).

Kavi, Jose. "Indian cardinal does a Pope Francis at church blessing". *Matters India: India's Complete Socioeconomic & Religious News*, 20 April 2015. <https://mattersindia.com/2015/04/indian-cardinal-does-a-pope-francis-at-church-blessing/> (consulted 1 October 2020).

Kelleher, James M. *Saint Mary's Cathedral – Pictorial Souvenir and Guide*. S.l., s.d.

Kennerley, Peter. *The Building of Liverpool Cathedral*. Lancaster: Carnegie Publishing, 1991, 3rd ed. 2008.

Kern, Margit. "Lokale Identitätskonstruktionen und globale Netzwerke – Gotikrezeption an Kirchen und Postgebäuden im frühen 20. Jahrhundert in Mexiko", in: Barbara Borngässer and Bruno Klein, eds. *Neugotik global – kolonial – postkolonial. Gotisierende Sakralarchitektur auf der Iberischen Halbinsel und in Lateinamerika vom 19. bis zum 21. Jahrhundert*. Frankfurt a.M. - Madrid: Vervuert, 2020, 199-212.

Kervick, Francis William Wynn. *Patrick Charles Keely, Architect: A Record of His Life and Work*. South Bend: S.V., 1953.

Kervick, Francis W. *Architects in America of Catholic Tradition*. Clarendon: C. E. Tuttle Company, 1962.

Kikuchi, Yuko. *Japanese Modernisation and Mingei Theory: Cultural Nationalism and Oriental Orientalism*. New York: Routledge Curzon, Taylor & Francis editor, 2004.

Kineth, Ruth. *'Licht in die Finsternis'. Kolonisation und Mission im Kongo, 1876-1908. Kolonialer Staat zwischen Kooperation und Konfrontation*. Münster: Lit Verlag Greven, 2005.

King, Stuart and Willis, Julie. "The Australian Colonies", in: G. Alex Bremner, ed. *Architecture and Urbanisme in the British Empire*. Oxford: Oxford Scholarship online, 2016, 1-40.

King, William E. "Abele, Julian Francis (1881-1950)", in: *North Carolina Architects & Builders*. North Carolina State University Libraries: <https://ncarchitects.lib.ncsu.edu/people/P000277> (10 October 2020).

Kitchens, Michael W. *Ghosts of Grandeur: Georgia's Lost Antebellum Homes and Plantations*. Brookfield (MO): Donning Company Publishers, 2012.

Klauder, Charles Z. and Wise, Herbert C. *College Architecture in America and its Part in the Development of the Campus*. New York-London: Charles Scribner's Sons, 1929.

Klein, Bruno. "El estilo gótico global. Viaje por las catedrales desde el Sena y el Rin hasta el Hudson y el Río de la Plata", in: Patricia Díaz, Montserrat Galí and Peter Krieger, eds. *Nombrar y explicar la terminología en el estudio del arte ibérico y latinoamericano*. Mexico City: Instituto de Investigaciones Históricas, 2012, 235-255.

Klein, Bruno. "Globale Gotik – Paris und Chartres zwischen Pampas und Prairie", in: Heiko Brandl, Andreas Ranft and Andreas Waschbüsch, eds. *Architektur als Zitat: Formen, Motive und Strategien der Vergegenwärtigung*. Regensburg: Schnell & Steiner, 2014, 163-186.

Klein, Bruno. "La arquitectura neogótica en la Península Ibérica y América Latina", in: Barbara Borngässer and Bruno Klein, eds. *Neugotik global – kolonial – postkolonial. Gotisierende Sakralarchitektur auf der Iberischen Halbinsel und in Lateinamerika vom 19. bis zum 21. Jahrhundert / Neogótico global – colonial – postcolonial. Arquitectura sagrada neogótica en la Península Ibérica y América Latina del siglo XIX al XXI*. Madrid: Vervuert Iberoaméricana, 2020, 49-60.

Klein, Bruno. "Warum Gotik", in: Hauke Horn and Matthias Müller, eds. *Gotische Architektur am Mittelrhein. Regionale Vernetzung und überregionaler Anspruch*. Phoenix, 5. Berlin-Boston: De Gruyter, 2020, 3-21.

Koelsch, William A. "A Gothic Architect in San Diego: Philipp H. Frohman and the New St. Paul's Church, 1920-1966". *The Journal of San Diego History*, 51 (2005) 1/2, 42-60. <https://sandiegohistory.org/journal/v51-1/pdf/2005-1_cathedral.pdf> (10 October 2020).

Koeper, Frederick. "Cram and the Late Gothic Revival", in: Marcus Whiffen and Frederick Koeper. *American Architecture 1607-1976*. London-Henley: Routledge and Kegan Paul, 1981, 286-290.

Kolsrud, Oluf. "Le statuaire de la façade", in: Olaf Nordhagen. *La cathédrale de Trondhjem. Documents et considérations relatifs aux plans actuels de sa restauration*. Trondhjem, 1919, 49-52.

Koschorke, Klaus. "Indigenization", in: Betz Hans Dieter, ed. *Religion Past & Present: Encyclopedia of Theology and Religion*, vol. 6. Leiden-Boston: Brill, 2009, 459-460.

Köth, Anke. "Verortung in der Zeit. Zeitliche Legitimationsstrategien im modernen amerikanischen Universitätsbau". *architectura. Zeitschrift für Geschichte der Baukunst*, 46 (2016), 176-189.

Köth, Anke. *Wolkenkratzerkirchen. Ein amerikanischer Bautyp der 1920er Jahre*. Dresden: Thelem, 2010.

Krebs, R. *La Iglesia de América Latina en el siglo XIX*. Santiago de Chile: Ediciones Universidad Católica de Chile, 2002.

Kuhn, João Carlos Santos. *Cidade, arquitetura e religião: A construção de uma metrópole católica em São Paulo (1939-1943)*. São Paulo: Universidade de São Paulo, 2018 (pdf).

Kulangsu, a Historic International Settlement. UNESCO World Heritage, 2017. <https://whc.unesco.org/en/list/1541>.

Kuthan, Jiří and Royt, Jan. *The Cathedral of St. Vitus at Prague Castle*. Prague: Karolinum Press, 2016.

L'Artisan Liturgique. Bruges: Abbey of Saint André, 1-14 (1927-1940).

La Catedral de la Plata. El mayor templo neogótico del siglo XX. Buenos Aires: MZ ediciones, 2000.

Lacroix, Laurier. "La chapelle de l'évêché de Sherbrooke: quelques dessins préparatoires d'Ozias Leduc". *National Gallery of Canada (Ottawa). Bulletin*, 30 (1977), 3-34.

Lai Delin 赖德霖, Wu Jiang 伍江 and Xu Subin 徐苏斌, eds. *Zhongguo jindai jianzhu shi* / 中国近代建筑史 [*History of Modern Architecture of China*], vol. 4: *Modeng shidai: Shijie xiandai jianzhu yingxiang xia de zhongguo chengshi yu jianzhu* / 摩登时代: 世界现代建筑影响下的中国城市与建筑 [*Modern Times: Chinese city and architecture under the international modernism*]. Beijing: China Architecture and Building Press, 2016.

Lampen, Michael D. *Grace Cathedral, San Francisco*. San Francisco: Grace Cathedral Corporation, 1980.

Landau, Tyrone. "Butterfield in Australia: High Victorian or Mainstream Gothic Revival". *Historic Environment*, 3 (1984) 4, 4-19.

Lane, Mills and Martin, Van Jones. *Architecture of the Old South*. New York City: Abbeville Press, 1993.

Lanford, Sarah Drummond. "A Gothic Epitome: Ralph Adams Cram as Princeton's Architect". *The Princeton University Library Chronicle*, 43 (Spring 1982) 3, 184-220.

La Vanguardia, 9 January 1965.

Lázara, Juan Antonio. *La edad media argentina. De la diversidad a la uniformidad estética La arquitectura religiosa neomedieval como emergente de las transformaciones estéticas e ideológicas en la Argentina de la primera mitad del siglo XX*. Thesis (PhD Arts), Universidad de Buenos Aires, 2016.

Lee, Pablo; Compte, Florencio and Peralta, Claudia. *Testimonio y memoria de la arquitectura histórica de Guayaquil*. Guayaquil: Universidad Católica de Santiago de Guayaquil, 1996.

Leite, Monsenhor Manfredo. *A Catedral de São Paulo*. São Paulo: Elvino Pocai, 1954.

Lemos McHale, Kate, ed. *Cathedral Church of Saint John the Divine and the Cathedral Close Designation Report*. February 21, 2017. <http://s-media.nyc.gov/agencies/lpc/lp/2585.pdf>.

Leniaud, Jean Michel, ed. *Répertoire des architectes diocésains du XIXe siècle*. Paris: École nationale des chartes, 2003. <http://elec.enc.sorbonne.fr/architectes/472>.

Lepine, Ayla. "The Persistence of Medievalism: Kenneth Clark and the Gothic Revival". *Architectural History*, 57 (2014), 323-356.

Lethaby, William Richard. "The Place of Gothic Art in Civilization. A lecture". *Architectural Review*, 7 (January 1900) 1, 17-19.

Lewis, David Frazer. *Modernising Tradition: The Architectural Thought of Giles Gilbert Scott (1880-1960)*. Oxford: Oxford University Press, 2014.

Lewis, Michael J. *The Gothic Revival*. London: Thames & Hudson, 2002.

Lewis, Michael J. "The Battle between Polytecnic and Beaux-Arts in the American University", in: Joan Ockman. *Architecture School: Three Centuries of Educating Architects in North America*. Cambridge (Mass.): MIT Press, 2012, 67-105.

Liaño Gibert, Soledad. "Rubió i Bellver en la Església Nova. Modernismo catalán en Son Servera (Mallorca)". *Locvs amoenvs*, 9 (2007/08) [2009], 363-384.

Lima, Francisco. *A Catedral*. Fortaleza: Cearense de Imprensa, 1978.

Lima Jr., Márcio Antonio. *O traço moderno na arquitetura religiosa paulista*. São Paulo: FAAUSP, 2016.

Liscombe, Rhodri Windsor. "Introduction. Writing into Canadian Architectural History", in: Rhodri Windsor Liscombe, ed. *Architecture and the Canadian Fabric*. Vancouver-Toronto: UBS Press, 2011, 1-33.

Liscombe, Rhodri Windsor and Sabatino, Michelangelo. *Canada. Modern Architectures in History*. London: Reaktion Books, 2016.

Liu Heung Shing 劉香成, ed. *China. Portrait of a Country by 88 Chinese Photographers*. Hong Kong-Cologne etc.: Taschen, 2008.

Lochhead, Ian and Stocke, Mark. "Christchurch Cathedral". *The Burlington Magazine*, 158 (2016), 36-37.

Löffler, Beate. *Fremd und Eigen. Christlicher Sakralbau in Japan seit 1853*. Berlin: Frank & Timme, 2011.

Löffler, Beate. "Geborgte Heiligkeit, gebaute Romantik. Die japanische Hochzeitskapelle als auratischer Raum?", in: Maximiliane Buche and Anna Minta. *Raumkult – Kultraum. Zum Verhältnis von Architektur, Ausstattung und Gemeinschaft*. Bielefeld: Transcript 2019, 79-95.

London, Christopher. "The Prag Mahal and Henry St Clair Wilkins' architecture". *Marg. A Magazine of Arts*, 51 (June 2000) 4. 40-57.

London, Christopher. *Bombay Gothic*. Mumbai: India Book House, 2002; 2nd ed. Mumbai: Jaico Publishing House, 2014; reprint Mumbai: Jaico Publishing, 2015.

Longstreth, Richard W. "Academic Eclecticism in American Architecture". *Winterthur Portfolio*, 17 (Spring 1982) 1, 55-82.

López Martínez, Sergio and Petrina, Alberto. eds. *Patrimonio arquitectónico argentino, Tomo II (1880-1920)*. Buenos Aires: Ministerio de Cultura de la Nación, 2014.

López Molina, Héctor. "Basílica del Voto Nacional". *Los ladrillos de Quito*, July 2018. <http://losladrillosdequito.blogspot.com/2018/07/basilica-del-voto-nacional.html>.

Loth, Calder and Sadler Jr., Julius Trousdale. *The Only Proper Style. Gothic Architecture in America*. Boston: New York Graphic Society, 1975.

Lúcio Costa: Registro de uma vivência. São Paulo: Empresa das Artes, 1995.

Luo Wei 罗薇. *Transmission and Transformation of European Church Types in China: The Churches of the Scheut Missions beyond the Great Wall, 1865-1955*. Unpublished PhD dissertation, KU Leuven: Department of Architecture, 2013.

Luque Alcaide, Elisa. *Iglesia en América Latina (siglo XIX). Renovación y continuidad en tiempos de cambio*. Barañáin: Ediciones de la Universidad de Navarra, 2012.

Mabona, Georges. *Sainte-Anne-du-Congo. Sanctuaire souvenir de la France libre*. Saint-Brieuc: Les Presses Bretonnes, 1988.

Macdonell, Cameron. "The American Pugins: Ralph Adams Cram and Bertram Goodhue", in: Timothy Brittain-Catlin, Jan De Maeyer and Martin Bressani, eds. *Gothic Revival Worldwide: A.W.N. Pugin's Global Influence*. KADOC Artes 16. Leuven: Leuven University Press, 2016, 95-105.

Macdonell, Cameron. *Ghost Storeys: Ralph Adams Cram, Modern Gothic Media, and Deconstructive Microhistory of a Canadian Church*. Montreal: McGill-Queen's University Press, 2017.

Maddex, Diane, ed. for National Trust for Historic Preservation. *Master Builders: A Guide to Famous American Architects*. Washington, D.C.: John Wiley & Sons, 1985.

Madrigal, Lorenzo. "Lourdes: Un milagro en grande que se hizo en silencio". *El Espectador*, 3 February 2014.

Magrill, Barry. "The Expansion of Religious Institution and Ontario's Economy, 1849-74. A Case Study of the Construction of Toronto's St. James Cathedral", in: Rhodri Windsor Liscombe, ed. *Architecture and the Canadian Fabric*. Vancouver-Toronto: UBS Press, 2011, 109-137.

Magrill, Barry. *A Commerce of Taste: Church Architecture in Canada 1867-1914*. Montreal: McGill-Queen's University Press, 2012.

Ma Hsingyo, William. *Pedagogy, Display, and Sympathy at the French Jesuit Orphanage Workshops of Tushanwan in Early-Twentieth Century Shanghai*. Unpublished PhD dissertation, Berkeley, University of California: History of Art, 2016.

Mâle, Emile. *L'art allemand et l'art français du moyen âge*. Paris: Colin, 1918.

Malingue, Maurice. *Sanctuaires et Pèlerinages de France*. Paris: Éditions du Louvre, 1952.

Marcelli Sánchez, Jesica. "Una mirada al neogótico mexicano del siglo XX. La parroquia de Nuestra Señora del Rosario de Guadalajara", in: Manuel Alcántara, Mercedes García Montero and Francisco Sánchez López, eds. *Arte y patrimonio cultural: Memoria del 56.º Congreso Internacional de Americanistas*. Salamanca: Ediciones de la Universidad Salamanca, 2018, 750-758.

Marigorta, José de. *Las dos catedrales de Vitoria*. Vitoria: Montepío Diocesano, 1959.

Marín, Dulce; Naranjo, Hilda and Orozco, Enrique. "Retrospectiva de las tendencias tecnológicas aplicadas en las obras religiosas de Jesús Manrique en San Cristóbal. Dos casos de estudio", in: *Semana Internacional de Investigación*. Facultad de Arquitectura y Urbanismo, Universidad Central de Venezuela, 2008, 1-23.

Martel, Fanny. *Adrien Dufresne et l'émergence de l'architecture religieuse moderne au Québec (1936-1964)*. Thesis (M.A.). Québec, 2011.

Marten, Bettina. "Die Almudena-Kathedrale zu Madrid. Abbild funktionaler und historischer Diversität", in: Barbara Borngässer and Bruno Klein, eds. *Neugotik global – kolonial – postkolonial. Gotisierende Sakralarchitektur auf der Iberischen Halbinsel und im Lateinamerika vom 19. bis zum 21. Jahrhundert*. Frankfurt-Madrid: Vervuert - Iberoamericana, 2020, 141-158.

Martinoli, Simona and Perotti, Eliana. *Architettura coloniale italiana nel Dodecaneso 1912-1943*. Turin: Ed. Fondazione Agnelli, 1999.

Masson, Matthieu 馬崇義. "Guangzhou shengxin dajiaotong de sheji he jianzao / 广州圣心大教堂的设计和建造" [The design and construction of the Sacred Heart Cathedral of Canton]. *Xixue dong jian yanjiu / 西学东渐研究* [*Research on Eastern Trend of Western Learning*], 7. Beijing: The Commercial Press, 2019.

Masure, Daniel and Houwen, Jaak. *Ieper. Kathedraal van Sint-Maarten en Sint-Niklaas*. German edition: *Ypern: St. Martinus - und Nikolauskathedrale*. Kleine Kunstführer 2425. Regensburg: Schnell & Steiner, 2000.

Matovelle, Julio Maria. *Imágenes y Santuarios celebres de la Virgen Santísima en la América Española, señaladamente de la República del Ecuador*. Quito: Tip. Editora de los Talleres Salesianos de Quito, 1909.

Maufe, Edward. *The Cathedral of the Holy Spirit, Guildford*. London: Pitkin Pictorials, 1972.

Maurín de Rufino, Elena. "Ernesto Vespignani, el arquitecto de Dios", in: Marcos Gabriel Vanzini, ed. *Basílica María Auxiliadora y San Carlos 1910-24 de mayo de 2010*. Buenos Aires: Asociación Civil Don Bosco Almagro, 2010, 45-53.

Mayer, Gabriel. *Franz Mayer of Munich and F. X. Zettler: A Short Historic Survey.* Munich: Selbstverlag, 2010.

McCarrick, Theodore et al. *The Stained Glass of the Cathedral Basilica of the Sacred Heart, Newark, New Jersey.* Strasbourg: Editions du Signe, 1998.

McCartney, Albert Joseph. "The National Presbyterian Church and Its Heritage in Washington". *Records of the Columbia Historical Society, Washington, D.C.*, 1960/1962, vol. 60/62, 44th separately bound book (1960/1962), 206-223.

McNamara Denis. *Catholic Church Architecture and the Spirit of Liturgy.* Chicago: Liturgy Training Publications, 2009.

McPherson, Albert B. *That uncomfortable genius: A study of building St. Paul's Cathedral, Melbourne and the role of its architect William Butterfield 1878-1884.* M.A. Thesis, University of Melbourne, 1980.

Medina Aráuz, Edy. "Basílica: Entre el gótico y la fe", in: Edgar Freire Rubio, ed. *Quito: testimonio, tradiciones y nostalgia.* Vol. 5. Quito: Libresa, 2004.

Meister, Maureen. *Arts & Crafts Architecture: History and Heritage in New England.* Hanover: University Press of New England, 2014.

Mercado, Soliani. "Relación luz-color en los vitrales del Santuario Inmaculada Concepción de La Azulita". *Proyecto Arte en Mérida*, 2009. <https://proyectoartemerida.wordpress.com/arquitectura/vitrales-de-la-azulita/>.

Merwood Salisbury, Joanna. "The 'New Birth of Freedom': The Gothic Revival and the Aestheatics of Abolitionism", in: Irene Cheng, Charles L. Davis and Mabel O. Wilson, eds. *Race and Modern Architecture: A Critical History from the Enlightenment to the Present.* Pittsburg: University of Pittsburgh Press, 2020, 118-133.

Mesecke, Andrea. "Pardal Monteiro, Porfírio", in: *Allgemeines Künstlerlexikon. Die Bildenden Künstler aller Zeiten und Völker*, vol. 94. Berlin-Boston: K. G. Saur, 2017, 298.

Mesecke, Andrea. "Pite, Arthur Beresford", in: *Allgemeines Künstlerlexikon. Die Bildenden Künstler aller Zeiten und Völker*, vol. 96. Berlin-Boston: K. G. Saur, 2017, 78.

Mesecke, Andrea. "Repullés y Vargas, Enrique María", in: *Allgemeines Künstlerlexikon. Die Bildenden Künstler aller Zeiten und Völker*, vol. 98. Berlin-Boston: K. G. Saur, 2018, 272-273.

Meyer, Jean. *Historia de los cristianos en América Latina, siglos XIX y XX.* Mexico City: Editorial Jus, 1999.

Meyer, Johan. "Cathédrale de Trondhjem. Aperçu abrégé de sa fondation, de sa décadence et de sa reconstruction actuelle", in: Olaf Nordhagen. *La cathédrale de Trondhjem. Documents et considérations relatifs aux plans actuels de sa restauration.* Trondhjem, 1919, 1-30.

Meyer, Katharine Mattingly et al. for American Institute of Architects. *Detroit Architecture: A.I.A. Guide.* Detroit: Wayne State University Press, 1980.

Milliner, Matthew. "Primus inter pares: Albert M. Friend and the Argument of the Princeton University Chapel". *Princeton University Library Chronicle*, 70 (2008-2009) 3, 470-517. <https://www.academia.edu/283858/Primus_inter_pares_Albert_M._Friend_and_the_Argument_of_the_Princeton_University_Chapel> (10 October 2020).

Mills, Edward D. *The Modern Church.* New York: Edition Praeger, 1956.

Minta, Anna. "A church for all purposes", in: Matthias Krueger, ed. *Im Dienst der Nation.* Berlin: Akademie Verlag, 2011, 261-285.

Minta, Anna. *Staatsbauten und Sakralarchitektur in Washington D.C. Stilkonzepte patriotischer Baukunst.* Berlin: Reimer Verlag, 2015.

Montero, Carlos and Mayer, Silvina. *Arquitectos e ingenieros poblanos del siglo XX.* Puebla: Benemérita Universidad Autónoma de Puebla, 2006.

Morales Tapia, Jesús. *La Parroquia de Nuestra Señora de Guadalupe de Cananea.* Hermosillo: Editora La Voz de Sonora, 1999.

Moreno, Daniel. "Casi listo, majestuoso templo de la Virgen de Guadalupe". *Periódico Correo al punto*, 8 January 2018. <https://www.facebook.com/periodicocorreo/videos/casi-listo-majestuoso-templo-de-la-virgen-de-guadalupe/1733816870003518/>.

Morgan, David and Promey, Sally M. *The Visual Culture of American Religions.* Berkeley-Los Angeles-London: University of California Press, 2001.

Mosquera, Sheila. "María Auxiliadora: Su artística restauración". *LaRevista*, 22 December 2013. <http://www.larevista.ec/cultura/sociedad/maria-auxiliadora-su-artistica-restauracion>.

Moya Pérez, Alfonso. "Las torres actuales de la catedral de Guadalajara", in: *Arquitectura religiosa en Jalisco. Cinco Ensayos.* Guadalajara: Amate Editorial, 1986, 163-196.

Moya Pérez, Alfonso. *Arquitectura religiosa en Jalisco: Cinco ensayos.* Zapopan: Amate Editorial, 1998.

Moyssen, Xavier. "El Tratado de Arquitectura de Léonce Reynaud en México". *Anales del Instituto de investigaciones estéticas*, 58 (1987), 155-159.

Mumford, Lewis. *Sticks and Stones.* New York: Dover Edition, 1955.

Muñoz Rodríguez, Pablo and García Ascensio, Miguel. *Piedra a piedra 2. Templo de San José Obrero, Arandas, Jalisco.* Aranda: Fundación de pensamiento arandense, AC., 2017.

Murphy, Kevin D., ed. *Skyscraper Gothic. Medieval Style and Modernist Buildings.* Charlottesville-London: University of Virginia Press, 2017.

Muthesius, Stefan. *The High Victorian Movement in Architecture: 1850-1870.* London et al.: Routledge & Kegan Paul, 1972.

Nagasaki City. *Survey Report on Oura Cathedral and Related Facilities.* Nagasaki, 2012.

Nasrani Syrian Christian Network (NSC). *History of Denominations.* <https://www.nasrani.net/2007/02/13/kerala-syrian-christian-the-tomb-of-the-apostle-persian-church-syond-of-diamper-coonan-cross-oath-divisions/>.

National Register of Historic Places Inventory – Nomination Form. <https://npgallery.nps.gov/NRHP/GetAsset/NHLS/66000562_text> (11 October 2020).

Negro, Sandra. "El acertijo de la arquitectura neogótica en el Perú y la antigua hacienda Unanue de Cañete". *Arquitextos*, 28 (2016), 62-75.

Netsch, Walter A. *Oral history of Walter Netsch* / interviewed by Betty J. Blum, compiled under the auspices of the Chicago Architects Oral History Project, the Ernest R. Graham Study Center for Architectural Drawings, Department of Architecture, the Art Institute of Chicago. <https://digital-libraries.artic.edu/digital/collection/caohp/id/18822> (10 October 2020).

Netsch, Walter A. Walter Netsch interviewed by Detlef Mertins. *SOM Journal*, 1 (2002), Ostfildern: Hatje Cantz Publisher. <https://web.archive.org/web/20100408014230/http://www.som.com/content.cfm/walter_netsch_interview>.

Netsch, Walter A. and Clement, Russell T. *Netsch, Walter A. FAIA: A Critical Appreciation and Sourcebook.* Evanston: Northwestern University Press, 2008.

Netto, Jeronymo Ferreira Alves. *Breve Histórico da Catedral de Petrópolis.* Petrópolis: Instituto Histórico de Petrópolis, 2010 (pdf).

Niglio, Olimpia. *Avvicinamento alla storia dell'architettura giapponese. Dal periodo Nara al periodo Meiji.* Rome: Aracne editrice, 2016.

Niglio, Olimpia. “La cultura eclettica e lo sviluppo del Neogotico. Lo stile dei colonizzatori oltre i confini Europei”, in: Martín M. Checa-Artasu and Olimpia Niglio, eds. *El neogótico en la arquitectura americana. Historia, restauración, reinterpretaciones y reflexiones*. Rome: Aracne Editrice, 2016, 25-44.

Niglio, Olimpia. *Paesaggio sacro e architettura cristiana nella prefettura di Nagasaki*. Rome: Aracne editrice, 2018.

Niglio, Olimpia. “La fortuna critica di John Ruskin in Giappone nella prima metà del Novecento”. *Restauro Archeologico*, special issue, 1 (2019), 268-275.

Niglio, Olimpia and Kuwakino, Koji. *Giappone. Tutela e conservazione di antiche tradizioni*. Pisa: Pisa University Press, 2010.

Nilsson, Sten. *European Architecture in India 1750-1850*. New York: Taplinger Publishing, 1969.

Nishkian, L.H. “Earthquakes, hazards and protection”. *The Architect and Engineer*, 119 (1934) 2, 23-25.

Noelle, Louise. *Arquitectos mexicanos desconocidos del siglo XX. Obra y pensamiento*. Thesis PhD. Sevilla: Doctorado en Historia y Estudios Humanísticos, Universidad Pablo de Olavide, 2018.

Noelle, Louise and Schávelzon, Daniel. “Monumento efímero a los héroes de la Independencia (1910). Federico Mariscal”. *Anales del Instituto de investigaciones estéticas de la UNAM*, 14 (1986) 55, 161-169.

Noppen, Luc. “Bourgeau, Victor”, in: *Dictionary of Canadian Biography*, vol. 11. Toronto: University of Toronto / Université Laval, 2003. <http://www.biographi.ca/en/bio/bourgeau_victor_11E.html>.

Norberg-Schulz, Christian. *Los principios de la arquitectura moderna*. Barcelona: Ed. Reverté, 2005.

Nordhagen, Olaf. “Considérations sur la conception architectonique de la façade occidentale”, in: Olaf Nordhagen. *La cathédrale de Trondhjem. Documents et considérations relatifs aux plans actuels de sa restauration*. Trondhjem, 1919, 31-48.

Obama Avine, Metodio José. *Evolución de la construcción en Guinea Ecuatorial: de soluciones primitivas a construcciones modernas*. Thesis (BS), Universitat Politècnica de Catalunya, 2018.

Obregón Pomayay, Katherine. “Aporte de la arquitectura neogótica en Jauja (Capilla del Cristo Pobre)”, in: Adolfo Gustavo Concha Flores, ed. *Historia, arquitectura y urbanismo en el Valle del Mantaro*. Huancayo: Facultad de Arquitectura de la Universidad Nacional del Centro del Perú, 2010, 217-226. <es.slideshare.net/gusstockconchaflores/historia-arquitectura-y-urbanismo-en-el-valle-del-mantaro>.

Ochsendorf, John Allen. *Guastavino Vaulting: The Art of Structural Tile*. New York: Princeton Architectural Press, 2010.

Ockman, Joan, ed. *Architecture School: Three Centuries of Educating Architects in North America; published on the centennial anniversary of the Association of Collegiate Schools of Architecture, 1912-2012*. Cambridge (Mass.): MIT Press, 2012.

Oechslin, Werner. “‘Quae sub humanum intellectum cadunt’, oder: Was das Nachdenken über Architektur betrifft”, in: Werner Oechslin, Thomas Büchi and Martin Pozsgai. *Architekturtheorie im deutschsprachigen Kulturraum 1486-1648*. Einsiedeln-Basel: Colmena, 2018, 11-141.

Olikara. “The Syrian Christian Church – An Architectural Overview”. Last updated 20 March 2014.

Oliver, Richard, ed. *The Making of an Architect: 1881-1981: Columbia University in the City of New York*. New York: Rizzoli, 1981.

Oliver, Richard. *Bertram Grosvenor Goodhue*. Cambridge (Mass.): MIT Press, 1983.

Ortega, Daniel. “Apuntes para la historia de Chapinero”, in: Marcela Cuéllar, ed. *Miradas a Chapinero*. Bogotá: Editorial Planeta Colombiana, 2008.

Padilla Rangel, Yolanda. *Después de la tempestad: la reorganización católica en Aguascalientes, 1929-1950*. Zamora: El Colegio de Michoacán A.C., 2001.

Palafox-Muñoz, Alejandro; Martínez-Perezchica, Ma. and Ortiz, Julia. “Nueva ruralidad y sustentabilidad social en el pueblo mágico de Calvillo, Aguascalientes”. *Revista Iberoamericana de Turismo*, 6 (2016), 64-81.

Pallarés, Mirtha. *Templos católicos neogóticos: Santiago de Chile 1850-1950*. Santiago: Editorial Universitaria, 2018.

Panikkar, Raimon. “The People of God and the Cities of Man”, in: Stephen Verney. *People and Cities*. London: Collins & Fontana, 1970, 190-219.

Pape, Carlos, ed. “1. Parroquia San Mateo Apóstol, Osorno”, in: *La Iglesia en Osorno, pasado y presente*. Osorno: Diócesis de Osorno, 2008, 144-147.

Pape, Carlos, ed. “13. Parroquia San Agustín, Puerto Octay”, in: *La Iglesia en Osorno, pasado y presente*. Osorno: Diócesis de Osorno, 2008, 172-175.

Pappas, George S. *The Cadet Chapel*. West Point, N. Y., 1958.

Paris, Peter J. et al. *The History of the Riverside Church in the City of New York*. New York-London: New York University Press, 2004.

Parsons, K. C. *The Cornell Campus*. Ithaca: Cornell University Press, 1968.

Partsch, Susanna. “Gurlitt, Friedrich”, in: *Allgemeines Künstlerlexikon*, vol. 66. Berlin-Boston: K. G. Saur, 2010, 72.

Pasuy, William and Sánchez Delgado, Gerardo. “Nuestra Señora del Rosario y la arquitectura neogótica en el departamento de Nariño (Colombia). Santuario de Las Lajas y Basílica de Sandoná”, in: Martín M. Checa-Artasu and Olimpia Niglio, eds. *El neogótico en la arquitectura americana. Historia, restauración, reinterpretaciones y reflexiones*. Rome: Aracne editrice, 2016, 161-166.

Patiño Franco, José Uriel. *La iglesia en América Latina: Estructuras eclesiásticas*. Bogotá: Editorial San Pablo, 2011.

Pattee, Richard. *Gabriel García Moreno y el Ecuador de su tiempo*. Quito: Editorial Jus, 1962.

Paul, Jürgen. “Chartres in Amerika. Ein Beitrag zur mittelalterlichen Ikonographie der Neuzeit”, in: Margrit Lisner and Rüdiger Becksmann. *Kunstgeschichtliche Studien für Kurt Bauch zum 70. Geburtstag von seinen Schülern*. Munich: Deutscher Kunstverlag, 1967, 287-300.

Pedlar, Neil. *The Imported Pioneers: Westerners Who Helped Build Modern Japan*. Kent: Japan Library Ltd, 1990.

Pendo, Mina. *A Brief History of the Riverside Church*. New York: Riverside Church, 1957.

Pepin, David. *Cathedrals of Britain*. Oxford: Bloomsbury, 2016.

Pereira, Sonia Gomes. “O Ensino da arquitetura e a trajetória dos alunos brasileiros na École dês Beaux-Arts em Paris no século XIX”, in: *Anais do XXII Colóquio Brasileiro de História da Arte*. Brasília, 2002, 6-7.

Pilger, Kathrin. *Der Kölner Zentral-Dombauverein im 19. Jahrhundert. Konstituierung des Bürgertums durch formale Organisation*. Kölner Schriften zu Geschichte und Kultur 26. Cologne: SH-Verlag, 2004.

Pilger, Kathrin. “Die Entwicklung des Zentral-Dombau-Vereins bis zur Vollendung des Kölner Domes”. *Kölner Domblatt*, 81 (2016), 18-35.

Pineda, Enrique. "Marcial Reséndiz Galván: Un hombre que le puso el pecho a las balas de la vida". *Vallarta Opina*, 2 April 2018. <https://vallartaopina.net/2018/04/02/local/ciudad/marcial-resendiz-galvan-hombre-le-puso-pecho-las-balas-la-vida/>.

Pinheiro, Maria Lucia Bressan. "Neo-Gothic architecture in Rio de Janeiro and in São Paulo", in: Martín M. Checa-Artasu and Olimpia Niglio, eds. *El Neogótico en la arquitectura americana. Historia, restauración, reinterpretaciones y reflexiones*. Rome: Aracne editrice, 2016, 101-115.

Pirotte, Jean. "Néo-gothique et fantasmes de chrétienté, du 19e au 20e siècle", in: Jan De Maeyer and Luc Verpoest, eds. *Gothic Revival: Religion, Architecture and Style in Western Europe 1815-1914*. KADOC Artes 5. Leuven: Leuven University Press, 2000, 255-265.

Politico y sociedad: el sinarquismo y la iglesia en México. Mexico City: Universidad Iberoamericana, 1992, 117-168.

Pradeep, Kumar. "Between the old and the new church". *The Hindu*, 17 April 2015. <https://www.thehindu.com/features/metroplus/between-the-old-and-the-new-church/article7113641.ece>.

Prieto Casanova, León. *Uyarq – universidad y arquitectura*. Santiago: Universidad de Chile, 1989.

Quinn, Frederick. *A House of Prayer for All People: A History of Washington National Cathedral*. New York: Morehouse Publishing, 2014.

Rabinow, Paul. *French Modern: Norms and Forms of the Social Environment*. Cambridge, Mass: MIT Press, 1989.

Radoin, Hassan. "French Territoriality and Urbanism: General Lyautey and Architect Prost in Morocco", in: Fassil Demissie, ed. *Colonial Architecture and Urbanism in Africa: Intertwined and Contested Histories*. Farnham-Burlington: Ashgate, 2012, 11-31.

Ramakotaiah, YV. "Medak Cathedral". <http://www.splendourindia.org/splen_Jun2009_half/Indian Treasures.htm>.

Ramazzotti, Luigi. "La cupola per St. John the Divine a New York di Rafael Guastavino", in: Claudia Conforti, ed. *Lo specchio del cielo*. Milan: Electa, 1997, 277-291.

Ramirez, Karen Niccoli and Neto, Henrique Lindenberg. "De igreja de taipa a catedral: aspectos históricos e arquitetônicos da igreja matriz da cidade de São Paulo". *Pós. Revista do programa de pós-graduação em arquitetura e urbanismo da FAUUSP*, 21 (2014) 35, 186-199.

Ramón Solans, Francisco Javier. *Más allá de los Andes. Los orígenes ultramontanos de una iglesia latinoamericana (1851-1910)*. Bilbao: Universidad del País Vasco, 2019.

Randles, Sarah. *Medievalism and the Gothic in Australian Culture*. Turnhout: Brepols, 2005.

Redacción. "Catedral con estilo único". *La Hora*, 23 November 2009. <https://lahora.com.ec/noticia/961602/catedral-con-estilo-nico->.

Redacción. "La nueva Catedral de Santo Domingo se hace con ayuda de los feligreses". *El Comercio*, 31 January 2012. <https://www.elcomercio.com/actualidad/ecuador/nueva-catedral-santo-domingo-ayuda.html>.

Reed, Thomas T. *A History of the Cathedral Church of St. Peter Adelaide*. Adelaide: Lutheran Press, 1969.

Regan, Brian. *Gothic Pride: The Story of Building a Great Cathedral in Newark*. New Brunswick, N.J.: Rivergate Books, an imprint of Rutgers University Press, 2012.

Reitz, Falk. "The Cheriapalli in Kottayam as an Example of International and Intercultural Influences on the Christian Architecture in 16th Century Kerala", in: S. D. Trivedi, ed. *The Glorious Heritage of India*. Vol. 1. Delhi: Agam Kala Prakashan, 2010, 69-79.

Répertoire du patrimoine culturel du Québec. "Alma, Église de Saint-Pierre". <http://www.patrimoine-culturel.gouv.qc.ca/rpcq/detail.do?methode=consulter&id=155166&type=bien#.X5wcci2X_dS>.

Répertoire du patrimoine culturel du Québec. "Basilique de Sainte-Anne-de-Beaupré". <http://www.patrimoine-culturel.gouv.qc.ca/rpcq/detail.do?methode=consulter&id=93392&type=bien#.XTWDJy3qjdQ> (17 October 2020).

Répertoire du patrimoine culturel du Québec. "Saguenay, Eglise de Saint-Marc-de-Bagotville". <https://www.patrimoine-culturel.gouv.qc.ca/rpcq/detail.do?methode=consulter&id=105554&type=bien>.

Repetzky, Henning. "Jensen-Klint, Peder Vilhelm", in: *Allgemeines Künstlerlexikon. Die Bildenden Künstler aller Zeiten und Völker*, vol. 77. Berlin: De Gruyter - K. G. Saur, 2013, 531-533.

Reyes Cruz, Raimunda. *Un ángel para los pobres. Vida del monseñor Francisco Velasco Marañón*. Xicotepec: Hijas del Corazón Eucarístico de Jesús y de Santa María de Guadalupe, 2018.

Riestra, Pablo de la. "El gótico posterior a la Edad Media", in: *La Catedral de la Plata. El mayor templo neogótico del siglo XX*. Buenos Aires: Manrique Zago Editores; Fundación Catedral, 2000, 20-29.

Riestra, Pablo de la. "Gótico y neogótico en la arquitectura de la Catedral de la Plata", in: *La Catedral de la Plata. El mayor templo neogótico del siglo XX*. Buenos Aires: Manrique Zago Editores; Fundación Catedral, 2000, 30-69.

Riofrío, Juan Carlos. *El Corazón de la ciudad, Catedral de Guayaquil*. Guayaquil: Biblioteca Municipal, 2002.

Ritter, Catrin. "Hager, Carl Otto", in: *Allgemeines Künstlerlexikon*, vol. 67. Berlin-Boston: K. G. Saur, 2010, 457.

Robinson, Rowena. "Negotiating Traditions: Popular Christianity in India". *Asian Journal of Social Science*, 37 (2009), 29-54.

Rodríguez Campos, William. "La iglesia venezolana entre los siglos XIX-XX". *Miscelánea Comillas*, 67 (2009) 131, 579-585.

Rogers, James Gamble III. "Reflections on James Gamble Rogers". *The Yale University Library Gazette*, 55 (April 1981) 4, 161-164.

Romero, Elsi Solvey; García, Viviana Carolina and Casanova, Betania M. "El neogótico en la arquitectura religiosa tachirense. Reinterpretaciones del estilo a lo largo del siglo XX", in: Martín M. Checa-Artasu and Olimpia Niglio, eds. *El neogótico en la arquitectura americana. Historia, restauración, reinterpretaciones y reflexiones*. Rome: Aracne editrice, 2016, 485-501.

Romero De Solís, José Miguel. *El aguijón del espíritu. Historia contemporánea en México (1892-1992)*. Mexico City: Instituto Mexicano de la doctrina social cristiana; El Colegio de Michoacán, Universidad de Colima y Archivo histórico del municipio de Colima, 2006.

Rousseau, François. *La croix et le scalpel: Histoire des Augustines et de l'Hôtel-Dieu de Québec*. Vol. 1: *1639-1892*. Québec: Les éditions du Septentrion, 1989.

Rozo Montaña, Nancy. *Giovanni Buscaglione, 1920-1940. Arquitectura religiosa en Colombia*. Thesis (M. teoría e historia), Universidad Nacional de Colombia, 2000.

Rüter, Ulrich. "Coomans, Jules", in: *Allgemeines Künstlerlexikon. Die Bildenden Künstler aller Zeiten und Völker*, vol. 21. Munich-Leipzig, 1999, 66-67.

Ryan, Susan. "The Architecture of James Gamble Rogers at Yale University". *Perspecta*, 18 (1982), 24-41.

S.A. *A. de la Herrán. Escultura artística*. <http://www.adelaherran.com/folletoEscultura.pdf>.

S.A. *Milagros de la Virgen de Agua Santa*. Baños: Padres Domínicos, 2013.

Sachs, William. *The Transformation of Anglicanism*. Cambridge: Cambridge University Press, 1993.

Sächsisches Staatsministerium der Finanzen, ed. *Das Schlingrippengewölbe der Schlosskapelle Dresden*. Altenburg: Verlag Klaus-Jürgen Kamprad, 2013.

Sadler, Arthur Lindsay. *Japanese Architecture: A short History*. Singapore: Periplus Editions, 2009.

Saint, Andrew. *The Image of the Architect*. New Haven: Yale University Press, 1983.

Salgueiro, Heliana Angotti. *Engenheiro Aarão Reis: o progresso como missão*. Belo Horizonte: Centro de Estudos Historicos, 1997.

San Martín, Iván. "Templos protestantes neogóticos e ingenieros civiles: entre la innovación constructiva, las inercias estilísticas y el simbolismo religioso". *Actas de Arquitectura Religiosa Contemporánea*, 5 (2018), 172-185.

Sánchez Hernández, Andrés Armando and Hurtado Mireles, Maximiliano. "El neogótico y su vínculo al culto en la industria en México. Contextos y ejemplos de templos y advocaciones católicas y protestantes", in: Martín M. Checa-Artasu and Olimpia Niglio, eds. *El neogótico en la arquitectura americana. Historia, restauración, reinterpretaciones y reflexiones*. Rome: Aracne editrice, 2016, 454-469.

Sánchez Vera, César. "La iglesia luterana de Puerto Montt". *Centro de Estudios del Patrimonio Histórico de la Provincia de Llanquihue (CEPH)*. <http://ceph-puerto-montt.blogspot.com/2010/11/la-iglesia-luterana-de-puerto-montt.html>.

Santos, Marcos Eduardo Melo dos. "A Catedral metropolitana de São Paulo por Maximilian Emil Hehl (1891-1916): História arte e ecetismo na arquitetura sacra". *Reveleto. Revista Electrônica Espaço Teológico*, 8 (2014) 13, 4-15.

Santos, Pedro Alberto Palma dos. *Métrica, proporção e luz: arquitetura sagrada moderna no Brasil*. São Paulo: FAAUSP, 2015 (pdf).

Schumacher, Thomas. *Großbaustelle Kölner Dom. Technik des 19. Jahrhunderts bei der Vollendung einer gotischen Kathedrale*. Studien zum Kölner Dom 4. Cologne: Verlag Kölner Dom, 1993.

Schumann, Matt and Schweizer, Karl W. *The Seven Years War: A Transatlantic History*. New York: Routledge, 2008.

Schyler, Montgomery. "Distinctive American architecture. A series of illustrations of the most notable work of the year – Chapel of the Intercession Trinity Parish, New York". *The Brickbuilder*, 23 (January-December 1914), 85-90.

Schyler, Montgomery. "Distinctive American architecture. A series of illustrations of the most notable work of the year – The new St. Thomas Church, New York". *The Brickbuilder*, 23 (January-December 1914), 15-20.

Scott, William. "Some notes on the Cathedral of Las Palmas with a Few Thoughts on Tropical Architecture". *Ecclesiologists*, 12 (1851), 29-45.

Scriver, Peter. "Empire-building and thinking in the Public Works Department of British India", in: Peter Scriver and Vikramaditya Prakash, eds. *Colonial Modernities: Building Dwelling and Architecture in British India and Ceylon*. London: Routledge, 2007, 69-92.

Scriver, Peter and Srivastava, Amit. *India: Modern Architectures in History*. London: Reaktion Books, 2015.

Scroggs, Marilee Munger. *A Light in the City: The Fourth Presbyterian Church of Chicago*. Chicago: Fourth Presbyterian Church, 1990.

Seasonwein, Johanna G. *Princeton and the Gothic Revival*. Princeton: Princeton University Press, 2012.

Sedlmayr, Hans. *Die Entstehung der Kathedrale*. Zürich: Atlantis-Verlag, 1950.

Segre, Roberto et al. "Um paradoxo patrimonial: a Catedral Metropolitana do Rio de Janeiro". *Risco: Revista de Pesquisa em Arquitetura e Urbanismo*, 14 (2016) 2, 67-81 (online).

Sestoft, Jørgen and Christiansen, Jørgen Hegner. *Guide to Danish Architecture. 1000-1960*. Vol. 1. Copenhagen: Arkitektens Forlag, 1991.

Shand-Tucci, Douglass. *Church Building in Boston, 1720-1970: with an introduction to the work of Ralph Adams Cram and the Boston Gothicists*. Concord: Rumford Pr., 1974.

Shand-Tucci, Douglass. *Ralph Adams Cram: American medievalist*. Boston: Boston Public Library, 1975.

Shand-Tucci, Douglass. "Ralph Adams Cram: America's Foremost Gothic Scholar Architect". *American Art Review*, 3 (May-June 1976) 3, 125-136.

Shand-Tucci, Douglass. *Built in Boston: City and Suburb, 1800-2000*. Amherst: Massachusetts University Press, 1999.

Shand-Tucci, Douglass. *Ralph Adams Cram: An Architect's Four Quests: Medieval, Modernist, American, Ecumenical*. Amherst-Boston: Massachusetts University Press, 2005.

Shearlock, David. *Truro Cathedral*. Eastleigh: Pitkin Pictorials, 1992.

Sicilia, Mary. *Building Honestly: The Foundations for the Cathedral Church of St. Mark*. Minneapolis, Minnesota: The Cathedral Church of St. Mark, 1991.

Sigel, Paul and Klein, Bruno, eds. *Konstruktionen urbaner Identität. Zitat und Rekonstruktion in Architektur und Städtebau der Gegenwart*. Berlin: Lukas Verlag, 2006.

Sigüenza, Grace. *Quito: patrimonio de la humanidad*. Quito: Soho Design, 2006.

Silva, Geraldo Gomes da. "Arquitetura eclética em Pernambuco", in: Annateresa Fabris, ed. *Ecletismo na Arquitetura brasileira*. São Paulo: Nobel, 1987, 176-207.

Simmins, Geoffrey. *Fred Cumberland: Building the Victorian Dream*. Toronto: University of Toronto Press, 1997.

Smith, Curtis. "Supplants Stone. Cathedral in Concrete". *The Architect and Engineer*, 119 (December 1934) 3, 27-28.

Smith, Michael G. *Designing Detroit – Wirt Rowland and the Rise of Modern American Architecture*. Detroit: Wayne State University Press, 2001.

Soetens, Claude. *L'Église catholique en Chine au XXe siècle*. Paris: Beauchesne, 1997.

Spence, Jonathan D. *The Search for Modern China*. New York-London: W.W. Norton and Company, 1990.

Spencer, Patricia C. *Helena, Montana: The Queen City of the Rockies and the Broadwater Hotel*. Mount Pleasant: Arcadia Publishing, 2002.

St. Andrew's Chapel. Preservation plan, Graduate Program of Historic Preservation, University of Pennsylvania, Preservation Studio, Fall 2010. <https://www.design.upenn.edu/sites/default/files/2010_St.Andrews_final_editied.pdf> (10 October 2020).

St. Mark's: A Parish Church and a Cathedral. Minneapolis, Minnesota: The Cathedral Church of St. Mark, 1953.

"St. Philomena's Cathedral, Mysore". <https://en.wikipedia.org/wiki/St._Philomena%27s_Cathedral,_Mysore> (13 May 2020).

Standaert, Nicolas. *Inculturation: The Gospels and Cultures*. Makati (Philippines): Saint Paul Publications, 1990.

Stanton, Phoebe B. "Pugin: Principles of Design versus Revivalism". *Journal of the Society of Architectural Historians*, 13 (October 1954) 3, 20-25. <https://www.jstor.org/stable/987703>.

Stanton, Phoebe B. *The Gothic Revival & American Church Architecture: An Episode in Taste 1840-1856*. Baltimore: The Johns Hopkins Press, 1968.

Stern, Robert A.M. et al. *Metropolitan Architecture and Urbanism 1890-1915*. New York: Rizzoli, 1983.

Steuer, Heiko. "Industrialisierung und Domvollendung", in: Hugo Borger, ed. *Der Kölner Dom im Jahrhundert seiner Vollendung*. Vol. 2. Cologne: Historische Museen der Stadt Köln, 1980, 271-293.

Stiles, Mark Douglas. *Reading Ruskin: Architecture and Social Reform in Australia, 1889-1908*. Sydney: University of New South Wales, 2010.

Stillwell, Richard. *The Chapel of Princeton University*. Princeton: Princeton University Press, 1971.

Stoler, Ann Laura. "Colonial archives and the arts of governance". *Archival Science*, 2 (2002), 87-109. <https://doi-org.wwwdb.dbod.de/10.1007/BF02435632>.

Storemyr, Per. *The Stones of Nidaros*. Trondheim: Norwegian University of Science and Technology, 1997.

Straub, Jeffrey Paul and Nettles, Tom J. *The Making of a Battle Royal: The Rise of Liberalism in Northern Baptist Life 1870-1920*. Eugene: Pickwick Publications, 2018.

Strickrodt, Silke. "The Brazilian Diaspora to West Africa in the Nineteenth Century", in: Ineke Phaf-Rheinberger and Tiago de Oliveira Pinto, eds. *AfricAmericas. Itineraries, Dialogues, and Sounds*. Madrid-Frankfurt am Main: Iberoamericana - Vervuert, 2008, 37-68.

Strong, Rowan. *The Oxford History of Anglicanism*. Vol. 3. Oxford: Oxford University Press, 2017.

Sturgis, Richard Clipston. "Three Somerset Towers and some Others". *Architectural Review*, 7 (January 1900) 1, 13-16.

Sundt, Richard A. "From Late Gothic to Gothic Revival in Latin America", in: Timothy Brittain-Catlin, Jan De Maeyer and Martin Bressani, eds. *Gothic Revival Worldwide: A.W.N. Pugin's Global Influence*. KADOC Artes 16. Leuven: Leuven University Press, 2016, 118-129.

Sunil, Edward. *A Study of Indigenous Church Architecture of Kerala State*. PhD Thesis. Roorkee: Indian Institute of Technology, 2005.

Sweeten Alan R. *China's Old Churches: The History, Architecture, and Legacy of Catholic Sacred Structures in Beijing, Tianjin, and Hebei Province*. Studies in the History of Christianity in East Asia 2. Leiden-Boston: Brill, 2020.

Symondson, Anthony. *The Life and Work of Sir Ninian Comper: 1864-1960*. London: Royal Institute of British Architects Publications, 1988.

Symondson, Anthony. *Stephen Dykes Bower: Twentieth Century Architects*. London: Royal Institute of British Architects Publications, 2011.

Tadros, Mariz. "Vicissitudes in the Entente between the Coptic Orthodox Church and the State in Egypt (1952-2007)". *International Journal of Middle East Studies*, 41 (2009) 2, 269-87. <www.jstor.org/stable/40206105>.

Takeda, John M. "Public and Private Church: The Experience of Japanese Anglicans, Past and Future". *Anglican and Episcopal History*, 65 (1996) 4, 412-441.

Tannler, Albert M. *Charles J. Connick: His Education and his Windows in and near Pittsburgh*. Pittsburgh: Pittsburgh History & Landmarks Foundation, 2008.

The Architect and Engineer, 119 (December 1934) 3.

The National Presbyterian Church Communications Committee, ed. *Facets of Faith: Seeing the Light through the Windows of the National Presbyterian Church*. Washington, D.C.: The National Presbyterian Church, 2011.

Thomas, George E. *Buildings of Pennsylvania: Philadelphia and Eastern Pennsylvania*. Charlottesville: University of Virginia Press, 2010.

Thomas, John. "The influence of Albi Cathedral: the use of historic precedent in nineteenth and twentieth century church design". *The Journal of Architecture*, 3 (1998), 85-105.

Thompson, Paul. *William Butterfield*. London: Routledge & Kegan Paul, 1971.

Thurlby, Malcom. "The Church of Our Lady of The Immaculate Conception, at Guelph: Puginian Principles in the Gothic Revival Architecture of Joseph Connolly". *Society for the Study of Architecture in Canada*, 15 (1990) 2, 32-40.

Thurlby, Malcolm. "Two Late Nineteenth-century Roman Catholic Churches in Toronto". *Ecclesiology Today*, 33 (May 2004), 30-40.

Ticozzi, Sergio. "Celso Costantini's Contribution to the Localization and Inculturation of the Church in China", in: *Cardinal Celso Costantini and the Chinese Catholic Church*, thematic issue of the journal *Tripod*, 28 (2008) 148, Hong Kong. <http://www.hsstudyc.org.hk/en/tripod_en/en_tripod_148.html>.

Tiedeman, R. Gary. *Reference Guide to Christian Missionary Societies in China from the Sixteenth to the Twentieth Century*. Armonk-London: Sharpe, 2009.

Tiedeman, R. Gary, ed. *Handbook of Christianity in China. Volume Two: 1800 to Present*. Handbook of Oriental Studies, 4/15. Leiden-Boston: Brill, 2010.

Toker, Franklin. *Pittsburgh. An Urban Portrait*. Pittsburgh: The Pennsylvania State University Press, 1986.

Tolles, Bryant Franklin. *Architecture & Academe: College Buildings in New England Before 1860*. Hanover: University Press of New England, 2011.

Treat Paine, Robert and Soper, Alexander. *The Art and Architecture of Japan*. Baltimore: Penguin, 1955.

Trejo González, Giovani. "Calvillo, Aguascalientes. De la naturaleza a la magia", in: Liliana López Levi, Carmen Valverde and María Elena Figueroa, eds. *Pueblos mágicos, una visión interdisciplinaria*. Vol. 3. Mexico City: UAM/UNAM/ Facultad de Arquitectura, 2017, 291-312.

Trémorin, J.M. "Autour de Notre Dame de Tong-lu. Tong-lu sous les Boxeurs. Après 1900". *Bulletin catholique de Pékin*, 16 (1929), 16-21, 65-70, 133-139, 203-205.

"Trinity Episcopal Church, Houston", in: *The Handbook of Texas Online*, Texas State Historical Association (TSHA). <https://tshaonline.org/handbook/online/articles/ietan>.

Tutag, Nola Huse and Hamilton, Lucy. *Discovering Stained Glass in Detroit*. Detroit: Wayne State University Press, 1987.

Tweed, Thomas A. "America's Church: Roman Catholicism and civic space in the nation's capital", in: David Morgan and Sally M. Promey. *The Visual Culture of American Religions*. Berkeley-Los Angeles-London: University of California Press, 2001, 68-86.

Ulrich, Laurent, ed. *Lille: la Treille, lumière du Nord. La grâce d'une cathédrale*. Vol. 10. Strasbourg: La Nuée Bleue, 2014.

Underwood, David. *Oscar Niemeyer and the Architecture of Brazil*. New York: Rizzoli, 1994.

University of Valparaiso, ed. *Dedication booklet, Chapel of the Resurrection*, University of Valparaiso, Valparaiso, Indiana, Sunday, September 27, 1959. <https://www.valpo.edu/chapel/files/2016/11/1959-Sept-27-Dedication-booklet-Chapel.pdf>.

Urbano, Judith. "Neo-Gothic Controversial Cases in Catalonia in the Nineteenth Century", in: Barbara Borngässer and Bruno Klein, eds. *Neugotik global – kolonial – postkolonial. Gotisierende Sakralarchitektur auf der Iberischen Halbinsel und in Lateinamerika vom 19. bis zum 21. Jahrhundert*. Frankfurt-Madrid: Vervuert, 2000, 109-122.

Utrilla Hernández, Alejandra. *La arquitectura religiosa en el siglo XIX. Catálogo de planos del acervo de la Academia de San Carlos*. Mexico City: Escuela Nacional de artes plásticas, Universidad Nacional Autónoma de México, 2004.

Utzinger, J. Michael. *Yet Saints Their Watch are Keeping: Fundamentalists, Modernists and the Development of Evangelical Ecclesiology*. Macon (Ga.): Mercer University Press, 2006.

Valderrama Rouy, Pablo. "La Virgen del Peñón, un santuario", in: Daniel Nahmad Molinari and J. Omar Ruiz Gordillo, eds. *Memoria del segundo encuentro de investigadores del Centro INAH Veracruz*. Veracruz: Instituto Nacional de Antropología e historia, 2010, 49-56.

Valdés Subercaseux, M. *Fray Francisco Valdés Subercaseaux. Misionero de la Araucanía y primer obispo de Osorno*. Santiago: Editorial Andrés Bello, 1985.

Van Hecken, Joseph. "Alphonse Frédéric De Moerloose C.I.C.M. (1858-1932) et son œuvre d'architecte en Chine". *Neue Zeitschrift für Missionswissenschaft / Nouvelle Revue de science missionnaire*, 24 (1968) 3, 161-178.

Van Reybrouck, David. *Kongo. Eine Geschichte*. Berlin: Suhrkamp, 2012².

Vanzini, Marcos Gabriel, ed. *Basílica María Auxiliadora y San Carlos 1910-24 de mayo de 2010*. Buenos Aires: Asociación Civil Don Bosco Almagro, 2010.

Varela, Luis Vicente. *Breve historia de la Virgen de Lujan, su santuario y su culto: desde 1630 hasta 1897*. Buenos Aires: Nicolás Avellaneda, 1897.

Vargas, José María. *Nuestra Señora del Rosario en el Ecuador*. Quito: Impreseñal, 1983.

Vargas Salguero, Ramón. *Federico E. Mariscal. Vida y obra*. Mexico City: Facultad de arquitectura, Universidad Nacional Autónoma de México, 1998.

Vargas Salguero, Ramón. *Historia de la arquitectura y el urbanismo mexicanos*. Vol. 3: *El México independiente*. Mexico City: Facultad de arquitectura, Universidad Nacional Autónoma de México, 1998.

Vastushilpalaya Consultancy Private Limited. "Mission and Philosophy". <http://www.vastushilpalaya.com/about>.

Vermeersch, Paula. "A construção da Catedral da Sé, São Paulo, 1913-1954", in: Barbara Borngässer and Bruno Klein, eds. *Neugotik global – kolonial – postkolonial. Gotisierende Sakralarchitektur auf der Iberischen Halbinsel und in Lateinamerika vom 19. bis zum 21. Jahrhundert*. Frankfurt-Madrid: Vervuert, 2020, 210-226.

Vieira, Juliana Polli. *A Igreja Matriz do Santíssimo Sacramento e a Constituição da Cidade de Itajaí*. Dissertation. Florianópolis, 2016 (pdf).

Vienne, Frédéric. "Admirateurs et détracteurs de la Treille", in: Laurent Ulrich, ed. *Lille: la Treille, lumière du Nord. La grâce d'une cathédrale*. Vol. 10. Strasbourg: La Nuée Bleue, 2014, 300-305.

Vienne, Frédéric. "La Deuxième Phase du Chantier, 1919-1965", in: Laurent Ulrich, ed. *Lille: la Treille, lumière du Nord. La grâce d'une cathédrale*. Vol. 10. Strasbourg: La Nuée Bleue, 2014, 114-137.

Voigt, Wolfgang and Flagge, Ingeborg. *Dominikus Böhm 1880-1955*. Catalog of exhibition DAM 2005. Tübingen-Berlin: Ernst Wasmuth, 2005.

Volgger, Peter, ed. *Architecture in Asmara: Colonial Origin and Postcolonial Experiences*. Berlin: DOM publishers, 2017.

Volwahsen, Andreas. *Splendours of Imperial India: British Architecture in the 18th and 19th Centuries*. Munich: Prestel 2004.

Walker, Robin. "A survey of early buildings in Nyasaland". *The Nyasaland Journal*, 13 (January 1960) 1, 51-61.

Watson, T. N. "Areas of concern". *Momentum*. International Council on Monuments and Sites, 25 (1982) 1, 29-42. <https://www.icomos.org/monumentum/vol25-1/vol25-1_4.pdf>.

Wayne, Andrews. *American Gothic: It's Origins, Its Trials; Its Triumphs*. New York: Random House, 1975.

Webb, Benjamin. "On the Adaptation of Pointed Architecture to Tropical Climates". *Transactions of the Cambridge Cambden Society, 1843-45* (1845), 199-218.

Webster, Josephine Faulkner. "Julian Francis Abele (1881-1950)", in: Dreck Spurlock Wilson, ed. *African American Architects: A Biographical Dictionary, 1865-1945*. Routledge: Chapman & Hall, 2004, 1-3.

Weil, Jorge. *Historia de Frutillar*. Puerto Montt: Editorial Universidad de Los Lagos, 2016.

Wickersham, George W. *The Cathedral Church of Saint John the Divine*. New York: Conroy, 1980.

Wiest, Jean-Paul. "The Building of the Cathedral of Canton: Political, Cultural and Religious Clashes", in: *Religion and Culture: Past Approaches, Present Globalisation, Futures Challenges (International Symposium on Religion and Culture, 2002: Macau)*. Macao: Ricci Institute, 2004, 231-252.

Wiest, Jean-Paul. "Le père Lebbe et son église de style chinois", in: Arnaud Join-Lambert, Paul Servais, Chung Heng Shen and Éric de Payen, eds. *Vincent Lebbe et son héritage*. Religio 3. Louvain-la-Neuve, 2017, 85-106.

Williams, Peter W. "The Medieval Heritage in American Religious Architecture", in: Bernard Rosenthal and Paul E. Szarmach, eds. *Medievalism in American Culture*. Medieval & Renaissance Texts & Studies 55. Binghamton, N.Y., 1989, 171-192.

Williams, Peter W. "The Iconography of the American City: Or, a Gothic Tale of Modern Times". *Church History*, 68 (June 1999) 2, 373-397.

Williams, Stanley T. "The Harkness Memorial Tower". *American Architect*, 120 (26 October 1921) 9, 315-316.

Wilson, Richard Guy. "Ralph Adams Cram. Dreamer of the medieval", in: Bernard Rosenthal and Paul E. Szarmach, eds. *Medievalism in American Culture*. Medieval & Renaissance Texts & Studies 55. Binghamton, N.Y., 1989, 193-214.

Winspear, Frank. "A Short History of the Universities Mission to Central Africa". *The Nyasaland Journal*, 9 (January 1956) 1, 11-50.

Wolfendale, Stuart. *Imperial to International: A History of St John's Cathedral, Hong Kong*. Historical Studies of Anglican Christianity in China 1. Hong Kong: Hong Kong University Press, 2013.

Woodword, Matthew. "The After-Lives of English Gothic", in: Laura Cleaver and Ayla Lepine, eds. *Gothic Legacies: Four Centuries of Tradition and Innovation in Art and Architecture*. Newcastle upon Tyne: Cambridge Scholars Publishing, 2012, 2-19.

Wubbenhorst, Paula. "America's Influence on the Cathedral of Christ the King in Hamilton". *JSSA/JSÉAC*, 29 (2004) 3/4, 41-50.

Wynd, Ian. *A History of St. Mary's Basilica*. Geelong: St. Mary's Parish, 2006.

Wysokowski, Adam. "Unusual Rebuilding Method of Historic St Mary's Cathedral in the Capital of Western Australia". *Civil and Environmental Engineering Reports*, 21 (2016) 2, 147-159.

X. "Objections". *Dossiers de la Commission synodale / Digest of the Synodal Commission*, 5 (1932), 475-485.

Yorke, Trevor. *Gothic Revival Architecture*. Oxford: Shire Publications, 2017.

Young, Ernest P. *Ecclesiastical Colony: China's Catholic Church and the French Religious Protectorate*. Oxford: Oxford University Press, 2013.

Zentralinstitut für Kunstgeschichte in München, ed. *Globale Räume des deutschen Kolonialismus. Begriffe und Methoden – Case Studies – disziplinäre Querverbindungen*. Thematic issue of *Kunstchronik*, 74 (2021) 7.

Zheng Yangwen 鄭揚文, ed. *Sinicizing Christianity*. Studies in Christian Mission 49. Leiden-Boston: Brill, 2017.

Zimmerling, Peter, ed. *Universitätskirche St. Pauli. Vergangenheit, Gegenwart, Zukunft. Festschrift zur Wiedereinweihung der Universitätskirche St. Pauli zu Leipzig*. Leipzig: Evangelische Verlags-anstalt, 2017.

Županov, Ines G. "'One Civility, but Multiple Religions': Jesuit Mission among St. Thomas Christians in India (16th-17th Centuries)". *Journal of Early Modern History*, 9 (2005), 284-325.

AUTHORS

Barbara Borngässer is consultant for modern and contemporary architecture of the international "Allgemeines Künstlerlexikon" (AKL/Thieme-Becker) and also freelance author and editor. She was cofounder of the Carl Justi-Vereinigung e.V. and is comember of the editorial board of the book series *ARS IBERICA ET AMERICANA*. She studied art history, archaeology, and Italian philology in Berlin, Florence, and Salamanca, and received her doctorate with a dissertation on fifteenth-century painting in Spain. This was followed by research on Baroque in Portugal and contemporary architecture in Barcelona. Borngässer has published widely on early modern and modern architecture with a focus on Spain, Portugal, and Brazil. Together with Bruno Klein, research fellow Martín Checa-Artasu, and Bettina Marten, she directed the research project Global Gothic – Neo-Gothic Ecclesiastical Architecture in the 20th and 21st Centuries, funded by the Deutsche Forschungsgemeinschaft (DFG).

Martín M. Checa-Artasu is a professor of the Department of Sociology of the Metropolitan Autonomous University (Iztapalapa Unit) in Mexico City. He is a member of the National System of Investigators of the National Council of Science and Technology of Mexico and a regular member of the Mexican Academy of Sciences. He was Mercator Fellow in the project Global Gothic: International Gothic Architecture in the 20th and 21st centuries. Since 2016 he is a researcher in the Italian Diaspora in Latin America project (EdA International Research Center, Rome, Italy). He holds a Human Geography Ph.D. from the University of Barcelona (2006) and a Bachelor's in Archaeology from the University of Barcelona (1994). Since 2009, his research explores a historicism in architecture in Mexico and Latin America from a geographical approach. His more recent publications as author or coauthor are (in Spanish) *The Gothic Revival in Jalisco. Basic Guide for the Appreciation of the Built Environment* (Arquitónica Editorial, in press) and *Adamo Boari (1863-1928). Architect between America and Europe* (Aracne Editrice, 2020). He has been the editor of the following books (in Spanish): *Architectures of the sacred in contemporary Mexico* (U.A. Aguascalientes, 2014); *The Neogothic in American architecture. History, restoration, reinterpretations, and reflections* (Aracne editrice, Rome, 2016); *Italians in Mexico. Architects, engineers, artists between the 19th and 20th centuries* (Aracne editrice, Rome, 2019); and *Architects and Artists in the Italian Diaspora in Latin America. Cultural Diplomacy in Action* (Aracne Editrice, 2021).

Thomas Coomans is an architectural historian, professor at the University of Leuven in the Department of Architecture, and program director of the Raymond Lemaire International Centre for Conservation. His former academic positions included teaching and research at universities in Brussels, Leiden, Paris, Montreal, Hong Kong, and Beijing. His teaching includes architectural history, building archaeology, and history and theory of conservation. Over the past thirty years, Coomans's research on various aspects of church architecture has included medieval churches in the Low Countries, monasteries of religious orders, Gothic Revival, reuse of redundant churches, and more. This research has resulted in sixteen books and more than 150 articles and book chapters, combining methods from the disciplines of history, construction history, building archaeology, iconology of architecture, and heritage conservation. His current research on Christian church architecture in China from the 1840s to the 1940s combines fieldwork in China—especially in collaboration with the School of Archaeology of Peking University—and research in Western archives.

Pedro Guedes is a Senior Lecturer at the University of Queensland in Australia. Prior to becoming a full-time academic in Australia, he practiced architecture in London and taught at the Architectural Association and Royal College of Art. His research interests include the architectures of encounter in colonial contexts and the entry of new technologies into building. He has published in *Architectural History*, *Fabrications*, *Architectural Theory Review*, *ARQ* (Chile), *Architectural Review*, *Architectural Design*, *A+U*, and *Japan Architect*.

Bruno Klein is an art historian and Chair for Christian Art of Late Antiquity and the Middle Ages at the Technical University of Dresden. After studying in Berlin, Paris, Cologne, and Bonn, he taught and researched at various German universities as well as in Paris (Sorbonne and EPHE), Fribourg (Switzerland), São Paulo, and Rome (Bibliotheca Hertziana). He is a member of the Saxon Academy of Sciences. Beginning with monographs in the thematic area of French Gothic (PhD) and Italian Romanesque (Habilitation), his research and publication activities are increasingly directed on medieval art as a whole, and on architecture from the Middle Ages to the present day. In particular, he is concerned with the globalzation of ideas and discourses on historical architecture. Together with Barbara Borngässer, research fellow Martín Checa-Artasu, and Bettina Marten, he directed the DFG research project Global Gothic – Neo-Gothic Ecclesiastical Architecture in the 20th and 21st Centuries.

Bettina Marten studied art history, classical archaeology, and sociology at the University of Hamburg, with a doctoral thesis on fortification in the sixteenth century in Spain. After, Marten has been involved in different activities: she has been as lecturer at the TU Dresden, and a instructor at the Goethe-University Frankfurt and at the Philipps-University Marburg. Together with Barbara Borngässer, research fellow Martín Checa-Artasu and Bruno Klein, she directed the DFG research project Global Gothic – Neo-Gothic Ecclesiastical Architecture in the 20th and 21st Centuries.

Olimpia Niglio is an architect and professor at the Department of Civil and Environmental Engineering, Faculty of Engineering and Design, Hosei University in Tokyo. Starting in 2012, she was a research fellow at Kyoto University, where she taught Urban Restoration and Architectural Conservation, and after at Hokkaido University. Visiting professor in many universities between Asia and Latin America. She is vice-president of Asian Cultural Landscape Association (SNU, Korea) and vice-president of ICOMOS Prerico (Places of religion and rituals). She is also a research fellow at the Korea Foundation. Her research areas and publications include comparative projects between East Asia and Latin America. She is coordinator of two international research projects: Italian Diaspora in the World and Cultural Diplomacy and Heritage.

Peter Scriver is a founder and Director (South and Southeast Asia) of the Centre for Asian and Middle Eastern Architecture (CAMEA) at the University of Adelaide, Australia. A pioneering scholar and critical authority on the architecture and planning history of modern India since the nineteenth century, his widely published historical and theoretical work has also spearheaded a growing body of critical scholarship on colonial modernity and the "Scaffolding of Empire" in the construction of the Global South more broadly. Scriver's extensive research on the British Indian Department of Public Works (PWD) has explored its instrumental role in the propagation and institutionalization of modern architectural knowledge in colonial India and beyond. Among other publications, his most recent book *India: Modern Architectures in History*, published with Amit Srivastava in 2015, examines the PWD's agency in disseminating Gothic styles and principles in the secular and sacred architectures of colonial-modern India.

Amit Srivastava is Director (India) of the Centre of Asian and Middle Eastern Architecture (CAMEA) based at the University of Adelaide, in Australia. Having trained and practiced as an architect in India, Srivastava's research focuses on the architectural and construction histories of colonial and postcolonial India. He is particularly interested in the transnational exchange of materials, skills, and construction processes across the Indian Ocean rim. Relevant publications include *India: Modern Architectures in History* (2015) and "Religion as Conceptual Scaffolding for Architecture" (2020).

INDEX OF PERSONS

A = Architect (Architect/Engineer/Firm)
B = Builder (Client/Patron)
C = Cleric

INDEX OF OBJECTS

The entries in the object directory are based on the designations in the contributions and were not schematized. As far as possible, denominational affiliations were added. Differences to the current naming cannot be ruled out, but are evident from the context.

COLOPHON

Final editing
Luc Vints

Copy editing
Lieve Claes

Layout
Alexis Vermeylen

KADOC
Documentation and Research Centre on
Religion, Culture and Society
KU Leuven
Vlamingenstraat 39
B - 3000 Leuven
http://kadoc.kuleuven.be

Leuven University Press
Minderbroedersstraat 4
B - 3000 Leuven
info@lup.be
www.lup.be